Hidden Teachings in Hinduism

Yoga, Bhakti, Mantra, Prana and the
Kundalini Pathway to Purifying the Koshas

WILLIAM BODRI

Copyright © 2024 William Bodri

All rights reserved. No part of this book may be used or reproduced in any manner whatsoever without the written permission of the publisher, except in cases of brief quotations in articles and reviews. The content of this book is for informational purposes only and is not intended to diagnose, treat, cure, or prevent any disease or health condition. Nothing should be considered medical advice. You understand that this book is not intended as a substitute for consultation with a licensed health practitioner. Please consult with your own physician or healthcare specialist regarding the information made available in this book. The use of this book implies your acceptance of this disclaimer.

Top Shape Publishing LLC
1135 Terminal Way Suite 209
Reno, NV 89502

Library of Congress Control Number: 2024939954
ISBN-13: 978-1-7370320-5-2

DEDICATION

To those within Hinduism seeking *moksha*, liberation or enlightenment. The *Upanishads* had to be written to supply details on ethics, culture and spiritual practice missing from the *Vedas*, and this book supplies much of the information related to *moksha* that is missing from the *Upanishads*. It is especially useful not just to householders but to sadhus, sannyasins, monks and ascetics who are cultivating to achieve liberation. It explains how to unravel the five *koshas* from each other that cover your *atman*, the spiritual practices of inner energy work that will do so, the twelve to fourteen year process of kundalini washing that will win you the first of the spiritual bodies of enlightenment, and how the enlightened saints thereafter are able to produce superpowers. After reading this book you will absolutely understand the practices within Hinduism for unbinding the *koshas* from one another and how this leads to transcendental liberation.

CONTENTS

	Acknowledgments	i
1	*Moksha* – Enlightenment	1
2	The Kundalini Process of Decoupling the *Kosh*as From One Another	47
3	Evolution, Hinduism and the Spiritual Objective	86
4	The Liberating Perspective of Advaita Vedanta	116
5	Detachment and the *Mahavakya*	154
6	Hatha Yoga to Cultivate Your Muscles and Prana	179
7	Pranayama to Open Your *Nadis*	191
8	*Bhakti* Devotional Worship	215
9	Mantrayana	245
10	Tantric Yoga for Inner Kundalini Practice	264
11	Superpowers	294
12	Takeaway Summaries	300
	Appendix 1: Chakras	305
	Appendix 2: Sample "Emptiness" or "Formlessness" Meditations From Kashmir Shaivism	321

RECOMMENDED STUDY

If you find this book of special value you should go beyond the limits of Hinduism to get a more complete picture of the processes of spiritual transformation and ascension that are non-denominationally found across the world. You are encouraged to read *The Secret Inner Teachings of Daoism*, *Correcting Zen*, *Neijia Yoga* and *Arhat Yoga* since they will give you a fuller picture of the kundalini process ignited by Hindu yoga, mantra, pranayama, tantric visualization, *bhakti* practices, and other spiritual *sadhana*.

CHAPTER 1
MOKSHA – ENLIGHTENMENT

Moksha is the ultimate goal of Hinduism, and it means attaining liberation from the never-ending cycle of reincarnation that rules human life and attaining freedom from the suffering that life entails. Another alternative for describing the spiritual liberation of *Moksha* is that it entails "freedom from rebirth in *samsara*."

The special characteristic of *moksha* rarely discussed is that it entails our attainment of transcendental spiritual bodies that reside on different heavenly planes of existence. Advaita Vedanta calls the attainment of these body-mind complexes "freeing your *atman* (your highest manifest self) from the *koshas*" that defile its purest state of existence. You essentially "negate," "extinguish," "remove" or "shed" lower *koshas* in order to reveal a transcendental *atman* of purified beingness. You undo any bindings with unnecessary, illusive physical and mental layers that have become bound to your presence as an *atman*, removing everything about yourself that is not true.

Moksha is the utmost aim of human life and if you attain the state of a pure *atman* free from defilements this constitutes enlightenment, the liberation of living in your highest possible state of existence. Enlightenment entails freedom from ignorance and a self-realization as to what you truly are as a being. Enlightenment means that your spiritual existence is so high that you can experientially realize that your *atman*, or highest possible and purest core self-entity, is the same as the Brahman as well as one with the universe and all things.

The *Upanishads* tell us that when a person or *jiva* (soul) attains *moksha* or liberation it means that their *atman* – the core or innermost essence of their self – experientially recognizes its unity with the Brahman that is the source of that soul and all creation. One's status becomes so refined that they *experientially comprehend* because of the perception of universal energies that their own true nature is the ultimate source of all existence, life and consciousness. Our deepest essence or composition, the substance of which you are ultimately composed, is the ground state of all existence … the primordial base or absolute substratum of manifest beingness. Everything can be resolved to this ultimate absolute residuum.

Sometimes the Brahman is split into two divisions where Nirguna Brahman represents a formless, limitless, undifferentiated essence lacking qualities or attributes while Saguna Brahman (Ishvara or Prakirti) represents a manifest aspect of Brahman with qualities and attributes, i.e. our universe. Purusha is another term commonly used to designate attributeless Nirguna Brahman as the self-so, uncreated, beginningless, formless (prior to beingness, undifferentiated without attributes), pure, eternal, and changeless (actionless or non-moving) substratum of the universe that has no perceptible qualities or characteristics.

The Brahman is the fundamental essence of the universe, its *deepest composition* that answers the question, "Of what is the universe made?"

On the other hand, the *Katha Upanishad* explains that *atman* is the innermost transcendental essence of each living being, and you must cultivate spiritual practices such as meditation to find it. You can think of the *atman* as the innermost soul of the individual or our innermost divinity, namely the highest core of a *jiva* (manifest self) while it remains a self-entity. According to the *Upanishads*, our *atman* and the Brahman are of the same substance which is true because the *atman* and all other things in the universe are equally composed of the same all-pervading substance of the Brahman.

You can intellectually understand this, but there is a stage of spiritual ascension where you can experientially perceive, know and understand that your *atman*, or highest core self, is actually composed of the Brahman, permeated by the Brahman, and so is essentially the Brahman even though your *atman* is a manifestation with apparent density while the Brahman is its ultimate undifferentiated and formless substrate.

When *atman* returns to Brahman it means that one's individual self has attained the peak of transcendental spiritual perfection. But what does that mean? It means that a *jiva*, whose body is an agglomeration of different layers of energy spanning different planes of existence, becomes liberated from the lowest, densest or most impure energies that pollute its highest and purest possible composition of manifestation.

When a *jiva* achieves that apex of purity by attaining the highest possible bodily existence of being nearly pure energy while still retaining a body that has consciousness, that *jiva* gains recognition of their compositional and vibrational unity with Ishvara (all of phenomenal existence) and then also recognizes their unchanging substratum as being the Brahman – the unmanifest static, permanent, ultimate source of All Creation.

The ultimate goal of Hinduism is to perfect oneself through the many cycles of birth and death, or *samsara*, so that one's innermost *atman* or highest potential of physical manifestation sheds nonessential lower energies belonging to more solid, denser or less vibrational planes of existence. It becomes more and more like pure energy when it becomes purified (free) of its impure taints that are these lower shells, and thereby achieves a *moksha* that escapes the *samsara* of the lower realms.

THE FIVE KOSHAS OF HINDUISM

To explain, the *Taittiriya Upanishad* states that the mind-body complex of man consists of five *koshas*, sheaths, coverings or layers which Sufism calls "veils" and Buddhism calls *skandhas* or aggregates. The sheaths are said to cover one another like the layers of an onion or segments of a collapsible telescope, but are actually various forms of energy from different planes of existence that become aggregated as matter within our level of existence, and we call our complete permeation by these higher energies as being "wrapped together." Matter, as you know from science, is really condensed energy but it can be decomposed into various planes of energy that can be separated from one another. The *atman* or immortal self is permeated by these five energy aggregates in the form of body doubles until it can free itself of these unnecessary shells and stand independent of them as a transcendent body free of the lower contaminants of superior existence.

We identify ourselves with these *koshas*, or sheaths, when our true *atman* is actually the Brahman, the fundamental substratum of the universe. However, we don't know this because our stage of existence lacks the ability to perceive the various planes of existence and how they intermingle within us as our composition while the Brahman remains their absolute permeating substratum. Since the absolute substrate of the universe never moves or changes but everything else does, and because we have no intrinsic enduring, unchanging core except for our fundamental substratum, Hinduism teaches us that the Brahman, our deepest composition, is our True Self. It is our True Self because our true self-nature never leaves us or changes but remains as it is in each and every circumstance.

The *Taittiriya Upanishad* and the Advaita Vedanta sage Adi Shankara spoke of five sheaths covering our *atman* in order to indicate that we have the potential to attain five transcendental spiritual bodies that reside on different planes of existence, and for a sage they can remain linked to one another so that he might access all five planes of existence. To accomplish this is the actual road of spiritual practice hidden within Hinduism but accomplished by its sages nonetheless.

The *atman*, which is man's truest soul and the "traveller of worlds," is thus said to be *covered* by the five *koshas* whereas you might more accurately say that the *koshas*, until they are unfurled from their crystallization, compression or aggregation within the human body, are *intermixed* as several different energy layer shells that can become unraveled from one another. According to Adi Shankara the five koshas are:

1. *Annamaya kosha*, or physical body (material envelope)
2. *Pranamaya kosha*, or energy body made of Prana
3. *Manomaya kosha*, or mind sheath (mental envelope)
4. *Vijnanamaya kosha*, or wisdom-knowledge sheath
5. *Anandamaya kosha*, or bliss sheath

Rather than aspects of consciousness, these sheaths actually refer to five types of energy condensed, compressed or agglomerated within living matter that can be released through the processes of spiritual cultivation. Just as solid matter has more tenuous phases of existence such as liquid, gas, plasma and so forth, the universe is composed of different energy planes of existence that interpenetrate and they are agglomerated in the realm of matter. However, through the practices of spiritual cultivation we can differentiate these energies from the human body and separate them out because they have a different "purity," frequency, vibration or density from one another. It is not that they actually have a higher frequency or vibration for that is just a way of talking used by Swami Vivekananda and other masters to make the process more intelligible.

You can think of your body as a compressed aggregate of energy while your mind specifically operates via a finer level of energy beyond that physical plane called Prana. For each spiritual body in the universe, its life force (pranic energy or "wind element") is a vital energy that powers both its life and consciousness, and that higher energy is composed of the aggregate of all the higher energy planes.

The enlightened sage Sri Nisargadatta explained that *prana-sakti* life force is the dynamic aspect of our being while consciousness is life's sentient principle, and the two aspects of life and consciousness are really one. Consciousness and life force are two components inextricably woven together as a single principle, which is why they can affect each other, and they always originate from the same form of energy.

Consciousness, which originates from the presence of a higher spiritual body composed of Prana, pervades and illumines your mind while your life is also dependent upon the existence of Prana within you. Hence, when your inner spiritual body is released from your corpse upon death (and thus "liberated" from the material plane of existence) then consciousness goes with it. The life force and consciousness of your released subtle body has its life and mind powered by a "wind element" that is a higher (vibrational) energy than Prana. In fact, in Chinese Taoism that energy is called Shen.

The *koshas*, sheaths or shells covering our *atman* core body are basically transcendental bodies composed of higher energies that can only be seen on higher planes of existence but they have become condensed or compressed into the realm of matter, which is an aggregate interplay of all higher energies and interpenetrating fields of existence. Yet they can be unraveled or uncoupled from each other and stand as independent existences.

The *annamaya kosha* – which Sri Nisargadatta calls the "foodstuff body" – corresponds to our physical realm of matter that is very condensed energy. You might colloquially say that matter is a condensing, compression, contraction, emanation or aggregation of higher energies such as Einstein proved, or that matter is an enfoldment of vibrational processes into a place that includes standing waves of vibrations which appear as particles. Matter is as if "frozen light" where light energy, rather than streaking off, becomes trapped or bound and localized in one place.

Yoga and the path of spiritual cultivation entails unbinding various vibrational energies or energy planes from being entwined with your body so that you can arise in a higher spiritual body that is independent of the earthly vibrational field of existence. Then you repeat that process to arise in each new spiritual body that is possible. Each transcendent spiritual body past the first one, which is known as the deva body or body of subtle energy, will retain its own structure that looks like your physical nature and have special capabilities greater than the human being since it is composed of energy. It will reside on a different realm of being or existence (i.e. spiritual plane, sphere, *loka* or field) according to its aggregate composition of vibrational components.

Therefore, transcending the *annamaya kosha* or gross physical body (*karya sharira* in Sanskrit) are the *pranamaya kosha* (inner subtle energy body made of Prana), *manomaya kosha* (mind-stuff sheath or Causal body), *vijnanamaya kosha* (wisdom sheath) and *anandamaya kosha* (bliss sheath) that each represent an agglomerated body of fewer and fewer energy types. In Tantra Shastra, the five sheaths are *paramjyoti, para, niskalasambhavi, ajapa* and *natrka* according to *Jnanarnava*, which is a Jain text on meditation.

When through the practice of spiritual cultivation – such as through yoga, meditation, mantra *japa, bhakti* and so forth – you first achieve the emergence of the subtle energy deva body that is your *pranamaya kosha*, then that subtle spirit body will still contain intermixed within it the higher energies of the *manomaya, vijnanamaya* and *anandamaya koshas* until you attain the next higher spiritual body that splits them off from its vehicle.

In other words, an agglomeration of the *pranamaya, manomaya, vijanamaya* and *anandamaya koshas* constitute the subtle body or deva body also known as the astral body whose Sanskrit name is *sukshima sharia*. Sometimes it is referred to as the *linga sharira* (astral body). Adi Shankara and the *Upanishads* don't tell you this, but this generation of a more transcendental body out of a lower one that is left behind is how you strip your *atman* of its coverings or sheaths.

The initial attainment of the *manomaya kosha* will also contain within itself the energies of the higher *vijnanamaya* and *anandamaya koshas* until they can be defused from it after you generate a higher body out of the *manomaya kosha* body composed of Shen energy.

If you can generate a higher body out of the initial *manomaya kosha* body then what will be left behind after the new body emerges on a higher plane will be the *manomaya kosha* standing pure by itself without the presence of the higher *koshas* within it that previously contaminated it through aggregation. You arise in a new body but you leave behind, attached to your new body, the living shell called the pure *manomaya kosha* that has become unbound from your higher nature.

This explains why different religions state that each spiritual body (and its corresponding heaven) can be ranked with different grades of purity, which also means that the different heavens or planes of existence will have different gradations of higher and lower frequencies or purities within themselves. You must achieve a higher transcendental body through purifying transformations in order to access and enjoy a new heavenly plane of existence, but that initial accomplishment must then be followed by yet more purification work to free your new body of energy impurities, which means freeing it of the *koshas* or energies that are still condensed within it by separating them out as new and higher existences attached to the old. The closer you get to generating a new body the higher the purity of your spiritual body on any plane of existence.

The next higher spiritual body past the *manomaya kosha* will be a combination of the *vijnanamaya kosha* and the higher energies of the *anandamaya kosha* (and beyond) as a composite, while the achievement of the *anandamaya kosha* will stand independent by itself resplendent. Correction: the composition of the *anandamaya kosha* will contain *all* the remaining higher energy planes of the universe since they will penetrate it with full permeation. They will serve as its life force and as the power behind its consciousness. Without the anatomical existence of the body and mind of the *atman*, which is essentially the *anandamaya kosha* or Superconsciousness body since you cannot proceed in any higher decoupling decomposition, the higher energies of the universe will still be there but they won't power anything.

You can call the *anandamaya kosha* the *atman* because it is still a sentient living being with consciousness, or you can call all those higher energies "pure consciousness" and identify them as your *atman* even though they are non-living entities. You can say they are the foundation of life, or the foundation of consciousness, or your witness-consciousness, or you can say they are primary consciousness whereas they are just energies. Or you can call the Brahman your *atman* since it is your ultimate substratum and True Self.

There are lots of way you can name things. It doesn't really matter because *what you are trying to do is cultivate as high a spiritual body as possible without reaching a stage of extinction or annihilation*. What teachings or terminology, stories, or skillful means you use to get people to cultivate in this direction are up to you. The only thing relevant is that you cultivate these higher bodies and go as far as you can go. In fact, any mistakes made in this text, and in other Hindu works (and they do contain them) will be corrected as soon as you die and achieve the subtle body because everyone is told the truth about all these things since devas can see the process of reincarnation. Thus you can't cheat them and there is no reason to withhold information in order to manage humanity.

You can take a Davaita dualist approach that the *atman, jivatman, Paramatma*, and the Ultimate Reality (Brahman) are completely different, or the Advaita non-dual approach that they are the same, or the Bhedabheda non-dualist and dualist approach that they are simultaneously non-different and different. It's irrelevant just as it is irrelevant whether you are a Hindu, Jain, Sikh, Buddhist, Christian, Sufi and so on as long as you are cultivating proper spirituality. The only thing really relevant is that (1) you exist with sentience, (2) your existence occurs because of a certain densification, condensing, congealing or freezing of energies and fields into an embodied form with consciousness, and (3) you want to attain the highest possible body that maintains self-awareness, replete with all perfections, and the ability to function with activities in the universe as you wish.

As soon as you attain the subtle body through enlightenment or though death you will come in contact with the true spiritual teachings that correct many errors that abound in religions, including some within Hinduism, and when you achieve the highest Immanence or Superconsciousness body you will also receive teachings that correct errant teachings given to people on lower planes of existence because you become privy to secret information as well. The only thing really relevant is that you exist with an attribute called consciousness that gives you the illumination of self-awareness, and that you can change your attributes and circumstances during life to achieve a higher stage of living and personification in the universe.

This is positivism, not nihilism, even though your existence is an illusion in terms of its ultimate substrate. Advaita Vedanta teaches that you are a non-intrinsic entity that has come about through a comprehensive interconnectedness of all things in the universe, your composite body is imperfect and your consciousness is a faulty illusion that functions with an errant self-notion at its core, but you still exist with a mind so you want to throw aside negativities and go about trying to maximize your life and its potentials. This includes learning how to use your consciousness correctly, and how to do things to accomplish what you want.

In terms of manifestation, as long as you exist on a plane of densified matter where a sentient anatomical existence remains possible then your appearance is an existence, and your life on that plane should then pursue happiness (the absence of suffering), achievement and purpose even though there is a deeper reality than your level of densification. Causality still exists on all the planes of manifestation, civilization and its benefits still exist, people must still cultivate virtue and seek accomplishments for their survival and flourishing, men and women still marry and produce offspring, and we should still strive to elevate ourselves and our culture because life life will still go on until it stops and there is reincarnation. Because we have life we can reach upwards striving for greater skillfulness, wisdom, elegance, elevation and perfection in our living. Hinduism simply provides us with foundational training for such a possibility and points us towards spiritually working to attain the highest possible body as liberation – the naked *atman* released from its shells.

What I use is that the *anandamaya kosha*, stripped bare of all sheaths, veils or other *koshas*, is your eternal *atman* that is the base form of your other *koshas* since they are all derived from it just as the physical body is derived from the subtle body. This is your highest, purest body that lives a *very long time* and its achievement is the equivalent of complete and perfect enlightenment, or liberation. It is as far as you can climb. At this stage you can see the realms of energy that penetrate everything below it, thus composing them, and can realize that you are not like a separate sentient cell floating in a sea of energy because those energies penetrate you infinitely and make you one with them. Your condensed emanation as a form is due to those energies so there really isn't any true such thing as a barrier of space between your body's existence and a sea of fields and energies that permeate it and produce it with contact at every point of its manifestation.

Therefore you are a seamless part of the fabric of the universe rather than a self-contained, coherent bubble within the ocean even though you seem like an independent bubble that is a tangible body. The point is that the Brahman is the ultimate Self, the whole universe is the same Self, the Brahman and the universe together are that one Self. Choose whatever perspective you like for whatever purposes you want to fulfill because you still have existence and you don't want to fall into bodiless extinction where you don't have a mind. You think you are a personal self but all those thoughts originate from a delusionary process of consciousness particular to sentient beings that are really just another phenomena in the universe, yet it gives you the illusion of independent existence and you'll always have that so use it to thrive and flourish while knowing the truth of your reality. That's all.

The pure *anandamaya kosha* is as high as you can go and the higher energies beyond our *atman* are sometimes called "pure consciousness" or the "energies of consciousness" that are still there without any sentient bodies but they cannot be known unless you have equipment at those stages of existence. Of course the science at the level of the Buddha body may reveal many facts about these energies that are the "consciousness of all minds." Those energies pervade the universe as a higher substrate which is why it is said that consciousness is everywhere and that the lower planes of the universe lie within consciousness. But of course the proper terminology rather than consciousness is energy or fields of energy.

Spiritual masters and traditions all use different vocabularies and it really doesn't matter what you choose to identify as what since the only real target is to cultivate to attain as high a transcendental body as possible. How you teach this to people through explanations may or may not be correct here or there but errors are and misdirections to get a good result for society as a whole are simply a matter of skillful means. Once you attain the subtle body you will be corrected as to what is true and false in the realm of spirituality since everyone in the heavens knows the path, can see how souls reincarnate, see demonstrations of the higher spiritual bodies and so on. There is no reason to keep anything secret.

When a higher transcendental body emerges from a lower plane of existence due to the purifying practices of spiritual cultivation then that new life of higher transcendental energies arises an independent spiritual body but remains connected to the lower ("impure" or unpurified) energies of the old body from which it had become differentiated and then separated. It remains connected to the previous body from which it arose as if tied to it by a string unless those connections are severed on purpose.

The linkage of all these bodies together is called the *sambhogakaya* of an individual. It is a collection of bodies, each residing on a different plane of existence, that are all connected to one another to form a single multi-dimensional (multi-planed) entity with many bodies. The movie writers will have a field day with this because our spiritual potential is not as they imagined things to be.

The *sambhogakaya*, which is called the Reward or Enjoyment body of an individual since its grandeur attests to their work at spiritual cultivation, isn't composed of just five bodies each within a different energy plane of existence. This is because the fourth body can generate multiple energy copies of itself, called *nirmanakaya*, in order to perform activities in the world while the fifth or highest body can generate *nirmanakaya* that can themselves generate *nirmanakaya*. A very old spiritual master will then have countless bodies within his *sambhogakaya* whose overall magnificence will attest to his many years of efforts at self-cultivation work.

When Krishna gave Arjuna a vision of his *Vishwaroop* (universal form) in the *Bhagavad Gita* this was a mental projection to Arjuna of the many bodies Krishna had emanated over time that belonged to his *sambhogakaya*, which is the collection of all someone's main spiritual bodies along with their *nirmanakaya* emanations.

You can see fanciful representations of Krishna's *Vishwaroop* in *Vishvarupa: Paintings on the Cosmic Form of Krishna-Vasudeva* (Neena Ranjan) although a more accurate picture of a *sambhogakaya* is found in the famous Taoist classic, *The Secret of the Golden Flower*. Tibetan Buddhism also has many illustrations on the way this works. You can also see a representation of how a human and subtle body are attached to one another in the *Xingming Guizhi* (*Principles of Balanced Cultivation of Inner Nature and Vital Force*) that also comes from China, and some of these pictures are available on the internet.

In summary, out of the physical body of matter or *annamaya kosha* is released a body of subtle energy composed of Prana called the subtle body, deva body, etheric body, soul, spirit body or astral body. That subtle energy constitutes the life force or vital energy of our physical nature, and that energy is also the energy that powers consciousness. Consciousness, which originates from the presence of a higher spiritual body within us composed of Prana, pervades and illumines your mind enabling it to function. Without the power of the *pranamaya kosha* within us ... without the presence of Prana within us ... then life and the mind cannot work.

It is the subtle body that does all the work of perception and conception in the body, which is why a child born who is missing parts of a brain sometimes has full mental powers and doctors cannot understand why. As an illustration, a fire cooks food with the help of fuel but the act of cooking is due to the fire (Prana) and not the fuel (physical body). Similarly, the acts of seeing, hearing, moving, etc. are actually done by the inner subtle body (the fire or Prana) that depends upon the gross physical body (the fuel) for its operations.

The fact that the subtle body can be released from being stationed within the *annamaya kosha* is explained in the *Taittiriya Upanishad (2.2.1)* which says, "With the self made of food (*annamaya kosha*) is another self, made of Prana (*pranamaya kosha*). The *annamaya kosha* is filled by the *pranamaya kosha*."

Consciousness depends on the presence of this subtle vital energy that leaves as a separate spirit when its tie with the physical body is broken upon death. Sometimes it can detach from the human body in near-death experiences when the tie between the two bodies is weakened, and thereafter an individual often tends to be a bit psychic or develops unusual mental powers because their subtle body is no longer closely tied to their physical nature. Science fiction fans might be upset to hear that robots are not alive and neither is AI programming, but since both do not have higher Prana bodies they can never be considered life forms nor as having consciousness, which are ludicrous notions.

In a human life, all its aspects are controlled by the subtle body.

The physical body is like a Laborer Caste and the subtle body like a Merchant Caste. The Merchant Caste (subtle body) has an intellect that calculates and compares things as good and bad in order to do business with the world, and then it employs the Laborer Caste (the gross physical body) to get things done as it plans because it is the higher master.

The important principle to understand is that the combination or fusion of the higher *koshas* with our physical nature is what fuels the body as its life force and empowers it to operate. Those higher aggregates constitute the force or energy that empowers the possibility of consciousness because it is impossible for matter to engender consciousness or life without higher transcendental energies.

When a deva, or subtle energy bodied individual, spiritually cultivates sufficiently then its own life force that the Chinese call Shen energy will become liberated as an independent higher spiritual body that then resides on a higher plane of existence. In other words, the *manomaya kosha* that is a combination of all the higher *koshas* will free itself from the shell of the *pranamaya kosha*.

When the *manomaya kosha* is sufficiently cultivated and purified through spiritual practices then from within it is released a *vijnanamaya-anandamaya kosha* composite as an independent life. When the *vijnanamaya-anandamaya* body–mind complex is cultivated then its own life force will eventually be liberated as a transcendental body that is the standalone *anandamaya kosha*.

This constitutes the *atman* or highest core of human existence, and the achievement is sometimes called perfect and complete enlightenment or the stage of no more learning. In Hinduism this is the real meaning of *moksha*, liberation or *nirvikalpa* samadhi, and in Buddhism this constitutes the achievement of *nirvana*.

The life force of this highest spiritual body attainment is derived from the remaining higher transcendental planes of existence. Those energies are a higher frequency subset of Saguna Brahman than that which composed all previous body existences. You can also call those higher energies Ishvara, the God from whom all things are said to have been emanated, since Ishvara is considered the creator of all phenomenal existence. Or you can consider Ishvara just the first emanate or singular highest plane of manifestation from which the rest of the universe arose.

Whatever you cannot reach and turn into another new transcendental body past the highest body-mind attainment of the *atman* or *anandamaya kosha* are energy planes that can be lumped together as "the source that pervades consciousness, existence and enlightenment." They power the consciousness and life of the *atman* so we can say that the material universe is composed of consciousness, which is just a manner of speaking rather than a fact.

The *Taittiriya Upanishad* and Advaita Vedanta sage Adi Shankara spoke of five sheaths covering our True Self, or unchanging identity, as a way to indicate that we have the potential to attain higher transcendental spiritual bodies that reside on different planes of existence but which remain linked to one another, at their interfaces of differentiation, so that one might use them to simultaneously access and enjoy all five planes, spheres or fields of existence.

Once again, the *annamaya kosha* (foodstuff body) corresponds to our physical human body of matter, or physical body-mind complex. Transcending this are the *pranamaya kosha* (energy or Qi body made of Prana), *manomaya kosha* (mind-stuff sheath or Causal body), *vijnanamaya kosha* (wisdom sheath) and *anandamaya kosha* (bliss sheath). When we spiritually cultivate we can separate each lower level of being, or *kosha* from a higher body-mind aggregate or complex, and we name these higher bodies differently according to spiritual traditions.

THE FIVE SPIRITUAL BODY EQUIVALENTS OF HINDUISM

Sadguru Sadafal Deoji Maharaj of the Vihangham Yoga tradition (a Nath Siddha tradition) also clearly stated that we can cultivate higher bodies. Starting from our gross physical body he said that we can also attain a subtle body, Causal body, Prime Causal body, and Superconsciousness body. In the Nath tradition the technical names for these bodies are the *Sthula deha, Sukshma deha, Karana deha, Mahakaran deha,* and *Hansa deha,* which are the same five bodies previously mentioned.

In Kashmir Shaivism the idea of the *koshas* is found in the five *kalas*, roughly translated as "worlds" or "planes" that represent the descent or emanation of pure consciousness into matter. In Sanskrit the traditional names for the physical body, subtle body and Causal body are the *sthula sharira, sukshma sharira* and *karana sariria.*

The Tamil saint Ramalinga Swamigal (Vallalar) taught that the stages of spiritual achievement start with the unripe physical body and then proceed to the attainment of a purified body of Prana (the subtle body of the devas), body of Vibrations (the Causal body), Wisdom Light body (Supra-Causal body) and then a Body of Immanence (Superconsciousness body). He wrote that through the fire of yoga the impure body or impure elements was slowly transformed into a pure body of pure elements.

He named these five bodies the *Stuhla deham, Suddha deham* (Perfect Body), *Mantra deham, Jnana deham* (*Divya dehan* or body of light, *Kailaya deham*), and Body of Immanence (Body of Wisdom and Bliss). Even though the *Suddha deham* is just the subtle body of Prana we normally achieve by cultivating spiritual practices, because this body is higher than our physical nature he calls it a "perfected body."

Sri Siddharameshwar Maharaj of the Inchagiri Sampradaya, a branch of the Navnath Sampradaya, taught that we have the potential of a physical, subtle, Causal, Supra-Causal (Cosmic body) and Paramatman body. He also calls the Supra-Causal body the Great-Causal body or *Mahakarana* body that is also known in the teachings of Vedanta as the Turya state, and told us that this is still the stage of an aspirant because there is one more body to go.

To better understand these bodies better, since much information is lacking in general Hinduism, we must turn to the spiritual teachings of other spiritual traditions that can supply more details than what has come down to us in the *Vedas, Brahma Sutras* and *Upanishads*. If the spiritual path is truly a non-denominational path then the other spiritual traditions of this world will have realized saints who have certainly have discovered the exact same stages of attainment and confirming their existence.

As the Sage of Kanchi (Jagadguru Sri Chanrasekharendra Sarasvati Swami) wrote in *The Guru Tradition*, "The Ayurvedic physician must accept what he may find beneficial for health in the Western or some other system but which is not contrary to the tenets of Ayurveda. Similarly, allopaths also must accept Ayurvedic methods of treatment that may be found useful."

In his book, *The Vedas*, he also notes that the Moslems rely primarily on the Koran for spiritual truths while Christians rely on the Bible, Parsees rely on the *Zend Avesta* and Buddhists on the *Dhammapada*. Hinduism, he noted, must look for spiritual answers in a large corpus of Hindu works rather than just the *Vedas* alone, and it must be willing to accommodate spiritual truths from elsewhere as well.

Consequently, Hinduism must be open to accept non-denominational truths from other traditions just as those traditions should be willing to accept the truths from Hinduism, for it matters not where math, science, medical knowledge or universal truth is discovered or revealed.

Facts are non-denominational, opinions are not, and when many religions will use a different vocabulary to announce the same truths promoted by Hinduism it is a type of proof confirming the spiritual path in Hinduism and in general.

THE EQUIVALENTS FROM BUDDHISM

One notable spiritual pathway from India that confirms the teachings of Hinduism is Buddhism. The ten primary avatars of Vishnu, or Dashavatara, includes Shakyamuni Buddha because like the ancient *rishis* he also revealed detailed teachings on *moksha* that originated among the enlightened masters of the highest heavens of existence and thus was able to fill in many of the gaps within Hinduism (just as the *Upanishads* were written to fill in the gaps left by the *Vedas* and other texts written to fill in their gaps so on). Much of Buddhism overlaps with Hinduism because it was born out of Vedic culture, but its uses a different vocabulary (the Buddhist term for the Brahman or Purusha is the *dharmakaya*) and provides clearer details on the stages of spiritual cultivation.

In the *Diamond Sutra* Shakyamuni Buddha clearly stated that there are five possible bodies for an enlightened human being by iterating the existence of the human eye, Deva eye, Wisdom eye, Dharma eye and Buddha eye. In other teachings Buddha referred to these bodies as the five *skandhas* instead of *koshas*, and matched these bodies with five stages of spiritual attainment that he called the stages of Arhatship.

Buddhism teaches that those who become enlightened are Arhats, which are equivalent to the Arahants of Jainism. The stages of Arhatship, or enlightenment, are the stages of the Srotapanna, Sakradagamin, Anagamin, Arhat, and Great Golden Arhat attainments. Each of these stages corresponds to a new spiritual body attainment yet most people don't know this because this information is transmitted in a muddled fashion for particular reasons.

The lowest stages of enlightenment that enable you to escape from the worldly plane of existence include the Srotapanna and Sakradagamin ranks of spiritual attainment, both of which refer to the subtle body attainment that resides in the energy plane called the Desire Realm. When you die your spirit, composed of Prana, ascends to this subtle energy or deva plane of existence that resides in what Buddhism calls the Realm of Desire or Desire Realm (*Kama Loka*) that for our world surrounds the material earthly plane. Joy is the condition of this heaven since the deva residents (who possess subtle bodies composed of Prana) are always happy and enjoying themselves in play and antics but the sentient beings who reside in this plane are still subject to strong desires and the pulls of sensuality.

The Srotapanna Arhat refers to a lower grade of purification of the subtle body's energy in this heavenly plane while the Sakradagamin stage of Arhatship refers to a higher stage of subtle body purification. The Srotapanna stage is equivalent to the first dhyana, or *vitarka* samadhi of Hinduism, while the Sakradagamin stage is equated with the second dhyana or *vicara* samadhi.

Buddhism calls the initial subtle body attainment of the deva body that frees itself from its physical shell, or stage of the Srotapanna Arhat (first dhyana attainment), the "Joyous Ground Born of Separation" because your spirit finally becomes liberated from the gross physical body. Naturally this produces great joy. The Sakradagamin (second dhyana) attainment is called the "Joyous Ground from the Production of Samadhi" because at this higher level of purification your mind becomes more stable because the energy of its consciousness becomes more purified.

Both of these subtle body stages correspond to the *Guyan Khand* Realm of Spiritual Knowledge in Sikhism, but you can basically just think of these classifications as the subtle energy or pranic plane of existence that extends across the universe. Buddha just called this the Desire Realm, and once you become a Desire Realm deva all these differences will be made plain to you so any errors being taught across traditions really don't matter.

Next comes the stage of the Anagamin Arhat, which corresponds to the Causal body that resides in the energy plane known as the Realm of Form (*Rupadhatu Loka*) that is distinctly different than the etheric realm that the subtle body resides within. Its residents have higher meditative and body accomplishments than those in *Kama Loka*, or the Desire Realm. The energy of this plane of reality corresponds to the combination of the *manomaya, vijnanamaya* and *anandamaya* energies that have not yet become undifferentiated from each other, or you can just say the heavenly plane of the Causal body or *manomaya kosha* when it has become devoid of the higher energy bodies that would normally be aggregated with it until defused through the processes of spiritual cultivation that churn one's energies to a higher state of purity.

Devas cannot see the Realm of Form where Causal-bodied beings exist just as we cannot see devas due to their rarified energy. Beings in the higher realms can see or sense beings within lower realms but those in the lower realms can never perceive those in the higher realms who can possess lower beings to control their thoughts and actions. When a deva finally attains a Causal body they cannot resist the temptation to possess their friends and do all sorts of antics.

Buddhism calls this Anagamin stage of Arhatship the third dhyana attainment and "The Wonderful Blissful Ground of Separating from Joy" because its stage of refinement is far separated from the joyous plane of the devas. When you attain the Causal body or Anagamin achievement, the joy experienced as a deva is recognized as a coarse factor of mental disturbance that you separate from through ascension by attaining this body of higher purity that can better experience stable equanimity and bliss.

To understand this, remember that various states of joy and happiness will have different breathing patterns than ordinary consciousness. They will also be accompanied by differences in the smoothness of your Prana (vital energy) circulation. Correspondingly, at this stage of ascension there is a further improvement in your energy circulation denoted by the cryptic phrase of "separating from joy." Joy is not absent, it is just that one's internal energy has transformed into a more elevated, refined energy that transcends that found in the deva realm whose residents are commonly characterized by continuous happiness and joyousness. One becomes more stable because the energies that power their consciousness are more refined.

The individual who cultivates the Causal body attains the third dhyana of Buddhism known as the *ananda* samadhi of Hinduism.

This body is composed of an energy of higher vibration or purity than the Prana that vitalizes our body and consciousness, and such individuals become capable of performing grand miracles such as giving sight to the blind, restoring limbs to the maimed and sometimes even raising the dead to life (but only of lower creatures rather than human beings). They can experience many more different worlds in the transcendental planes than a subtle-bodied being possibly can.

Transcending the Anagamin is the stage of the full Arhat who has attained what Sri Siddharameshwar Maharaj of the Navnath tradition calls the Supra-Causal body. It resides in the energy realm or *loka* heavenly plane of existence called Formlessness (*Arupadhatu Loka*), and the body has many shape-shifting abilities. In Buddhism this is equivalent to the volition *skandha* attainment, which matches with the *vijnanamaya kosha*, and Buddhism also calls this the stage of "*nirvana* with remainder" because the "remainder" means there is one more body attainment to go.

Buddhism also calls this stage "The Ground of Clear Purity from Casting Away Thought" because of the extremely high degree of mental purity you can now experience in your attendant mind-stream of this body attainment, and because the body attainment is very pure as well. At this stage your internal energy that empowers the production of consciousness is so good that your mental realm is capable of great concentration, stability and quiet.

When you finally are able to attain this body by cultivating the internal energies (life force) of the Causal body you will exist with a body vehicle whose structure doesn't deteriorate quickly because of the long-lived nature of its compositional elements (often referred to as "light"). Therefore it is said you will live practically forever as an "immortal" that can escape the lower realms of reincarnation forever because those bodies need never become aggregated with denser energies anymore.

If it must die, this etheric body is so high that it can carry strong memories of a life with it into a new incarnation, which even happens to some extent when lower level Arhats are reborn, and it can also self-generate copies of itself as independent life existences too. These possibilities insure a type of continuity, unbroken continuum or immortality of life from a different aspect other than deathlessness.

With the attainment of the Supra-Causal body you escape further incarnations in the lower material realms forever because of its transcendental composition that is absent of the lower fields of existence, and with this "immortality" you escape the cycles of birth and death in the lower realms of existence.

The Supra-Causal body is also known as the Clear Light body, Wisdom Light body, *jnana deha*, Dharma body, Rainbow body, or Arhat body. It is said to be "one with the universal life" comprising the lower levels of energy because it can sense the happenings in all the lower energy fields of Nature because its energy realm interpenetrates them at a very high stage of permeating refinement. Hence it can be a "witness of the universe" able to freely hear and comprehend the minds of lower sentient beings (whose thoughts are composed of lower energies readily accessible to this body's more transcendental level), and able to access their knowledge and wisdom.

When someone attains this body we say "their wisdom opens up" (which is why it is called the Wisdom body) because they no longer need to enter into someone and read their neurons to know their thoughts as is necessary for subtle-bodied devas and Causal-bodied individuals. Rather, they can sense thoughts in the environment, or they can still use *nirmanakaya* energy emanations, which are energy copies of their bodies (body doubles), to access the brains of many individuals as well as intelligent animals such as snakes, parrots, dogs, elephants, etcetera. They can also perceive the etheric tapestry pattern of the past and future (called the *akashic* record) for the lower realms of existence, which we call "prophecy" when it refers to what is to come, so many traditions give this attainment a name involving "wisdom." The Supra-Causal or Wisdom body is referred to as the volition *skandha* in Buddhism and *vijnanamaya* ("wisdom") *kosha* in Hinduism. It corresponds to the *Karam Khand* "Realm of Grace" in Sikhism.

This stage of achievement is also called the fourth dhyana attainment where one becomes a full Arhat, which is the classical meaning of "becoming enlightened." In Hinduism this is the *ananda* samadhi. This everlasting body is the attainment that people normally think of when they hear the word "enlightenment," and the attainment of this transcendental body is considered Sivahood, or "*nirvana* with remainder" because it is "formless" yet imperfect since there is one remaining attainment left that is a still higher level of physical purification. Hence, the remainder means that it is not yet fully purified or decoupled from a lower energy realm from which it can escape.

As mentioned briefly, this Supra-Causal body can generate energy copies of itself, called *nirmanakaya* emanations, which can be projected as independent entities in the world to perform specific deeds to help people. For instance this body can therefore twist and turn in all sorts of shapes without restriction that then enables it to create all sorts of kundalini energy movements and effects (such as feelings of hot or cold or vibrations) within any human body it enters. When you meditate and feel strange energy movements inside you it is usually attributed to your "kundalini energy," but this is usually the energy from the *nirmanakaya* emanation of a transcendental spiritual master. Surprise, it's not due to you!

The strange currents of hot or cold energy people feel inside themselves during spiritual practices are also typically due to higher beings helping them move their energies with their own. The phenomenon of *shaktipat* (where a guru "sends you his energy") is exactly this – a *nirmanakaya* body emanation sent inside you to move your Prana by using its own *nirmanakaya* energies to move yours. It is not a self-generated activation of your own energy that comes solely from yourself. The experience of *shaktipat* is a spiritual guru's energy moving inside you because one of his body doubles goes inside you to move your energy and give you a particular experience that he learned how to give. Sometimes a guru will tap you on the shoulder, look at you in a strange penetrating way, wave a fan, speak a word or shout at you before you experience *shaktipat*, and you would normally assume that this is what causes it but of course, this is unnecessary play acting to make you know it came from the teacher. Countless phenomena in the field of spirituality are chicanery but no one wants to tell you.

Transcending the stage of the Arhat is the stage of the Great Golden Arhat, Buddhahood or Tathagata body that Buddhism calls Complete and Perfect Enlightenment, or the Stage of No More Learning. This is the stage of "*nirvana* without remainder" or *nirvikalpa* samadhi in Hinduism because no higher body vehicles are possible, and hence there is no remaining body to be cultivated. Hence, this is the stage where the *atman* returns to Brahman. That is to say, the stage where *atman* realizes its highest possible penetrating unity with the energies of the universe while still retaining a body-mind complex.

This is the highest or purest stage of the *atman* in Hinduism within the hierarchy of bodily sheath attainments. In Islam it is the *insan al-kamil* or perfect, universal man, and in Chinese Taoism it is the real or true man. It is a body composed of the highest transcendental energy plane we can reach while still maintaining a body.

It is referred to as the consciousness *skandha* in Buddhism, the *anandamaya* ("bliss") *kosha* in Hinduism, consciousness *skandha* in Buddhism, the Stage of No More Learning (No More Training or Non-Practice) in Tibetan Buddhism, the stage of God consciousness in Kashmir Shaivism, and the tenth Bodhisattva *bhumi*, and stage of "*nirvana* without remainder" in Buddhism because it is said that no higher body vehicles are possible. In Hinduism this is *nirvikalpa* samadhi.

Once you first attain the Supra-Causal body of a full Arhat that is equivalent to the *Sach Khand* "Realm of Truth" attainment in Sikhism, there is still a higher body attainment possible that is composed of the highest fundamental energies of Shakti, Saguna Brahman, Paramatman, Prakirti or Ishvara where a body formation is still possible because linkages can still exist between its rarified components.

What is very important, and a principle that Buddhist always miss is that these higher spiritual bodies can also be matched with various samadhi achievements. As stated, the first and second dhyana of Buddhism, which correspond to the *vitarka* and *vicara* samadhi of Hindu Yoga, represent the Srotapanna and Sakradagamin stages of the subtle body attainment that you achieve from purifying your Prana. In the *Surangama Sutra* the subtle body attainment, which is attained by breaking free of the *form skandha*, meaning your physical body, is called the "mind-body" attainment to hide this correspondence. The third and fourth dhyana correspond to the *ananda* and *asmita* samadhi of Yoga which represent the Anagamin and full Arhat stages of attainment.

In other words, to compare traditional yoga teachings with Buddhism and Tantra, the *vitarka*-samadhi corresponds to the first dhyana. *Vicara*-samadhi is samadhi with a more subtle basis of support, and therefore corresponds to the second dhyana. The "more subtle basis of support" means that the practitioner's Prana is more refined and thus their consciousness is more refined. Do you see how everything matches up? *Ananda*-samadhi is corresponds to the third dhyana and *asmita*-samadhi corresponds to the fourth dhyana of liberation.

The samadhi attainments are not something you actually cultivate. Spiritual masters and teachings will tell you that you are cultivating samadhi so that you sit there and meditate but this is a misdirection because the samadhi really correspond to body attainments, but they won't tell you that. They will lie. Spiritual masters simply want you to meditate, they want you to notice your mind is getting clearer, and they want you to label that benefit with some name so that you keep practicing and think you are making spiritual progress. If humans develop clearer minds and start watching their consciousness and acts of behavior more this is how the population becomes more civilized, purified or elevated over time. This is how you manage a population and gradually raise it above its animal nature since very, very few people will be able to attain the higher spiritual bodies starting as a human but you don't want anyone demoralized knowing that. You still want them to practice.

So actually the fact is that you want to cultivate transcendental bodies but few people can do that so everything is posed in terms of samadhi attainments. The samadhi attainments do, however, refer to a clarity of consciousness that accompanies each new higher body of energy so masters aren't really lying either. They are just not being 100% truthful. It's like Jedi master Obi-Wan Kenobi telling Luke that Darth Vader murdered Anakin Skywalker because in a way he did.

When a guru is sitting motionless in samadhi it is not because his mind is free of thoughts but *because his spiritual bodies have left to traverse the world,* but masters hide this fact that all their possible sources of consciousness were absent by saying they were absorbed in a thoughtless samadhi experience.

On this note, Sufi Sheikh Muhammed Hisham Kabbani stated clearly in *The Hierarchy of Saints* that the enlightened often travel from their locations, leaving behind their bodies, to help people who need help and their bodies remain motionless during their absence so you should not disturb them. Chinese Buddhism and Taoism also tell us never to touch those bodies, and certainly don't pull on them or shake them in any way, but to call back a master's spirit by ringing a chime next to his ear. Usually when a master is sleeping his body is roaming the world so the same warning holds.

When the Indian saint Ramakrishna would sit motionless "in trance" some students thought his mind was in some beatific samadhi but he too was just absent from his physical shell and traveling about in his higher spiritual bodies. They thought he had to be fed or he would die but this was just nonsense. The Supra-Causal and Immanence bodies also do not need sleep but of course this is a necessary for the physical body.

Consciousness becomes more pristine and clear as you progress in physical ascension since your vital energy or life force, which powers the consciousness of your mind, becomes more purified with every new body because they are the next level of transcendental energies. In other words, the attendant, concomitant ordinary stage of consciousness for each transcendental body is identified as a specific samadhi because, for purposes of expediency, spiritual traditions do not want to publicly reveal to people that this is their real meaning.

The time, however, has come for a full disclosure and for you to understand what spirituality is all about.

By posing spiritual attainments as samadhi attainments of mental purity you pull people into the practice of meditation, cultivating their minds, and policing themselves along the lines of virtue and ethics in thoughts and deeds. This gradually raises us above our animal nature of selfishness, greediness, and violence. So it is good to get people to learn meditation any way you can.

Another benefit of posing the transcendental bodies as mental attainments reached through meditation practice is that meditation provides an opening for higher beings to use their *nirmanakaya* to wash the Prana of humans when they are not, through thinking, clinging to their inner Prana movements that would oppose such washing efforts. This is just another proof of the actual fact that you cannot reach enlightenment unless you engage in inner energy work.

The Buddhist sutras talk about someone who sat in meditation for eons but still did not reach enlightenment, which was because he did not engage in inner energy work. Meditation alone will achieve you nothing. A famous Zen text, *The Transmission of Light*, states "In the distant past, Ananda (Buddha's student) had awakened the aspiration for complete perfect enlightenment in the presence of the Buddha called King of Emptiness, at the same time as did the present

Buddha Shakyamuni. Ananda was fond of intellectual learning, and that is why he had not yet truly realized enlightenment. Shakyamuni, on the other hand, cultivated (inner) energy, whereby he attained true enlightenment."[1] This is the teaching to remember. You can study Advaita Vedanta, the six schools of thought and Hindu philosophy all you want but you will not reach liberation except through spiritual practice that entails *both* meditation *and* inner Prana cultivation work.

Thus you can refer to the stages of spiritual achievement in various ways as *koshas*, transcendental bodies, ranks of attainment, heavenly levels of being, or samadhi-dhyana states of mind. We will soon see that there are even more ways to delineate these stages such as by naming the energy of your body's composition at each stage, or how you feel at each level of accomplishment.

Remember that most spiritual traditions describe spiritual ascension in terms of purified states of mind in order to lead practitioners away from doing kundalini type inner energy work because that will invite the interference of devas who will then play with your Prana and possibly interrupt your life severely. They want most people to do meditation work instead where higher beings can work on you at leisure, but which then takes many lives. Smart people realize that the spiritual path actually entails inner energy work, and that there is no such true thing as a non-conceptual state where you know your pure nature (a cognition of nothingness). You cannot perceive your absolute base state of being although you can think about it and be aware that is exists because of logic. Teachings on empty mind and no-thought and thought detachment are just meant to motivate you to engage in lots of meditation practice.

Shakyamuni Buddha also partitioned each body attainment into a greater and lesser degree of purity (due to the purification work the adept undergoes) called *bhumis* where the 1st and 2nd *bhumi* refer to the Srotapanna subtle body attainment, the 3rd and 4th *bhumi* refer to the Sakradagamin subtle body attainment, the 5th and 6th *bhumi* refer to the Anagamin Causal body attainment, the 7th and 8th *bhumi* refer to the Arhat Supra-Causal or Prime Causal body attainment, and the 9th or 10th *bhumi* refer to the Great Golden Arhat, Immanence or Superconsciousness body attainment of Perfect and Complete Enlightenment that is the core *atman* finally revealed by having

---

[1] *Transmission of Light*, trans. by Thomas Cleary, (Shambhala Publications, Boston, 2002), p. 9.

attained release from its denser energy pollutions.

The life force of this ultimate Buddha body, which is the vital energy that also powers its consciousness, is composed of the remaining energies that cannot be reached in a body-mind vehicle and hence are termed the life force or consciousness *of the universe*. The *jiva*, which is kept alive by association with the Pranas, when stripped bare to become the *atman* is itself all those higher energies of the universe.

Thence, the five *koshas* of Vedanta correspond to these five bodies of the spiritual path. If you cultivate these five transcendental spiritual bodies then you are also cultivating the five *koshas*, which are the *skandhas* of Buddhism, and its *Surangama Sutra* is all about "breaking free from the *skandhas*" in order to attain perfect enlightenment, which means achieving these progressive body attainments because a new body breaks free from the old.

The *vijnanamaya-anandamaya kosha* complex corresponds to the enlightenment of the Arhat (a Supra-Causal body attainment) and the *anandamaya kosha* (bliss sheath) refers to the Immanence or Superconsciousness body attainment of Perfect and Complete Enlightenment, or Great Golden Arhat stage of Buddhahood, that is the pinnacle of human spiritual achievement. This is the *nirvikalpa* samadhi of Hinduism or "Advaita Siddhi" that is the highest stage of realization of the Self.

Vajrayana (Tantric) Buddhism words these five bodies differently than Hinayana and Mahayana Buddhism. It teaches that we have a physical body and the potential to achieve an independent Impure illusory body (subtle or deva body), purified illusory body (Causal body), Wisdom light (Clear light) or Dharma body that is the Supra-Causal body of the Arhat, and then Buddha body or Tathagata body that corresponds to the Superconsciousness or Immanence body of Hinduism. The ultimate foundation of all these bodies is the fundamental substratum which Buddhism calls the *dharmakaya* or Buddha-substrate.

Once again, together these bodies stay linked together as you attain new ones and can be considered a single unit called a *sambhogakaya* "Reward body" that reveals the extent of your spiritual cultivation work. The *sambhogakaya* is also called an "Enjoyment body" because you can use these various body attainments, made of very different fundamental energies or "winds," to traverse and experience (enjoy) the different energy planes of existence. You can be in those planes while transcending them, and thus enjoy them. If you withdraw your highest spirits into a body on a lower plane of existence you can then experience it as the inhabitants do who have the same sense organs and level of consciousness. Naturally it takes time and training (practice) to learn how to use the various spiritual bodies linked to one another so that the highest body is conscious of all their doings.

For a human being to become fully enlightened you must cultivate a *sambhogakaya* that is a set of transcendental spiritual bodies linked together: the physical, subtle, Causal, Supra-Causal and Immanence bodies (the human eye, deva eye, wisdom eye, dharma eye and Buddha eye of the *Diamond Sutra*). However, spiritual schools do not provide many teachings on this because spiritual masters in general didn't want people to know too much about anything other than the subtle body achievement that is the very next rank above the human realm, which everyone reaches upon death, and which should be the immediate target of all your spiritual cultivation efforts.

If you do not achieve the deva (subtle) body attainment then you cannot achieve any of the higher spiritual bodies that lead to true *moksha* or liberation. Therefore you only need to talk about this body and the virtuous behavior, good deeds, higher inner life and spiritual practices that will win you its achievement.

There are many different names used by Vajrayana Buddhism and Dzogchen of the Yungdrung Bon tradition to signify these same stages of attainment, so the terminology used here may be different than what you normally encounter. The cardinal point is that the various *koshas* or densified energy components of a human being that cover its core *atman* must be differentiated through purification efforts and then separated out from one another so that the *atman* stands alone, resplendent, and in that way you attain *moksha* or liberation. You cannot go any higher than that. *Moksha* means "the state of being released" and one of the connotations of this is for the *atman* to be released from all the unpurified, unnecessary energies that are aggregated with it.

Basically, the subtle body is what you achieve from cultivating the various spiritual paths and practices of Hinduism, or from equally subscribing to the intensive inner energy purification practices of other religions. The subtle body is an independent life that is free to traverse the lower heavenly realms of the material plane of existence. Your subtle body is not confined to this little biospherical globe called the earth, but just like your physical body your subtle body needs to be transported to other areas of the universe to experience them whereas the higher transcendental bodies can make some of these trips on their own.

The Causal body is the next higher body superior to your subtle body made of Prana and is also known as the Mental body, Wisdom body, Mantra body, body of vibrations, *pranava deha*, man's spirit, Grace body, or purified illusory body. It is composed of a higher energy that is more transcendental or refined than the Prana of the subtle body and therefore enables greater superpowers than the subtle body. It is free of all lower gross matter and impurities, but it is considered a denizen of the Realm of Form since its field of existence still has many solid-like structures that have not been decomposed into more foundational energies. It is equivalent to the third and fourth Bodhisattva *bhumis* and it is hard to pass through this level to attain the Supra-Causal body in the Formless Realm that is essentially entirely free of the lower realms of matter. The Causal body is also referred to as the conception *skandha* in Buddhism and *manomaya* ("mind-stuff") *kosha* in Hinduism. Furthermore it is the stage of an Anagamin Arhat. In Sikhism the Causal body corresponds to the third level of spiritual attainment that matches with the *Saram Khand* "Realm of Spiritual Efforts."

The Supra-Causal and Immanence bodies that have very long life existences have already been dealt with.

Hinduism teaches that through spiritual activities such as meditation, mantra, yoga, pranayama, reverence and devotional worship you will purify your physical body (dense matter), subtle body and mental body that are the lower three *koshas* in order to attain "the state of final release," or *Kaivalya*, that is the Supra-Causal body attainment. Then there is one more attainment to achieve.

Being free of the lower realms and now understanding one's own true condition as belonging to the unity of all things in the one soup of Shakti (an attainee realizes that there is no such thing as a separate independent existence because one is part of everything seamlessly), at this stage one recognizes that they are part of the one Ocean of Shakti – a single fabric that is the manifest universe – and becomes free of ignorance, delusions, and misunderstandings as regards the origins and evolution of life. Thus one becomes emancipated from *Maya* (delusions and ignorance) because one now understands. Devoid of ignorance a man or woman realizes his eternal existence in the infinite ocean of Shakti as Shakti itself.

In Hinduism you are ultimately pursuing *kayasiddhi*, which means you make various spiritual efforts of many types, including worshipping deities, to attain a perfected immortal body as described by Tirumular, the founder of the Shaiva Siddhanta Tamil Siddha system of spiritual cultivation. The eight *siddhis* manifest in the subtle body that is the first of the higher spiritual attainments, and the yet higher spiritual bodies have even more *siddhi* that are rarely mentioned in scriptures.

Sadguru Siddharameshwar Maharaj said, "You must learn to discriminate the gross, the subtle, and the steady from Parabrahman and recognize it. It is eternal. Then give up untrue form and select the only 'True Thing,' 'Paramartha.' Even after the destruction of the eight bodies, (four of the jiva and four of Ishvara) our True Form lasts forever."

The four *jiva* bodies are the coarse, subtle, Causal and Great-Causal bodies that are still not the naked *atman*. The famous *Dasbodh* written by Samartha Ramdas reports that the four Ishvara bodies of manifestation include the huge gross body (Virat) made up of all the five elements in the universe, the subtle body of God (*Hiranyagarbha* or Golden Womb) that is the universal energy, Causal body of God (*Avyakrut*) that is the unmanifest causal body, and Great-Casual body of God, Primal Illusion, *Moolamaya* or Moola Prakriti body. These represent the universal planes of existence of energies and matter within which the spiritual bodies appear.

THE EQUIVALENTS IN SUFISM

The Indian Sufi master Meher Baba also taught that we have a gross body, subtle body, Mental body, Universal body and Shiva-Atma or Paramatma body. The *bhautic sharir* is the gross physical body, the *adhyatmic sharir* is the subtle body and the *mansik sharir* is the mental body (Causal body). A Sadguru is someone who attains the highest state of enlightenment, namely the *atman*.

Some schools of Sufism call Creation an emanation or effusion from the absolute that occurs in a process of Divine Descent.

According to this scheme the First, Original or Primordial level of existence is Allah, an incorporeal unmanifesting existence that is the fundamental substratum or source essence identified in every other religion or spiritual school as the perfect formless foundation of all existence. This is Parabrahman, Brahman, Nirguna Brahman or Purusha in Hinduism.

Allah is *Alam-i-HaHoot*, the Realm of He-ness (Is-ness). This is the primordial Divine Essence prior to manifestation and it exists as Alonehood (*Ahdiyat*) since there is nothing other than itself. According to Sufism, *Ahdiyat* is primordially pure and incapable of being conceived. Aloneness means without phenomena or attributes, hence *Alam-i-HaHoot* is "The Unknowable and Incomparable Realm."

In other words, this foundational essence certainly exists but it has no attributes or qualities so it cannot be exemplified with anything. Thus thinking cannot make any mental representations of it which is why Islam refuses to let anyone make images of Allah. Allah is at the primordial level of non-Creation and pre-existence. Allah is a state that hasn't manifested into any phenomena, attributes or qualities, including empty space, but somehow everything emanates from this pure substratum despite its absolute purity or aloneness that lacks any causes for its own existence.

From Allah, the First or Real, emanates the existence of a second. According to Sufism this is an utterly incorporeal substance called *Alam-i-YaHoot* (the Realm of First Manifestation) that is an existence dependent on its substratum and it appears different from its own essence (Allah) yet is not a separate, independent entity. It is *Wahid-ul-wujud*, or a singular Unitary Existence since it encompasses Everything infinitely. This first emanation, from which all else will arise, is equivalent to the Ishvara or Saguna Brahman of Hinduism and the Tathagatagarbha or Womb Matrix of Buddhism.

In Islam *Alam-i-HaHoot* is said to have no attributes (like the *nija-shakti* first emanation taught by Gorakhnath) and yet the first manifestation of *Alam-i-YaHoot* is by definition an attribute or quality of the primordial ground state that is pure and incapable of change. This is like the partitioning of the Brahman into Nirguna Brahman (non-manifestation) and Saguna Brahman (manifestation). This first stage of divine descent/manifestation is also called the "Light of Muhammad."

To explain this one must say that the attributes of God are neither other than God nor identical with Him. God permeates everything since everything is God-substance so appearances are nothing but God. They are appearances and thus seem different or apart from His infinite undifferentiated formlessness but they cannot be other than Him since they are Him. Thus they appear to us through illusion or a type of *Maya* that is basically our illusory operations of consciousness. Without consciousness there is no universe because there is no way to know it.

This is why a yogic text like the *Siddha Siddhanta Paddhati* by Gorakhnath states that *Anama* – the Nameless origin (fundamental nature) that is self-existent, self-made, and self-manifest like Allah or the Brahman – gave birth to the first evolute of *nija-Shakti* (like Ishvara or Saguna Brahman) that is eternal, pure, motionless, imperceptible and equivalent to an undisturbed state of consciousness. The first evolute was described as a peaceful, pristine state of consciousness because this skillfully leads you to meditation practice in line with this description – you should meditate with a formless, empty mind similar to an undisturbed awareness that does not attach to whatever arises within it. It cannot be empty or blank because then the state of no-thought is not consciousness, so the best analogy is that it is like empty space within which all things arise but which itself does not cling to anything or interfere with things.

In fact, the only reason any evolutes of the Brahman are described as consciousness, or the reason that the fundamental substratum of the Brahman is described as consciousness (ex. "Luminous Mind") in spiritual schools is to have you understand that *everything you perceive* is your consciousness (your mind) and to encourage you to meditate in such a way that you don't hold onto your thoughts. You are taught to detach from the fabrications that arise within your consciousness. This mirrors the nature of empty space that lets all things appear within in without resisting them or clinging to them. The same can be said for the Brahman that lets Shakti or Ishvara arise within it without ever interfering with anything at all.

During meditation practice you should let thoughts appear in your mind, stay clearly aware of everything that arises, but you shouldn't mentally cling or attach to the products of your consciousness. Instead you should let them flow as the proper operation of consciousness unless you are engaged in a state of concentration where you must remain focused on specific thoughts with stability and perseverance. In this way you are practicing pristine awareness, attention, luminous mind, non-attachment, mindfulness, clear presence, or a state of operational beingness just like the absolute nature of existence that is our underlying substratum. The descriptions within spiritual schools are just expedient means designed to lead you to this type of meditation practice.

Within Sufism the first evolute of *Alam-i-YaHoot* is described as "like awareness." Although it is really a vibrating energy level, radiation, or plane (field) of manifestation ... which perhaps entails many different levels of energy ... it is called awareness because those higher constituents of the universe penetrate the Buddha body as what powers the operations of its consciousness. This is why this realm is also called the "Light of Muhammad" where light refers to consciousness, illumination, awareness or cognition. *Alam-i-YaHoot* is therefore said to be able to know of its own existence, so the descriptive schemes of Ibn Sina and al-Farabi call it the "first intellect."

Once again, this is simply a form of skillful means that motivates ordinary people into meditating by creating an image of this first formless emanation in their mind. The fact that it is called awareness or intellect reflects the fact that the consciousness (and life force) of your highest transcendental body runs on this energy, and because you cannot attain a higher body than an Immanence Buddha body you can colloquially call all the higher energies beyond it, which includes *Alam-i-YaHoot*, "pure consciousness" or the "Light of Muhammad" in Islam.

Only a sentient being can have consciousness because a field or plane of existence lacks appropriate structures for thought formation whereas the anatomical body-mind vehicles of sentient beings have them, so this is just a method of explanation that prompts you to practice meditations where you are just pure awareness without thoughts. You would be practicing emptiness meditation if you were trying to experience nothingness within your consciousness, which is actually a form of non-thinking, non-existence or extinction.

The emphasis on consciousness has only this purpose of promoting meditation practice since "emptiness meditation" is the major method of achievement on the spiritual path. It doesn't matter what is or isn't true about the first emanates of the universe as long as you are cultivating the higher spiritual bodies, and more accurate teachings will become available to you with each new achievement. Hence, the injunction is to just get started with meditation practice.

In Sufi cosmology the next realm of manifestation is *Alam-i-LaHoot*, which is described as the realm of absolute unity. This is what you realize yourself to be part of when you attain the Immanence or Supra-Causal bodies of Hinduism. This is the realm of manifest existence recognized by the Supra-Causal and Immanence bodies, Arhat and Great Golden Arhat, the Buddha body and Dharma body, the volition and consciousness *skandhas*, the *vijnanamaya* and *anandamaya koshas*, and the 7th through 10th Bodhisattva *bhumis*.

The next level of emanation is *Alam-i-Jabrut*, which refers to the realm of the Causal body. It is the domain or plane of residence for the third degree Arhat (*Anagamin*) or *vijnanamaya kosha* and it can be divided into many grades of purification.

The next level of emanation is *Alam-e-Malakut*, or Realm of Souls, which naturally refers to the plane of pranic energy across the universe populated by devas who have not yet achieved the Causal body or higher. This is the realm of beings composed of Prana or subtle energy.

The final level of emanation is the Realm of Physical Bodies, or *Alam-i-Nasut*. This is the tangible world of matter upon which we reside. Our highest spiritual body is concealed within the cover of this realm while being penetrated by the energies of the other higher realms as well, until we strip off these layers to arrive in progressively more naked existences to reach the highest realm possible that can still support a tangible manifestation of a body-entity, which is *Alam-i-LaHoot*. The life force of beings on this realm, and the energies that power their consciousness, whether bundled together or not are referred to in the catch-all plane *of Alam-i-YaHoot*.

Sufi master Ibn Habash Suhrawardi taught that there are planes of existence through an analogy in his philosophy of Illuminationism. He said that the Supreme Light of Lights *(Nur al-Anwar)* was pure immaterial light where nothing manifests. This, of course, corresponds to the Nirguna Brahman substratum of existence that is Purusha, Parabrahman or the *dharmakaya*. Manifestation then unfolds from this Light of Lights in a descending order of ever-diminishing intensity, which is akin to the varying frequencies analogy of Swami Vivekananda, and through complex interactions the lights give rise to energies and forms that produce mundane existence on each level of beingness. All these realms interpenetrate one another but when you attain a higher spiritual body you free yourself from a lower aspect of densified energy that is unnecessary for your existence.

Illuminationism is similar to the ideas within Jewish mysticism which calls these layers of emanation a "thickening of the light."

In *Druze* we have the physical body of the material plane as well as the Universal Soul sphere representing the subtle body, the Logos (Word) sphere representing the Mental Plane or Causal body, the Cause (Precedent) Sphere relating to the Arhat stage of enlightenment or Supra-Causal body, and the Immanence sphere representing the Superconsciousness Buddha body stage of existence.

As explained, the great Indian sage Gorakhnath, founder of the Nath Hindu monastic movement and one of the nine Navnath saints, similarly explained that there are five stages to the self-unfoldment of the Divine Shakti, meaning five stages, fields, spheres or planes of self-manifestation. As with Sufism, Buddhism, Hinduism, Taoism, Confucianism, Jainism and all other religions, these stages or planes of existence correspond to five possible physical existences, each composed of different energies that reside on different realms of being unknowable to each other through the senses.

THE EQUIVALENTS IN CHINESE TAOISM

If we turn to the spiritual schools that developed within China, Chinese Taoism calls the subtle body achievement the stage of the "Earth Immortal." It uses the term "Immortal" to denote the ranks of spiritual attainment, rather than the stages of Arhatship used by Buddhism, to denote the fact that these bodies have very long lives.

If an "Earth Immortal" (who is free from matter due to their subtle body) achieves the next higher transcendental body attainment, which is the Causal body, one next becomes a "Spiritual Immortal." At this stage one's body-mind complex (*sambhogakaya*) has a physical, subtle and Causal body linked to one another where the Causal body is your center of life. You possess all three body attainments.

Upon any stage of spiritual eminence (attainment) where you possess multiple bodies connected to one another we can no longer call you a member of the human species, but something more elevated or divine.

Taoism calls the next achievement, which corresponds to the full Arhat stage of Buddhism or Supra-Causal attainment of Hinduism, the stage of the "Celestial Immortal" while the final Buddha body stage of Perfect and Complete Enlightenment is called the "Universal Immortal" that corresponds to the Superconsciousness or Immanence body of Hinduism. In Buddhism this is also called the stage of No More Learning.

Taoism further explains that you work at refining and perfecting your physical body to perfect or purify your Qi (Prana) for spiritual ascension. This means you spiritually cultivate your physical nature and its life force to attain the independent subtle body of Prana or that is an Earth Immortal. You cultivate, purify, transform and perfect your internal energy so that what arises out of your physical body composed of Jing (semen) is an independent deva body composed of your purified life force subtle energy, called Prana or Qi.

Taoism says that next you work at refining and perfecting your Prana (Qi) body, which means that independent subtle body attainment that is the Earth Immortal, to perfect your Shen. Shen is the name that Taoism gives to the life force energy of the subtle body that upon sufficient purification can leave the shell of the subtle body to become an independent life of its own called the "Spirit Immortal."

Thus Taoism says that out of transformed Jing (the physical body) arises Qi (the subtle body) and out of transformed Qi arises Shen (the Causal body). This is an important simplification of the whole process to understand.

Next Taoism states that you work at refining and perfecting your Shen, which means the Causal body attainment equivalent to the Spirit Immortal, and by purifying the life force of that Shen body you can release a Supra-Causal body composed of what Taoism terms Later Heavenly Energy. This is when you become a "Celestial Immortal."

If you then spiritually cultivate that Supra-Causal body and its life force, which is known as Primordial Heavenly Energy, you can attain the highest spiritual attainment of the "Universal Immortal," Great Golden Arhat, Tathagata body and so forth.

Summarizing, while our physical human body is composed of flesh that originates from a union of egg and semen (Jing), the next highest body is composed of Qi, which is our vital internal energy that keeps us alive. From within that subtle body composed of Qi you can release a yet higher spiritual body composed of Shen energy, which is then known as the Causal body in Hinduism or Anagamin stage of the Buddhist Arhat. Hence the life force of the subtle Qi body is called Shen. From within the Causal body of Shen you can release a higher Supra-Causal body composed of Later Heavenly Energy through even more cultivation effort, which is the Buddhist stage of the full Arhat and Taoist stage of the Celestial Immortal. Most schools use terms like wisdom and dharma, or light and rainbow, or even invisibility and emptiness to describe this body because these are good analogies for some of its capabilities.

This body achievement is considered "enlightenment with a *remainder*" because the "remainder" means that there is one more purification level to achieve, and thus more purification work can be performed on the energies of that body to generate a yet higher body vehicle. From within the Arhat's body of Later Heavenly Energy, which is the stage of Taoist Celestial Immortal, you can release the highest possible spiritual body attainment, which is to achieve the Great Golden Arhat, Immanence body or Tathagata body attainment of the pure *atman* or *jiva* that is composed of just Primordial Heavenly Energy. This is considered the *true man or real human being because it is our highest core body*.

In Taoism, spiritual cultivation can thus be divided into five steps:

Transforming grain (food) into Jing,
Transforming Jing into Qi *(Lian Jing Hua Qi)*,
Transforming Qi into spirit *(Lian Qi Hua Shen)*,
Returning spirit to emptiness *(Lian Shen Huan Xu)*, and
Combining emptiness with the Tao, *(Lian Xu He Dao)*.

A rough way of translating this is that you eat grain (food) to maintain your life (Jing), and then the subsequent spiritual transformations are that "Jing (the physical body grown from semen) transforms into Qi (the deva body), Qi transforms into Shen (the Causal body), Shen transforms into Emptiness (the Supra-Causal or

Clear Light body of an Arhat empty of the lower realms of form existence) and you must achieve a higher stage where the essence of an Emptiness body (devoid of matter attributes) returns to unity with the fundamental substratum of Nature (that composes this body along with its own life force and consciousness)."

Adi Shankara wrote a commentary on the *Taittiriya Upanishad* where he said that your true nature is to be discovered by removing or negating each of the five *koshas* one by one. Islam, as you know, calls them veils. Well, when you generate the subtle body out of the physical body then your subtle body (deva body) becomes your new center of life. In this case the physical body is removed from your structure by being *stripped off*, so it is "negated." Those energies are stripped away from you like a veil that is removed. Shakyamuni Buddha similarly said that breaking through the *skandhas* is like untying the knots of a string in sequence. Thus, all of the *koshas* must be removed in sequence and the process to do so involves internal energy purification.

Adi Shankara told us about the process but he didn't want to explicitly reveal that it was really about body attainments where one body arises out of another after sufficient cultivation work, and it then becomes the new center of your life so that we can say the previous bodies are removed or negated. You can see that every spiritual tradition describes the process differently without anyone really wanting to give all the details for various reasons. In his *Master Key to Self-Realization*, Sri Siddharameshwar Maharaj also called this overall process "negating" your lower bodies and said the process is one of "progressive elimination."

In the *Surangama Sutra*, Shakyamuni Buddha explained that the *skandhas*, *koshas*, veils or spiritual bodies arise by piling themselves upon one another with the purest pattern originating from the "*skandha* of consciousness" that is your underlying Buddha body or *atman*. Shakyamuni Buddha described our job of spiritually cultivating to attain higher transcendental bodies than our physical nature (in order to reach supreme enlightenment) as like *untying the knots of a knotted string in sequential order*. The various bodies are gradually overcome or transcended one by one starting with the physical body, next the subtle body, and then the other bodies in sequence. Their energies are stripped away to eventually reveal a naked *atman* because each time you break away from or transcend a body you arise in a new body composed of the most purified energies of the old body and leave it behind on a lower plane of existence. It remains connected to you but its no longer your center of life, thus it is negated. Instead of using the term "negation," Shakyamuni said that an old body is "extinguished" when you attain a higher transcendental body through countless purifying transformations of your physical nature that resides on whatever plane of existence it is on. Ascension in a higher body basically means that the previous body is separated from, but Buddha used the terminology that the previous body is extinguished.

This, once again, is the same as Adi Shankara's teachings on "negation" and the Taoist teachings that the bodies arise out of one another by cultivating the internal energy within each one by turn. In ancient times no one wanted to say clearly that you were basically cultivating new spiritual bodies where new ones could arise from their impure counterpart. Telling the truth would lead to troubles.

Nevertheless, you basically detach from a body and its unpurified energies that are not necessary for a new body existence on a higher plane of being. Spiritual masters across the world have typically used all sorts of allusions and imprecise (but close) terminology and explanations to give you a general idea of this overall process of spirituality but without spilling the beans to reveal things clearly.

THE EQUIVALENTS IN CHINESE CONFUCIANISM

Some Hindus are familiar with Buddhism and Taoism but most are totally unaware that Chinese Confucianism – which was blessed by the three enlightened masters of Confucius, Mencius and Wang Yang Ming – also has descriptions for the stages of spiritual achievement that correspond to each of these transcendental bodies.

Mencius called the subtle body achievement the stage of "Faith" or "Belief." This is because upon this Srotapanna attainment you gain access to the astral heavens of the subtle body where you can converse with other spiritual beings and obtain access to true, unvarnished spiritual teachings that put away with many false teachings in the world. Therefore you develop *trust, confidence, faith and belief* in the path of cultivating the higher bodies since all the devas around you knows this is the path, see the process of reincarnation being performed on devas who die and must return as humans, see demonstrations of the higher transcendental bodies by enlightened spiritual masters who have no reason to hide anything in this realm, and even meet beings from other world systems. Thus Mencius called this the stage of Belief or Faith.

The next stage of spiritual progress in Confucianism is called "Beauty." In order to keep progressing spiritually upwards you must cultivate the life force of your subtle body to a higher stage of purity to reach the stage of a Sakradagamin that all devas are hoping to reach. This is "beautifying" yourself because your Prana becomes more purified. Devas run around from spiritual master to spiritual master waiting for them to use their *nirmanakaya* projections to purify their bodies. They hope, at a minimum, to achieve a stage of purification just prior to the next body that is the Causal body attainment or Anagamin stage of Arhatship because this will insure rebirth in heaven rather than on earth.

Hinduism tells us clearly that heavenly beings are actively involved in spiritual cultivation. They run from enlightened teacher to teacher for purification blessings on their body to reach a yet higher transcendental body composed of the higher class of energy that Taoism calls Shen. Since (1) an ordinary deva born in heaven, (2) a human who attains the deva body through cultivation, and (3) humans who have died all possess the same type of astral deva body composed of Prana but at different degrees of purification, the deva level of the subtle body attainment is differentiated into two classification levels. In Buddhism these levels are the first dhyana and second dhyana, which simply refer to a lesser or greater degree of purification work on their body pertaining to the subtle-bodied heavenly devas. In Hinduism these are the *vitarka* samadhi and *vicara* samadhi that refer to one state of mind and another more refined state of consciousness. One class will be reborn on earth because they didn't purify themselves enough and the other class will be reborn in heaven.

Mencius called the spiritual cultivation efforts of this stage "extending and fulfilling," which means that by further energy and *nadi* channel purification of your body you can reach a higher degree of its purification but without yet liberating from within yourself the next higher body composed of Shen. In other words, you must *extensively* ("extending and fulfilling") cultivate your subtle body composed of Prana to reach a more purified level of your body-mind complex. This is exactly what is done in Hinduism through devotional worships, *bhakti*, yoga, pranayama and other spiritual practices even though they might not achieve for you the subtle body attainment. In any case, you first attain the deva body and then you continue fully cultivating the purity of its inner energy, "extending and fulfilling it," which is also called *beautifying it or perfecting it*. You must do this before you can generate an additional body out of its essence composed of a yet higher energy than Prana ... just as you free a subtle body made of Prana out of your physical body shell due to spiritual practices.

Mencius said that from the stage of Beauty as a base, "extending and fulfilling it until it shines forth is called great." "Greatness" or "Grandness" is the name for the next spiritual body attainment composed of Shen, namely the Causal body. It corresponds to the third dhyana attainment of Buddhism, the Anagamin stage of the Arhat, the *ananda* samadhi, and the Shen body attainment in Taoism. The Causal body is a body tethered to the subtle body but composed of a more refined substance than Prana so it resides on a higher plane or vibrational field of existence. The aggregate of all higher planes of existence constitute the actual life force energy of the subtle bodies composed of Prana.

The third body of the *manomaya kosha* clearly corresponds to a Causal body, Shen-based Spirit Immortal or Mantra *deha* body that is called "Greatness" by Mencius. According to Vajrayana Buddhism, on the spiritual path your impure illusory body (subtle or deva body) can generate from within it a purified illusory body, free from all gross matter and impurities, which is exactly this stage of attainment.

It is basically the result of purifying your subtle body, which means that a pranic body has interpenetrating throughout it the potential of a body double of more transcendental nature that starts to become greatly differentiated from the rest of the subtle body's energy if that individual cultivates sufficiently. As the ties that bind it to the unpurified subtle body lessen due to becoming differentiated it can then gain release and emerge from the shell of the subtle body. This happens after that individual cultivates a lot of spiritual practices to purify the vital (life force) energy of their subtle body. It is basically the result of beautifying or cultivating one's Prana and fulfilling the full potential of it.

This transcendental achievement of the next higher spiritual body is the stage Mencius called Grandness or Greatness that is equivalent to the Anagamin Arhat or Causal body. The Nath Yoga tradition within Hinduism calls it a "body of vibrations" that refers to its composition of a higher form of energy (Shen) than Prana (Qi). Every new body you achieve is composed of a more refined, purified, or higher vibrating (higher) form of energy or substance than the body it is born from, and so it always remains invisible to residents on the lower plane of existence from which it arose. All the higher realms of energy interpenetrate the lower realms of vibration so it is just that a higher frequency of aggregates arise in a new body of its own.

Mencius said that to reach the stage of Greatness and then transform it will enable you to reach the stage of the Sage, which is the next stage of achievement. This is the Supra-Causal enlightenment stage of a full Arhat whose mind-body vehicle is composed of a substance that transcends all lower energies, including Qi (Prana) and Shen, which is why it can sense vibrations or perturbations within all the denser fields of manifestation. The superpowers at this stage are tremendous, which is why it is the stage of the sage.

This is the capability of the "enlightenment" of a full Arhat so Mencius calls this stage of becoming a "sage." This newest Supra-Causal body or liberated *vijnanamaya-anandamaya kosha* complex – which is still attached to your previous Causal body – is composed of a substance, essence or energy so pure that our only comparison of its purity is invisible clear light that has become completely separated from matter. It belongs to a field where light and matter have become fully separated from each other.

White light can be split into many colors and this body has the similar ability of being able to separate off energy copies of itself called *nirmanakaya* emanations, which are like different colors or wavelengths of light. They are controlled by the host body, or Supra-Causal Arhat body, but can be sent off across the world to do things such as give people thoughts, visions, dreams, emotions, impulses, motivations, energy and so on. These *nirmanakaya* projections can even cultivate the their own body's energy so as to be able to generate their own higher body that corresponds to the subsequently ascendant stage of the Immanence or Buddha body.

Consciousness at this stage, as with all stages of spiritual ascension, is still dependent upon the structure and processes of your body vehicle since your body is still an exact replica of your physical body. Are you any wiser than a human at this stage of attainment? You might be able to know more because the sensory reach of your senses becomes exceedingly large (called "infinite without boundaries"), and because you can know and understand the contents of more minds and because you can perceive the past and future (prophecy) in certain circumstances. However, you still have the same thinking processes that you did prior to this attainment unless you keep perfecting yourself and learn the greater abilities of these new bodies. You must still study and train at every new level of existence. The superpowers that each new body is cable of demonstrating don't just happen naturally because you must train to master them.

Every new body is simply a replica of your previous lower body where all of these bodies depend upon your original human body as the base template, and thus your thinking processes stay the same with each new body. You simply attain new powers and abilities with each new body, such as the eight *siddhi* that become available immediately when you become a deva after death or when you attain that body by becoming a spiritual master. Each new body feels more blissful (comfortable) than the previous because its construction is composed of higher forma of energy, and consciousness works a bit faster too and seems more pristine. The really big difference are the new skills you gain with the new body *whose capabilities you must train to master*. Once again, you don't just attain a new body and then ... Bingo! You have all these new skills. You must train to attain them.

The eight siddhis of *anima* (ability to shrink one's body), *mahima* (the ability to increase one's body size), *laghima* (the ability to become lighter), *garima* (the ability to become denser/heavier), *vasitva* (the ability to possess a human and take control over them), etcetera, for instance, are only the capabilities of the higher spiritual bodies and not a human body that learns yoga. Devas can shrink their bodies down to a small size, solidify their bodies enough to be able to rap on matter to make a sound in a room, and can shrink in size to enter into your brain that is the siddhi of *parakaya pravesanam* – the ability to enter the bodies of others which also includes a full body possession.

An enlightened spiritual master can use the audience time when a bunch of devas collect in your brain to show them how the processes of thinking and feeling are generated within consciousness since it is basically a mechanism. An enlightened guru will have them watch the neurons of your brain firing with pranic energy and electricity when you create and store memories, form thoughts or retrieve memories stored in your neurons. Devas will practice giving you thoughts at that time that provoke Yin or Yang emotional responses, such as guilt (Yin) or sexual desire (Yang), to prove to their teacher that they have a certain level of skill in affecting consciousness, and this happens to everybody but especially to those going through a kundalini awakening. They will be tortured with such things for years, and not a single thing you did or thought in your life will be hidden.

Each higher spiritual body attainment will have more capabilities and can accumulate more experiences than the lower body from which it was generated, but the memories of the higher body are not imprinted in the lower ones unless it withdraws into the lower one to operate it, like a snail that withdraws into its shell, and thinks about those memories so that they then become stored in the lower nature. Thus they all have separate lives. In fact, a spiritual master like Pramukh Swami Maharaj might seem like they have an excellent memory to remember all the details of building a temple, but they simply use their higher bodies to search the memories of their human body if they forget anything and this makes them look memory impressive.

When a master is operating in the world while his higher body is busy elsewhere in higher realms he will often seem as if not present, and only when the higher bodies return to rest in his lowest physical shell will he seem to make wiser decisions than when he/she seems absent. He seems to be in the world but transcends it, which is why he can preach about detachment, "money doesn't matter," sexual abstinence and so on since he is operating on a different plane so the human factors don't touch him. To be sure, he or she will have their own problems at those higher levels but they will look at the lower planes as if dreams since they are not the center of their lives. Many are married upstairs but preaching *brahmacharya* below, hence they certainly need money for their family, but the hypocrisy in preaching is just a way to encourage you to conserve your energies and devote yourself to Prana purification work.

In progressing upwards, when an enlightened person's cultivation level becomes so high that nobody knows how high it is,

Confucianism calls this the final stage of becoming a "Shen" (divine), which is equivalent to the highest level of the Buddhist enlightenment *bhumis*. This stage of divineness is akin to the Perfect and Complete Enlightenment of the Great Golden Arhat, Immanence Body, Superconsciousness body, and Buddha body or Tathagata body. It can also generate *nirmanakaya* projections that have the ability to themselves generate *nirmanakaya* projections! This is the naked *atman* stage of attainment.

As previously explained (but the repetition helps), humans who attain the subtle body attainment reach the Srotapanna Arhat stage ("stream-enterer") of enlightenment which corresponds to the initial step of climbing the actual ladder of spiritual progress. Devas who start out at this level (due to being born in Heaven) and cultivate their body to a higher stage of purity reach the Sakradagamin stage of the Arhats. This is just a higher stage of subtle body purification whose attainment means that upon death the deva-attainee will definitely be reborn in the realm of devas (Heaven) rather than the human realm. No one wants to be reborn in the human realm.

As explained, Buddhism differentiates these stages of purity as the first and second dhyana, Hinduism as the *vitarka* and *vicara* samadhi, and Confucianism differentiates them too. Spiritual practice is all about purifying your inner vital energy or Prana that is your life force along with your personality, thinking (inner life) and behavior that are the results of the movement of your consciousness powered by your Prana. This is how you achieve spiritual ascension.

Prana, of course, represents an aggregation of all of the higher fields of energy above the material plane that is a condensing of them all although the densifications can be unbundled.

For this reason you should cultivate the purification of your Prana during this life through relevant spiritual exercises and activities because even if you don't succeed in attaining enlightenment this lifetime you will have a healthier life and be far ahead of everyone else who didn't cultivate when you die because you will have purified your subtle body to some degree. Along these lines there is nothing wrong with the road of *bhakti* and worship. You have to elevate your inner life, your character and behavior as well as your internal energy because these all go into purifying your Prana so the critical, crucial question is how to best accomplish this.

As devas, everyone in the Heaven of our earthly plane is

cultivating their body to reach the second dhyana (a more purified state of their body) during life which then assures for themselves a rebirth in Heaven when their life is over rather than rebirth in the lower earthly plane of material existence as a human once again. This is something to think about.

SUMMARY

As a short summary so that the grand objective of Hinduism, *moksha*, is clear to you, according to Hinduism the five spiritual bodies are the physical body, subtle body, Causal (Mental) body, Supra-Causal body and Immanence body of superconsciousness that is also known as the Buddha body in Buddhism.

These bodies when separated are also called the *annamaya* (food), *pranamaya* (energy, Qi or Prana), *manomaya* (mental), *vijnanamaya* (wisdom or intellect), and *anandamaya* (bliss) *koshas* or sheaths that Islam calls veils. Most Hindus know our potential spiritual bodies as the unpurified sheaths that cover over our naked *atman*.

In Buddhism these sheaths are referred to as the five *skandhas*: the form *skandha*, sensation *skandha*, conception *skandha*, volition *skandha* and consciousness *skandha*. They correspond to the form body, deva body (composed of subtle energy, your life force, your vital energy or Prana), Wisdom body, Dharma body and Buddha body (as mentioned in the *Diamond Sutra*). The higher body attainments (past the physical body) also correspond to the four dhyana, four stages of Arhatship, and the Bodhisattva *bhumis* where every two *bhumi* levels refer to one body level attainment. All these bodies reside in heavens that can be partitioned into different gradations of purity as well.

Vajrayana Buddhism says we have a physical body and the potential of an impure illusory (subtle or deva) body, purified illusory body, and wisdom light or clear light body. The final Tathagata stage body is equivalent to Complete and Perfect Enlightenment, a stage of "No More Learning" or "*nirvana* without remainder" because there are no more bodies to go. When all the bodies are achieved in their separate form and remain linked together this is called the perfect *sambhogakaya* (Reward body or Enjoyment body).

In the Nath Yoga tradition the components of a *sambhogakaya* are the physical body or *stuhla deha*, purified subtle body or *suddha deha*, body of vibrations or mantra *deha*, wisdom light body or *jnana deha*, and then the body of Immanence.

In Islam these are the gross body, subtle body, Mental body, Universal body and Shiva-atma body. These correspond to the realm of the physical body (*Alam-i-Nasut*), realm of intelligence (*Alam-e-Malakut*) that corresponds to the subtle plane, realm of power (*Alam-i-Jabrut*) that corresponds to the Causal plane, the "second manifestation" or realm of Absolute Unity (*Alam-i-LaHoot*) that corresponds to the Supra-Causal and Immanence plane (also known as the "Soul of Mohammed" or *Rooh-e-Qudsi*), and the realm of first manifestation (*Alam-i-YaHoot*) that is also known as the "Light of Mohammed" (*Noor-e-Mohammed*) since the name is an allusion to the energies that power consciousness.

In Taoism the five bodies are said to be composed of Jing, Qi, Shen, Later Heavenly Qi and Primordial Heavenly Qi. Qi means Prana, which is the "wind element" of spiritual texts that essentially means energy. Each new body attainment corresponds to the rank of being a new type of Immortal and the stages of the Taoist Immortals are equivalent to the stages of the Buddhist Arhats. The higher bodies are the stages of the Earth, Spiritual, Celestial and Universal Immortals.

In Confucianism the five bodies correspond to the stages of Faith, Beauty, Grandness, Sage and then Divineness taught by Mencius.

Once you attain the final Buddha body or Immanence body of superconsciousness (Perfect and Complete Enlightenment) you cross the ocean of *samsara* as far as can be done, and then you become qualified to take others across it as a guru.

A true enlightened guru, unlike the charlatans that sometimes populate Hindu culture for money, is like a boatman who plies his boat filled with passengers and takes them across the swollen river of *samsara*. He can do so because he has body attainments, which is the secret hidden in Hinduism that is now revealed. Through his efforts he follows people across innumerable lives and tries to elevate us to the highest level of spiritual attainment.

CHAPTER 2
THE KUNDALINI PROCESS OF DECOUPLING THE *KOSHA*S FROM ONE ANOTHER

Einstein proved to mankind that matter is a form of condensed energies while Hindu culture, as well as Buddhist and Moslem culture, state that our bodies are agglomerated complexes of various *koshas* or body shells that can be disentangled from one another to release several types of transcendental bodies. When we die an exact copy of our body arises as our soul or spirit that exists on a higher plane of energetic existence all around us called the "earthly heavenly plane," and the vital energy or life force *of that body* can be cultivated to attain a higher independent life as well.

This can go on for a total of five bodies, which is the meaning of the *koshas* that are known as *skandhas* in Buddhism and veils in Islam. Our spiritual bodies are exact replicas of our human body because they are aggregations of energy that permeate the shape and structure of every part of our physical matrix. The practices of spiritual cultivation differentiate our energies into distinctive components and thereby enable a release of these higher bodies embedded within our nature. Just as the all-pervading higher planes of energy interpenetrate the matter of this world, they can be unwrapped from one another through a progressive purifying process of separation that weakens their interfaces of union.

During the processes of religious practice you strive to purify the aggregation of the *pranamaya* and higher *koshas* so that a spirit body of Prana (which contains all the higher *koshas* within *it*) can be released as a spiritual life independent of the human physical shell within which it resides as its animating force. What you have to understand is that the *koshas* cover the *atman*, so-to-speak, but it is actually that the *koshas* are energies penetrating each other as an agglomeration that needs to become differentiated so that the *koshas* can be released as independent spiritual lives.

However, an easy way to explain this is to just call the *koshas* shells or sheaths while Buddhism refers to them as *skandhas* or aggregates since each *kosha* sheath – until it is freed as an independent body on its own – is an aggregate of all the remaining higher *koshas* that together compose a body on a specific plane of being. Prana, for instance, is an aggregate mixture of higher energies from the upper planes of existence instead of a singular energy called Prana. The highest owner of all these bodies is the *atman*, which does not admit that any of these coverings are its uncontaminated body.

A key principle concerning the nestling within themselves or bundling together of potential spiritual bodies within each other is the teaching from the *Upanishads* that the *atman* cannot be reached through learning or the intellect. This means that you must reach it through the yogic means of washing each energy layer so that it becomes extremely purified enough that it looses its connection with its lower impure energies that it is joined with and then becomes released.

Hinduism also speaks of various transcendental worlds and planes of existence such as Brahmaloka, Vishnuloka, Sivaloka, and so forth. There are competing notions of Hindu cosmology explaining the *lokas* or planes of existence, such as those in the *Puranas* and *Atharvaveda,* and when you add in the notions from Buddhism, Jainism and other religions there are even more. Hinduism certainly believes in the existence of other planes of existence than just the gross, corporeal material universe and believes in the possibility of communication between their beings and the human race.

One skillful way of thinking about the universe is that its realms, fields or planes of existence are similar to a spectrum of light that has a gradient of colors or intensity, or of a spectrum of higher running to lower vibrations where the highest etheric realm finally becomes the densest material plane of densification that is solid matter. When energy vibrates exceedingly fast it begins to look like there isn't any motion at all such as when a fast running river looks extremely smooth on its surface, which might explain how the first emanate of creation appears like the primordial substrate and yet differs in quality due to very fast movement.

You can think of the spectrum of the universe as creating a differentiation in scale between pureness and impurity, lightness and heaviness, Yang and Yin, high vibration and low vibration or upper and lower for each realm of manifestation. In terms of the *gunas*, the ideal mode is *sattva* (an equilibrium that seems non-moving like the ultimate nature) while *rajas* represents a manifest purity, lightness or speediness and *tamas* represents slowness and densification or impurity. We live in the most *tamas* realm of existence.

Spiritual progress is the task of cultivating physical bodies that climb the gradient ladder of purity for each plane of emanation or existence. This doesn't just happen by chance because it requires active and conscious effort. It involves engaging in methods to purify the life force internal to each body so that it can escape its shell to live an independent life in a higher form of existence. For each realm of being you spiritually cultivate your internal energy in order to purify it and thereby free your "soul" or "spirit" from the "material body" of that plane of existence. You do this by so purifying that energy through various forms of churning so that it gradually becomes highly differentiated from the corpus of that body and a repository of unpurified vital energy that maintains its life but which cannot yet be purified.

When we die the spirit or soul of man is automatically released into the heavenly plane of existence surrounding the earth, which is one type of decoupling and ascension. Through spiritual practices you can purify your internal energy (Prana) so that its higher fractions become more differentiated from lower fractions, and then due to that widening difference a spirit body can be released from the rest of the human shell whilst alive. This makes you a saint or sage although there are grades to the ranks of achievement.

The process for doing this is illustrated in the Hindu story of the *Samudra Manthana*, or "Churning of the Ocean of Milk," found in the *Vishnu Purana*. In this story a milky ocean (which represents our body that is composed of 70% water, and which was initially created by the white liquid of semen) is churned to produce *amrita*, which is the elixir of eternal life.

In this story *amrita* represents the higher life force energies of the long-lived transcendental spiritual bodies and the churning of the Ocean of Milk represents the separation of denser from lighter aspects of the Prana within our body (which is the ocean) just as butter is separated from the wateriness of milk due to continuous stirring.

The story is a veiled reference to various cultivation exercises that stir the Prana of our physical body so that its Prana becomes purified and then that energetic body aggregate, which constitutes a body double, can ascend as a separate life by disconnecting itself from the denser impure energy of the physical body that remains.

Some describe this process by saying that we *differentiate* the lower from higher (pure and impure) energies or essences of the body to attain the higher spiritual bodies. Some describe this saying that we *purify* our body's spiritual energy through religious cultivation and then disconnect, untangle or separate out that purest fraction of life as a separate life existence. Some describe this process by saying that we raise the *frequency* of our internal energy aggregate, which is a perfect copy of the human body, by slowly ridding that Prana aggregate of impurities via spiritual practices that then raises its vibrational rate higher than the rest of the body. There are many ways to describe this.

Through an arduous spiritual purification process of inner washing or cleansing gradually the quality of one's Prana differentiates itself markedly from the quality of the Prana composing the interface linkage between matter and its vital life force. It's like stirring sludge in a tub where the central portion being stirred becomes more watery or more differentiated than the stubborn, denser, unstirred, harder-to-transform sludge that sticks to the rim of the tub. Because the body-Prana bond weakens due to spiritual washing practices the two can become separated, which normally happens only at death, while a sage can break free from his material body and ascend the realm of matter. Naturally a residue of Prana remains to keep the physical nature alive and like taffy that is pulled out into a string the new spiritual body remains connected to the corpus of the old body unless the connection is 100% severed.

In the story of the *Samudra Manthana* the massive mountain, Mount Mandara, was used as the stirring rod in a great churning process of the Ocean of Milk. The devas and *asuras* had to churn the ocean for a long time, which tells us that it requires years of purification work on the human body for the ascension of the deva body to arise out of it. In fact it will take twelve years or more, with thirteen and fourteen years also being common.

Devas and *asuras* both participated in the churning of the Milk Ocean but only the devas received the blessings of *amrita*, which was produced out of the stirring, to represent the fact that *asuras*, known for their tendency for evil deeds and pursuing carnal desires, cannot achieve the higher transcendental bodies until they become purified of their lower traits.

During the churning, which essentially represents the process of purifying or detoxifying one's internal energy or Prana, the poison *halahala* was also produced. This essentially means that during the process of purification non-heavenly dregs are separated from the pure which is exactly the process we have been revealing. It is like stirring a vat of liquid where the centrally stirred section becomes more fluid while the unmixed residues sticking to the sides become more viscous and solid, hence a differentiation of quality or purity. The human body undergoing the process will suffer from all sorts of skin problems, sicknesses and other issues as it progresses through this process that is essentially a purification process of detoxification and then ascension or transcendence.

Among the items released by stirring the Ocean of Milk was Lakshmi, the goddess of wealth and prosperity, who thus represents the vast consequence of great good fortune issuing from the churning purification process. Shakyamuni Buddha, in the *Diamond Sutra* of Buddhism, accordingly says that achieving enlightenment is more valuable than all the riches in all the galaxies of matter. Once you attain the deva body, for instance, no one wants to return to the earthly realm even if they are made kings and queens of great power and riches.

Kamadhenu or *Surabhi*, the wish-fulfilling cow (the brain), *Kalpavriksha* the wish-fulfilling tree (the nervous system) whose branches bore every type of fruit, and the desire-satisfying gem *Chintamani* (the brain stem) also arose out of the Ocean of Milk. They represent the purified consciousness of the subtle body that arises from this process. Hindu culture typically uses peacock feathers to represent all the neurons and neural connections in a brain but in this case the brain and nervous system were represented in different images. A virile seven-headed flying horse, *Ucchaishrava*, also arose out of the Ocean of Milk to represent that the method produces your purified subtle energy body of ascension, which is a purified Prana body of seven chakras or body sections.

When *amrita* is finally produced, only the devas, representing those individuals who cultivate virtue and goodness in life, receive it while *asuras* do not indicating that only those who cultivate ethics, morality and virtue can attain the higher spiritual bodies of enlightenment (represented by our *koshas*). Those of higher virtue and status won't help you ascend unless you qualify in terms of purity and virtue in your mind and behavior. The process of generating a higher body, which means freeing a higher, more etheric spiritual aggregate from its denser shell at each plane of existence, requires a churning of the energies within that body shell which is achieved via the cooperation of countless enlightened spiritual masters lending you their energies. It is a tiring process for them so if your merit is lacking they won't be working on your case yet. When you are ready, and when many others in your region have also achieved a sufficient level of virtue so they are qualified to join in a group ascension, then you are likely to succeed.

The process of stirring or churning the Ocean of Milk, which represents the Prana or life force aggregate of our body, entails friction so that warmth is produced as a byproduct. That is why strong heat is felt during the process of kundalini awakening, which is a "burning" process of purification where your internal energy is moving around inside you and purifying your Prana through frictional contact. Because this can eventually lead to the decoupling of the subtle deva body from the physical body, kundalini energy is called the "fire of separation" although there are many stages when the body becomes very cold during the stirring because your Yin energies are being stimulated with purification work. The purifying energy is usually supplied by the local guardian spirits and enlightened spiritual masters who are moving your energies with their own, but normally you must cultivate various exercises and spiritual practices to initiate this process yourself.

One must note here that the main purport of the *Vedas* is sometimes said to be fire worship, or Agni Upasana, which might actually refer to the hot kundalini energy purification necessary to wash all your tissues so that your inner subtle body can escape its mortal shell. Hinduism has many analogies like this in its great body of teachings.

CHURNING OR ROTATIONAL METHODS FOR MOVING YOUR PRANA TO WASH IT

The *Yoga Yajnavalkya* teaches us that the method of *pratyahara* can be used to mentally guide our Prana through circuits inside our body to purify its internal tissues, which is similar to the churning within the *Samudra Manthana*.

Kundalini Yoga, *kriya* yoga, and *anapana* practices involve moving the Prana of your body in various ways guided by your will (thoughts), which is also basically the *nei-gong, neijiaquan, neijia* or *neidan* work of Chinese Taoism. These methods involve practicing to pull or push your Prana with your mind such as by rotating or revolving it hundreds to thousands of times in specific patterns within your body to wash tissues.

Another yogic method of washing your tissues entails first mentally fixing your Prana with focused concentration in various body locations. Then you mentally take it (move it by pushing it with your mind) slowly, step by step and stage by stage, to other sections of your body. For instance, Yogi Boganathar of the Tamil Siddhars has a washing circuit where you lead your Prana from your big toes to your ankle, knee, thigh, genitals, navel, heart, neck, uvula, nose, space between the eyebrows, forehead and crown of the head.

The *Nitya Natha Paddhati* of the Yoga saint Gorakhnath, who founded the Nath Hindu monastic movement, reveals "sixteen containers" where you can lead and concentrate your Prana: big toes, anus, rectum or sphincter, male genital organ, lower abdomen (entrails), navel area, heart, throat, uvula, naso-pharynx, root of the tongue, base of the upper teeth, tip of the nose, base of the nose, point between the eyebrows, and eyes. You can also *hold* your Prana at these or other vital points within the body, and also rotate the Prana when it masses at those locations.

Nyasa Yoga is another Hindu cultivation method that also teaches us to guide our Prana using our thoughts and will. Using your mind you rotate your Prana around your bones, organs, body regions and appendages in order to wash those tissues enough to be able to detach from the *annamaya kosha*, or material physical body, in an elevated spirit body that constitutes our *pranamaya kosha* and the remaining potential of all our other higher *koshas* that can be released from within it as independent entity vehicles as well.

Nyasa practice is said to be a method of "consecrating your body to the divine" because you are trying to produce the first divine body, the deva body, by washing your internally energy in an orderly fashion with the help of divine sources. Many other rituals of Hinduism are designed to bring the Divine into your body and mind with the cardinal objective of purifying your Prana through the presence of those transcendental, heavenly energies.

Hence, Nyasa involves consecrating your body to a deity, which invites assistance for washing your Prana from higher enlightened beings associated with that deity, and then making efforts to purify your body's inner energy while simultaneously engaging in stimulating visualizations to raise your energy while mentally leading your Prana from location to location, such as marma point to marma point, while reciting mantras at each spot. Essentially, you systematically rotate to different parts of your body the purification work necessary to wash the Prana in that region while also empowering each location with a bit of extra energy to make it easier to wash.

Yoga Nidra is the similar practice of rotating your consciousness to various parts of the body by focusing on those points and drawing the Prana to that location. You can pull Prana to a location from other areas of your body, or try to pull it in from the environment in which case this becomes an absorption practice. Thus, Nyasa Yoga, Yoga Nidra and *pratyahara* use your consciousness (thoughts and willpower) to move your Prana internally so that you wash your tissues along special routes that eventually involve all the regions of your body.

Chinese *nei-gong* also uses this same method of mentally guiding your Qi, which is the Chinese word for Prana, which is possible because our Prana and consciousness (thoughts) are linked. This linkage between our thoughts and our vital energy, where one can move the other, is the basis of the well-known body-mind dualism confirmed by science.

During Chinese *nei-gong* spiritual exercise you feel your Prana at certain points within your body and then take, move or lead it step by step and stage by stage to other locations, which will help remove various disorders in those regions by opening up any constricted *nadis* in those locations. Through willpower you can lead your internal energy to any area within your body because "where your intent is your Prana will condense." Prana that floods a region will "wash" the region thus warming and softening it. This behavior will then purify and strengthen your inner subtle body in that region. You must do this for a long time with all sorts of related exercises before you can prompt a kundalini arousal into happening.

Pranayama uses control of your breathing to move your Prana and wash your inner energy. *Kumbhaka* pranayama, in particular, makes use of breath retention methods to increase your lung capacity, stimulate the creation of more capillaries, force open up your Prana channels of circulation (*nadis*), and improve your inner Prana flow. Furthermore, pranayama enables you to control your body, senses and thinking through your breathing. Your mind can be controlled and your inner narrative of wandering thoughts can die down through this practice so it is said that through control of the breathing "the mind subsides." If you don't control your mind you will always become dazed by thoughts and merge with them or fuse with them so that you forget yourself, your state of presence, and your state of observing watchfulness. Mind-control means peace.

A basic principle of Yoga and Tantra is that your Prana energy will follow your thoughts because consciousness is powered by Prana, and therefore you can guide it around your body to go where you want because the two are essentially the same energy. Your Prana is connected with your consciousness, which is why your thoughts and willpower allow you to move your Prana around inside your body so that you can wash your inner *pranamaya kosha* (subtle body that is the yet to emerge Srotapanna or deva body attainment) with rubbings of your own vital energy.

Through frictional churning (and other energy movements) led by your mind you eventually purify the Prana of your subtle body for its emergence as an independent spiritual body on its own, which is why Buddhism calls it the "mind-born" body. This is a bifurcation point at which you transition to a new life. If you go deeply into pranayama practices this can help you gain control of your mind because of the connections between respiration, your Prana (physical energy) and consciousness (thinking). At its ultimate heights, pranayama and other cultivation practices enable you to achieve an exalted *sattvic* mental state that is clear, peaceful, and calm rather than just a temporary tranquility.

The ideal of mental peace is where your mind can retain an undistracted focus without distraction on whatever you are doing rather than wander around or jump from one distraction to another because it constantly becomes entrained with a new fascination. Mental peace also entails the ability to control any unwanted afflictions that appear within your mind due to the algorithms of consciousness that cause things to arise in your mind automatically even if you don't want them. This happens because you are not the controller of consciousness because consciousness is just a process that even gives birth to your I-thought sense of self-existence.

Pranayama has the capacity of bringing you some conscious control over your Prana, which plays a role in producing your thinking, and this control can enable you to attain a greater or lesser degree of mental peace on call. In short, if you can control your breathing you gain a degree of control over your thinking. Special forms of pranayama can also cause you to build more capillaries which helps with spiritual cultivation as well.

The mantrayana practice of reciting mantras in tune with your breathing, and the singing of *bhajans*, are practices that rely on different principles to wash your Prana. They use sound energy to stimulate your Prana and to also move it around inside your body to wash the tissues of your inner subtle body.

Instead of singing to do this, you can arouse strong emotions within yourself by listening to music to change the tonality of your Prana and accomplish a minor washing this way as well. By listening to music of various emotional types – energizing, defiant, triumphant, amusing, relaxing, dreamy, annoying, nostalgic, happy, inspiring, joyful, scary or tense, sad or depressing, etc. – you can create internal energy sensations within your Prana that stimulate it and thus wash it due to that activation. If you like, you can also perform inner energy exercises simultaneously to beneficially take advantage of charged mental-emotional-Prana states within you.

Kumbhaka pranayama uses constrained breath retention to help force open the impediments or obstructions to the Prana flow within your body. The *Gheranda Samhita* contains eight different *kumbhaka* pranayama techniques you can use and Tibetan Buddhism has several as well including *Jiujie Fofeng* "Nine Winds" breathing (see *Neijia Yoga* for complete instructions). When practiced correctly, this type of pranayama will help clear out the circulatory blockages of Prana flow within you and thus speed your attainment of the independent deva body by "opening your *nadis*."

The one idea of pranayama is to learn how to control your breathing in order to be able to influence the Prana within your body. The purpose, beyond the mundane results of thought control and improved health and longevity, is *to cultivate your inner subtle body*. Every part of your body can be filled with Prana, and when you are able to actually do this you not only wash it but will gradually become able to control your entire body.

Yoga, Pilates, the martial arts, natural bodyweight training exercises and sports or exercise in general use the approach of stretching to eliminate any knots or obstructions that impede the free circulation of Prana flow within your physical and subtle bodies. You first start with mastering your physical body and then move to practicing control of the Prana in every muscle of your body.

This is the physical exercise pathway for quickly developing your independent spirit body. It takes a long time to accomplish this but that time can be shortened by the practice of yoga, Pilates, dance, the soft martial arts and any other exercises that also teach you to master your inner Prana and its circulation.

It is especially easy to push the Prana of your body upwards or downwards into your upper or lower torso in tune with the power of your breathing. As is usual, the frictional rubbing of Prana over itself causes an abrasive (frictional) cleansing of its nature where the pure or more refined energy eventually differentiates itself more and more from that which is less pure and of greater viscosity, so-to-speak, due to not yet being transformed.

The more refined or purified Prana is what differentiates itself from the rest of your energy and escapes as your first spiritual body of enlightenment that is the subtle body or deva body. It is more purified than the deva body that ordinary mortals obtain when they die and arise as spirits because you have performed lots of cultivation work to wash it again and again to attain its independence while you are alive. Hence, it is more like a Sakradagamin than Srotapanna stage of Arhatship.

Basically, pranayama when done correctly is one of the techniques that helps you transcend your physical nature in a spiritual body by using your breathing's connection with your energy to push it around inside you and wash your tissues. You amplify its effectiveness when you change your emotions while breathing in order to wash your energy with different qualities of Prana to affect all its dimensional attributes.

Visualization, on the other hand, uses mental concentration to collect and mass your Prana around your bones or other body parts and thus wash them and the surrounding tissues due to the concentration of Prana in the region of focus. Kaula Tantra, in particular, uses ecstatic visualizations, often with an arousing erotic content, to excite your entire body's Prana so that you can then more easily move it using your will to wash your *nadis* via mental guidance.

Mantrayana, as previously explained, uses sound power to vibrate your Prana and then push that energized life force energy around your body to wash its tissues and *nadis*.

The Path of Heroes, or *Viramarga* method, has you rest in a *bhava* absorption where you fix yourself in a given strong mental attitude for a prolonged period of time. During that period when you are absorbed in a dominant attitude, you try to feel the energy of that attitude penetrating all throughout your body in order to wash your Prana with the total penetration of that energy flavor.

Bhakti yoga uses the imagined unification with a *deity* to invite enlightened masters (of a specific tradition or your locale who are helping out) into your body, meaning their *nirmanakaya* emanations, so that the presence of those energetic presences visiting you will wash your Prana and thus purify it. This is why *bhakti* is recommended as a spiritual practice since God does not need worship, nor did God create man for the narcissistic purpose that He become worshipped. *Bhakti* yoga is just a simple and easy method, suitable for householders, for purifying your Prana but masters don't want to tell you that. Through *bhakti* you will gain connection with a lineage of enlightened masters that will help you.

Another method for washing your Prana, which is similar to the *Viramarga* method of holding onto a dominant attitude, is to forget yourself while holding onto great, boundless, immeasurable emotions to alter your Prana while radiating those energies everywhere into the environment. Through this technique of mental absorption and radiating Prana you will slowly wash your internal energy with the energized Prana connected with those emotions. Those attitudes might be of infinite compassion, infinite kindness, infinite humility (self-surrender), infinite equanimity, infinite mercy, and so forth.

Yoga, Pilates, dance, sports and martial arts use stretching, muscle control and the Prana control connected with these arts (mastery of internal Prana movements guided by your will) to cultivate the Prana of your body. Cardiovascular sports go a step further by requiring a harmonious coordination of your physical movements with your respiration, blood circulation and Prana flow together where they achieve their optimum peaks for performance excellence. In other words, you must drive the internal circulation of your Prana to an optimum state of harmony and excellence, and then retain that state so that the optimal excellence of its circulation can wash your body of obstructions.

Fasting forces your body to rely on its inner subtle energy body rather than material food (just as breath retention forces your body to rely upon its Prana for survival when breath is temporarily unavailable), thus strengthening the integrity and efficiency of your inner subtle body.

This short synopsis should make it easy for you to realize that countless techniques, most of which fall under the umbrella of "spiritual cultivation," are used across the world to purify the Prana of your inner self, which is basically differentiating the most purified or high-grade energy of your body from the most impure, denser or lowest grade impure energy. It essentially involves differentiating the Yin and Yang Pranas of your body from one another and refining the nature of your Prana in general.

To do so successfully you must daily practice a set of different types of spiritual exercises that all work at purifying your Prana via different principles in order to start transforming your Prana for the independent subtle body attainment.

The general rule of spiritual cultivation progress is: the more that you simultaneously practice different types of spiritual exercises with ardor and consistency the better and quicker will be your results.

GUARDIAN SPIRITS, DEVAS, DEITIES, AND ENLIGHTENED MASTERS MUST HELP

One notable feature of Tantric Hinduism, which largely deals with purifying your Prana, are fanciful colorful pictures of various deities residing within the human body. The reason you've been given these pictures is to prepare initiates for the fact that higher-bodied spiritual beings will have to lend you their own energies in order to purify your Prana through churning, as in the story of the Ocean of Milk, and they will be entering your body for that process. In fact, spiritual beings are going in and out of your body all the time at all stages of your life and humans simply don't know this.

In any case, countless devas and *asuras* were involved in the story of the *Samudra Manthana* because when you go through a true multi-year kundalini purification process that makes you a saint it will involve innumerable devas and enlightened beings entering into and out of you all the time for purification sessions.

A second secret to this churning purification process concerns feminine and masculine energies called Yin and Yang or moon and sun energies (energies of Surya and Chandra). In Hinduism, yoga, Ayurveda and Indian martial arts the life force of the body is typically divided into five *vayus* or winds, but more fundamental is its partitioning into the two components of Yin and Yang, or the masculine and feminine principles, as represented by male deities and their consorts or by the sun and moon. In Christianity, St. Francis of Assisi wrote the *Canticle of Brother Sun and Sister Moon* to refer to these two fundamental types of Prana within the human body.

The *Brihadaranyaka Upanishad* mentions that the *Purusha* divided itself into male and female, which we should think of this as Yang and Yin energies that are polar opposites. Yang energy is like the warm rays of the sun and Yin energies are like the cool light of the moon. In the *Samudra Manthana* the *asuras* represent Yin energies while the devas represent the Yang energies of the human body. The secret is that the human body is composed of two fundamental types of Prana, Yin and Yang, male and female, solar and lunar or positive and negative, and both must be purified during this churning process! This is incredibly significant information you need to understand.

Many Hindu sages state that the process of transformation that releases the subtle body from the earthly shell after its purification requires at least twelve years of kundalini rotations, which they simply call *tapas, sadhana* or spiritual practice.

Ramana Maharshi said, "The *sastras* say one must serve a guru twelve years for enlightenment."

Of the eighty-four Mahasiddhas of India, Mahasiddha Pankajapa (Sankazapa) spent twelve years cultivating to attain enlightenment that involved paying homage to a statue of Avalokitesvara,

Mahasiddha Darikapa was a king who served as a slave to a temple whore for twelve years while cultivating to attain enlightenment, and Mahasiddha Lucikapa (Lutsekapa) spent twelve years practicing the *Cakrasamvara Tantra* and meditating on the nature of the mind before attaining the subtle body, ...

The sage Matsyendranath, who is considered is considered one of the eighty-four Mahasiddhas and a pivotal figure in Tantra, Yoga and the Natha traditions (the first human teacher of Hatha Yoga and thus its traditional founder), is said to have cultivated within a fish's belly, and then emerged after twelve years of practice.

Matsyendranath's student Gorakhnath cultivated *tapas* for twelve years at Badrinarayan after which he attained yogic powers. These powers equate with the subtle body achievement that is the first stage of enlightenment.

Sri Shivabalayogi Maharaj said that he attained enlightenment after twelve years of arduous cultivation practice.

Swami Sivanandaji Maharaj did vigorous cultivation work for twelve years in order to attain enlightenment.

Samarth Ramdas spent twelve years as an ascetic cultivating Rama *bhakti*, and then attained enlightenment at age 24.

Ramakrishna Paramahansa spent twelve years in spiritual practice while the Buddhist sage Asanga spent twelve years meditating in his cave.

Mahavira, who revived Jainism in India, meditated as an ascetic for twelve years and then attained enlightenment. Bahubali, a revered figure in Jainism, is said to have meditated motionless for twelve years in a standing posture with climbing plants growing around his legs (symbolizing *nadis* opening), and afterwards became a pure liberated soul who attained omniscience. Vardhamana Mahavira, the 24th Tirthankara who founded Jainism, undertook ascetic practices for twelve years before becoming enlightened.

Kabir meditated for twelve years and then finally got superpowers, meaning enlightenment, while Sai Baba of Shirdi said, "I stayed with my master for twelve years."

The subtle body of Prana that becomes a deva body is released from its *annamaya kosha* shell after you pass through a kundalini purification process that takes twelve years *minimum* to reach completion. Vajrayana Buddhism calls this subtle body the "impure illusory body" when it is released while Adi Shankara calls it the *pranamaya kosha* with the understanding that all the higher *koshas* are still embedded within it until they too become decoupled from within it as separate existences. That is why the subtle body is considered "impure."

The next higher body, which Hinduism calls the Causal body, is referred to as the "purified illusory body" in Vajrayana and *manomaya kosha* in Advaita Vedanta (where you understand that it still has inside itself the unreleased *vijnanamaya* and *anandamaya koshas* until they decouple). It arises out of the life force of the pranic subtle deva body whose life force energy is called Shen energy by the Chinese Taoists. For each new body it takes about three years to achieve the next higher spiritual body of attainment.

Hence, you must go through a process lasting at least twelve to fourteen years involving warm Yang (and cold Yin) kundalini energies rolling around within you on a continuous basis to attain the liberating subtle body attainment, and then it requires about three years for each new higher body attainment to be achieved. Hence, after the attainment of the astral deva body – which takes about twelve to fourteen years of active around-the-clock kundalini purifying transformations where your Prana is constantly circulating around within your body to purify its energies through frictional contact – it requires another three years to attain the Causal body, and then three years for the Supra-Causal attainment, and then three years for the final attainment known alternatively as the Superconsciousness, Immanence body, Great Golden Arhat, Universal Immortal, Buddha body or Tathagata body achievement that is your naked *atman*. Each body contains all of the remaining *koshas*, sheaths or shells that are potentials embedded within a body until they are released through kundalini energy purification.

Spiritual masters will not give you any information on this process but they all go through it if they become truly enlightened. The more bodies you achieve the higher your stage of attainment and the more superpowers or miracles you can demonstrate on the earthly plane. The higher the purification efforts you undergo for your Supra-Causal and Immanence (Buddha) bodies, and the higher the skills you cultivate, the more *nirmanakaya* emanations you can project out of them. Since the *nirmanakaya* emanations are energy doubles of your Supra-Causal and Immanence Buddha bodies they are composed of a certain stage of energy, and therefore you can even cultivate them separately so that each one can also attain its own higher Immanence attainment. Each body, while remaining connected to the original parent unless it becomes totally detached, can actually act like a separate Buddha.

This is one of the reasons that spiritual masters keep working on purifying the bodies of humans in the world. It is not just out of a kindness to help all beings become enlightened. From doing so they also gain the benefit of greater powers and skills for their immortal bodies because when they do this by using their *nirmanakaya* emanations or parent bodies then older and more accomplished enlightened beings will teach them various tricks and skills and work on purifying their bodies even further, thus the benefit. The older will use their own more purified *nirmanakaya* bodies to purify the *nirmanakaya* of juniors, as well as their host bodies in attendance, so that those bodies might further ascend. This would give a helpful master even more powers and capabilities.

An individual who starts the micro-macrocosmic circulations in his or her teens usually achieves the enlightenment stage of a full Arhat before age forty. Some examples of spiritual greats who become enlightened in their early twenties include Ramana Maharshi, Ramakrishna, and Bhagavan Nityananda. These individuals became enlightened at such a young age because they were already residing in the higher heavens but specifically descended to earth to help people. Hence they all started their kundalini transformation process in their early teens with friends working on them, and each did report to students that strong energy sensations were continuously surging within their body starting from a young age.

From the point of view of the outside world, upon the subtle body accomplishment you may still use your physical body but you are actually liberated and are now a *jivanmukta* (liberated being) or Arhat because you also have a deva body that becomes the new center of your life. When some achieve the subtle body attainment of enlightenment at a young enough age they will take on a heavenly wife to be their companion for the long journey ahead so the idea of *brahmacharya* (celibacy) really only holds in most traditions for the earthly plane. Thus, many enlightened masters will preach to you about celibacy so that you don't lose your energy but they themselves are really married "upstairs" and you just don't know it.

Like everyone else Sri Ramana Maharshi, Ramakrishna

Paramahansa, and Bhagavan Nityananda each went through twelve years of kundalini transformations to achieve their deva body, three years to achieve their Causal body and then three years to achieve the stage of the Supra-Causal body or full Arhat. After this your remaining target is working to achieve the Immanence, Buddha, Tathagata or Great Golden Arhat stage of the Universal Immortal that is the fully unsheathed *atman*. Prior to attaining the initial deva body or Srotapanna stage of Arhatship each of these individuals engrossed themselves in a stage of Intensified Yoga practices involving meditation, *bhakti*, yoga, *tapas*, mantra and other spiritual practices to generate the independent subtle body achievement. This is the standard sequence of practice. No one can escape it.

If you go through this twelve-year Prana purification process you will experience many different types of energy sensations within your body, and you pass through many emotional experiences just as Rama and Arjuna both passed through many emotional experiences during their wars. Swami Muktananda reported in his autobiography that he felt various sensations of heat or pain during this process at the base of his spine, a heaviness in his head, experienced involuntary movements, felt energy flows throughout his body, experienced unusual breathing patterns, would see inner lights and would experience strange sounds, visions, voices and many other extraordinary experiences. Ramakrishna also described various Prana sensations but his descriptions are quite inadequate compared to what you really need to know. The sensations range all over the place from lightness, heaviness, itching, roughness, smoothness, weightlessness, heaviness to warmth and cold and all sorts of other experiences. Ajit Mookerjee once wrote,

> The ascent of Kundalini as it pierces through the chakras is manifested in certain physical and psychic signs. Yogis have described the trembling of the body which precedes the arousal of Kundalini, and the ion of heat which passes like a current through the Sushumna channel. During Kundalini's ascent, inner sounds resemble a waterfall, the humming of bees, the sound of a bell, a flute, or the tinkling of ornaments. In closed-eye perception the yogi visualizes a variety of forms, such as dots of light, or geometrical shapes that in the final state of illumination dissolve into an inner radiance of

intensely bright, pure light. The aspirant may experience creeping sensations in the spinal cord, tingling sensations all over the body, heaviness in the head or sometimes giddiness, autonomic and involuntary laughing or crying; or he may see visions of deities or saints. Dream scenes of all kinds may appear, from the heavenly to the demonic. Physically, the abdomen wall may become flat and be drawn towards the spine; there may be diarrhea or constipation; the anus contracts and is drawn up; the chin may press down against the neck; the eyeballs roll upwards or rotate; the body may bend forward or back, or even roll around on the floor; breathing may be constricted, (sometimes it seems to cease altogether, although in fact it does not, but merely becomes extremely slight); the mind becomes empty and there is an experience of being a witness in the body.

There may be a feeling of Prana flowing in the brain or spinal cord. Sometimes there is a spontaneous chanting of mantras or songs, or simply vocal noises. The eyes may not open in spite of one's efforts to open them. The body may revolve or twist in all directions. Sometimes it bounces up and down with crossed legs, or creeps about, snake-like, on the floor. Some perform *asanas* (yogic postures) both known and unknown; sometimes the hands move in classic, formal dance patterns, even though the meditator knows nothing of dance. Some speak in tongues.

Sometimes the body feels as if it is floating upwards, and sometimes as if it is being pressed down into the earth. It may feel as if it has grown enormously large, or extremely small. It may shake and tremble and become limp, or turn as rigid as stone. Some get more appetite, some feel aversion to food. Even when engaged in activities other than meditation, the aspirant who concentrates his mind, experiences the movements of Prana-shakti all over the body, or slight tremors. There may be aches in the body, or a rise or drop in temperature. Some people become lethargic and averse to work. Sometimes the meditator hears buzzing sounds as of blowing conches, or bird-song or ringing-bells. Questions may arise in the mind and be spontaneously answered during meditation.

Sometimes the tongue sticks to the palate or is drawn back towards the throat, or protrudes from the mouth. The throat may get dry or parched. The jaws may become clenched, but after a time they reopen. One may start yawning when one sits for meditation. There may be a feeling of the head becoming separated from the body, or "headlessness." Sometimes one may be able to see things around one even with the eyes closed. Various types of intuitive knowledge may begin. One may see one's own image. One may even see one's own body lying dead. From some or all of these signs, one may know that Kundalini Shakti has become active. The Kundalini produces whatever experiences are necessary for the aspirant's spiritual progress, according to habit-pattern formed by past action.

Swami Muktananda, initiated by his spiritual preceptor, describes in his own autobiographical account his heaviness of head, sensations of heat and or pain at the base of the spine, the involuntary movements, flows of energy through the body, unusual breathing patterns, inner lights and sounds, visions and voices, and many other extraordinary experiences. In another recent autobiographical record, Gopi Krishna describes his experiences when Kundalini was aroused spontaneously, without spiritual preparation or the guidance of a guru.

Ramakrishna, who followed the discipline of kundalini-yoga under the guidance of a female guru, Brahmani, achieved in three days the result promised by each of the rituals. He described his experience as hopping, pushing up, moving zig-zag. He directly perceived the ascent of the Kundalini, and later described to his disciples its various movements as fishlike, birdlike, monkeylike, and so on.[2]

Sometimes you will hear devas speaking to you, or hear spiritual masters masquerading as deities during spiritual *sadhana* leading up to this. Many types of visions are possible that will be as real as the sights you see with your physical eyes. You might even see visions of events in the outer world that turn out to be true. At times, you

---

[2] *Ancient Wisdom and Modern Science* ed. by Stanislov Grof, (SUNY Press, Albany: New York, 1984), pp. 125-127.

might be able to see the whole system of nerves, veins, and arteries, the digestive and eliminative tracts in your body in multicolored light, which spreads throughout all your *nadis*, or you might see different forms within your body or within someone else's body. You might even see your Prana flowing through your *nadis* with increasing intensity as your body and Prana purification continues.

Of course, these are all illusions. They are visions *projected into you by humans who have become enlightened* who want to demonstrate their powers to their students and peers on how *they* do things. They project a *nirmanakaya* emanation into you and it overrides your consciousness to give you these visions. This is how they give you thoughts as well for there is no such thing as telepathy; this is the way it works.

Ramana Maharshi aptly stated that a spiritual practitioner might "see before him bright effulgences, etc., or hear (unusual) sounds or regard as real the visions of gods appearing within or outside himself. He should not be deceived by these and forget himself."[3]

THE SURANGAMA SUTRA

The best guide to navigating the many possible experiences once again comes to us from Buddhism, whose teachings arose in India based on offshoots of Vedic culture. In particular, the teachings we need for guiding ourselves reside in the "Fifty *Mara* Deva States" chapter of the *Surangama Sutra* given by Shakyamuni Buddha. Specifically, this chapter is called "The Fifty *Mara* States of the Five Skandhas Affecting Practitioners During Meditation."

Remember that much of the information that Shakyamuni Buddha taught came from the transcendental heavens or was pulled together from the milieu of the spiritual traditions of India that existed around 2,500 years ago. That is why he is sometimes considered one of the Avatars of Vishnu for he filled in many cultivation details that were missing in Indian teachings.

The first ten of these fifty types of delusionary experiences concern some common types that ordinary people will typically run into over the years such as feeling that their body is empty, experiencing unusual internal energy sensations within their body

---

[3] *The Spiritual Teaching of Ramana Maharshi*, (Shambhala Publications, Boston, 1988), p. 26.

whose initiation is not of their own doing, having visions of things inside their body, seeing the bodies of enlightened spiritual masters seem to etherically change their shape in some way, hearing voices in the sky or within their head, seeing light surround objects or other living beings, seeing amazing objects appear in space, seeing visions of spiritual lands and deities (which are fake like all these other things), being able to see in the dark, seeing events happening in the distance far away, and so forth.

As an example, devas and masters within the Swami Muktananda tradition train to be able to project a blue dot sparkle in your mind that then appears as if it is floating in the outside world whereas the vision is just inside your mind. In the Vajrayana tradition of Buddhism students are told they may experience something in their mind like a mirage when due to meditation practice their earth element Prana dissolves into their water element Prana; an experience resembling smoke when their water element Prana dissolves into their fire element Prana; an experience like a ball of fireflies when their fire element Prana dissolves into their wind element Prana; and an appearance of light when their wind element Prana dissolves into their consciousness. You might see these imaginary visions, but these explanations are all nonsense. You are being cheated just to help encourage your practice.

For instance, the great Tibetan master Tsong Khapa wrote that there is a visionary experience known as "appearance," like seeing moonlight in a cloudless sky, when you reach a certain state of mental emptiness due to meditation practice. This "appearance" then dissolves into a higher mental emptiness experience known as "very empty" where one sees an inner vision of a yellowish red light like the light at sunrise. Next is an experience of "great emptiness," linked to a vision known as "proximate attainment" that is of utter darkness, like that of a night sky pervaded by thick darkness. After this the person emerges from the darkness and a state of mindlessness to experience "utter emptiness" or "clear light" where there is a vision of a color like the clear sky at early dawn that corresponds to the clear light that is the actual basis of consciousness.

These teachings are all nonsense and were simply invented so that masters could practice their visualization projection skills as well as encourage students to continue practicing meditation because they received those visualizations. There is no such thing as automatic visions attached to any stage of cultivation attainment, which is a misleading misdirection provided within the *Visuddhimagga* treatise of Buddhist practice as well.

These are all fictitious visions given to practitioners, called marks or signs of progress for meditative progress, that the masters of traditions themselves project inside students. They are *Mara*, delusionary experiences that are not real. They are, plain and simple, illusions but you won't think so when you experience them. You will mistakenly take them as real and think you've reached some profound stage of progress when those very same people who projected them are stoking your pride so that your Yang Prana arises as well.

Another example is when you *feel like* you know something about an individual (psychically) when that's impossible, and those feelings and psychic knowledge are being projected into you by someone else. You might know you aren't the doer but you don't know this is coming from devas and enlightened spiritual masters. Many people are smart enough o know they are not the source.

Basically these and the many other events reported in the first ten *Mara* states of the *Surangama Sutra* happen all over the world. They are all events where enlightened teachers (and their students) enter your brain to demonstrate how to project visions, sounds, thoughts or feelings or use their energy to move yours. At those times with their teachers in attendance, devas in particular will practice giving you thoughts and play tricks on your mind. That's what higher beings do because consciousness always runs on vital energy, and all the higher beings have bodies made of higher refined vital energy that enables them to override your own. This means they can affect your consciousness by overriding your mind with their thoughts, or by using a *nirmanakaya* energy emanation. The images and sounds you see on the spiritual path are therefore just *Mara*, which means fakery, delusions or illusions.

It is the second set of *Mara* states mentioned in the *Surangama Sutra* that pertain to the twelve-year kundalini purification process. This is the information that is the most important for your spiritual aspirations and yet it is missing in Hinduism, which is why I wrote this book to fill in the gaps. The *Surangama Sutra*, which arose from the spiritual practices of the ascetic traditions in the India of Shakyamuni's day, provides clear examples of what spiritual practitioners will go through as they are trying to "break free of the form *skandha* (*annamaya* sheath or physical body)" to be liberated in an independent subtle body that then makes you a Srotapanna Arhat of junior enlightenment.

During the twelve years of the internal alchemy warming kundalini purification process where Prana is rotating through all your *nadis* and meridians (your entire body) continuously, various enlightened masters will be putting you through countless Yin or Yang emotional experiences to arouse, stimulate or excite different types of energy within you because that makes it easier to wash all the qualities of your Prana (which responds differently according to your emotions). They will also be letting their students train in giving you various thoughts and sensations so *that by helping their students they personally get something out of sacrificing their time working on you.*

The second set of ten *Mara* states described in the *Surangama Sutra* tell us that during the stages of internal alchemy (kundalini transformation) you will be put through various strong emotional experiences such as the following:

- Great sadness or pity (Yin)
- Excitement and boldness (Yang)
- Hopelessness and forlornness (Yin)
- Pride and arrogance (Yang)
- Dread, anxiety and distress (Yin)
- Purity, peace and joy (Yang)
- Intense self-satisfaction and feelings of superiority (Yang)
- Infinite lightness and purity (Yang)
- Fear of death or absolute extinction (Yin)
- Boundless love, desire or even lust (Yang)

This short list is only indicative of the many emotions that will be aroused within you in order to stimulate your Prana during the overall process of spiritual cultivation. That purpose is to arouse a different energy inside you in order to wash your Prana. Enlightened masters and devas do this in order to alter the temperament of your Prana during the times when they are washing it. If you are lucky, an enlightened teacher will put you in different Yin environments or have you perform different Yin activities so that appropriate situations arise to arouse and wash your Yin Prana rather than just sickness, which is a great time to cultivate Yin Prana.

Shakyamuni Buddha gave us explicit teachings in the *Surangama Sutra* on the fact that this is the process you must go through, and like Sri Ramana Maharshi he also gave us warnings not to let the devas lead you astray into doing things against common sense or break the laws of society that will get you into trouble when you are experiencing this. They will absolutely, definitely, certainly cast self-discipline aside in the process of learning how to control human beings – you – and will get you into trouble because the power goes to their head and it is funny for them to make you dance at their whim or mislead you. Hinduism portrays the idea that awakening your kundalini will produce all sorts of havoc, but the troubles are not due to Prana but to devas and all sorts of misconduct.

As another example, the guru Matsyendranath took on the student Gorakhnath as a disciple when he was twelve years old and sent the boy to Badrinarayan to do *tapas* for twelve years, meaning the exercises of spiritual cultivation. Just as Shakyamuni warned, it is reported that *asparas* and other *devatas* came to molest Gorakhnath (as he was going through this process) but he triumphed over their temptations and shenanigans. Sometimes you must just humble yourself with patience and endure until the enemy gets tired of their shooting. Every session headed by a lousy enlightened master is eventually replaced by another who might be less of an asshole.

You can best understand why heavenly beings try to provoke the emotions of people going through this process if you examine the famous Finnish thermal body heat mapping pictures, readily available on the internet, which indicate where various emotions are typically felt within the human body. One such study of these thermal heat maps is called "Bodily Maps of Emotions" by Lauri Nummenmaa, Enrico Glerean, Riitta Hari and Jari Hietanen, and you should look up these pictures on the internet.

It can easily be seen from these pictures that each human emotion excites your inner energy (Prana) in a different sort of way, thus changing its quality, temperament or flavor. That excitation is felt strongly in unique areas of the body for different emotions.

You should study these pictures of "emotion-induced bodily sensations" because *this knowledge is the secret basis of many cultivation techniques in Hinduism* meant to stimulate "dominant attitudes" or arouse your positive (masculine or Yang) or negative (feminine or Yin) emotions. The basic cultivation method of all spiritual schools is to enter into an emotional state that accordingly arouses sensations inside your body that will, in turn, stimulate or arouse your Yin or Yang energy because that arousal will wash the energy of your subtle body made of Prana.

Repeat: A basic cultivation method of spiritual traditions across the world is to use a method of practice to arouse different strong emotions or attitudes within you. Strong emotions or attitudes affect your internal energy because they cause internal sensations that arouse your Prana. When that happens, the activation of strong Prana flows within you, such as when you get exceedingly frightened, will wash the Prana of your whole body completely, and this is what they want.

From these valuable thermal imaging studies you will see that Yin and Yang emotions cause different energy responses within your physical body. Positive Yang emotions such as happiness, love or friendship are felt throughout your entire body while some emotions are felt strongly only in specific locations. You already know from personal experience that your internal energy feels different during different emotions just as your breathing pattern may change in response to different mental states as well. This is the principle used to wash the various flavors of your Prana to prepare your spiritual body for emergence.

Certain emotions or attitudes like anger, pride, victory, domination, etcetera will stimulate your masculine Yang energy throughout your body and especially cause your energy to arise in the upper part of your body. This is why Vajrayana Buddhism employs the arousal of "divine anger" and "divine pride" in various spiritual cultivation practices, which is in order to temporarily raise the Yang energy of practitioners rather than to cultivate these attitudes as permanent personality traits. As another instance, during sexual intercourse the happiness, excitement, joy and pleasurable feelings of sex can envelop you completely, at which time you can then use sexual intercourse's ability to stir your internal energy as an activity for Prana cultivation too.

Feelings of anger, pride, courage, triumph, heroics, victory, domination, confidence, euphoria, exhilaration, enthusiasm, joy, cheerfulness, awe, optimism, sexual excitement, love, amusement, strength, willpower, mirth, brightness, aliveness, ... and attending weddings or other happy ceremonies or festivals, active exercise, fighting, masculinity practices, sunshine visualizations, pranayama cultivation, positive planetary aspects etcetera are all situations that raise or "stimulate" your body's solar energy or Yang Prana.

When you stir up great devotional emotions for a deity you can enter into a deep state of Yang or Yin Prana depending on whether you became absorbed in positive or negative emotions. You can also do this independently of any spiritual rituals, ceremonies, or *bhakti* activities of any form by *becoming absorbed in self-generated positive mental states or strong attitudes* that will stimulate your Prana so much that the resultant positive energies will pervade and wash your subtle body throughout.

If you regularly do this you will lean toward developing those characteristics as personality traits, and in those cases you must break the limiting barriers of your comfort zone that define your normal emotional range so that you are really energizing your energy by overwhelming your normal emotional limits. You want to galvanize your Prana to an unusual degree that is far beyond the standards of your normal personality in order to strongly wash its nature. Don't worry that you will become wild with that energy as a permanent personality trait because after this type of emotional absorption you will immediately slide back to your normal steady state routines for holding yourself (your "set points") unless you are actively cultivating a new trait continuously. Like the highs of sexual bliss, afterwards everything typically returns to normal once again.

When you perform meditation practices that hold onto feelings of infinite joy, universal loving-kindness, boundless compassion and perfect (infinite) equanimity this is another form of this technique where you try to strongly exhilarate all the Prana inside your body using boundless emotions as a prompt since becoming enmeshed in an "infinite" emotion causes you to throw away your ego-concepts and *go beyond yourself with a limitless thrilling energization connected to that emotion*. That will certainly wash your Prana, which is the whole point of the exercise.

When your practice at this is so good then when your emotions stir you inside that energy will totally infuse you with internal sensations and delight. Then the practice is no longer just a mental phenomenon but becomes a physical phenomenon too, and that's what you want. You want your mind to be affecting the energy sensations within your body through self-stimulation, which is the basis behind many spiritual practices that *use imaginary cognition as a prompt*. You want to be enlivening, stirring up, thrilling, shaking or electrifying the Prana of your body in a rousing fashion in order to activate it, and through that movement thus wash it.

This is the basis of many *bhakti* techniques too where you are supposed to arouse the feeling of extremely large positive or negative mental-emotional states within yourself in order to activate your internal energies. The target is to energize and wash the Prana of your subtle body that constitutes the *pranamaya* and higher *koshas*.

From these thermal images you will also see that negative emotions such as fear, terror, disgust, shame, anxiety, nervousness, guilt, inferiority, embarrassment, hopelessness, contempt, sadness, depression, shame, jealousy and envy will cause your body's Yin energy to be stimulated. When cultivating Yin energy you will sometimes feel coldness in your body or a coolness like vapor surrounding you and rising into the sky (sort of like the feeling of light air conditioning) which is a blessing from higher spiritual beings trying to help you transform your Yin Prana. Yin energy is cool, which is why it is often compared to the light of the moon. Yin Prana is therefore called lunar energy and sometimes feminine energy.

Another blessing of Yin Prana purification is a chilling state within your body temporary becomes so cold that your teeth actually chatter, your body shivers and you must wrap yourself in blankets for about 15-30 minutes or so. It is not a sickness (like malaria or the flu) because it will last no more than a few minutes and then suddenly depart. Feelings of coldness within the body are typically a sign of Yin Prana arising, and sometimes during cultivation you will suddenly feel various types of cold energy washing you that are another type of blessing for your spiritual efforts.

As stated, the emotions of fear, fright, terror, shock, hurt, anxiety, sadness, worry, sullenness, disappointment, loneliness, isolation, hopelessness, helplessness, resignation, vulnerability, rejection, unimportance or inferiority, insignificance, feeling unwanted, feeling let down, feeling confused and lost, feeling on guard and nervously uncomfortable, inner turmoil and travail, physical pain, intimidation, humility, self-surrender, yearning, hunger (fasting), depression, suicide, guilt, embarrassment, shame, humiliation, grief, apathy, disgust, revulsion, jealousy, treachery, sneakiness, greed, ... as well chills or the flu will all stimulate, vibrate, energize or raise your Yin Prana.

In particular, spiritual masters in many traditions particularly like to arouse your Yin energy using fright or disgust, which is especially a common feature in the Aghori Shaivite sadhu tradition that uses cremation ground ceremonies, mantras for ghosts, and meditations on dead bodies. There is no special magic behind this. The enlightened masters just want to put you in situations where you become very afraid since fear and anxiety arouse your Yin energy so that it can be differentiated form your Yang energy.

When trying to purify a practitioner's Yin Prana, enlightened masters typically put individuals through very fearful or painful emotional experiences and sometimes even use their own *nirmanakaya* energies to cause physical annoyances, irritation or pain within their student's bodies to arouse their Yin Prana. This is especially so during the last years of the internal alchemy rotations to free your subtle body from its shell during which time one's feet become extremely cold due to the fact that your Yin Prana is being worked on incessantly in that region. All of this is quite distressing to practitioners who don't know what is going on and the lack of understanding prompts many to consider suicide due to the excessiveness of the process or lack of sufficient protection from the attending masters who are more interested in their own deva students or showing off their skills than in your welfare. That's just the way things are. This is why most Hindus going through the process do so under the supervision of a living master.

In Christianity the monks of Mount Athos going through the twelve-year kundalini transformation are taught that everything happening is the work of devils, which adds fear-based Yin Prana to the pain-based negative energy, but actually it is just a washing process for your Prana that is going on. Being only human, unfortunately the specific devas involved in the process sometimes get carried away and go astray in provoking you with all sorts of efforts to raise your anger (Yang Prana) or fear and pain (Yin Prana).

Let me put it another way. The *Taittiriya Katakam* (1st *Prasna*, last *Anuvakan*, 4th mantra) states, "One who merely performs Yajnas (sacred fire rituals) without feeling the presence of God is merely feeding the fire with firewood and raises only smoke. He is a fool. He will never realize the Self." Strong feelings must be involved in the process of washing your Prana in order for you to attain *moksha* or liberation.

These teachings are only explaining to you what goes on during the twelve years of intense Prana purification, where you are put through intense emotional ups and downs in order to wash your Prana, that you must go through to achieve the first junior body of liberation that is the subtle body attainment that can roam free of your physical nature. Naturally, only a few people are qualified which is why each country only has a few genuine masters of saints at any moment in time.

THE 12 MINOR HARDSHIPS OF NAROPA

The secret hidden in Hinduism, which Shakyamuni revealed in the *Surangama Sutra*, is that on the road of spiritual practice your Prana needs to become washed through experiences that arouse emotions that strongly stimulate your positive energy. This is necessary for everyone, and so Shakyamuni explained the secret basis behind what is happening during those twelve years.

These principles are also taught in the story of the Mahasiddha Naropa (circa 956-1040), who was born into a Kashmiri Brahman family. He spent twelve years with his teacher Tilopa on the banks of the Bagmati river at the site of the Pashupatinath Temple in Nepal before he attained *siddhi*, which means the subtle body attainment that is the first stage to final *moksha* or liberation. Whenever a story involves twelve years they are usually talking about the kundalini washing experience that must take place during which time your Prana is rotated and rotated in various ways (and undergoes many other strange Prana manipulations) with hotness and coolness until you attain the independent subtle body, which is only the first stage of Arhatship or junior enlightenment.

The story of the "Twelve Minor Trials (Hardships) of Naropa" recounts various Yin and Yang energy experiences that Naropa went through before he could meet Tilopa, but few people understand the hidden meaning of this story. In this story the student Naropa goes looking to meet his future master Tilopa and encounters many shocking experiences during his journey. The idea being transmitted is that each of those experiences strongly stimulates his emotions and consequently the Yin or Yang energies throughout his body become activated and washed a bit from the attending devas and masters. We must be given some leeway in interpreting which emotions were stimulated during the experiences he encountered, but it doesn't really matter because the story is only meant to teach you that *this emotional priming has to happen* in order to wash your Prana.

For the first trial Naropa encountered a leper woman covered with wounds who could not move, which caused disgust and repulsion to arise within him (and thereby stimulated his Yin energy) as well as compassion.

In the second trial he came upon a dog infested with lice and maggots that were eating its rotting flesh, and various emotions of compassion and repulsion thus arose (stimulating his Yin and Yang energy).

For the third trial he encountered a man trying to play devious tricks on his parents who asked Naropa to help him. Refusing this man with criticism, indignation and detestation strongly aroused Naropa's Yin and Yang Prana.

Next in the fifth trial he met a man who was tearing up a corpse for its intestines, and naturally Naropa felt fear and abhorrence from seeing such a ghastly sight (arousing his Yin Prana).

Next in the sixth trial he came upon a man having an open stomach wound that he was washing with water and who asked Naropa to help him wash the injury. Afraid and disgusted but also feeling compassion, his Yin and Yang energies were strongly evoked.

For the seventh trial he became interested in marrying the daughter of a king because his sexual desire was provoked strongly (thus stimulating his masculine Yang Prana).

For the eighth trial he came upon a hunter with his hounds who asked Naropa to join him on a hunt. This either spurred his sense of excitement, fun and courage (thus arousing his Yang Prana) or fomented abhorrence (Yin Prana) because of the killing, but Naropa refused and continued on his journey.

Next in his ninth trial he encountered a couple by a lake who cooked a non-vegetarian meal for him that he declined eating, so the man said in anger that he would kill Naropa's parents. The unruly, unpredictable and vehement unreasonableness frightened Naropa thus stimulating his Yin Prana.

In the tenth trial he came upon the terrifying scene of a man who had impaled his father upon a stake and imprisoned his mother in a dungeon, both of whom asked him to free them from their murderous son. Fear, worry, anxiety and feelings of unjustness at the misery he viewed arose within him to wash his Prana.

In the eleventh trial he came upon a hermitage where he was received with pomp because of his status, thus raising his pride (and Yang energy). On the premises was a beggar named Tilopa cooking fish and the residents started hitting him. Naropa became confused and perplexed with Tilopa's doings and teachings, thus arousing his inner Yin energy once again.

In the twelfth trial he came to a wide open plain populated by people with strange abnormalities, and the strange sights prompted disgust, fear and other Yin emotions to arise.

Remember this principle: the only way you can achieve enlightenment is if your Prana becomes purified, and the only way this happens is if hundreds of masters lend their energies to the process of helping to purify your body's energies by scrubbing them with their own energies (using *nirmanakaya* emanations) while raising the Yin and Yang aspects of your pranic life force. Basically, they must activate all the modalities of your Prana so that all the possible energies of your physical body can be easily washed after being stimulated into arising through your physical tissues.

You need to depend upon others in order to attain enlightenment because you cannot achieve this through just your own efforts alone. This is why you should do as much of this work as possible through your own personal *inner energy* practices that employ the lessons and understanding you are receiving. Also, remember that you cannot just cultivate positive inner Yang energy but must cultivate Yin energy as well. This is why some masters live in strange desolate places filled with Yin Prana, which is to absorb the Yin Prana of that location.

Now you can understand why many spiritual masters force their students to **approach things they find repulsive such as cemeteries and places that might scare you.** This is meant to help stimulate your Yin Prana, which people hardly ever do of their own initiation. Nevertheless you will find countless mantras in the spiritual literature of Hinduism that call forth *asparas*, ghosts, demons and so forth that are really just spiritual masters masquerading in disguise (while keeping ancient traditions alive) to provoke and cleanse the Yin energy of worthy candidates through such trickery. Higher spiritual beings just love masquerading as deities or this and that to play tricks on human beings.

Any local deva in the vicinity of a purification session on you will also want work done on his body as well and will come within you for some teaching sessions if an enlightened master is working on you for purification purposes. Hence, if the process wasn't abusive involving lots of undeserved pain then thousands of unqualified devas would clamor to be worked on within you as your Prana is being rotated daily during the twelve years of kundalini washing that grants you the stage of the subtle body achievement. The process is so painful and abusive at times that no devas become envious of you, and hardly anyone who goes through it explains what happens during this period. Higher being train in using you rather than just helping you. It is like being the tail end of a whip where you are getting frayed day by day as Causal-bodied, Supra-Causal and Immanence individuals demonstrate their skills at how lightly or strongly they can control their Prana by simultaneously giving you and the deva audience pain here and there. Hinduism and Tibetan Buddhism have tantric pictures of deities standing on the bodies of men crushing them to denote this fact.

This is why masters don't want you doing inner energy work unless they give you permission, which means their protection, otherwise you will eventually invite a diluted amount of such interference onto yourself. Nevertheless, everyone goes through it. Enlightened beings will possess and then use your body like a mechanism since essentially that is what you are although you think you are an independent true self-entity rather than a created cog in the workings of the universe.

Let me explain this a different way. The process is like the Milgram Shock Experiment but in this case devas will inflict pain on you at the request of their teacher to demonstrate their skills, and they won't care a bit whether they hurt you too much or not.

It is also like the Stanford Prison Experiment where there were good guards and bad guards who abused students who were acting as fake prisoners. In the Stanford Prison Experiment, good guards on the shifts when the worst abuses occurred never did anything bad to the prisoners themselves but not once during the experiment did they ever intervene to stop the activities of the bad guards who abused the students. They never once confronted them and asked, "What are you doing? Remember those are just college students and not prisoners." The good guards allowed all the abuses to happen and their inaction facilitated evil and abuse, allowing it to happen. Similarly, all the masters are having fun during your washing process so they typically lose their discipline in preventing any abuse of you unless you are one of their old buddies (which is someone who becomes enlightened in their early 20s) or supposed to take over a tradition where they need you. It is unbelievable but how you are treated is ultimately a matter of your tradition (some are more abusive than others), your location and relationships.

When ordinary devas see and experience the incredible pains that you must suffer through the kundalini process (for instance, assaults that last hours to your ears, nose, head, face, teeth, asshole, right side, knees and so forth) then no one complains that they aren't being worked on. This is why you should undertake a lot of purification efforts yourself to speed the process, and develop the neural patterns for the various geometrical ways of washing your Prana to speed the process, which will often be neglected at times by spiritual masters overseeing it.

THE 10 TRIALS OF LU DONGBIN

Chinese Taoism also has its own relevant story that illustrates these same principles of (1) the *Surangama Sutra*, (2) Naropa's hardships and (3) the thermal mapping pictures which reveal where emotions strongly evoke sensations that stimulate the energy within your body. We must remember the Sage of Kanchi's advice that we must draw such information from elsewhere if it is to help our own spiritual efforts as most of this information is hidden from Hinduism.

The Chinese story concerns the ten trials of Lu Dongbin, a famous Taoist who became enlightened. Those ten trials, like Naropa's hardships and the ten trials of the *Surangama Sutra*, also teach us what to expect when going through the transformational experiences of internal alchemy that wash your Prana so that your astral deva body can differentiate itself from the rest of your Prana and break free of its physical shell.

The twelve minor trials of Naropa teach this same lesson and Shakyamuni Buddha also gave explicit teachings in the *Surangama Sutra* on the fact that this was the process you must go through with warnings not to let the devas lead you astray into doing things against common sense and the laws of society during this time. Otherwise you will get into trouble.

These principles are taught to us in the Ten Trials of Lu Dongbin which also, unbeknownst to Taoists, refer to the Prana purification or cleansing phase of the twelve-year kundalini transformation period where he also passed through various strong emotional states in order to wash his Prana:

In the first trial Lu Dongbin was caused to feel great sadness (Yin energy was aroused) because he thought his family members were dying.

In the second trial he felt great anger (his Yang internal energy was aroused) because he was cheated of money in the marketplace for his goods.

In the third trial he responded with compassion (Yang energy was aroused), and then indignation and irritation (Yin energy was aroused) because he gave money to a beggar who then kept asking for more and more.

In the fourth trial he crossed paths with a hungry tiger which incited great fear (his Yin Prana was aroused).

In the fifth trial he resisted the pull of strong sexual desire that arose within him (Yang energy was aroused) when a beautiful girl tried to seduce him. In the Aghori tradition of India the masters will sometimes ask an attractive enlightened heavenly maiden to produce a physical *nirmanakaya* emanation to attract a young adept's attention to provoke his sexual interest from afar.

In the sixth trial he felt dejected, depressed and at a loss (his Yin energy was aroused) because his entire estate had been completely burglarized.

In the seventh trial he experienced great astonishment and happiness (his Yang Prana was aroused) in the face of greed (Yin energy was aroused) when he discovered that some bronze utensils he bought were actually made of gold, so he returned them.

In the eighth trial he aroused fearless courage (his Yang energy was aroused) despite nervousness (Yin energy was stimulated) by drinking a magic potion said to either kill you or make you enlightened.

In the ninth trial he experienced great worry and terror (his Yin energy was aroused) due to a flood, but then he composed himself.

The tenth trial is the most enlightening. Lu Dongbin was alone reading a book in his room when countless ghosts, demons and monsters suddenly came from every corner of the world to attack him (his Yin Prana was aroused). This type of illusion often happened to the Christian saint Padre Pio and the Tibetan adept Yeshe Tsogyel (c. 757), which you can read about in her autobiography. This is common for anyone going through the process.

Despite the attacks, Lu Dongbin kept on doing his chores without paying the demons any attention, ignoring them entirely. This is the instruction provided for us even though our emotions are provoked to become unbalanced during these operations. One of the monsters yelled that Lu Dongbin had wronged him in a past life and now needed to sacrifice his life. Without any fear Lu said, "Go ahead and take my life since I took yours in a past life. This is fair."

Suddenly **Lu Dongbin** heard the clapping of hands, a shout in the air, the sky turned blue and all the ghosts and devils vanished. Standing there was his master, Han Zhongli, who had been looking and laughing at him while all these events were happening. In other words, Han Zhongli (and other enlightened spiritual masters who were helping him) had been supervising the charade of illusions and emotional promptings (while the energy of his inner subtle body was being worked on).

This short tale again symbolizes what happens when you go through the advanced stages of internal alchemy for the twelve or more years it takes to purify your body's Prana so that your subtle body can become purified enough to differentiate itself from the rest of your body's impure energy, and the thinning of the interface between the two then enables your spirit body to finally break free of your physical body. The masters will provoke all sorts of strong Yin or Yang emotions to arise within you to wash your Prana, and will in particular will often masquerade as devils or angels to raise your Yin energy through fright during the purification process.

The Aghori tradition of India is an expert at this as is the Chöd tradition of Tibet that also involves willingly doing what is undesirable or putting yourself into unpleasant circumstances because of the effect on your Yin Prana. Jain monks become overly fearful of hurting even the tiniest insects while Orthodox Christians recite prayers to God lamenting that they are sinners. All of this is done to raise one's feminine Yin Prana.

Speaking frankly, the tail end of the kundalini internal transformation process can be extremely painful. While you are going through the long procedure, which is being overseen by spiritual masters who are purifying your Prana through various manipulations of *nirmanakaya* emanations from their higher bodies, devas and lower level spiritual beings are all passing in and out of you because they are being worked on at the same time. They surround you daily because they all want purification work on their own subtle bodies so that they can raise themselves from the stage of the impure subtle body to a purified subtle body or achieve the Causal body if possible. When going through the process you become a nexus of activity.

The established enlightened beings also want work performed on their various *nirmanakaya* emanations so that those emanations can also become purified to gain the ascension of a higher body attainment from within them as well. If the enlightened masters from ancient times are working on you they are also working on helping many devas in your vicinity at the same time using hundreds of *nirmanakaya* emanations, and this includes teaching higher skills to the local guardian spirits. You are never going through the process alone because all the "audience" voices you hear are of devas and higher beings being worked on at the same time. They certainly like playing tricks on you (because all devas are used to doing that to human beings) and as a general rule will never give you any useful information, hence conversations with them are meaningless and useless. Just ignore them.

There will also be one main deva going through the process within you whom you may or might not hear based on your tradition and your maturity in being able to understand what is going on. He, of course, will be abused as much as you with higher teachers taking over *his* body and speaking through him, such as making jokes, but he (or she) has more protection during the process than you because he can directly complain to his teachers about excessiveness. But he suffers too unless he can master the skill of hardening his body (*garima siddhi*) which offers some protection. Usually nothing that your deva companion says will be worthwhile or helpful and usually anything said is someone else speaking through them.

There is a famous tale about Napoleon Hill, author of the famous book *Think and Grow Rich*, who used to hold an imaginary council meeting in his head to give him ideas and solve his problems. It was composed of the imaginary figures of Thomas Paine, Ralph Waldo Emerson, Thomas Edison, Charles Darwin, Abraham Lincoln, Luther Burbank, Napoleon, Henry Ford and Andrew Carnegie. Initially these imaginary council meetings went fine until the personalities started to act on their own that were out of his control, and then Napoleon Hill stopped this practice out of a fear of insanity. Hill did not understand that some enlightened individual had hijacked his mental operations in order to show his own students how to manipulate certain operations in human consciousness, which all devas are taught how to do because controlling human thoughts is how they normally help people. However, that enlightened teacher really wanted to have some extra fun in the process. On the spiritual trail devas and enlightened masters will often pretend that they are good guys (angels, saints, gods, etc.) or devils and demons and terrorize people to provoke our Yin Prana into arising but this often borders on dangerous extremes because they lose control of themselves in all the fun they have when manipulating people.

All devas want to attain the higher spiritual bodies of enlightenment, which are the bodies that make miraculous superpowers possible. Superpowers don't just happen like you see in the movies where you magically think some special thoughts and Presto! ... a miracle happens. They arise because someone manipulates the energy of their own higher bodies, or manipulates a *nirmanakaya* emanation of energy to do something, or because someone's higher spiritual body has the ability to control the energies of lower realms since that master trained to use the connection between his thoughts and lower energies such as electricity.

Thousands of local devas around you want enlightened masters to work on transforming their Prana via their *nirmanakaya* emanations, and to dissuade an incredible amount of unqualified wannabes from training sessions within you they make the process especially painful at times so that many leave (while they also put those thoughts to leave into the minds of the unqualified attendees). If you have to suffer incredible pain and anguish due to an abusive process then nobody complains, "Well, why does he or she get to go through it and not me?" No one is jealous when they see the pain and abuse you have to suffer.

These are some of the secrets hidden from main-stream

Hinduism but contained in other spiritual traditions whose teachings often originated in India. Hopefully this information will help every future generation of Hindus going through this painful process.

CHAPTER 3
EVOLUTION, HINDUISM AND THE SPIRITUAL OBJECTIVE

According to Hindu scriptures the origin of the manifest universe is Purusha, the eternal substratum that lies at the foundation of all existence. Also known as the Brahman (or Parabrahman or *dharmakaya*), Purusha is an underlying substrate that endows everything with existence because it is *satyam*, the pure permanent existence itself out of which the universe is woven. It is also *anatam*, which means limitless, infinite, endless, immeasurable, all-pervading, and supreme.

Purusha or the Brahman or the *dharmakaya* is a limitless substratum within which, or out of which manifest existence appears. It is singular (non-dual, non-composite, without parts or divisions, undifferentiated), a self-so existence (uncreated by anything else), infinite, without form, without parts, actionless, changeless, immovable, tranquil, without transformations, eternally pure, faultless, undecaying and therefore eternal. Beyond it there is nothing so it is superior to all things.

As the fundamental substrate or substratum of the manifest universe, Purusha or the Brahman is the core substance penetrating all of manifest reality and the ultimate substance of manifestation that seems like a freezing, solidification, or densification of its empty formlessness that is thereby perceived differently than what it really ultimately is, which is why we say Nature is an illusion. It is the union of Shiva and Shakti in one form. It exists in unmanifested and manifested forms, the forms of both being and non-being.

The house of Creation is built out of the substance of Brahman, so everything you see is the Brahman and consciousness is the Brahman too, or you can say "its source is the Brahman." The Brahman manifests as the universe and is therefore the ultimate nature of life.

It is the Brahman and only the Brahman that manifests as consciousness, which is just another process that has arisen within the manifesting universe. Among other things, consciousness produces an apparent but illusory view of the universe that it different for different types of sentient beings. The view that consciousness produces for us seems to work fine, but is all based on the illusion of a self-knower, its thinking is often illogical and biased by wrong perspectives, and it paints a false picture of the world. Yet that picture works with consistency and enables survival for our type of organism, so we go with it and should!

The universe actually has no other giver of experience and no witness other than the Brahman that is the indwelling Self in all, although of course Brahman does not witness anything since that is just a way of speaking. With consciousness, the witness is just consciousness speaking to itself or reflecting things to itself in a loop. Speaking in the same manner you can also say that the Brahman is not just the ultimate nature of consciousness and enjoyer of the consciousness of all sentient beings (without being found by our senses) but also the ultimate life force behind the life force. You can also call the Brahman "pure consciousness" but it is just a formless substrate without parts or differentiation so it is by no means an active consciousness that forms thoughts or images.

Although actionless because it is changeless or non-moving, you can also colloquially say that the Brahman has sovereignty over everything, governing the universe, since it is the foundational, primordial, ultimate absolute substrate that transcends all as well as the first cause of the universe too. It is the cause of all transformations or achievements although non-dual, without any attributes. It manifests various adjuncts to *appear* as manifoldness by manifesting itself as the subsidiary agencies which cause the various cosmic processes. Transcendentally the Brahman is ever free of conditions so it is never under the bondage of cause and effect that causes change, and the changes that appear in the universe are only seen because of the illusory nature of our consciousness.

The Brahman is without any prior antecedents so in being without cause it is self-existent or self-so, and it never changes its qualities because of its singular, pure, non-composite, non-dualistic nature. It has always been and will always continue to exist throughout all times of past, present and future since it has no beginning and no end and because it cannot change.

Thus Brahman or Purusha or the *dharmakaya* is eternal and everlasting, always remaining what it is, and never becomes anything other than itself due to changelessness. Purusha is actionless so it always remains the unmovable Self inside all things, including us. It is our permanent self-nature that dwells in all *jivas* and includes within itself all divinities. It pervades every being, sustains every being, enjoys every being and always remains the same. Hence we say it is that which moves in every body keeping them all functioning by functioning as their life force, and we can colloquially say that the Brahman has innumerable eyes, meaning countless forms of consciousness since it is their Self. Basically it remains aloof from transmigratory existence that is a subcategory of the overall transformations of phenomena that are all unreal appearances.

To understand Purusha it is wise to consult the *Astavakkra Samhita* (Swami Nityaswarupananda), *Avadhuta Gita of Dattatreya* (Swami Chetanananda), and *Traditional Theory of Evolution and Its Application in Yoga* (Gharote, Devnath and Jha). Also helpful would be *Maya in Physics* (N.C. Panda), *The Ribhu Gita* (translated by Dr. H. Ramamoorthy), and *Dasbodh* (Sri Samartha Ramdas). These books summarize the nature of the Brahman, Purusha, Parabrahman, or Paramatman and its manifestation as the cosmos or Prakirti (Shakti).

Somehow unmoving Purusha gives birth to Prakirti or Shakti, the manifest universe of energies, forms and vibrations that we call attributes, characteristics, qualities or phenomena. No one knows how the creation of something that is always moving originates from something that never changes or moves which is thus impossible to transform, so Hinduism deals with this event by calling creation the desire, play or sport of the divine in order to dismiss our ignorance and not deal with the topic at all. Advaita Vedanta says it is all an illusion so there is no reason to fret about it.

Don't ask why or how manifestation took place. Everyone is in ignorance about the details although perhaps in other worlds the physics are good enough to explain matters. The important thing is that your physical body is not your true identity because the ultimate substratum is your identity. It is the unchanging part of you that never transforms so it is your permanent self, your True Self, or your fundamental self-nature. Your physical body will not remain your identity because it is only a *brief* appearance in the realm of manifestation ... unless you cross a threshold to achieve a body with a physical state of immortality, or where there is death and a continuity of memories in rebirth that would then constitute a type of immortality as long as that cycle of rebirth can continue.

Purusha has always existed, alone and pure (homogenous) without a second, and always remains changeless. What is change? It is the appearance of another characteristic of a substance while the previous characteristic has disappeared. Somehow through a process we don't understand called the sport, play or *lila* of the divine, the manifest universe of Prakirti or Shakti has appeared. However, the universe is only apparent, not the Reality, so it cannot be a true change of the substratum. The substratum always remains itself and so what we see must be an illusion that superimposes a densification on top of something formless like empty space.

The Brahman or Purusha is the only Reality ... not the manifest existence that we perceive. We *do perceive* a world of forms and phenomena, so they are apparently true through self-evidence, but in actuality it is all only Brahman the unmanifesting substrate. The true reality that is your True Self, Brahman, is so formless, empty or refined that it is beyond the capabilities of the intellect and imagination yet you are that final ultimate truth.

The situation is like Brahman being an immeasurable clump of gold that takes the form of many different shapes such as rings, pendants and bracelets that all seem different from one another but are equally just the single element gold. From the standpoint of the gold they are just itself (gold) which might assume different forms but the substance of gold itself never changes. There is nothing else that exists other than the gold just as factually nothing else exists other than the Brahman.

Nothing is happening to the element gold if an ornament appears, nothing has happened and nothing is going to happen. However, from the standpoint of consciousness, which is flawed in the sense that it cannot penetrate *Maya* to see the ultimate substrate, appearances seem like compressed condensings or agglomerations different from one another when they are actually just one single foundational thing that has one taste.

Within Prakirti, Shakti or the cosmos, which is constantly changing, transforming or evolving through a nebulous chaos of uncountable complex interactions we call cause and effect, life eventually formed over time. Eventually consciousness developed within life and over time the attribute of complex consciousness evolved for some life forms with the appropriate anatomical apparatus as we have now.

Of course, from the standpoint of Advaita Vedanta we would say that nothing has happened at all since everything is all the Brahman and only the Brahman so no real changes have occurred, and that is true if we take the world "real" to mean unchanging reality that is a dependable truth unalterable and absolute. There is no such true thing as sentient beings, deities, dharma, cause and effect, codes of behavior, and so on because the manifest universe is all insentient, inanimate, inert Brahman and that ultimate absolute nature is a singular, formless, undifferentiated entity without qualities or attributes just like pristine empty space. It is the ground state of existence that lacks any form of manifestation or appearance so how can there be such real things as morality or dharma or souls or cause and effect?

That invisible reality which cannot be perceived through thinking or the senses. That presence that existed before the universe and you were created will continue its existence even after you expire. Permanent omnipresence is your stateless state prior to your beingness of manifestation.

Now, somehow through a complex chain or evolution or set of transformations we have the fact that a combination of the eternal self-existent primordial nature (universal substratum), the five elements (energy and matter) and consciousness produced your bodily form. Your presence certainly emerged through an infinite set of complex interactions spanning the history of all manifestations yet we don't know how anything originally appeared and we certainly don't know all the laws of cause and effect pertaining to your existence and consciousness either. Your manifestation along with the universe and everything within it, all appeared out of your fundamental substratum of base existence but we cannot trace any major details other than your ancestors parents mating in sequence to produce you.

The world of manifestation is here, we are in it and we are it, but actually we are not intrinsic, separated living beings with true selves but just the ground state essence yet don't realize it. Self-generated from the unmanifest to the manifest, from the formless to the form, the universe was produced without any external stimulus as a natural impulse and now it has produced us. We are the universe, and we are the fundamental substratum. Whether an illusion or not, we exist with a sometimes faulty attribute called consciousness that lets us exist as (imagined) selves so we have the chance to make the best of our sentient lives if we apply ourselves correctly. The teachings of spirituality, and Advaita Vedanta or Buddhism in particular, simply tell us what we truly are. We *both exist and are not true existences*, but because we have existences with the miraculous attribute of consciousness in an insentient universe we should seek the most out of our lives.

The energies of a manifest universe somehow eventually appeared and differentiated themselves in a multitude of ways although there is only one single underlying unchanging reality. Through complex interactions those energies produced more energies. Energy fields, particles, atoms and elements were formed as well as space, and the manifest universe composed of various planes of existence and material forms took shape over time.

Within that universe of forms and energy life eventually evolved as a manifestation, and then complex life, and then life with consciousness. Eventually, animal life with higher consciousness developed that includes the humans on our planet, and it went through its own various stages of development. The same can no doubt be said for other worlds in the universe that had the right conditions for developing complex life. The *Vishnu Purana* and *Yoga Vasistha* clearly state that there are an uncountable number of worlds in the universe with their own forms of life that are sometimes too remarkable to be believed.

In order to maintain itself, the human species adapted itself to all sorts of living conditions otherwise its various experimental branches died out. Out of whatever forms remained, humans eventually grew in numbers and cognition to organize themselves into societies with rules of order and conduct. Those rules or traditions insured the maintenance, survival and procreative continuance of those groups and the ability for those groups to cooperatively live together otherwise they died out. Those individuals who did not align with the values of their group, and who exhibited low levels of empathy for others and a lack of moral considerations, would end up with low social status and not be desirable mates for others. Thus, over time the human brain evolved ways to induce social moods that were in the best interests of your genes, and humans began to value a social status determined by contribution to the group rather than just dominance.

Consciousness is the big issue in this discussion, the great miracle of existence because the majority of the universe is insentient. You are a body-mind-energy complex with the attribute of consciousness, but you already know that your inherent nature existed before your bodily form and will continue to exist after your bodily form expires. You don't need any proof of your our existence because it is self-evident to your mind. You know it and that's enough. But the big false misunderstanding that your consciousness makes is that you are an independent individual with a mind, ego and intellect that is unconnected to anything else when you are actually Nature, the manifest universe, as well as the ultimate substratum. That is your true nature. You don't have a life of your own. You don't stand alone as a separate existence in space but are defined by the entire universe and cannot be removed from it since there is nowhere else to go due to its infinite nature.

This misunderstanding as to who and what you really are happened because you developed an ego-sense that gave you the feeling of being a separate identity from everything, and you began to feed off this information without analyzing matters. Now it's come to the point where you think you are a specific self-enclosed entity but you are actually formless and immortal without any such thing as consciousness. In reality you are formless, unborn, without a beginning or end because you are the Brahman. Your true self-nature of what you actually are was probably something you never even knew about until you came in contact with this information which you can also learn by studying Advaita Vedanta.

You bought into the dream of consciousness, even though the world it produces for you is an internal illusion that is similar to what is out there but not the real picture. You accepted all the thought forms and mental fabrications you have built in your mind as being real although your mind is just a function of algorithms, habits, *samskaras* and impressions that run an illusory process called consciousness that is not really sentience but just a process. If you were really the owner controlling your consciousness then you could do so completely but you cannot since your ego-sense is just an outcome of your organism and its processes. Because you didn't analyze matters you believe you are a somebody whereas you are a nobody. Or you can say that you are all things, or the original beingness without a body. Or you can stick with conventionality and say that you are the appearance of a separate individuality, which is just fine.

From a practical standpoint, to live a life with existence and be part of the great collection of consciousnesses you must live as if you are just a person, but be self-realized in knowing what you ultimately are. You must know the answer to "who am I?" and because you possess consciousness, a mind that experiences pleasure and pain, you must seek ways to find peace and joy in life and free yourself from suffering and impermanence.

The ascension to the higher realms of being by achieving transcendental bodies, and achieving the Great Transformation of crossing the threshold from the "Realm of Form" to the highest planes or heavens of the "Formless Realm" by attaining the Supra-Causal and Immanence bodies, is the solution to many of your problems even though any of those physical bodies are not your ultimate identity because they are not your ultimate core substance. What you ultimately are is a permanent, unchangeable core nature that is the Brahman. Yet to eat and not be eaten, and to survive, thrive and procreate so that the human species continues, you must live according to the laws of cause and effect that define the universe and your existence that you know because you have a mind. Everything you experience might be a mental construct but you must still adjust yourself to the forces of Nature that might imperil your existence.

Even so, spirituality requires that you need to recognize the illusion of consciousness, called *Maya*, in that everything you see and experience are appearances in a personal faulty dream of your consciousness. Furthermore, we are part of a grand illusion of concentration or agglomeration whose ultimate decomposition is the stateless ground state of undifferentiated base reality. All things can be resolved to this residuum. At one time your body didn't exist previously and neither did your consciousness or the universe. They are all part of an ever-changing dream that lacks real substance, which is why it changes … the reality we perceive is an unreal drama lacking permanent substance. All things are appearances in this dream of effervescent, scintillating, ever-vibrating and transforming Manifestation called the universe. There are no multiple universes as scientists like to talk about because their existence must be lumped into the one term "manifestation" whose root source is always the singular formless substratum.

Therefore, how you should operate your consciousness in your dream life is to just loosen your hold on mental attachments to see everything without exception as a dream. Then pain becomes less and you can respond to negativities in life with less affliction because you recognize that it is all a dream that will pass. You can adapt to situations much easier when you don't cling to how you want things to be because you recognize that the situation will pass and that your reactions are all mental constructs. Of course you must also cultivate a skillfulness of your mind, such as the ability to avoid suffering, adapt to changes, and transform your own states of consciousness. You might recognize that your mind produces a *Maya* or illusion but you must still function according to the conventionalities of the dream otherwise you will certainly expire. You must also station yourself in a state of alertness or clear presence so that you can better select your thoughts and avoid being just a robotic actor that automatically follows the habits of mental algorithms.

When you view life as a dream then your mentality can lighten up so that problems do not affect you as much due to this liberated mindset. It is like when you have the subtle body connected to the human physical body and can see the world through both sets of eyes. Your new center of life is the subtle realm, but you can still see the physical realm and operate that body as a shell while realizing that its affairs are not so important since your true life is elsewhere and you can cast it off without as second thought. You are in the world but not of the world so it is as if you are acting in a dream knowing that you are at the same time separate from it.

In the ultimate sense you are the unshakable, all-pervading, fundamental substrate that never experiences birth or death. What you are ultimately in essence has always existed. However, what you seem to be is a "dream being" with consciousness that enjoys the experience of life but suffers birth and death within it.

The physical world we live in appears to be solid but that is only our mental perceptions at work that make it seem so. Only wisdom and knowledge about the workings of consciousness enables you to understand what you are truly perceiving – which is a just a mental product within your consciousness that is your mind only. Only wisdom and knowledge enable you to understand what you truly are.

Everything we perceive of the world outside us is an illusion, representation, similitude or model of the world fabricated inside our minds. We live in an imaginary world of our own creation. We are prisoners of our minds in that what we always experience is Mind-Only or Mere-Consciousness. What we perceive as reality is just our consciousness. The universe as experienced from the perspective of an observer is his consciousness. It is just his consciousness only.

Our minds create conventional constructions that are not ultimately real in how we perceive them and certainly not the real things in themselves. The vision we create of the world seems to function with inviolable facticity of unbreakable cause and effect, and seems to be aligned with what everyone else perceives, but who says our world view is the correct one ... are there others possible? Who says that our way of perceiving the world and interpreting it as the objects we see is the correct one? Everything is empty of a firm reality just as are atoms when you deconstruct them into their finest level of pre-particle energies.

If you can stop identifying with the various forms that arise in your mind you will attain a degree of unrivaled mental freedom and flexibility because of realizing that what you are seeing is an inexact illusion created by the algorithms of your mind, and that you are actually selfless because you are the root substrate of not just consciousness but of all those shapes and appearances. You are the ultimate foundation that underlies everything including your appearance and the appearance of the world. That absolute, ultimate foundation is your true "I" or True Self which we call the Brahman, *dharmakaya*, Purusha or Parabrahman or many other names.

You are that eternal substratum of existence, the intangible, imperceptible reality and nameless power or energy which has been called by many different names in cultures and religions such as God, ultimate truth, ultimate reality, Brahman, Nirguna Brahman, Parabrahman, source nature, primordial essence, ground substratum, foundational state, *dharmakaya*, Ein Sof, etc. You are that boundless, imperceptible reality that underlies everything as its ultimate substance. *Everything is that reality and you are a selfless part of it.* There is nothing other than that reality. That invisible presence is very subtle, in fact more subtle than the sky or empty space.

The world which appears to be real is seen because you have sentience and because your mind has reasoning abilities and can create fractional (abbreviated) illusory pictures of a certain level of congealing, condensing, emanation or densification of that all-pervading underlying substratum that is the ultimate substance of everything. You cannot see that ultimate substance or perceive it any way to perceive what things really are. The projector that enables you to know about it and to perceive the world and yourself is your mind – consciousness.

Advaita Vedanta says that your problem is that you give importance to the illusory projections instead of recognizing that your mind is the projector of all you see and that this thing called consciousness is just a mechanistic process in the realm of cause and effect without any real self-doer entity behind it experiencing anything as a witness. The workings of consciousness are the witness so now you can stop letting unfortunate events bother you so much. Prior to your manifest beingness there was no body and no knowledge and even now there still is no true individual self or life doing any experiencing or understanding but just a process going on that gives rise to perception and understanding without there being any ultimate self, experiencer or doer within it. Therefore everything you have amassed as experience is not who you are.

We are all part of one universe. It may seem real, look real and feel incredibly real but solidity and stableness exists only as an appearance that can be ultimately decomposed, by discarding the illusions, into the unchanging underlying essence.

Nonduality means there is only one absolute, singular, ultimate reality that is the same unchanging essence that composes everyone and everything. Your body and mind can function only because of the partnership between that underlying nature as its support and absolute substance and because the five elemental body has evolved as an apparatus that provides illusory consciousness and an illusory life that is also a factual life in terms of conventionality. The world is really the projection of your ultimate nature that never changes, and you can say that *it does exist as an appearance* but not as a true ultimate thing-in-itself. Since it does exist in some way (as an appearance) we must deal with life as it appears and make things for the best rather than fall into nihilism. However, the unnameable source that is the ultimate source by which you think, perceive, experience and act, is the real deal or bottom line. It is who you are, what you ultimately are. You are not an individual self, you are that thing – the Brahman.

Let's put this another way to dispel with nihilism and instead see the positivism, grandeur and grand potential of our sentient existence. We *do exist* at some stage of condensing or concentration of universal energies and forces rather than as an insentient formlessness that does not have a body. We exist due to the comprehensiveness of the universe in creating everything about us including an errant consciousness and not-so-perfect body. As long as we live we should strive to flourish in life.

While Vedanta teaches us that our level of concentration or densification of energies is not the way the universe really exists but is just a false appearance (because there is a deeper reality than that stage of condensing), and while you can realize that the way you see the world at your level of densification is also an illusion, it *does exist* for you. Nothing negates that. It will continue existing for a long, long time and so will you as long as the processes or reincarnation are retained. It is just that through the wisdom of understanding you no longer ignorantly believe that the world exists in the way you perceive it to be. That's all. You still live and have simply shed your ignorance.

Furthermore, if you learn how to use your mind correctly you can take more conscious control of your life by breaking free of limiting patterns and not simply be pushed here or there by the forces of the universe or the past conditioning and automatic beliefs established within your mental algorithms. If you become a neutral witness of your mind where you become aware of your automatic patterns and conditioning then this is the first step to freeing oneself from them. Attention allows you to be in the present moment (where you can experience reality without distortions caused by extra mental garbage) while self-observation allows you to look within without distractions, and together these two principles amplify awareness and the sense of beingness or aliveness. They allow you to station yourself in the present where self-witnessing can disrupt the automatic patterns of consciousness by stimulating the awareness of one's being.

Therefore nothing negates the optimistic objective of treasuring, expanding upon, enjoying, beautifying and elevating the body, mind, energy and experiential possibilities of our existence – its *sat, chit, ananda* and *ikigai* possibilities. Because we are living beings our lives have a continuity to them so rather than tossing up our hands and saying that nothing matters the wisest thing is to perfect ourselves and live lives to the fullest extent that seek experiences, accomplishments, *eudaimonia* and progressive growth for ourselves and others!

SAT, CHIT, ANANDA

What does human life desire because it has consciousness? Hinduism says it desires *sat, chit, ananda*. Of course a human being also pursues the four *Purusharthas* that include *Moksha* (liberation), *Dharma* (righteous behavior), *Kama* (pleasure) and *Artha* (prosperity) but we will not deal with these four because we will only focus on *moksha*.

Because of the reasoning abilities of consciousness humans would rather exist rather than not exist *(sat)*, so they act in ways to avoid death and maintain their existence for as long as possible. Because of having a mind *(chit)* a man knows that consciousness or cognizance is a precious attribute to be preferred over insentience where you exist as an unknowing part of the universe, although the universe is indifferent to your fate. Consciousness is the miraculous wish-fulfilling gem of the cosmos since it lets part of the insentient universe know of its self-existence and qualities no matter how imprecise the dreamy illusion.

What does consciousness want? The absence of suffering, and the experience of happiness or bliss in its place. Because of being a body-mind-energy complex it desires *ananda* or bliss that includes physical comfort as well as mental peacefulness, positive emotions, and the absence of suffering or unsatisfactoriness in both body and mind.

In terms of the characteristics of our existence, our mind actually exists because we have the animating Pranas or higher *koshas* of energy within us that constitute our life force and powers our consciousness. They are released as an agglomerated entity or spirit upon death, so we are actually a body-mind-Prana complex rather than just a body-mind complex, but we can use "body-mind" or "mind-body" as a shorthand.

As a human entity (body-mind-Prana complex) we have our own unique personality (of mindset, dispositions, perspectives, attitudes, values, ethics, virtues, faults) with its own unique conduct, behavior or manners that you daily express in your activities. You also have a fortune, fate or destiny in life keyed to the moment you left the womb as a separate entity, and you have the opportunity to develop a life purpose for yourself that can provide your life with meaning and significance. Instead of just *sat, chit, ananda* we should say that a human life also desires *ikigai* which means having a sense of purpose or motivation for one's life, i.e. a sense of purpose, a reason for living or life purpose. You want to be volunteering your actions for purposeful causes and guide your life according to your *ikigai*. You need to give meaning to your existence so that you are not just existing, and most people do this through relationships or an *ikigai* of service to others.

As a body-mind-energy complex that wants to avoid death and suffering and experience bliss or peace and happiness, we have just specified the very few things we can and should be cultivating in our life: * our physical body; * our consciousness (its clarity and capabilities); * our Prana or life force (that constitutes the aggregate of our higher spiritual bodies composed of energies transcendent to the dense material plane of matter); * our personality, disposition, perspectives, attitudes, ingrained tendencies, and habits (our attributes); * our conduct or behavior and activities (applications of our will); * our life path or destiny (our astrological fortune keyed to our birth time initiation); * and our life purpose or *ikigai* that gives direction to our activities.

We can cultivate our physical body through proper nutrition, athletic exercise (such as sport) and the spiritual practices of yoga, dance, or martial arts that in themselves can lead to attaining the higher spiritual bodies.

We can cultivate many special abilities of our consciousness such as having a super memory, forward planning or mental rehearsals using the imaginative powers of visualization, the capability of doing arithmetic in one's head, gaining control over the circulation of vital energy inside one's body, and so on. The abilities of consciousness are countless. As pertaining to the mind, the three major things to gain control over are our thinking, emotions and willpower.

One of the major problems with consciousness is that we are only fractionally in control of its workings or contents, thus we cannot control our emotional moods, concentration and focus, or banish mental disturbances and afflictions when they arise. This makes us subject to mental disturbances or afflictions, disturbs our inner peace, creates a lack of focus and inattention, and hampers our ability to concentrate or persevere in a line of activity. This is because, as an example, our emotions arise in response to whatever happens; they don't happen for you but are an automatic reaction that you have no control over. Since they are just an automatic reaction they can easily arise as afflictive disturbances within our mind unless you learn how to gain control over emotional processes to be able to transform them at will. We can engage in exercises to learn how to gain some control over some of the normally uncontrollable, automatic workings of the processes of consciousness but this takes time to learn, yet is the process of spiritual cultivation. After you learn what you really are it becomes paramount to gain control over the workings of your consciousness.

To gain control over our Prana, or life force, we can turn to the yogic teachings of various inner energy exercises taught to us by the Hindu sages, and the schools of Yoga Tantra offer many such teachings. This can enable us to attain the higher bodies that, when unfurled as separate existences, are the *koshas* of Adi Shankara.

To transform our personality, which has a natal astrological component to it as well as a temperament due to our genetics, parental conditioning, our education and social conditioning, etc. we have to choose a model of ideal conduct, maintain mindfulness of our thoughts and behavior in terms of whether they stray from that ideal, and then engage in self-correction when deviations occur. Fundamentally, we want to bring our actual selves – in thoughts and behavior – closer to the template of our admirable ideals and strive toward our highest potential. We cannot achieve salvation any way other than by transforming our mind and behavior, making them different from what they were originally before we undertook the spiritual path, and then our minds and actions can become deified through our self-efforts and the grace of spiritual masters who lend us their *nirmanakaya* emanations to help us.

In other words, we must always be practicing a form of self-observation, mindfulness or watchfulness over our thoughts and behavior to perfect them, to elevate them, to raise them up. You want to be thinking and acting in the ways that you admire in others so that you climb to higher peaks of virtue and excellence, which in turn will cause you to become like the ideals you truly admire.

You want to be altering your automatic thoughts, your internal map of values, your own character and your behavior because in redesigning yourself – which is always in a state of *becoming* or transformation – you want to be changing yourself so that you begin to align with your highest ideals and values as closely as possible. You want to be working toward embodying your ideal self through your thinking, habits and behaviors and to do this you need to learn continuous self-appraisal (self-surveillance or self-observation) and restructuring that is accomplished through mindfulness and self-correction.

To become more effective in our worldly activities we must learn that there are optimal ways of navigating our lives in terms of doing things and performing most any task, and for the purposes of survival, safety, expediency (skillfulness), thriving or happiness it behooves us to learn those methods for every thing that we do.

Our fate, fortune or destiny can be known through astrology or consultations with enlightened sages whose highest bodies can look down upon the patterns etched in the lower etheric realms of Nature, and with their input and advice there are usually various remedial measures we can employ to change the trajectory of our life and destiny. The possible remedies include changing our living location, changing our job, changing our personality, asking heaven for help, resting motionless during periods of bad fortune so that it passes without affecting us, and so on.

An enlightened sage can also help you decide upon your life purpose, which can then provide a direction for your life that goes against your current fate and destiny, thus helping you to change it as is your right in a changeful universe where nothing is permanently fixed.

AVATARS GUIDE MANKIND IN ITS EVOLUTION

The earliest eras of Hindu civilization revolve around the Rigveda and stories of the Vishnu Avatars Rama and Krishna found in the *Ramayana* and *Mahabarata*.

In Hinduism the Dashavatara or ten primary Avatars of Vishnu recount the tale of evolutionary change in our world that eventually produced the human being. Those Avatars started with the fish (a water creature of simple consciousness), then tortoise (a water-land creature that grew a shell to protect itself from being eaten), boar (which represents the stage of aggressive land animals), man-lion Narasimha, dwarf (pygmy), Parasurama (Brahman warrior), Rama, Krishna, Buddha and Kalki.

The man-lion Narasimha is probably a powerful proto-human (a man-animal hybrid with a homo-sapiens type body) like Bigfoot (Sasquatch) that has a simple consciousness. When the hair on his face is brushed back Bigfoot actually does look somewhat like a lion. He can give off a roar like a lion although he usually communicates in whistles, grunts, moans, howls and screams. Although he does not have claws many stories show that he is strong enough to pull up tree trunks, rip a man's limbs off when fighting and he disembowels his prey, such as deer, with his hands. Narasimha probably symbolizes this creature, which is "not a man nor animal nor demon or deity," but most Hindus do not know of this correspondence. He generally lives a peaceful, solitary life in the deep wilds avoiding people and does not congregate in large communities, hence he is rarely encountered. Bigfoot represents a pre-civilization phase of mankind that is peaceful but which can become aggressive.

Next comes the pygmy or dwarf who symbolizes a stage of human development that is not yet the full stature of man. He represents the barbaric stage of the earliest primitive hunter-gatherers who did not yet develop agriculture or elaborate, highly organized culture and social structures like the state. His tribal communities were held together by the need to forage for food and relied upon fear as a unifying force since lots of things could kill man at this stage of cultural development such as animals and diseases. The simple tribal communities at this stage of development lack well-developed spiritual teachings, writing, the arts and math and science, as well as laws and large-scale social organization. They did not yet figure out the rules to follow that would enable large populations to grow and thrive in their environments.

Parasurama, a warrior priest known as the "axe-wielding Rama," represents the sixth Avatar who appeared during the turbulent stage of warring mankind where man developed kingdoms by conquest and force and afterwards rulers suppressed and tyrannized the people. This is humanity's prior historical stage of warriors ruling mankind without regard to dharma. Although a Brahman born to a sage, Parasurama used force to deliver the world from the oppression of the Kshatriya rulers who killed his sagely father. He symbolizes a civilizing influence on mankind when the virtuous, who tend to avoid violence and harm to others, must apply violence and force as a corrective discipline in service to a higher spiritual cause.

Next came Lord Rama, an Avatar of Vishnu who appeared as an exemplary human at a time when agriculture, large cooperative societies and peaceful kingdoms with central civilized governments had sprung up that were held together through the development of culture, religion and dharma. By this time civilization, culture and religion had systemized people into being good beings. Lord Rama represents peaceful civilization and appeared during a time when society was regulated by state laws and the duty to follow religious dharma (rules of conduct and reverential worship) that served to produce order and reduce violence in society. Rama opposed Ravanna, who although an enlightened Brahman himself (as symbolized by his many heads and superpowers) abused his abilities to break society's laws and the dharma of proper behavior by taking Lanka from Kubera and stealing Rama's chaste wife for his own lust. The colorful story of Rama's war against Ravanna, which includes many notables such as the monkey-man Hanuman, is found in the *Ramayana*.

Lord Krishna represented the next stage of development where mankind's consciousness had become more clever and the state had developed in complexity as well, and where a portion of the governing elites were now engaged in the decadence of immorality and unrighteousness which arises during the growth of prosperity. In the *Bhagavad Gita* Lord Krishna revealed great spiritual truths, and in the *Mahabarata* war he showed that when mankind was threatened by unrighteousness because individuals of elite status began to abuse their power with deviousness, mankind should still follow dharma while eliminating the evil that afflicted mankind. He simply did it via a different way than Rama or Parasurama, yet the lesson holds that it is our duty to purify the world of evil. One of Krishna's purposes was to teach mankind to use the human mind to outwit evil opponents, overthrow them, or eliminate them through force when necessary for he killed the demons Putana, Trinavarta, Bakasura as well as his evil uncle Kamsa, Chanura, Shishupala and others. He taught that we must reestablish justice when the behavior of powerful individuals extends toward greed, deviousness, violence and harm, arrogance, hubris and just basically deviates from righteousness to oppress the people.

Next came Shakyamuni Buddha, who represents the superior man of power, status and effulgence who gives up the throne of a kingdom or glory of a conquering king to instead solve the problem of suffering and sorrow in the world and how to transcend it via practices that lead to enlightenment. He clearly revealed the many practices and pathways for achieving the higher bodies of enlightenment that he called the stages of Arhatship, dhyana, *bhumis*, *skandhas*, heavens, and our various spiritual bodies.

In our present day the average human being who is not a monk, sadhu or sannyasin is naturally more virtuous than in the past due to many generations of continual civilizing influences and the continuous perfuming of the population by teachings on non-violence, non-harmfulness, virtue, ethnics, morality, righteousness, law, human rights, merit-making and good conduct. He is also more educated than the present day sadhu, monk or sannyasin and can even surpass the skills and talents of the governing elites, which is a great difference than in the past when these were the two most educated classes. He also tends to be more ethical since he is tested everyday with temptations whereas the spiritual renunciate is not hardened from any fire of testing because of artificial isolation from society that only requires conformance to a code of conduct and schedule of worship. In general, the professional religious class is less talented than the average human of today because it has no standards of performance or self-improvement other than being able to adhere to the conformity of behavioral rules. The governing elites, on the other hand, are prone to corruption from their constant exposure to the temptation of graft where they can gain access to redirecting public funds to themselves or colleagues for gain.

While he may not have the royal status and heavenly powers of a Rama, Krishna or Shakyamuni, a man of today who always adheres to personal self-improvement and self-development by correcting his own faults and behavioral flaws (such as by always abiding in the truth and insisting on righteousness), who creates or promotes new progressive methods for benefitting people, and who just keeps doing good deeds for the world, can surpass the good done by all the former Avatars, saints and sages.

Once individuals become enlightened by attaining the highest transcendental bodies with countless permanent *nirmanakaya* emanations, they can do even more than having just a human body. However, the potential fault here is that of the Kshatriya rulers, Ravanna, the Kauravas and others who attain power because power may corrupt you, which it usually does. Due to their exalted status, powerful elites fall prey to hubris and then abuse their power as a common error. Because of hubris they disregard righteousness and tend to assume for themselves permissions they do not have simply because they have the power to do so, and then they commit wrongs that affect others.

This is a lesson that also comes to us from the Iraqi foreign tale of the God-man Gilgamesh who was two-thirds god and one third man (perhaps indicating a mortal who had also attained the subtle and Causal bodies). Without dharma to guide oneself and without adherence to a code of ethics or the restraints imposed by law, such individuals typically end up abusing people who cannot defend themselves because they use their powers (or superpowers) to attain status, money, and the satisfaction of their desires.

Look at what happens to the fake gurus of Hinduism who surround themselves with the trappings of wealthy lives. Even Godmen can gradually forget the continual path of self-improvement that won them their heavenly status because upon attaining their elevated status they typically start focusing on learning more superpowers to gain what they want in life while entirely neglecting the cultivation of ordinary skills to do so. Then they use those powers to control rather than help others.

Power and egoistic pride have the ability to corrupt anyone, so just as Yang at its peak becomes Yin what was once totally pure and virtuous eventually turns into its opposite where it must be wiped away and replaced by purity once again. Purity oxidizes over time so remedial measures must be taken. Thus Shakyamuni Buddha warned that his dharma teachings would encounter a dharma ending age, and

Hinduism foretells that Vishnu's Avatar of Kalki is due to appear to remove *adharma* (unrighteousness) in the world when the barbarism of cruelty, evil, greed, violence and ignorance rises to new heights among the elites and their underlings who end up controlling societies.

Thus we come to our present day when you are being taught the secrets within Hinduism beneath the outer façade of temples, *pujas*, colorful festivals and reverential worship. The hidden truth is that spiritual enlightenment is not a mental state of detachment that provides liberation but is all about attaining the higher transcendental bodies of existence that are hidden away in its various teachings. To accomplish this you must first qualify yourself by becoming a virtuous individual of merit and helpfulness to others who can control himself through self-discipline so as not to engage in harmfulness.

Whether or not you give up the worldly life to cultivate spiritual practices, or whether you remain in the mundane world at home while cultivating spiritual exercises, the path will always involve the cultivation of virtue, ethics, morality, righteousness, fairness, self-improvement, a higher inner life, good behavior and good deeds. The path will also, for various reasons, entail meditation practice and various spiritual exercises that are basically inner energy work that purifies the first of your four possible transcendental spiritual bodies.

After you attain that first body of liberation – the subtle body that becomes freed from its physical *annamaya* shell – you will be taught the rest of the spiritual path without any of the muddying misdirections, falsities and defilements that have ended up polluting religions over the centuries.

Which spiritual path is therefore correct? This is the wrong question because all the paths are fraught with errors and misdirections. The only thing that is important is that a spiritual path takes you quickly, safely and virtuously to enlightenment. To be a good Hindu, Sikh, Moslem, Jain, Buddhist, Taoist, Christian and so on requires being a virtuous human being. With that as the foundation you must then cultivate virtuously and efficiently to attain the first transcendental spiritual body that is primarily attained through inner energy exercises that purify your Prana so that it can become differentiated from the heavy, densest portions of your manifest being, and then that differentiation of becoming more purified can enable it to separate itself off as a separate living entity.

You might subscribe to this or that religion and its moral standards for life but the only real objective is to achieve the highest transcendental body stage of existence that you possibly can. Each spiritual body will have its own internal energy serving as its life force that also powers its consciousness. That internal energy will represent *an aggregate of higher transcendental energies* that you can lump together or divide into separate planes or fields of existence, but there is a limit to body achievements where you cannot achieve any higher bodies anymore because you would be decomposing whatever is necessary for composing a body with particles into energies and thereby disbanding with the structural forces that would hold a body together as a recognizable, functional form.

Without a body you would have no apparatus for consciousness because you would just be energy, which is what you ultimately are anyway. However, the point is that at some point the next stage of decomposition, liberation or "breaking free" would be that you would lack any physical structures at all and a body is certainly necessary for the ability to create thoughts and perceptions.

Hence, in your highest possible body you can call the remaining higher left-over aggregate of transcendental energies "pure consciousness" because they power your highest body's consciousness and vitality, but that aggregate is just a set of energies rather than consciousness or life force. If you want to call it consciousness or life force then by all means do so even though they are just energies. If you could actually become that then it would constitute a dissolution of your mind.

If the energies are so high frequency that they appear entirely stationary or non-moving, like the unchanging Brahman, then you can even say that Brahman is pure consciousness or awareness if you like. It doesn't matter what the truth is because *the only thing that matters is that you achieve a body of as high a transcendental composition as possible*. You don't seek the annihilation, extinction, nothingness or oblivion of not having a body and mind but want to preserve *sat, chit, ananda*. Therefore, the self-concept should also remain otherwise you are just natural vibratory processes functioning as they are designed, but you understand that you are that anyway.

Without a body or consciousness you are just a natural portion of the manifest universe of Shakti or Prakirti that is composed of fields or energy, particles and space. Space itself might even be the densest or highest frequency form of energy since it seems empty of attributes and cannot be broken just like the Brahman. But, once again, that's irrelevant since the only thing important is to secure for yourself the highest and best possible body and conditions of existence.

You are always evolving in some direction, and the best course of action is to take an active role in this process to evolve into your highest and best self that includes a more perfected body and becoming the kind of person you highly approve of and deeply admire in terms of character, thoughts and actions. Next, strive to live the life you want.

Since the higher energy planes are of extremely high frequency or vibration they will appear as if they are not really moving at all whereas they are vibrating extremely fast. Hence, consciousness for your highest composite body will be calm, peaceful, vivid and blissful. Shakyamuni Buddha even called your highest body the consciousness *skandha* to denote the fact that you are reaching the base of active consciousness with this body achievement, while Adi Shankara identified our highest shell as the *anandamaya* bliss *kosha*. The base of this highest existence would be all the higher forces that you would then call your life force powering the consciousness of that highest body vehicle. Hinduism calls that highest body the *atman*, Immanence body or Superconsciousness body to refer to the higher transcendental energies powering the consciousness and life force of your very highest possible body vehicle.

You can call your highest possible physical body your *atman* or highest self. You can call the highest left-over aggregates of unattainable transcendental energies your true "*atman*" because they are universal in powering the consciousness of all sentient beings since they are their permeating substrate of consciousness, so those forces can be called pure consciousness if you choose. Or, you can call the fundamental substratum your *atman* or True Self, but you will never be able to realize the Brahman (Purusha) with cognizance. It is just like the contents of a *Sahasranama* that sometimes refer to a deity as the fundamental nature, sometimes as the manifest universe Shakti (Prakirti), sometimes as a personal deity, sometimes as the deity's powers, and sometimes as a spiritual guru.

In all cases the arguments and names for this and that are

irrelevant because all you want to do is simply attain the highest and best body possible on the transcendental energy planes that compose the universe! This solves many of your problems of existence, except for the problem of what then to do with your life which is the question of developing an *ikigai*.

If you go further than a certain level then the structure of your body's composition will break down into its component energies and then you would just become flowing energy without any structure. Presto, you're gone. As energy without form you would therefore be oned with the universe (which is the case already) *but without consciousness*, which would be the extinction of your manifestation as a living sentient entity. Do you think that is the meaning of enlightenment? Do you think this is the highest desirable possibility for mankind? The true spiritual path is to understand what is your true nature and also strive to become the best of what you are possible to become while knowing your true self-nature so as to help guide your decisions as to how you should use your attributes.

Insentience is not the meaning of *sat, chit, ananda* otherwise annihilation is the meaning, and annihilation or extinction are not the meaning of *moksha*, liberation, enlightenment or *nirvana*. Thoughtlessness is not the meaning either. At some point of progressing through the higher energies the remaining body structure starts falling away, so it's inevitable that at some stage you cannot go any higher and still retain a living protoplasmic body structure composed of particles where you also remain a living sentient being, or any type of physicalled entity. It might actually be that this happens at a sixth, seventh or even higher possible transcendental body, but this fact is hidden from us and religions just settle on revealing five. That would be irrelevant knowledge anyway because you still must follow the same pathway of ascendance.

All the spiritual teachings that you run into are simply expedient means or skillful methods to get you to cultivate the higher bodies, that's all! It doesn't matter what errors, falsities, lies, fables or misdirections are told to you in religion as long as they get you to start cultivating to become a virtuous, non-violent, non-harmful being and achieve the highest possible transcendental bodies for your existence.

You can call the higher left-over aggregate of transcendental energies Brahma, Shiva, Vishnu, Krishna, or Devi for the very same reason that those remaining higher energies are the substrate of the consciousness of all lower-bodied beings, and thus even though there is no apparatus within those energies for a world soul or deity-self to exist you can refer to them as a deity if you like. It's all irrelevant because the only task is to get you to cultivate to achieve the highest transcendental bodies possible, whatever they may be. Nevertheless it is true that those energies are the "consciousness of all minds" if you refer to those energies as the power of consciousness and vitality.

You can call the higher left-over aggregate of transcendental energies Ishvara for the very same reason that this set of energies represents the substratum of all creation, but you are not accounting for how many planes or layers of energies Ishvara would entail. In a perfect world of correspondences you would want Ishvara to represent the first emanate, energy shell or plane of emanation from which all else in manifestation is born as in Sufism's first evolute of *Alam-i-YaHoot* or the brightest light in Ibn Habash Suhrawardi's philosophy of Illuminationism, but here you are clumping many possible energy planes or gradations together as one.

As before, in any case it's all irrelevant because the only task is to get you to spiritual cultivate to achieve as high a transcendental body as possible using whatever virtuous and expedient pathways that are available and once you achieve the first of these, the subtle body, you will be taught the exact science, pathway and practices you need to do the rest. All the deceptions and errors and misleading misdirections will be corrected for you once you attain the heavenly deva body. Many of the stories about deities in Hinduism, for instance, were simply invented to provide you with various teachings. Hinduism is filled with lots of mixed-up teachings but the pathway is made clear once you attain the subtle body of a deva. I have strived to give you many missing details and unveil the secrets hidden within Hinduism that you can use for your benefit.

A lesson about lying to the public once again comes to us from Shakyamuni Buddha who in the *Lotus Sutra* told the story of a father who *lied to his three sons* by promising them wonderful toys because this was the only way to get them to exit a burning house about to kill them. In the story the three sons represent the three realms or *lokas* of Desire, Form and Formlessness that classify all the possible stages of physical bodies for sentient existence.

In another case Buddha told a man that there was no such thing as God and then he told another man that there was a God, explaining to his students that he taught each individual what each needed to hear in order to keep making spiritual progress.

Whether this is true or that is true and whether the religious scholars argue over this or that in their books, the only relevant objective is to *cultivate the higher transcendental spiritual bodies of attainment*. This is the truth hidden in Hinduism that is being revealed to you directly.

DIFFERENT SPIRITUAL TRADITIONS HAVE EVOLVED

The point is clear: it doesn't matter whether Adi Shankara, Ramanuja and Madhvacharya argue over what is the truest Vedanta, and whether that tradition should be the Bhedabheda, Advaita, Dvaitadvaita, Vishishtadvaita, Tattvavda, Suddhadvaita, Achintya-Bheda-Abheda, Neo-Vedanta or the philosophy of the Swaminarayan Sampradaya. The point is to find a road that will get you to cultivate the higher bodies that achieve *moksha*, "the state of being released" which entails liberation or escape from the lower bodies and lower planes of existence, and then to cultivate correctly accordingly.

Let the various spiritual traditions of the world create as many contradictory teachings as they like as long as each one, which appeals to a different type of mentality, contains virtuous practices that take people to purifying themselves and achieving the first subtle body achievement. From there you can learn the rest of the path because nothing is hidden to heavenly residents since they can see what is normally forbidden for us to know. The process of enlightened beings assisting souls with reincarnation is not hidden, the multiple bodies of spiritual masters are not hidden but demonstrated for all to see, alien worlds and their beings are not hidden because they visit us all the time, superpowers are not hidden but are explained, and so on. They can then dispense with some of the dishonesties within religions that were created to help pacify and guide the masses.

So it doesn't matter whether the Vishnuites or Shavites are right as to the ultimate deity. In the *Shiva Puranas* it would be stated that Shiva, the ascetic yogi, is the Supreme being and that Vishnu worships him and takes orders from him. In reading the *Vasihnava Puranas* you will find just the opposite where Shiva is subservient to

Vishnu, the King of Kings, who defeats him in various ways. Incidentally, the first three Alvars (Poigai Alvar, Bhoothath Alhar and Pey Alvar) were tremendous devotees of Vishnu but also showed great respect to Shiva proving friendship between the two sects.

The point is that any arguments between the two groups as to who is supreme doesn't matter. Once again, the only thing that matters is that you pick a spiritual road of practice that suits you and that by following it you thereby achieve the higher body attainments. *This is the purpose of Hinduism* other than to help create and maintain an orderly, thriving, peaceful society comprised of a very large number of individuals living together.

Hinduism contains many different spiritual pathways and practices inside it, each which appeals to a different type of mindset or propensity so that you are attracted enough to one that you will follow with ardor to the extent that it takes you to this highest of objectives. Enlightened spiritual masters stand behind all these paths willing to help take people upwards towards enlightenment just as others did for them.

It really doesn't matter that you follow Jainism, Buddhism, Sikhism, Christianity, Islam, Judaism, Taoism, Confucianism, Shintoism, Shugendo, and so forth either if and only your path of practices takes you to the enlightenment of the higher body attainments. The saints of Orthodox Christianity, or the Sufi masters with their powers, and the enlightened monks of Buddhism and Taoism prove that these pathways can also take people to the higher bodies of enlightenment which is because they have enlightened spiritual masters standing behind them as well. It is a *non-denominational path* that everyone know about who becomes enlightened. All the various divisions and arguments made by ignorant scholars are irrelevant in the face of this open truth hidden in Hinduism.

There are uncertainties and misleading teachings, scriptures and errors everywhere including within the vastness of Hinduism itself, especially when it comes to specific guidelines for human behavior. All these different pathways within Hinduism and the great world differentiate the way people live by altering the character of their lives and communities but the only thing that matters is that you purify your mind, body and behavior and cultivate the higher transcendental heavenly bodies to leave the burning house of *samsara*.

This is what is hidden in Hinduism. You can worship this or that deity or follow this or that Sampradaya, and an entire group of enlightened people who have vowed to help humans escape the lower realms of existence will work on you to help you attain enlightenment. If you worship a different deity then it will be a different set of individuals with their own lineage and customs who will help you. The way it works is that your local temple is managed by enlightened guardians who perform local functions and who masquerade as the great main deity. They are connected in a network to all other temples honoring the same main deity, who has a big honcho or team presiding over all of them, and also connected to individuals who became enlightened by worshipping that deity or who are simply local helpful residents.

There are always a large collection of enlightened masters surrounding every locale performing various functions that take care of humanity. They respond to our prayers when possible, perform administrative functions for mankind, and help us with various activities. Most of their efforts are spent working on purifying the bodies of devas because they are already composed of pure Prana which is easier to purify than human bodies. Hence, you must be exceptional as a virtuous individual, or someone who is spiritually cultivating hard, to get the work required to become enlightened in this life. They will perform all sorts of work to help you ascend or just purify your mind and behavior even if you are not destined for enlightenment in this incarnation, yet you should do as much inner work as possible to purify yourself in mind, body and actions.

Whether you worship this or that deity it usually doesn't matter, and so the world is filled with different religions. The only thing that really matters is that you follow the practices of a lineage having devoted enlightened masters who will help you solve your problems during life and help you attain enlightenment. This is why I recommend that you establish a connection with a personal deity, a family deity, the local temple deity, and the main temple deity in your area.

All the enlightened individuals running these operations, such as the local guardian spirits, have their own skills, abilities and specialties as well as limitations. No one is good at everything. The enlightened masters managing all these temples are the ones who help to answer prayers in a locale, solve people's problems, and purify their pranic astral bodies that become released upon death. They are overloaded with work so you should also try to find a living enlightened master as well.

You can argue about this holy scripture saying this and that scripture saying that, or this religion being right or supreme and this one being wrong and lesser. Remember that it's all irrelevant because the only thing that really matters is that you cultivate the higher transcendental spiritual bodies using a pathway to support you. Once you break free of the physical body by attaining the subtle deva body you will discover that lots of things are wrong in *every religion*, which are primarily designed to wire people's minds in a certain way with good mindsets that also enforce moral standards such as family values, kindness, personal sacrifices of sharing and caring, delaying gratification, and the idea of treating others well so that people can live together peacefully and cooperatively (without violence and crime) while avoiding degeneracy. Religion has a central importance to the socializing of society. Don't put it down!

You can research all the religions of the world for relevant teachings and guidelines and spiritual practices. Some provide moral teachings or codes of conduct, such as the differing rules for the subsects of Shaivism and Vaishnavism or the rules of the Swaminarayan tradition. Religions serve as a unifying social mechanism for society and quite a few contain strange or false notions that go against science or logic. Their presence doesn't matter if this doesn't harm you or others. You just want to follow the practices that make you a more ethical, moral human being and provide you with progress in attaining the higher spiritual bodies. You want to push aside and leave the unhelpful alone, especially teachings that lead to hubris such as the idea that only your group is chosen, excellent or matters.

Hindus are blessed to have so many qualified spiritual pathways available within India along with many enlightened masters stretching all the way back to ancient times who are willing, wanting and waiting for you to work toward the objective of attaining your *atman*, which happens when you reach the Immanence body of full enlightenment. They are devoted to helping you just as we say a Paramahansa, *jivanmukta* (liberated one) or enlightened guru will help you cross over to the other shore, which is to cross the threshold from the human to Arhat attainments.

What is the ultimate target? A higher body, that lives an

incredibly long life, in a higher and more enjoyable transcendental realm of existence where your mind is more clear, more controllable and more free of afflictions. Naturally you must cultivate an ethical personality, virtue, a higher inner life, good deeds and the lack of harm towards others to get started at deserving this by purifying away your negative tendencies, which doesn't just magically happen without training. You must also find for yourself a constancy of purpose for your existence that would make a limitless existence of countless years worthwhile.

To qualify for the effort that must be put into you by teams of individuals to purify your energy bodies you must be worthy in respect of character, behavior and merit.

CHAPTER 4
THE LIBERATING PERSPECTIVE OF ADVAITA VEDANTA

In the highest spiritual traditions people are taught the view of self-realization, which is a collection of insights that answer the questions: "Who am I, what am I?" Once you understand the truth of your real self-nature it is called realizing the nature of your self, or self-realization.

Self-realization involves intellectually understanding something whereas the transcendental spiritual body attainments are the actual ranks of *moksha,* enlightenment, or liberation. Enlightenment is an actual physical body attainment rather than mental experiences or understandings composed of thoughts and perceptions.

The ground state substratum of the universe has produced the universe, and you. You are a seamless part of it where the causes and effects of the universe compose you so you are not something inherent, intrinsic or independent that stands on your own. A human being is nothing special; humans are not the center of the universe. The universe has no purpose for your creation so you must find *ikigai* for yourself and reach for the best existence you can get by cultivating the highest transcendental body possible that is the *atman*.

You are the universe. You are not actually part of everything but *are everything* because the universe is just one body of manifestation which looks like it is made up of all sorts of different things but it is only one evolute with various fields of agglomeration. At your stage of physical existence you cannot see all the fields of energy or any energies criss-crossing your body that interpenetrate your being to create you, nor can you see the singular unity of it all that comprises a singular body of manifestation. Only when you reach the highest transcendental bodies can you perceive this and realize your unity with the universe and the Brahman.

You can think of yourself, or the universe, as a great ocean composed of space and atoms (particles). Or you can think of yourself and the universe as a great ocean of molecular and energetic transformations continuously surging around like a cauldron of chemical transformations. You can think of the universe in the image of a tremendous mixture of innumerable currents or energy-matter streams flowing in marvelous directions, or going deeper you might view it simply as an ocean of vibrating energies that don't really compose anything, or a glob of quantum foam vibrating without producing any real patterns.

However you envision your existence and the manifest universe, your manifestation *is the universe* and you are also always just the underlying fundamental nature that appears to be a vast ocean of manifestations that is empty of a true reality of its own. Hence you are nothing at all. However, in terms of appearance you should see the whole universe as yourself, and should also be able to see it in different ways that are also all yourself. You are an iota of this singular manifestation that you can view or perceive in various alternative ways, and that's what you are including being an organism with the capability of consciousness and self-directed actions.

At the liberated stage of enlightenment *jivas* are freed from the shackles of matter because they transcend it by having crossed the threshold of form through attainment of the Arhat stage of the Supra-Causal or Immanence (Tathagata) bodies. The lives of these enlightened individuals are so mysterious and great and they are the guides who initiate students so that they can themselves reach the perfection of the mystical experiential union of the *atman* with the Brahman.

As a *jiva* or soul, you want to reach the stage of the *atman* where you are fully living as the *real, highest, purest* or *most perfected* man or woman inside you because you have become liberated from all binding impurities. You want to become the true living man or woman you are where all your energy and consciousness are fully awakened with glory and power. You attain this stage of being by stripping off the baggage of the lower *koshas* that hold you back from being your truest, highest, purest perfected self.

The human, deva and Causal bodies do not reach this far. However, while any Arhat walks the earth we can say that their consciousness transcends it because they are living in a higher body than the material plane, and the very highest body or *atman* has as its life force and consciousness the primordial energies of the universe that are closest in emanation, purity or vibration to the Brahman itself.

Adi Shankara said, "From non-attachment comes freedom from delusion; where there is freedom from delusion there is abidance in Self-knowledge, which leads to freedom while alive."

The mental practice of non-attachment is mankind's proper way to handle the mental products that come and go within our consciousness. When we don't get entrained or enmeshed with our mental fabrications this also makes it easier for higher enlightened beings to use their *nirmanakaya* energy emanations to enter us and through that superimposition purify our thoughts and Prana. The mental mode of non-clinging produces no resistance to higher beings transforming your Prana since your thoughts, connected to your Prana, are not being held tightly in this or that way when you are practicing detachment.

Because of these benefits, to help learn detachment from thoughts and sensory perceptions yogis, sannyasins and sadhus are taught mental detachment, mindfulness, self-observation and the like and the various truths of existence that help them abide in a state of detachment so that they can release themselves from mental clinging. It is as if they then center themselves in their subtle body to watch the movements of their physical body and thereby practice a little bit of ascension.

Advaita Vedanta and the Vedic scriptures teach the liberating view of self-realization that are principles you mentally comprehend rather than an actual stage of spiritual achievement. Let us explain several of these in brief.

(1) The first principle is that all things are actually the absolute substratum of existence, the Brahman, and only falsely appear to be separate entities. The name you call the Brahman, Purusha, *dharmakaya* or absolute substratum in your mind doesn't matter. All

things – including living beings and their consciousnesses – are in essence, this singular foundational substrate, substance, nature, power or essence.

Your existence before having a bodily form was in the nature of this eternal substrate empty of phenomenal attributes, and your existence this moment is still composed of this eternal nature that looks like it has somehow been condensed into a firm, stable materiality that is actually that unmanifesting formless essence. You are that absolute reality that is an unmanifesting, undifferentiated substrate lacking all qualities, phenomena or attributes whose best descriptive analogy is that is it just like space. There is only this one reality as the absolute substance of existence.

Right now you exist as a physical form with consciousness but your real existence is prior to this body of yours, the existence of the world, the universe, to creation, to everything. You existed prior to your physical beingness because the foundational substrate of reality always existed prior to manifest existence. Actually, you are still that foundational substrate that hasn't changed at all.

Prior to your physical existence you had no desires, consciousness, awareness, knowledge, perceptions, relationships, or associations because nothing tangible, conceivable or perceivable existed in the non-manifesting Brahman. There was no perceiver, no perceiving and nothing to perceive ... no energies, quantum bits, objects, phenomena, marks, signs, attributes, qualities, nothing at all.

You only acquired awareness, thought, perception, language and knowledge because you somehow attained a bodily form capable of sentience. What you are experiencing now is just a dream existence provided to you via a mind that creates an illusion of the world as appearing a certain way whose deepest and most underlying substratum – its deepest non-reducible composition – you cannot see. Your beingness is somehow as a living conscious entity with a form that the entire universe produces like a thread within itself whereas you are actually an underlying stateless, thoughtless, intangible existence.

Everything is actually that same underlying absolute reality that is empty of phenomena and qualities yet because we have consciousness we make an illusory picture in our mind that it appears a certain way even though we know that stable appearance is incorrect because the reality around us is unstable (always changing) and lacks solidity all the way down to its roots.

Unless you achieve a physical immortality for your conscious beingness, or something that resembles it, what has appeared as your body will disappear one day and then merge with the rest of the insentient universe due to the conservation of energy. Put simply, out of nothingness something, your body and existence, appeared after a long evolution and one day that something will go back to nothing unless something is done to help it continue its existence in some way, such as reincarnation or the final achievement of the highest, nearly immortal spiritual bodies. That is the objective of the path of spiritual practice.

(2) You are basically just another internal portion of the manifest universe, Nature, without an intrinsic beingness or self-nature of your own. You are devoid of any permanent, enduring, homogenous self-core that is always permanently yours as your own-nature.

Reality is characterized by impermanence and dependent arisings, which is what you are. You are just an instantaniation or momentary phenomenon defined by current conditions while forever changing into something else.

You are always a different person than the one you were a moment ago. Everything about you, down to the tiniest iota, is always changing so you have nothing unchangeable about you that you can call your own. You are not a stable, inherent self-so existence has a permanent core of an own-nature because you only exist through all conditions and they are always changing so your manifest essence is always changing.

You were created not through a bunch of causes and effects but through ALL the cause and effect interdependencies of the universe that produce you through a complete perfusion. Therefore, everything is what you are.

You are part of the single universe of manifestation, whatever the form of your entityship, but you cannot see at your stage of solidity (condensing) that you are interfused or integrated with all other manifest parts of the universe just as you cannot see atoms. The universe, or Shakti, is a single vibrating entity without separate parts even though it appears as if separate phenomena exist.

You have no intrinsic, inherent, self-so, uncreated, independent self-nature of your own but only exist because of all dependencies and relationships in the universe. In other words, you are a temporary, dependent, composite creation subject to conditions and will change as those conditions change, which happens every moment. Nothing about you is stable or permanent so how can you be an intrinsic soul with an enduring permanent self-core destined to last?

Man is therefore merged with the universe without mediation (a body without borders since every man is smeared into the universal fabric) rather than an intrinsic, inherent, real being. A man is not an independent self and has no separate self-nature. Humans have no being (beingness) of their own but are just an enfoldment of processes that appear in Nature. Consciousness, one of our many properties, produces the illusion of being separated from the rest of the universe due to insufficient sensory inputs and ignorance.

Man's existence *and his consciousness* depend on the other happenings of the universe because they arise in dependence on all its conditions and they change every moment as the universe changes. We simply hold onto an errant false notion that we are something unique, separate and different from the universe. However, the universe is all just one manifestation, and at its root is a singular, final, non-composite substrate or pure substratum that is Purusha or the Brahman. The Brahman is what we ultimately are, so the Brahman is our true self-nature, or True Self since it never leaves us.

When something happens in the universe it is not because of a single set of causes or because man is the doer but because the entire universe as a unity, its wholeness, gets into the act. No one is thus the doer of anything; it is the manifest universe that is the doer. Or you can say that God alone, the unshakeable substrate, is the all-doer even though God is not a being with consciousness and doesn't move so doesn't do anything. The Brahman lacks qualities and attributes such as the composition of parts necessary for consciousness so the Brahman, being inert and changeless, is not really the doer or witness except in name only. Faulty as we may be in our minds, we are actually the illusory consciousness of the Brahman.

Since nothing is intrinsic in the universe because every single thing is composed of all the conditions of the entire universe, this means that nothing is a self-so entity that stands on its own. Therefore nothing has an independent own-nature. All things exist in dependence on everything else and this perfect interfusion characterizes all beings.

A single thing exists contingent on the existence of the entire universe, and since this applies to everything then all things are essentially permeating or interfusing with all other things for one grand simultaneous arising of individual manifestations that are all conditional upon one another, and constantly jiggling in movement due to the ever-changing transformations that define them. They are all related to one another, they are all dependent arisings.

Everything has a dependent, composite nature of agglomeration rather than an own-nature composition of pure this-thingness. Everything has a composite composition rather than an unchangeable own-nature core that would constitute a true permanent self.

You, yourself, are therefore not a real independent soul, *jiva*, self or being but just a small smear within the universe connected to everything else. You are part of the environment that just happens to possess the miraculous attribute of consciousness that can give rise to self-realization, namely the ability to understand what you really are and what you are not. You can understand what your true self-nature is, you can create some understanding of your environment, and it's really a miracle that you can do this.

We say that you are living and are sentient (have consciousness, self-awareness or cognizance), but those are terms we made up because to the inanimate universe we are actually inanimate processes too and there is also no such true thing as consciousness either although on the conventional level it is consciousness that pervades and illumines your mind and it is through the functioning of your mind and body that you can know consciousness.

Consciousness powers your mind, and your mind is just an inanimate process within the universe functioning the way it does according to dependencies rather than a real soul or person being involved in it. Or you can also say that the universe is living because of all the life it produces, and conscious because all the conscious life within it makes it conscious where the upper surging forces within it are the equivalent of life force even though there is no such true thing as life. Consciousness is powered, or made from the same energies.

(3) As a component of the vast inanimate universe we have the

marvelous, miraculous luck to be a form of life that has this attribute, property or characteristic called consciousness, sentience, mind, cognizance, awareness, illumination or Knowledge that is a process itself produced through the intersection of countless mental events, biochemical reactions, subtle energy and our anatomical structure. Consciousness not only produces perceptions of the self and world, thoughts, emotions, will, memories, and other subtle objects (*vrittis*) but illuminates (reveals) to itself those same products or activities.

Consciousness is not an I-self ego-entity but just a process created within a body vehicle that has the capability of sentience as long as its structural host remains living, which means that the body-mind complex that produces consciousness must be supplied with life force energy that is transcendentally higher than the realm of the body. In other words, consciousness is an attribute of a certain type of living object whose structure permits it, and the mind of consciousness that produces thoughts and perceptions depends on subtle energies higher than the world of matter. Consciousness is not a thing that transcends the universe since a mind is part of the universe and its countless doings that affect it. Consciousness that appears on a certain plane of existence depends, in part, on a higher plane of existence than the plane upon which its body vehicle appears.

Knowledge (consciousness) is automatically being generated in a "sentient being" as a process and this body of Knowledge is doing everything such as thinking thoughts, producing perceptual images of an outside world, coming to conclusions and guiding the activities of the body within which it occurs. Knowledge is always just producing itself; there is no independent being, entity, soul or *atman* producing Knowledge for it is just the process of Knowledge itself that is producing Knowledge without an inherent soul being involved. But actually, the whole universe is producing the Knowledge within a sentient being yet this is hard for us to accept. This is also why astrology affects us.

There must be a witness in order for there to be the knowing of anything, but the "I-thought" within the processes of Knowledge-making that serves as the witness is created by the Knowledge-making rather than there being a real sentient being creating Knowledge, which is why the "ego" does not control whatever arises in the mind.

Advaita Vedanta tells us that it is Knowledge within us that makes and experiences Knowledge so a Knowledge-making and understanding process is what experiences Knowledge in a self-referential feedback-process, and we call this sentience. Vedanta says that no real sentient being, soul, self or spirit is involved in this process of Knowledge-making and that it simply occurs according to conditions.

A Knowledge-generating machine, process or object is experiencing Knowledge by, in effect, talking to itself in an illusory manner where it creates the false concept of being an independent self in order to function. Knowledge is talking to itself in a delusory circular fashion that produces comprehension for itself because it (wrongly) takes itself as an entity, soul, person, being, I-self or knower in its self-talk. No one is there, and yet there is understanding. There is life, but no one who lives a life.

(4) One of the characteristics of the processes of consciousness is the function of creating an "imaginary" perceptual picture of the world from the physical senses. Consciousness has separate algorithms, subroutines, or techniques for how it interprets signals from the senses to build up a picture of the world in the mind. It also has systems for anger, fear, lust, playfulness (joy), seeking, grief, etcetera where that circuitry is shared with other animals.

Within the brain consciousness concocts for you an *imaginary picture* or similitude of the world as a mental representation, map or model of external reality but the fidelity to the outside world is not so good. That mental image is just an approximation of whatever is out there built with enough detail for fitness, meaning with enough similitude of details so that you can survive rather than perceive fully and correctly. The mind creates a worldview based on the need for survival rather than as a representation true to what the world actually has in terms of characteristics.

The worldview created by the mind is incomplete in terms of the dimensions it represents. Furthermore, of the dimensions it reveals to us our mental world image is faulted with abbreviation or rounding errors so that you can never experience the true complexity of manifest reality as it truly is. No sentient being can do so.

There *is something out there in manifestation* at our level of condensed energy-matter existence rather than a nothingness. It is never the case that nothing exists at all but that no phenomena exist with their own intrinsic natures, which would mean that they are separate phenomena. They exist according to conditions.

Furthermore, our sense perceptions and consciousness do not apprehend the world out there fully or correctly. We only perceive a fractional part of it with our limited senses, and turn those perceptions into objects according to our own subjective mental definitions. However, even that fractional part that we perceive is poorly processed by our brain and consciousness because our perceptual senses and mental apparatus have processing limits. Our brains cannot process all events simultaneously happening in the environment. They end up producing a highly edited, abbreviated image that we can comprehend that is good enough for the purposes of survival rather than something that duplicates the outside world with fidelity. So, we only produce false objective knowledge – a mental illusion of the world – that lacks fidelity with the real world.

Thus there *is something out there in manifestation* at our level of condensed energy-matter existence, rather than a nothingness, but we just cannot accurately perceive it.

What you perceive of the world is just a mind-only representation inside your consciousness. Everything that appears to exist is made of your consciousness – you are only ever seeing consciousness stuff, namely mental images created by your mind rather than the naked reality of the world. What you are seeing right now is your mind only, a mere representation, and not the world. You never experience the world. You only experience a limited mental representation of it.

The world really doesn't exist in the way it appears to us. We only observe the universe in a certain way, rather than the way it really is, due to our existence stage of physical aggregation and our anatomical structure that has limitations on its sensory perceptions and its capability for constructing mental formations. We can never then know for certain how the world actually appears. Our views of the external world are merely illusory appearances created in our consciousness because that is what consciousness does, as a biological process for sentient beings, in order to make the phenomena of living beings able to survive. We create a mind-only image of the world's appearance that has a useful facticity for us, and seems aligned with what everyone else commonly perceives due to our shared traits, but it is not how the world really appears. What we perceive is how it appears to us but that is not the way it really is. Yes there is a world external to us rather than a nothingness but we cannot perceive it correctly.

(5) Our consciousness has separate algorithms for processing the inputs from our senses of seeing, hearing, tasting, smelling and touching where those separate functions make those inputs intelligible to us. If we were able to go into the consciousness of animals we would find that they have similar but different algorithms, as well as different sensory mechanisms, so they see the world differently than us in the mental pictures they create of it in order to survive.

All these mental pictures of the world, in all the different types of sentient beings, are based on sensing and interpreting different types of vibrations (frequencies) in the environment. Hearing comes from sensing sound vibrations, sight from light vibrations, touch from the sensations (vibrations) felt by tactile nerves, and so forth. Your body, too, is just a complex vibration within the universe that you can tangibly feel through sensations (due to nerves) and you can see it, smell it and so on. In terms of manifestation, you are essentially a bundle of vibrations or processes that come together rather than a sentient being, and the same goes for your consciousness. It is not just your body and spirit that produces consciousness but the whole universe of processes that does so yet for convention's sake we limit all our explanations to the perimeter of the human body.

To explain this better you need to understand that some animals have different sense organs than humans and different ranges for the range of their perceptual senses. Thus they perceive the world differently than we do. For instance, if a tree falls in the woods then the effect will be a change in air pressure. This is a fact. However, *there will be no sound* if there is no being capable of hearing the crash due to the lack of a hearing sense being present; instead there will just be a change in air pressure. You need the sense organs of the ears and the algorithms of hearing consciousness to transform those changes of air pressure into the sounds of a tree falling. If there are not any beings with the requisite sense of hearing then there is no such thing as sound although there are changes in air pressure. Sound is a conscious experience that the mind creates. That's why people always ask the question, "If a tree falls in the woods and no one is around does that crash make a sound?" The crash produces a change in air pressure, but you need a sense of hearing to turn the crash into a sound. The point is that if you don't have the requisite sense organs then various features of the world do not exist for you!

Many animals have unusual sensory skills where they can sense energies invisible to us like magnetic or electrical fields, UV light, infrared light or changes in polarized light. Before the development of science our ancestors did not even know such forces existed. The echolocation abilities of bats are an example of sensory abilities we do not have that are also based on sensing vibrations.

Naturally many types of energies exist in the universe but to a normal human life it is as if they are non-existent if we have no apparatus to sense them. We create our mental representation of the world without knowing about any of these characteristics whereas animals include them, and thus our own mental image is only a fractional similitude or model of the world that is entirely *imaginary*.

Among human beings some people even perceive the world to a better extent than others due to varying degrees of sensitivity in their sense perceptions or because they have different ways of processing their sensory inputs. Two simple examples are color blindness in human beings and synesthesia where an individual might see changing shapes in their mind when hearing music. Essentially, animals and human beings experience the world differently from one another and *there is no way to say which way is the correct way.*

We also process things in our minds differently from one another because we all use different algorithms. Physicist Richard Feynman, for instance, found out that he counted verbally in his head while a mathematician friend counted using visual pictures, and so each was limited in what they could do when they were counting because of either using optical images or the inner narrative to count. But returning to the main argument, the fact is that animals and humans experience the world differently from one another and no one can say which is the correct way. Some methods are just better than others for certain purposes.

We therefore never fully perceive an object or thing-in-itself, and never can even though we can use instruments to extend our realm of perceptions. We perceive an object *together with a mental interpretation of it*, which is really just a mental representation or map, and that is all that we can experience. Basically we experience an imagination, illusion or delusion made up by our mind where our internal mental images are imperfections fraught with error. There aren't really any things at all in the way we think of them because any thing we conceive of with our mind is actually only a combination of other things that only appear in a certain way at a particular time, and it is only us who conceptualizes this aggregate collection of things into a false identity that we call a specific object.

Our senses give us inputs that we must interpret, we color the images we create of those inputs with the algorithms and memories of our minds, and then we can perceive things. One sentient being sees the world with three senses, another with four senses, another with five senses and then a sixth can see it with all these enumerated qualities along with an additional one. A sentient being with seven senses can perceive an object having even more qualities! The more senses you have then the more qualities are added to your picture of the world. Hence you are never seeing objects completely, nor correctly either because what you see is limited by the fidelity of your senses and the algorithms of your Knowledge-making that have a finite processing capacity for creating a picture in your mind.

If we consider that there are different beings on other world systems with different sense capabilities and mental algorithms for processing those inputs then how to perceive the world correctly or best cannot be answered. There is a world external to our body filled with objects at our stage of agglomeration or condensing of energy vibrations into tangible matter, but how they truly exist in their fullness cannot be known. We create limited mental representations of them that do not fully reveal all their attributes, characteristics or dimensions. They only exist as particular objects (in our mind) because we experience them in a limited fashion through their presence to our senses and consciousness. Thus, objects or phenomena don't have a true existence as we experience them, but only become perceptibly known after we apply our ideas of existence upon them. This means that our view of the world is entirely a man-made fiction. We don't perceive the world as it really is. We always experience the veil of *Maya*, a dream or illusion rather than the real world. No sentient being can escape this because the nature of consciousness itself is illusory by definition.

Another example of this is the fact that we cannot see the world during our eye movements. Our neural processes deliberately wipe out the visual experience of seeing the world during every time we move our eyes so that you are effectively blind for about 2 hours every waking day. We think we see a stable world but it is constructed every time we move our eyes. We are unaware of the underlying mental processes that create a stable picture of the world, but feel they create a coherent picture. We are not aware of the illusory processes that create the self-notion either but they are nonetheless existent too.

It is a delusion to believe that the illusionary picture we create in our mind of the world's appearance is how it really appears. Somehow we create a picture in our mind, and then we invert those images to project them as a world outside us when it is really just happening in our head.

How extraordinary is consciousness, the great miracle of existence in the universe, that it can do this! It is so miraculous and extraordinary. It is the greatest treasure of existence because it makes self-awareness possible even though it is a fiction. It enables us to know with cognizance, as well as to have desires that we can also self-direct ourselves to fulfill. How extraordinary!

Thus it is said that the wish-fulfilling tree *Kalpavriksha* (the nervous system), the wish-fulfilling cow *Kamadhenu* (the brain), and the desire-satisfying gem *Chintamani* (the brain stem that produces thoughts) miraculously arose out of stirring the Ocean of Milk, and these objects were classified as treasures because they are ultimately responsible for consciousness. What thing is more valuable?

Furthermore, how incredible it is that we do not even normally realize that what we perceive is *Maya*, an illusion, and we don't even realize that we are not independent from the world but embedded into a singular matrix of the universe through uncountable lines of force that link us with everything else in existence as one unity, one body.

(6) There is even a time lag required for the mental processing required to create a picture of the world from your senses. In other words, you never see the world as it is *now* but only some version of it is represented in your mind from several hundred milliseconds in the past because that's how long it takes for your brain to create an image.

Since everything that exists does so only momentarily before transforming into something else due to the continuous jiggling of the universe that affects everything, all things are really just instantaniations that appear limited, stable and unchanging only for an instant.

Because of the time lag required for mentally processing perceptions, which is not to mention that we cannot even perceive the universe in micro-dimensions or in countless qualities that other beings can, we cannot perceive most of the changes that occur in Nature. Once again this makes our picture of the world faulty.

To make matters even worse, we also tend to process perceptions slower when our attention is temporarily distracted.

The amazing thing is that our mind constantly creates pictures of world, turns them into intermittent mental states, and the sum total of all these instantaneous flashes one after another create the illusion of existence.

(7) Furthermore, our *thinking processes* of Knowledge-making are not just slow but often illogical in making conclusions. They are prone to faults (such as when you make a math error or misinterpret an optical illusion), and easily biased or distorted due to the influence of our personal memories, emotions, incorrect assumptions and false perspectives. We only create subjective Knowledge prone to error rather than objective Knowledge in our minds.

Also, during the operations of consciousness it is Knowledge itself, rather than an I-self, that is experiencing thoughts (knowledge) and perceptions even though you think it is a self-being. Knowledge produces Knowledge, and the experiencer of the Knowledge is Knowledge as well without any true being, soul, spirit, personality, *atman* or *jiva* being involved in the process of knowing. There is no living self within it! You are just a seamless part of the environment.

The workings of Knowledge produce a biased, subjective point of view or perspective that is never universal absolute truth and sometimes these views are so far off the mark that we must term them false and errant just from the standpoint of logic. Essentially you construct *personal imaginations* in your mind that are conditional judgments applying only to you, which is one of the many reasons they are called *illusory thoughts*.

(8) Again, we erroneously conclude that we are an inherent self-

contained self, but our view of being an intrinsic self is a delusional (imaginary) set of thoughts automatically created as the basis of consciousness where this delusory perspective is built up during the infant-child stage of automatic conscious actions in order to gradually make higher thinking possible. The self illusion serves the useful purpose, for instance, of providing a focal point for gluing experiences together from the past, in the now and in the future. It also allows us to treat others as individual selves rather than a bundle of processes.

We are a bundle of processes or influences and develop the feeling in our minds that there is something inside us we call the self. Our I-thoughts of selfhood give us the sense that "I" am thinking "my" thoughts when in fact nothing of the kind is happening. Knowledge is just talking to itself without any intrinsic self being involved. Evolution has built into us the internal development of a sense of singular autonomy, the I-self, but those thoughts are fake. They are a delusion or illusion that keep the processes of living going. What we call the "I" or "individual" or "self" is simply a combination of ever-changing physical, mental and higher energetic forces or energies.

Yes, there is a body that is your vehicle or entity-nature you take as part of your "me" even though all of the molecules within its composition have been replaced over the years. Furthermore, you cannot see that your body is actually borderless because it is smeared into the rest of the universal forces and energies (through infinite connections) without space being a separator. You only feel yourself to be a separate and unique individual (self) because of an error consciousness makes in wrongly self-identifying with a fictitious centralizing device of ego-sense and ego-idea that are created within its processes. The sense of self is an active computation that the brain must perform, which we might call the "running of the self module," that helps you create the idea that "I'm still me. My personal identity has continued," even though all the components that make up the self are always changing. The self-concept is a created illusion and to assume that you have a permanent self or unchanging core is an mistake.

You are just a living container that is always changing with an internal Knowledge process that produces a mind. You are seamlessly connected to the universe without mediation, but you cannot see this at your stage of existence (whereas higher bodies can) nor perceive the infinite parts that compose you, and you operate or function as your process is designed to do in the universe according to your anatomy that has evolved with a process called Knowledge-making so that you could survive to maintain existence. You have also evolved in a social environment rather than having evolved to think about others as a bundle of processes, which is what everyone one essentially is, just as you have not evolved to see the world correctly but for purposes of survival.

Who is the manifest you? The whole universe is getting into the act of composing you and having you think in a certain way, so the whole universe is the maker of you and doer of you rather than an I-self you that you take yourself to be. You are universal because the universe is your true manifest body.

The five elements of earth, wind, fire, water and space are universal and so is the I-am thought that you rely upon to identify yourself since it is just the product of a process that is really inanimate although we call it animate. During the process of thinking it is essentially the thought processes of consciousness that are doing the thinking rather than a separate, stable, eternal "I" or self that is an independent, inherent, uncreated *atman*, soul, *jiva* or sentient being, and that process derives from your construction, upbringing, etc. with the whole universe getting into the act of determining what thoughts come up within your mechanisms.

Nevertheless that I-thought of being a self must be there for consciousness to operate while an inner, higher subtle body needs to be there for there to be life, but it too falls under the same conditions of being a creation without a self.

An awareness of your self – the I-thought, self-thought or ego-sense – must always exist in order for consciousness to operate. It must be there for there to be an awareness of anything. The way that consciousness works is that our knowledge of ourselves is always there in every moment of cognizant consciousness. The awareness of things other than the self can only be known in a field of presence constituted by a subject's awareness of itself. So every experience of something other than ourselves is also at the same time an experience of ourselves experiencing that thing so the I-sense is there in every moment of knowingness. That's why the I-sense had to be developed within the processes of the mind, but that doesn't mean that it is true.

It is a falsity, a false conclusion.

The thinking process itself, Knowledge, is automatically doing all the thinking, cognizing, understanding or knowing without any real individual, self-entity, I, soul, self, *jiva* or *atman* being involved. It's just another process of the universe going on that is connected to and influenced by everything else in the universe but because of limitations (and ignorance) it "mistakenly" creates a false self-identity and thinks it is something separate from the universe (Nature) due to space, and thinks it is different from what it actually is. Being generous, we might say that we are actually a small cellular part of the total embodiment of the universal mind that is non-different from Creation and not independent of it. *We* make the universe sentient together with all other beings with consciousness.

As the Vedanta sage Nisargadatta Maharaj states, the self-concept is a fiction or falsity, a *Maya*, an illusion, a delusion, an imagination. The processes of consciousness, Knowledge, give rise to an assumed, apparent I-self that thinks it is the doer when that very I-self is just a mental product of myriad conditions that produce it within the processes of consciousness as a consequential result. Knowledge is the doer, not an I-self, and Knowledge itself is ultimately a product of the universe, Nature, which is the ultimate actual doer.

What you think of as the "I" is an illusion, just a collection of mental processes that the mind puts together into the idea of a unified self that isn't really there. For instance, when we perceive an object in the world we conceive of it with our mind. The object, however, is really a combination of other things that only appear in a certain way to us as an object when we conceptualize this aggregate collection of things into a false identity that we call the specific object. The object, however, doesn't really have an independent existence of its own.

The designation of something as an object depends on it having parts composing it in aggregate, and the object we identify with our mind is only a concept, name or mental label that we apply to something that doesn't have an existence on its own. We only conventionally conceptualize something as being real. The self is the same way. We say there is a self and talk about ourselves using words like "I" because it is convenient and useful for daily matters but in reality there is no such thing because it is just a name we give to a temporary collection of aggregates.

Knowledge, when it provides understanding to itself, is just a process of Knowledge producing more Knowledge that also includes an illusion of understanding. There is conceptualization and intellectualization going on, but no being who is actually doing the thinking and producing the conceptions. It is as if you are a living mechanism with memories and energy that spins out the thoughts of consciousness. Knowledge, the processes of consciousness, rather than a self-being that is a conceptual product of Knowledge, is actually doing all the thinking and the understanding.

We are not the actual doer of things for it is the whole universe that is doing the doing. We are like machines that can know we are machines, but by knowing this by throwing aside our previous ignorance of the fact we can find ways to cease simply being reactive organism mechanisms. We can even gain some control over the automatic processes of consciousness.

Doing and thinking exist but there is no real doer or thinker within those processes, yet there is still doing, thinking, understanding and experiencing and a false doer can gain some control over its own processes and enjoy life if it acts correctly, so what is better? At the core of this, however, there is no real individual, soul or self as the doer. But that's okay because you can still live with the illusion because to possess a mind you cannot live without it it's acceptable even though errant.

In other words, Knowledge is experiencing Knowledge without there being an intrinsically real person in the process. There is understanding, but there is no being experiencing the understanding. *Knowledge is experiencing the understanding*, and so understanding is there for that Knowledge without there actually being a sentient knower within the process. There is just Knowledge doing everything. There is just Knowledge operating on its own without any inherent self witness being involved.

So be it. You can still enjoy life.

Knowledge is not an I-self ego entity. Knowledge is just Knowledge – a point of view or perspective – a construction of a large set of self-referential mental operations and memories that constitute Knowledge. There is an apparent self involved in the processes of Knowledge that is also a product of Knowledge, a false or fake self involved in Knowledge-making and understanding (that is itself just Knowledge) to make the processes of consciousness operate but there is no intrinsic self or permanent witness involved in all this. There must be a witness in order for there to be the knowing of anything, but the "I-thought" that serves as the witness in cognition is just a fake construction from the processes of consciousness rather than a real sentient being, which is why it does not control the processes of consciousness itself. If it was the real ruler of consciousness then it could control all the thoughts which arise in the mind. There is just a conditional process of knowing operating within a protoplasmic organism according to the various mechanisms derived through evolution that rule the process.

The act of cognizance or awareness is Knowledge knowing Knowledge without an intrinsic living being involved in that process, and yet understanding is there. It's the universe that is there. It is the never-changing Brahman that is there as the support and ultimate substance of it all. You may think that you live but actually you are "being lived" by the universe.

The sense of self thinks it is calling the shots of thinking and doing the understanding or comprehension when there is no true self-being behind those thoughts. If there were really a self or true host behind then process then it would be able to control its mental realm as it wants, but the assumed self cannot do so. That's because it is also a product of thoughts rather than the thinker. Consciousness arises due to algorithms rather than due to a being who creates it. The thoughts of consciousness, Knowledge, just arise automatically within the mind according to the mechanisms or algorithms that rule Knowledge thought-making without a self-doer actually making them.

Every thought, feeling, sensation or mood is accompanied by an "I" that believes it is a whole person and acts in the name of the whole person, but no such real thing produces the mind or is connected with the mind. In every moment of thought a different constructed "I" arises. This non-continuousness is why we make decisions that are seldom carried out. We also sometimes think, move or feel without being aware of what is happening, which we can call the automatic functioning of consciousness through a plethora of I's. There is an illusion about our stability and unity but we are always a different person than we were a moment ago. The automation of I's appearing one after another is initiated by external and internal influences. You are actually manufactured by automatic reactions to influences, out of your control, that activate your various personalities to appear one after another. You are thus manipulated by your karmas unless you learn to take control of such processes.

So Knowledge without a self is doing all the thinking and doing. It is just a process that is going on. Knowledge is the doer of deeds, *which also means that your attributes are not fixed and can be altered with the right efforts.* Furthermore, because this is what you are you have no reason to cling to any forms of suffering or other things that arise in your mind. You can *change things as you wish* if you strive to learn the methods for mastering and transforming your consciousness. You don't have to settle for a destiny or fate either linked to your current personality or characteristics because you can change these attributes of yourself as well as your actions and thereby forge an entirely new future.

(9) Thus man, as a fluctuating energy process embedded within the fabric of the universe with a special attribute called consciousness (that other forms of inanimate Nature lack), acts as a channel of energy that shapes events through the ideas he holds or acts upon. He is strongly influenced not just by his genes that produce his anatomy, his education, upbringing and training, local circumstances, or his pondering and experiences etc. that fill his consciousness with thought patterns (memories) but also by universal forces such as those encapsulated in astrology (keyed to your birth time) and *feng-shui* or *vastu* (keyed to your location) or climate and so on. He is a process that was not generated for a purpose but which, because he has consciousness, needs to find a meaning for his existence.

Because your multiple bodies (*koshas*) are essentially energy, the planets of Jupiter, Saturn, Uranus, Neptune, etc. have a particularly strong influence on you, which is why astrological forces are so significant and should be noted for your life. The sun and planets not only emanate forces such as light, heat, magnetism, and cosmic rays, and not only produce gravitational impacts on the earth and your own body, but they have an effect on your physical, mental and spiritual components. For instance, the human body has its own electrical field so external electrical fields must certainly influence its inner electrical fields, meaning that if the electrical field of a planet or the solar system undergoes variation there must be a corresponding disturbance to the earth's field, and in turn an effect on a man's psychological reactions due to his field being affected. You are simply a creation of the universe, embedded within its matrix that runs on automatic even though you mistakenly believe there is a core self inside you separate from everything, so for that self-notion to gain better control of its life it must understand these forces and learn how to deal with them skillfully.

Consciousness runs on the power of Prana, which is composed of the higher vital energies encapsulated in each of the *koshas*, so your thinking and particularly decisions for actions are affected by invisible planetary forces that modulate these energies. Thus, as stated, the whole universe is involved in producing the workings inside your consciousness. In fact, which one of your personalities appears is a function of your reaction to the influences of the universe within and outside you.

One way of looking at this is the view of Ramanujacharya that you are controlled by the universe in so far as you constitute its body, and thus are a dependent mode within it. You are an aspect, portion, fragment, process, attribute, or function of the universe that operates like a gear pushed this way or that by its other various moving forces. Your sole essence is as an ancillary of the universe rather than existence as an intrinsic, inherent, independent self-being. You exist imminently in the manifestation of the universe as an aspect of its potential, as its actual conditions (its body or "personality"), and as a portion of its consciousness. Thus you are affected by the rest of it rather than exist through a solitary mode of beingness.

The entire universe gets into the act of producing you as part of itself through a vast set of interrelationships, and the same goes for the mental objects that arise within your consciousness. Why do you feel a certain way? It is not just because of your body and current circumstances and prior memories etc. but because of planetary and many other influences that originate far from you.

The fact that all phenomena affect one another and enter into each other's manifestation is called *mutual perfuming* or *mutual interpenetration*. It means that no phenomenon is permanent because they all have apparent existences dependent entirely upon other factors, infinite in number, that are always changing so they are always changing. Everything exists in mutual dependence on everything else, everything is related, and this is the mode of any apparent reality. All the factors of reality that appear as existents depend functionally upon each other, or you can say they all enter into each other with perfect permeating interfusion.

A living being looks like a separate entity different from its surroundings due to a superficial analysis of seeing it separately in space that ignores it flowing into everything else. Its existence is actually within the ocean of Shakti and its appearance comes about because of the innumerable interdependencies within Shakti that define it. Hence, a living being, soul or entity is not some self-so independent or inherent entity, but *is* Shakti. It is a localized space within Shakti whose form and appearance is caused by infinite conditions enfolded into that region by interpenetrating it, but you just cannot see them because your sense organs and consciousness have not developed to enable this. Thus you now know what humans are in the grand scheme of things.

The appearance of any one thing is an *unfoldment* of cause and effect that fully encompasses the entire universe into a localized enfoldment, but we don't normally think this way even though this is the truth of manifest reality. We normally only see a localized space (rather than infinite components) where our mind identifies a phenomenon, but we can correctly say that the entire universe *enfolds* to produce that entity, event or phenomenon.

We can say that Saguna Brahman or Ishvara (the manifest universe and hence the Brahman with qualities) is the indweller of all beings and phenomena. All beings dwell in Ishvara that is the Supreme Cosmic spirit that controls the universe together with all sentient beings inside it since they all together form the body of Ishvara. Ishvara is in turn the Brahman, so Ishvara and the Brahman, or Nirguna Brahman and Saguna Brahman, or Purusha and Prakirti, is the completeness of existence that is the union of form with formlessness or manifest being within the container and substance of the unmanifest substrate. The inner controller or thread that connects everything in manifestation is Ishvara. Then again, you can also say that everything is the unmoving, changeless Brahman.

(10) Through repetitious behavior, or through practices such as forward planning, visualization where you fully imagine yourself in the situations you want, you can mentally rehearse and persistently work to create a new future for yourself through your conduct and daily activities. Every time you visualize doing or repeat the same

action, follow the same path or activate a specific behavioral pattern it becomes more defined as a neural circuit in your brain, and it then gets closer to becoming your default habitual behavior and way of being.

Your entire life runs on the neural patterns and software in your brain, namely the algorithms of consciousness for how to think and do things, but you can use those principles to actually recreate your programming and create a new future if you work to change your characteristics to new ones that don't presently exist. You can actually take greater control of your consciousness to create new attributes and characteristics in yourself whereas inert matter cannot. How extraordinary!

Your brain, wanting to be efficient, will take the easiest, most familiar mental route in producing thoughts and actions so the repetition of a new behavior, and visualization of a new behavior, will gradually make your efforts your new natural way of doing things over time. This is one of the keys to spiritual self-cultivation, as is the practice of mindfulness or inner watchfulness where you station yourself in the role of an observer, lodging yourself in your higher bodies so-to-speak, where you observe your mental and physical doings on each plane of existence in order to police them and correct them.

You can actually create a new fortune other than what is already set to occur through the impersonal universal laws of cause and effect that manifest according to conditions, and which sages in the higher realms can see etched out as a pattern in the lower vibratory fields of ether. How do you change your fate or destiny? By working to upgrade or elevate your current parameters of personality, psyche and behavioral conduct, which is the basis of spiritual practice.

Because you have consciousness you can actually change your mental programming, or algorithms of consciousness, to become less robotic (unconscious) during whatever you are doing and can point your thinking and actions in direction where you start becoming whatever you want. You can start working to achieve whatever you want even if it is beyond your current programming and status of self-development. You simply need to develop yourself by growing. You are always in a state of becoming or transformation but few people grab the reins of this process to guide it as its leader and become what they want.

You can even strive to always be living in your innermost ideal that is the *raison d'etre* of your existence that you have decided upon, and you will learn some of the spiritual cultivation methods to move towards that goal.

For your personal existence and for the pursuit of your *atman* you want there to be a progressive manifestation of your highest spiritual self through your efforts. The more you become self-directed and remain in a state of present awareness that oversees all your thoughts and actions the less robotic you then are as a universal manifestation and the more you become your highest self the *atman*.

THE VIEW OF LIBERATION THAT CONSTITUTES SELF-REALIZATION

The "True I" refers to our underlying fundamental substrate that is the ground state substance of all existence, permeating everything, since it is truly the self-nature of all. The physical body is not your true "I" for in oneself there is a higher psychic being, and beyond that there is the whole cosmos of creation, and of course transcending creation as its substance is the fundamental substratum that is your unchanging self-nature.

When each of us speaks "I" we are actually all referring to the same underlying Self as the core inside us. When you say "I," what you really are referring to is your absolute original nature (the fundamental substrate of the cosmos) inside you that never leaves, which means that all "I's" are fundamentally equal since they all point to the same thing – the single shared root of the Brahman.

You are the embodiment of universal consciousness. Each being with consciousness is actually part of the consciousness of, or for, the one substrate of the Brahman or Purusha that some call God but it isn't a personal being at all since it has no attributes. Or you could say that each sentient being is part of the consciousness of Prakirti or Shakti, and call this God as well even though these are all just inanimate energies. In both cases it's irrelevant because the objective in life is to attain the highest spiritual bodies possible where you still maintain an existence.

Nevertheless, "I" could also be used to refer to the singular ocean that is the manifest universe, too. And of course, from a conventional sense "I" refers to just yourself for without this convenience of referring to yourself as "I" you could not communicate with others, even though when you shed the ignorance you realize that they do not exist as separate living beings either. The personal "I" is what you use to climb the ranks of spiritual achievement and you never abandon it but simply recognize that it is fallacious and then continue living your life in an adjusted way.

In truth, everyone who says "I" is referring to the same absolute infinite substance ("God") since we are all cause and effect appearances of its essence that reflect its infinite potential. Since everything is composed of this substance then everything is ultimately one wholeness that seems as if it is diversity linked in unity, but the cosmos of multiple planes of existence and manifold forms is really just a oneness when seen in its ultimate state of decomposition.

What you learn after enlightenment as a Hindu is the same thing you learn after your enlightenment as a Sikh, Moslem, Buddhist, Christian, Jew, and so on, namely this ...

(1) Your existence as having an independent, intrinsic, non-composite selfhood is a conceptual illusion, a false imagination, an errant belief, a false conclusion. You incorrectly see yourself and phenomena as distinctly differentiated stable individualities because of perceptual and conceptual mistakes made by your senses and mind. You are in fact connected to all things and each other in the one brotherhood of manifestation, but that rarely inspires people to help one another like brothers and sisters.

There is just a oneness in front of you in unity with the universe but you cannot perceive this the way it truly exists. You can only perceive the universe at a specific level of agglomerated energies where it seems as if the environment is a collection of condensed energies that become (seemingly) separated things. You can intellectually understand this, but until you attain the higher transcendental bodies this is just information that is hard to believe.

(2) All phenomena arise in dependence on other conditions so they also have no being (beingness) of their own. They are empty of an intrinsic existence, a self-generated existence, an inherent existence, an own-nature. As conditions or forms that arise based on countless *not-themselves conditions* they have no beingness on their own since they are dependent constructions. Their existence depends on

an infinite number of other factors rather than them being self-generated. Thus they are devoid (empty) of any core self or own-nature that stands solely on its own for they are non-homogenous, non-permanent entities.

As it actually stands, all things are co-existent simultaneous arisings that require all other things for their appearances. They appear in manifestation only because each is infinitely connected to all others that makes the appearance of one thing possibly so, and the whole is one single fabric of varying intensities that constitutes manifest reality.

Every single thing in the universe is a collection of endless causes and conditions, and lacks "own-being" as an inherently existing singular phenomenon. In other words, all things lack an intrinsically existing self because other things comprise it – so it is made of parts or component pieces that are not-self.

Every thing is a conditional or dependent thing. Nothing has a self-so own-nature but is a dependent construction composed from the existence of everything else.

Let us take the example of a flower. What is a flower other than a compendium, a conglomeration, an agglomeration of diverse processes or conditions in a localized region (a ripple in the fabric of Shakti) whose components are themselves not flower-nature elements? *There is no innate flower-nature there within a flower* because it appears after all these different separate components assemble together to create a flower. Many independent elements, unrelated to one another, must connect together to create what we call a flower. Since there is no such thing as an inherently existing, permanent, intrinsically-so "flower nature" that produces a flower this conclusion carries forth for humans too.

There is no permanent soul or self-nature within you but there are many independent elements that have come together to compose your existence. A flower is itself just an agglomeration of other-than-a-flower conditions, in fact infinite conditions, and because its existence *is due to these other conditions* without there being anything of itself within its appearance/origination (that is purely the flower-essence) its manifesting pattern is empty of being intrinsically so, empty of an independent existence, empty of a true existence, and lacking of a self-so nature. There is nothing within its compositional elements that is a flower at all because the flower is an aggregate phenomenon of non-flower elements. It is just a karmic formation – a product of infinite interdependent origination – a pattern of appearance within an infinite Indra's web of simultaneously-so intersecting conditions. *It is a nothingness since it totally lacks attributes and phenomena and yet through interdependence is everything.*

Individual phenomenon are not only interdependent simultaneously arisings based on the existence or influences of everything else but are interpenetrating, interfusing, mutually inclusive and all-pervasive *within each other*. You consist of all things and they also consist of you (where one is in all and all are in one) because reality is one manifest unity of presentation within one single substrate.

Everything in the universe is involved in cross-defining everything else which produces an effervescent, scintillating, ever-vibrating or jiggling ocean of instantaniations that we take as stable phenomena because we cannot see the tiny changes always taking place.

There is one unity of existence so while all things may look separate they are perfectly interfused or interconnected and contingent upon one another, but all things ultimately derive their existence from the same source where there is no differentiation. The problem is that you just cannot perceive this. You can only intellectually understand these truths of Advaita Vedanta.

(3) Because all phenomena are connected to one another they are impermanent, transitory, non-homogenous, conditional constructions and always incessantly vibrating in a state of indeterminacy. Matter, for instance, is made up of vibrating atomic components that are made up of further components that are themselves just bundles of energy within fields of energy that are vibrating everywhere always. Thus phenomena are always changing from the quantum to sub-atomic to macroscopic level while seeming stable at our own level but lacking anything permanent as an innate own-nature (permanent core) that can be grasped. They may look stable but they only exist as instantaneous appearances, or instantaniations, where we cannot see their structure transforming every moment due to our lack of sufficient sense perceptions.

That being so, you incorrectly see them as solid, distinctly differentiated and stable individual phenomena because of perceptual mistakes made by your senses and mind at your stage of existence. Solid objects, consisting of atoms comprised of even smaller particles, seem solid but are mostly empty space and condensed energy. Everything in the universe is transitory or impermanent and thus mutable with the sole exception, which is eternal and true, of their unchanging fundamental substratum.

The various schools of Hinduism all agree that the manifest universe is the play of an underlying unchanging permanent core substance that is our self-nature, and no one can explain how the universe can arise or how it has arisen from something that is changeless, actionless, eternal, immutable and as pure as a invisibility that lacks any qualities.

The universe is known to us because we have consciousness, but our consciousness is delusory in that it doesn't work correctly. It doesn't create a true picture of the world nor function with absolute rationality. We just create a movie in our minds of what is happening around us without realizing the true nature of the movie or the projector, and then we take that moving dream to be reality. Our consciousness makes an image of the universe that is a delusion, illusion or mirage even though the mental similitude representation it creates has a profound facticity or fidelity to cause and effect.

Another problem with consciousness is that is continuously contaminated by all sorts of unwanted mental arisings that you cannot control *because you are not its ultimate master*. You don't create consciousness because in your organism it creates your sense of you. There is no self giving rise to consciousness that is its master. Knowledge-making functions on its own as just another operational system within a living being. Whatever arises within a mind automatically appears due to the algorithms or mechanisms of consciousness that are responsible for its operations rather than because you want them. The algorithms of consciousness run our lives by themselves while informing us of their decisions, which we usually then feel (and assume) to have been made by our sense of "me" when there is no me involved in any of those determinations. They make decisions before you're even conscious of them. This once again proves that your self-thought or ego-sense is fictitious.

The I-sense is not a true self or master of its processes but a product of its processes. Consciousness also commonly makes mistakes of logic or miscalculation and becomes warped by false perspectives, prejudices and biases that populate the memories and algorithms upon which it operates. It is not entirely trustworthy, just as when it makes a wrong judgment by taking a mirage as being real (until the error is discovered).

The key problem on the road of spirituality is that consciousness mistakenly assumes there is a permanent master at its core that we call the soul, and then holds onto attachments, desires and so on to your organism's detriment. Whatever our embodied soul is, its absolute essence is the underlying substratum that is liberated and spotless. The *atman* is the closest vehicle of existence you can attain to being pure Brahman while still retaining an identity of consciousness without extinction, annihilation or extermination.

(4) You cannot ever correctly, objectively perceive the external world of dependent reality around you to know what it truly is (the ground of the world, or things-in-themselves) because there are limits to your sense organs and your mental processing abilities, which are imperfect and inadequate to the task. All you can perceive is an apparitional, provisional mental reality (of your mentality-only) that is a representative illusion made by your mind.

For instance, when you perceive objects it is because the objects you conceive of in your mind are actually a combination of other object parts (that perhaps we do not perceive), and it is only your mental processes that conceptualize this aggregate collection of object parts and features into a false identity that we call a specific object. You mentally create a representative world and then mistake what you conceive as the way things really exist.

Your mind creates a similitude approximation or representation of the world using the objects you conceive, yet that false *Maya* mental fabrication (together with other personal subjective biases) enables you to survive and maintain your existence, *sat*. You are an imperfect and inadequate mechanism that knows of your own existence and creates your own reality through patterns in your mind, namely thoughts or *chit* (consciousness). The ideas you choose to hold, true or false, good or bad, create your own reality. You can follow thoughts and actions that lead away from suffering, unsatisfactoriness and to happiness or *ananda* (bliss), or not. The choice is up to you. In your mental operations, you actually have the chance to choose what actions or directions to pursue.

(5) Besides your (false) sensory image of the world that you build up in your head even your conceptual, "objective" thinking operations of consciousness are fraught with errors in rational logic and interpretations of perceptions, prejudicial biases and other imperfections. You sometimes make errors in arithmetic, do you not? Thus it is rare to experience a factual, truthful perspective of reality and your existence. Because our thinking processes are subject to errors, this is why we must always observe our thoughts with clear mindfulness so that we can subject them to self-correction.

(6) You are definitely imperfect. Furthermore, you don't always function in the way you want to function as regards your thinking and behavior because your I-thought or self-concept is not the ultimate master. Things are just running on their own without a self being involved. This accounts for why you are often impelled by your desires even though your mind says "no."

Also, you often get caught up in false stories your mind concocts (false perspectives or mindsets) or habitual ways of doing things that you cannot escape from. Sometimes you just cannot control your behavior, or your mind, because they are not yours. As examples, because of what we are and how we operate we all have troubles with managing or transforming our emotions, eliminating unwanted mental afflictions, ending habits we have developed, or maintaining focus, perseverance and concentration for a course of thinking or action even though our self wants to do these things.

You also tend to create a *false image or false identity* for yourself that isn't true along with false *limiting beliefs* that become difficult to unlearn even though they are mistaken. Through the practices of rational logic, self-observation, mindfulness and introspection we can separate ourselves from the mental habits, limitations and pretensions that have enslaved us from childhood and return ourselves to our highest possible self to achieve liberation.

This also means not mentally losing oneself (one's overseeing presence of self-awareness) in the flux of outer circumstances but maintaining a heightened naked über-awareness of one's thoughts, actions and circumstances grounded in the present. Only by transcending your normal mental operations through a self-observation (mindfulness) free of distractions can you defy the automatic mental responses that arise within your consciousness in response to external stimuli, which are not of your own volition, and go against the grain to resist long established thought patterns, habits and tendencies that are like automatic programming. In short, mindfulness helps you center in the present moment where you can experience reality more fully without distortions, and also become *more alive* because you are giving full reign to consciousness free of limiting patterns.

Lastly, because you largely operate on autopilot like an automaton that is unconscious of what it is doing most of the time, you must not only remain present and fully aware of what you are doing but also always be remembering your *raison d'etre* you have chosen as the ultimate purpose for your life and innermost ideal. You must continuously try to exemplify those values, goals and behaviors in all aspects of your life every moment so that there is a progressive manifestation of your highest self in the form that is you.

(7) Most perplexing of all, you cannot even mentally fathom or perceive the singular pure fundamental substratum of the universe that is the ground state of all being – the substance of what you truly are – and thus you can never know your real self, your true self-nature, your True Self, your unchanging identity. You can think about it but never perceive this formless substance through your senses (or any type of senses) or through any mechanism.

No such thing as an actual emptiness of phenomena, a nothingness, unmanifestness, qualitylessness or absolute void can be experientially realized as Knowledge. This is because thoughts are things so they are the antithesis of nothingness. They are the opposite of the lack of qualities or attributes like empty space. You can make an image of your fundamental Self, the Brahman that is the absolute substrate of everything, but then that mental representation would not accurately represent the Brahman because any image has represented the Brahman as a phenomenon when it is a phenomena-less state.

(8) However, from the standpoint of manifestation you exist as an *atman* that is covered over by various sheaths that can be removed, through spiritual practices, and you can attain a high enough transcendental state where you realize the unity of your *atman* with

the Brahman and the energies of existence that define and span the universe.

It does not matter what religious notions you believe or what spiritual practices you perform as long as you know that <u>the target is to attain the first transcendent spiritual body</u> – the subtle body or deva body – above the human level because upon that achievement you will be taught the rest of the spiritual path in the heavens. Any errors you've mentally picked up from incorrect spiritual teachings can then be corrected through instruction and understanding.

Sadguru Bausaheb Maharaj explained how the understanding of Jnana Yoga, the flower of Vedanta, leads to liberation. Once you know what the mind is you can achieve liberation from clinging the longing for objects and can direct yourself to learning how to use consciousness (yourself) correctly. Once you realize that you are God rather than an independent self, and therefore a non-doer because it is the whole universe that does something rather than any subset of its components, you realize the God is doing all the work and you are ultimately a non-doer since you're just a part. You aren't even an intrinsic self. You are a non-doer, and understanding this you become a *liberated soul* because of your realization.

You achieve "liberation through oneness" when you realize your unity as part of the single fabric of the impersonal universe that is experiencing innumerable changes of its body every moment without any true selves or souls being involved in those transformations. It is all just surging energy that is going through transformations where agglomerations of form (condensed energy) and energies appear and then transmute into new states because of complex laws of transformations, but there are no actual parts to this and from the standpoint of the ultimate foundational substrate (true self-nature) nothing is happening at all. It just appears as if it is happening because of an illusory perspective called consciousness. All that exists is the Brahman in disguise.

Everything you can personally perceive as the universe is just a small fraction of what is happening, and you cannot even perceive that small part completely, clearly, or correctly. Nonetheless, everything that is happening, including your own thoughts and perceptions and actions, is the whole universe moving rather than you as a doer doing something or thinking something. The universe is doing your doing and thinking that are just processes within it.

Everything interpenetrates with perfect interfusion, so the whole universe is in you and you are also it. With this realization of what is actually going on in the world and your life you become *liberated by knowledge*, which is the road of Advaita Vedanta.

When you attain the highest spiritual body you can perceive the energies that interpenetrate all objects to form them and rather than just intellectually you *experientially realize* that you are just a consequential result of all these impersonal forces that compose you and the universe as one unit. This is like the ancient Rishis who, because of their high body attainments, became aware of the vibrations that resulted in the creation of the world (the "cosmic breathing" as it were), and turned these sounds into mantras.

We say that the ancient Rishis realized the mantras within themselves due to a high state of dhyana, which simply means that they had attained the highest transcendental bodies that could vibrationally sense the energies of the universe that penetrate and compose everything because of their bodies' elevated energetic composition. When you reach the transcendental stage where you feel oned with universe, meaning that you feel in unison with all energies and objects, then you can sense (find) certain background vibrations that can be turned into mantras in order to vibrate your Prana and thus help to purify it.

The Rishis might not have seen or heard in the usual sense but they could feel the vibrations, or sounds of the universe, within them due to their impact. Even today, if you recite the mantra of an ancient seer they are sure to hear you and respond. When you read the lives of Hindu saints, or the saints of other traditions, they sense what you are doing so and check you out to see if there is any way they can help you. Some masters will even tell unusual stories about themselves so that when astounding tales are retold to others, or you read about them in books, they can sense vibrations of shock connected with their name. This makes it a little easier for enlightened masters to hear stories of themselves that penetrate through the dense fog of all other thought forms of the earth, and then they can more easily find you to investigate whether you are worthy of their assistance as a possible beneficiary. This is also why masters sometimes give themselves giant convoluted names like "Sri Sri Sri Bhagavan Guru ... Maharaj Swami Paramahansa" with so many adjectives, which is because the name then becomes an unusual mantra that can more pierce through the busy mental realms of ether that they listen to.

Realizing your unity with this whole due to an experiential realization of your own composition as energy that pervades all the realms of being, and understanding the fact of your ultimate selflessness (and the fact that your consciousness is constructed from all this), this is attaining the Godhead with the fact being that God is impersonal. Everything is the Godhead, or the Brahman since there is nothing other than That, but your own quality of being the Brahman (Purusha or Parabrahman) is not recognized by sentient beings until they receive teachings like this to dispel their ignorance, or until their bodies and accompanying minds reach the highest planes of existence. Then they can start to understand the highest source that pervades pure enlightenment, and experientially become truly liberated ones from all the lower planes of existence possible as well as the guides of mankind.

Even though vibrations infinitely criss-cross the universe in wavy fields of flux, the Brahman/Purusha is not in a state of vibration, and deep inside us always stays in a state of quiescence.

Of course, some might argue that the highest realms of existence are energetic realms of increasing greater frequencies, and therefore there is no end to the speeding up of these vibrations where the fastest motion seems calm and unperturbed as if not moving at all, so perhaps the ultimate state of existence is actually the fastest realm of existence and only appears changeless and static. This then, would explain how Creation came about as a decreasing gradient of frequency and resultant transformations. Space, for instance, might be a solid block of energy that is actually the densest form of matter since you can bend it but not break it, and within space virtual particles are always being born that spontaneously pop out to create winds and waves of energy.

It could also be that the fundamental substratum, the Brahman or Purusha, and manifestation have both always been simultaneously existent without one giving birth to the other, and the densest or slowest frequency becomes non-movement that connects with the highest frequency that appears as non-movement. We don't have the physics to comprehend any of this yet, but perhaps other worlds have reached some more definitive conclusions.

It doesn't really matter, nor does the fact matter that we are virtual sentient beings, because the primary objective that solves so many issues is to achieve the highest existence possible where our *atman* stands stripped bare of lesser energies, and this means cultivating the ladder of spiritual body attainments to get there. It can perceive the lower realms that are inferior to its own so it knows its realm is better.

Advaita Vedanta, and many other school of Indian philosophy, explain that the universe comes into being out of nothingness, formlessness or an emptiness of attributes, which is called *ex-nihilo* in western spirituality. This leads to an admirable set of cultivation principles that champion meditation and mental states that imitate characteristics of the Brahman such as *desirelessness, the cessation of suffering, blissfulness, pacification, equanimity, naturalness, patience, tolerance, mentally not clinging, not being bound to form or characteristics, freedom from bondage*, etcetera. Such states speed the attainment of the higher spiritual bodies. From the practical standpoint of our provisional existence, this is all that is really relevant rather than the truth about the ultimate truth since we cannot perceive anything truthfully anyway. It's all about transcendental body together with your personal characteristics and behavior and activities in the end.

The most effective cultivation systems across the world say that the Brahman (the absolute ultimate substratum of reality) is akin to "a stainless substance empty of attributes, or emptiness" while some compare it to "pure consciousness" to raise the analogy of a pristine, empty mind free of inner dialogue. This produces an inducement to achieve mental peace through the stillness effects of meditation practices.

During periods of mediation practice where your mind becomes detached from its thoughts or other fabrications, it is easiest for higher spiritual beings to enter your body with *nirmanakaya* emanations to help purify your inner subtle body without having to fight against your Prana and the movements of your consciousness that control it. So the truth doesn't matter whether we do or don't know how Creation came about as long as we have established a motivation to practice the very methods in consciousness that will allow us to climb up the rungs of body existences to escape the lower realms of *samsara* and improve our conditions permanently.

Because withholding the truth might be an elaborate form of

skillful means, this is something to think about. In another sense, once again the truth is irrelevant because *the only thing that matters is that you cultivate the highest spiritual bodies!* This cannot be stressed enough. Some of the schools of Vedanta, for instance, were invented simply to encourage worship as a cultivation method for the masses.

You cannot say that you are anything more than a vibrating oscillation or resonance within the cosmos that appears to have a solid structure even though you are empty of solidity and lack an own-nature. You only exist due to the congealing forces of interdependencies, and thus you have an apparent existence with various characteristics and internal properties such as consciousness. Your life philosophy should not be one of nihilism because you have the choice of elevating and perfecting your attributes and the experience that sentient cognizance gives you of life no matter what form it takes or how long it lasts. This is the path you should take!

Whether you think of God as Vishnu, Shiva, Narayana, Ishvara, the Brahman or some other nobility your consciousness comes from God because it is part of God, it is God. Your life serves as part of the consciousness of God, and because consciousness is what you have as your primary characteristic of existence it behooves you to purify and extend it as much as possible to a fuller awareness accompanied by clarity, calmness and wisdom.

You are an apparatus made of vibrations that has the characteristic of a mind, as imperfect as it is. That's what you are. This is the knowledge of the manifest self; knowing this is self-realization. However, you can also pursue joy, happiness or bliss with the mode of beingness that you appear to be, and that is proper spiritual practice rather than seeking annihilation or extinction to be one with the Brahman through insentience, inertness and non-existence. To the universe it doesn't matter but because you have consciousness it does matter and should matter.

Advaita Vedanta points out that you can achieve liberation by intellectually understanding this, but the real spiritual path of *actualization* requires you to attain the spiritual bodies of liberation that transcend the lower realms of the material universe where, with each new ascension, you can see how matter is composed of energies and all the energies interpenetrate and cross-depend upon one another while having an ultimate motionless, pure substrate or substratum beyond manifestation as their absolute substance, support or fundamental core.

The base of existence is what you are, but so what? You must cultivate to seek the highest of life which is the transcendental bodies and good deeds/behavior that put an end to suffering in the lowest realms of reality forever.

You are the Brahman, the transcendental state, and one with all manifestations through unity, including a brotherhood with all living beings since they are all part of your being, but due to intellectual ignorance you do not know this or understand this and due to the lack of a true experience of this we say that you are ignorant and deluded. However, with this information you are now liberated from the bondage of ignorance. Now you have been introduced to the view of enlightenment, liberation or *moksha* from Hinduism that you can achieve by working to attain the higher transcendental bodies and ultimately the liberated *atman*. This is your birth right since that is what you ultimately are as a created being.

CHAPTER 5
DETACHMENT AND THE *MAHAVAKYA*

The *Mahavakyas* of Hinduism are short aphorisms used to express the highest Advaita Vedanta teachings that the *atman*, or personal self, is the same as the ultimate reality Braham: "I am That," "You are That," "All of this is the Brahman," "This verily is that," "I am the Brahman," "This self is the Brahman," "The Brahman is one without a second," and "Consciousness itself is the Brahman."

In the *Chandogya Upanishad* we find Uddalaka Aruni, the father and teacher of Svetaketu, telling his son nine times, "You are the Brahman, dear son." We should take from this the fact that all beings have unity in a common base – the Brahman (Purusha) – which means that the existence and subsistence of all attributes is actually due to a common underlying substratum. The universe is the Brahman, and from the aspect of manifestation you are also the universe. You can think of yourself as a fragment of the universe or process embedded within the universe but essentially you are the entire universe – the body of the bodiless – and you are also the universal consciousness. You are the Brahman that has become condensed into an apparent appearance.

What fills the universe is what you should regard as your body and there are various ways to think of what fills the universe. You basically are the universe whether you think of the universe as a collection of atoms in space; an ocean of continuous transformations involving atoms, molecules, energy and fields of force; as flowing streams of force and matter that have congealed together in waves, currents and objects that appear as phenomena; as a giant ball of ceaseless ungraspable energy vibrations; or as just the fundamental ground state substratum (the Brahman) that is sometimes called Emptiness or the Great Void since it is empty of all qualities and phenomena. These are all good meditations for visualization practice that will attract the attention of enlightened beings who are looking to help intelligent people who are studying the path to become enlightened.

You are beingness without a body because your real body is bodiless. Your real body is the infinite empty substratum empty of all forms just like empty space. From that aspect you personally are empty of manifest existence, or you can be considered all of Shakti (that has an infinite manifest body) that is the realm of manifestation, or you can be considered just an iota of her grand ocean of Creation when you limit yourself to being just a small physical entity with consciousness.

You are empty of an independent intrinsic existence on your own yet are *all* of manifest existence, and that manifest existence is essentially the absolute substance of unmanifest beingness that is the underlying substratum of manifest existence, so you are nothing at all.

Since the All of Manifestation is essentially the one primal primordial substratum at its root, it means that you are ultimately bodiless, birthless and imperishable since you are essentially the ground substrate. You are all or nothing, or both, or an apparent living entity within a sea of multiplicity where you are linked to each and every iota of it without realizing it.

To the average person walking on the street this talk is all nonsense because they just go about their life assuming they are an independent sovereign sentient being, and everything works out just fine. However, the yogi, sannyasin and sadhu are taught to engage in special meditations that hold various perspectives in their mind so that they can come to an understanding equivalent to those with higher bodies. What fills the universe is what you should be considered your body and there are many alternative ways of describing what fills the universe that can help your understanding.

THE EARTH ELEMENT VIEW OF SOLIDS

They are taught to first consider that their body is a collection of atoms and space, and that the earth and entire cosmos is also just a collection of atoms and space. There is no place where one collection of atoms and space stops and another begins because the whole universe is just a collection of atoms and space, so there aren't any "objects" anywhere that exist with proper parts. In other words, there is just a universe consisting of atoms and space without any patterns. The only time there are objects is when our minds take atoms arranged in various spatial patterns as objects; without the addition of consciousness to do so there are just atoms and space.

Everything is composed of independent atoms and different qualities emerge from the aggregation of atoms. From this viewpoint the interaction of elemental atoms and energies produces the different qualities of universe. For instance, gold atoms in suspension appear purplish red in color to our eyes but when they aggregate as a metal they take on the quality of being golden yellowish in color. Their aggregation together produces a quality of color and the malleability we know of for gold. How atoms aggregate together is determined by cosmic laws but the biggest body of aggregation is simply the entire universe.

Our senses and consciousness give the false impression that there are composite material objects but there is only one giant universal soup of atoms or particles without any arrangements into objects whatsoever. It is our minds that make objects through our own mental processes that create a mental illusion. We put our own mental labels, names, forms and definitions on what we see and then we have objects.

When you meditate and realize "I am That" or "You are That," and when you take the entire universe of atoms (or particles instead) and realize that you are really that agglomeration which can be decomposed into one absolute underlying substratum, this is realizing "All of this is the Brahman." To understand this view of being part of an infinite soup of particles in space and hold it in your mind is the meditation on the earth element (atoms, solidity) extending across the material universe.

THE FIRE ELEMENT VIEW OF TRANSFORMATIONS

Yet another meditation is to think in terms of the entire universe being "on fire" where it is "burning" because it is undergoing ceaseless energy and matter transformations. When you realize that atoms are forever undergoing transformations with other atoms to form molecules while releasing or absorbing energy for those processes you can understand that the whole universe is just a cauldron of excitations, transformations or complex interactions involving heat and energy. You are also just that cauldron of excitations or transformations. Seeing the universe in this way is called the fire element meditation on the existence of the universe.

There are many types of universal fire samadhi where you practice seeing the universe as one body of fire, or energy or chemical reactions so you don't need to stick with just this one. For instance, beryllium chloride reacts violently and exothermically with water giving off a steamy hydrogen chloride gas. This is a type of fire reaction and the universe is filled with such reactions everywhere. Perhaps a new chemistry is possible from understanding such transformations. Perhaps a new chemistry would be possible for humanity if we had some way to expose water to the "vibration" or "frequency" of beryllium chloride to produce an exothermic reaction that releases hydrogen without the actual compound.

THE WATER ELEMENT VIEW OF FLOWING AGGLOMERATIONS AND CURRENTS

If you decompose this grand cauldron of universal atoms and energies into just seething energies because the atoms have been decomposed into their energetic nature (where atoms are decomposed into even more basic energy mechanisms such as quantum fields) then the congealing of particles and fields into flowing streams or currents forms the meditation on the water element view of the universe. Alternatively, if you think of the atoms and energies congealing into forms such as worlds and people and objects that are moving here and there in various paths, this is also the water element view of the universe too based on the agglomeration of simples into larger objects or currents that make their own way in their worlds. You are this also.

Once again the yogi, sannyasin and sadhu are taught to think about this view of the universe where energies and matter throughout the cosmos agglomerate through forces that put them into forms that proceed in their own currents or patterns. They are taught that this is another way to view their manifest nature while also realizing "I am That," "All of this is the Brahman."

The particles in the universe that form matter do not exist everywhere at once. When the congealed agglomerations of particles and their movements are further decomposed then the particles are themselves realized as just excited quantum fields that carry energy throughout the universe such as the Higgs field (which gives mass to elementary particles), electron field (that produces electrons), QED electromagnetic field (that produces photons), the weak and strong nuclear fields and so on. The fields ensure that all particles of the same kind, like electrons, have the same characteristic properties throughout the universe. They also ensure that there is a universe-spanning mechanism for every point of spacetime to create elementary particles from appropriate excitations.

This means we are all electric creatures floating in an electric sea of this electric universe. We are all creatures of light floating in a universal sea of light. We are all creatures of mass floating in a sea of mass, and so on. All these fields flow through us constantly with the universe as the source.

THE WIND ELEMENT VIEW OF ENERGY

Particles emerge through the process of decoherence from the underlying fields that span the universe, and there are over a dozen such fields as well as gravity. Across different locations in space and time the value of all quantum fields fluctuate, and your physical body is just this – an ocean of quantum fields always vibrating or fluctuating or changing in value. This produces endless fluctuations of energy and particles in the universe, and this ocean of seemingly indeterminate fluctuations is the view of the universe as being the wind element, which is a giant ocean of seething energy fluctuations. Once again, this is the wind element view of reality, and you are also this.

THE SPACE ELEMENT VIEW OF EMPTINESS

Furthermore, if you realize that within the universe is a smallest unit of time during which there is no change in any part of it, and that during this time you focus on realizing the universal container of empty unmoving space that is holding the manifestation of all the energy and particles, this is the space element meditation of the universe. Just think of empty space infinite in all directions and this is the meditation on empty space, but how can you say you are that? When you realize that the whole universe is not moving (like the substratum) for the "universal reset" instant of time shorter than the fastest possible change, and that the universe of space still holds everything during that moment of stationariness, then you can realize that you are that container of space with all things within it.

Fields and particles all move around within the great container of empty space which functions like an empty womb that always gives birth to something new within it, and you are also just that – infinite space within which everything appears.

Since space can be bent by matter due to gravity this means that space is not the ultimate substrate of the universe. Empty space appears within something else more ultimate, and its ultimate substrate is once again the unchanging Brahman that is empty of phenomena. The Brahman is compared to empty space that seems to lack attributes but space is a type of form so it is not the ultimate Brahman.

The universe is essentially its fundamental substrate that appears as a manifestation although it remains ever and always itself – the changeless, unalterable, actionless, motionless, permanent Brahman. It is an infinite formlessness empty of everything, just like empty space, yet this transcendent voidness of qualities exists everywhere as the base of creation. You are ultimately nothing other than the Brahman as well. Everything is composed of the Brahman so everything is the Brahman because the Brahman extends everywhere and permeates everything as its ultimate substance, the absolute ground state of existence. The Brahman is the substance of all beings. Everything that exists is the Brahman in disguise. To understand that is part of self-realization.

What is *self-realization*? Self-realization is understanding what is the true nature of your existence. It means understanding your true self-nature, understanding the nature of your true self as to who and what you ultimately are. When you say "I" it is only a matter of expression because "I" really means your true self-nature. When true reality or your underlying Self has taken form through manifestation you refer to it in language with the word "I." Thus to understand your true self you must transcend the normal outer forms of identity that you are used to using.

Self-realization also entails realizing what you are not since to the manifest universe there is also no such true things as living beings or consciousness. Also, as an entity that is a temporary agglomeration or portion of a single ever-changing fabric, you lack a constant, solid, stable permanent core in the realm of manifestation. You are simply an energetic phenomenon continuously transmuting as you pass through endless transformations.

Hence in the realm of manifestation there is no such thing as an enduring self. Manifest reality is characterized by impermanence and dependent arising, or interdependent origination that is in a state of continuous flux that gives rise to only momentary appearances ("instantaniations") because of infinite interrelationships and interfusions continuously changing. Where is an intrinsic self in this?

What we perceive as things (objects) or events are stable, conventional constructions invented by our minds that simplify all that. The objects or events we cognize within our minds are not ultimately real even though they *are conventionally real* since they are characterized by an unbreakable facticity of cause and effect, and everyone else seems to perceive them in a similar confirming way (event though the way we perceive them isn't correct). The consciousness processes of our species simply evolved a way to make a picture of the world in a logical, consistent manner for our process of life to function, and this involved the evolutionary creation of a process called consciousness in a living organism that could create a workable picture of the world for survival. Consciousness also needed the creation of a false self-identity inside its workings to make them operate.

"Self-realization" means understanding the true nature of your ultimate selfness or beingness, who and what you really turn out to be in your absolute essence of beinghood, so it means understanding these facts. All your spiritual bodies, as high as they can go, are still really just the formless, empty fundamental essence of the universe that has somehow been condensed into forms and energies. Your composite, conditional spiritual bodies have a structural solidity to them on their own planes of existence that can allow them to maintain very long lives of *sat, chit* and *ananda* that are preferable to that of our lowest realm of corporeal gross matter. This is why we seek to attain them through spiritual practice, which is to then experience a consciousness of *ananda* (bliss), deathlessness (*sat*) and an escape from the endless cycle of reincarnation managed by masters within the lower realms.

Ikigai, or the self-selected purpose of your existence so that it has meaning, significance and fulfillment, is a decision you have to make for your own life rather than just the goal of pursuing a blissful, enjoyable existence. Without a life purpose of significance that provides fulfillment and satisfaction a long life becomes meaningless. A life purpose also provides you with the impetus for improvement, i.e. self-improvement and the motivation to improving situations too. You do not want life to just be a battle for survival while sometimes chasing after temporary pleasures, gratifications and creature-comforts.

Hence enlightened spiritual masters fill their life with special vows or pledges of compassionate activities to help others who also have consciousness, and who thus are brothers and sisters in manifestation and ultimate spirit. Since everything is the Self, by making everyone happy the Self is pleased so sages try to make people happy because of realizing, "They are of my own nature and of my own forms, so their happiness is my happiness."

Thus the *Mahavakya* aphorisms of Hinduism are the basis of self-realization, which is the "mental" enlightenment of finally understanding what your self-nature is, what your source nature is, what your core Self ultimately is, what your True Self ultimately is. This is *what you are* rather than some type of independent homogenous spiritual self or soul. You are a conditional existence assembled together due to conditions but your eternal nature is the single foundational substrate of all existence.

In the *Siddha Siddhanta Paddhati* the sage yogi Guru Gorakhnath (responsible for the Nath Sampradaya) explains the different layers of phenomenal creation and says that you and the universe are ultimately *anama*, the nameless origin or *nija-sakti* that is eternal, pure, motionless, imperceptible and "undisturbed consciousness." Through some means it becomes *para-sakti* – existence, inscrutable, indivisible, infinite, unmanifest. Its next stage of evolution is *apara-sakti*, which is characterized by emanation, expansion, bursting, pulsation. Then he traced out yet further evolutes until coming to the realm of matter.

Gorakhnath, as I have said, stated that the controversies between dualism and non-dualism in ancient India are irrelevant or useless from the practical point of view of daily life. And why? Because from a practical angle you can use either view to cultivate the target of clear consciousness with the clearest consciousness belonging to the highest transcendental bodies residing on higher planes of manifestation described by his teachings. It doesn't matter which view you subscribe to as long as you attain the highest spiritual bodies possible.

SADHU MEDITATIONS

In order to achieve this understanding many Hindu sadhus, sannyasins, yogis and monks are taught to disconnect their mind from the concept of being the doer of actions because the universe itself is the single manifest entity doing everything through the internals of all its interconnected, interfusing, interpenetrated parts and conditions. You are not the doer because you have no intrinsic self; the universe is the doer. Similarly, you might also say that the Self that is the underlying substratum of the manifest cosmos is the ultimate doer of everything because it is the only permanent, unchanging and thus real Self. However, it is not a living Self because it is inanimate, and furthermore it does not move so calling it the Ultimate Doer is just a way of speaking. Of course this is just a mental trick for meditation practice.

Sometimes Hindu sadhus, yogis, sannyasins and monks are taught to unite their minds with the Brahman since it is the ultimate cause of everything as the absolute essence, so it is the real (ultimate) doer in their life. To help them learn detachment they are taught that they should surrender themselves completely to the Brahman (either the absolute universal substrate Purusha that is *Nirguna* Brahman, or an ultimate deity like Ishvara who is *Saguna* Brahman) and offer Him everything they have including their thoughts and behavior so that they can live their lives in peace.

Hindu sadhus, yogis, sannyasins and monks are taught that they are not actually their physical body so *they should live like someone without a body* as a way to once again become detached and thereby attain a serene sense of peace through mental detachment where they liberate themselves by letting go of everything, including the results of their actions and any self-identity they had created. They are taught that they are formless, boundless, and bodiless because that is their true unchanging identity – the Brahman. This mental perspective is also a meditation method that impels you to stop clinging to mental objects. Because you do not cling to your thoughts or emotions that are your fabrications of consciousness, your open mentality gives enlightened spiritual masters and guardian spirits a chance to work on purifying your Prana for ascension without much push-back that would normally occur due to the connection between our thoughts and our Prana.

Some Hindu sadhus, yogis, sannyasins and monks are taught to disassociate from all mental objects that their mind fabricates and to focus their continuous attention on the sense of "I," which is the center of our thoughts and perceiver of our personal perceptions. This is the approach of Ramana Maharshi. The theory is that if you focus on the I-sense and stop consciousness from connecting with all exterior phenomena then the individuality of the "I" can no longer exist, so it will have to withdraw and disappear ... and you can then realize the inherent unreality of our concepts of being an intrinsic sentient self. The idea is to cultivate a practice so that all sense of "I" is interrupted but without blocking the I-sense by strongly holding onto other thoughts to interrupt it.

Some Hindu sadhus, yogis, sannyasins and monks are taught not to identify with their ego-self (I-ness), or with the sensory perceptions for knowing their body or the world, or with their thoughts (emotions, desires, urges, attachments, sufferings, will, etcetera) or any other subjective aspects of their conscious beingness. They are taught not to identify with their body, mind, thinking (discrimination), emotions, will, or their sensory perceptions of the manifest cosmos of elements that surrounds us. They are taught to practice giving up the I-concept to achieve an unattached mental state of formlessness or "emptiness" that simply flows without attachments because we are all actually just the thoughtless Supreme Nature, the Brahman, which is the fundamental substratum of Creation.

This is your True Self, your ultimate and absolute true-nature, your unchanging identity that is pure and eternal and never changes. Hence, devoted Hindu sadhus, yogis and monks are taught that if they detach from their thoughts, desires and emotions in their spiritual practice then their minds will gradually calm down and they will find an internal peace as if nothing exists, and that this peacefulness is the bliss men seek because it imitates the peaceful nature of the Brahman, yet non-existence is not our way nor should it be.

Therefore many Hindu sadhus, yogis, sannyasins and monks are taught that if they give up their ego and remain absorbed in the Brahman, or God, then they will experience peace or bliss, which will happen because they will start quieting their mind and gradually touch upon inner peacefulness since this is a type of emptiness, empty mind or formlessness meditation. Of course it is actually impossible to "give up your ego" because consciousness needs the I-thought as a center for its workings to operate, otherwise without a self-concept consciousness could not know thought-forms and without consciousness you would be mindless like the natural world. Therefore you cannot be "conscious without thoughts" – such as achieving an empty mental state (samadhi) of nothingness or oblivion – because when you are conscious various mental operations are always operating behind the scenes (occurring below awareness) even when thoughts are shut down unless you are in deep sleep or your spirit body has left for another location.

Actually, what is actually being taught to sadhus, yogis, sannyasins and monks is to let go of mental contents – including any attachments to the products of consciousness – in order to let the mental realm flow and better experience mental peace, and it doesn't really matter how you achieve this because countless practice roads are available. Christian monks and priests are told to "find peace in the contemplation of God" in order to receive the same benefits of peacefulness, mental stilling. Buddhists are taught to cultivate the "bliss of emptiness" but also the states of Prana transformation that help purify your inner subtle nature.

Some Hindu sadhus, yogis, sannyasins and monks are taught that they are empty of an intrinsic, inherent, independent, non-conditional homogenous self and lack all the attributes or qualities pertaining to a self ... and that objects are free of an intrinsic own-nature too. The purpose of pondering this perspective is so that they abstain from identifying with a self-notion, and detach from the world but primarily to achieve some release from identifying with the self-notion. The purpose is so that they become liberated from mentally stationing themselves in identifying as a self or with the products of their consciousness and thereby achieve peacefulness through this angle of practice.

The Indian siddha sage Thayumanavar instructed, "Ever-permanent, without any blemish, without any ignorance, without support, ever-full, undecayingly pure, far as well as near, like the Light beyond the three luminaries (Sun, Moon and Fire), the One Charm that includes all, overflowing with Bliss, undiscernible to mind or speech, standing as the Colossus of Consciousness—on that vastness of the beginning of Infinite Bliss, let us meditate." This is telling us to practice meditation on the purity of our foundational nature that, since it has no qualities, is empty of phenomena.

The enlightened Yoga master Tirumalai Krishnamacharya said, "Knowing all objects to be impermanent, let not their contact blind you. Resolve again and again to be aware of the Self that is permanent." This is a different way of instructing you to practice mental detachment or emptiness meditation because the only permanent element, of which he speaks, is the fundamental substratum of yourself and the cosmos. Enlightened yogis repeatedly speak of this truth so that you recognize who and what you ultimately are because this understanding is the basis of self-realization and liberation from being bound by your mental states.

These various instructions on detachment are called *Vairagya* and serve as various types of meditation practice for individuals ordinarily involved in busy daily activities. Then there are the sitting meditation practices (empty mind meditations) of Zen or Daoism and the stationary *asana* positions of Hatha yoga to help you cultivate mental detachment and internal peace (emptiness) as well.

There are also the standing Trinity Posture (*San Ti Shi*) of *xingyiquan*, the Eight Mother Palms holding postures of *baguazhang*, and various martial arts *shuzuang bu* (Tree Stump) standing postures where you silently hold a stable, stationary position while patiently maintaining an empty mind. These, too, if you hold yourself in these positions with a mind of detachment or emptiness, will lead you to inner Prana transformations and great *gong-fu* attainments because if you become truly empty through detachment during these times then enlightened beings will have great success in purifying your Prana without any stubborn push back.

Hindus should know about all these practices rather than just the standard ones promoted within India or Hinduism such as *bhakti*. You should know about the non-denominational principles of spiritual practice and how different spiritual schools approach the task of cultivating the body and mind (consciousness) to purify both.

HUMANS HAVE A TASK AS BEINGS OF CONSCIOUSNESS

Our tasks as humans, as beings with the attribute of consciousness, is to learn how to expand our awareness; how to control our thoughts; how to handle mental afflictions that automatically arise within consciousness and handicap its workings; how to maintain focus, attention and concentration; how to transform or manage emotions; how to think logically, rationally and self-correct our thinking; how to create the proper mindsets, attitudes, dispositions, or perspectives; and how to develop countless mental skills or abilities such as being able to count in your head, develop a super memory using mnemonics, visualize (mentally rehearse) a situation, use logic and reason to deduce conclusions, link with and mentally move your internal Prana energy in various ways, become absorbed in a state of flow, use your breathing to change your biochemistry and mental state, and so forth.

In other words, consciousness has many possible abilities or skills and you want to learn to master them to expand the capabilities of your mind. You also want to just widen the scope and depth of your awareness, and reduce any limitations to your awareness because your field of consciousness is limited by the barriers of your *samskaras*. You want to get rid of such restrictions. As a being of consciousness shouldn't you be doing this … making the absolute most of yourself and specifically maximizing your one special characteristic that distinguishes you from the rest of the universe? You absolutely should be developing *all the capabilities of your mind and awareness* and your *ability to create an enjoyable life existence* for yourself and others.

This is what Hindu sadhus, sannyasins, monks and yogis should be practicing in their daily activities. All your experiences are conventionally real, but ultimately illusory and groundless because the picture you create of the world is a similitude representation, your thinking is often rationally faulty or biased by emotions and wrong perspectives, and because your central idea of being an intrinsic self is also incorrect. The world is neither perceived *correctly* or *fully* through your limited senses and sense processing capabilities nor are your mental sense images understood properly since you have adopted an entirely fictitious reference frame of what they and what *you* ultimately are.

Nevertheless, you have life and are the universe, the embodied consciousness of the universe, so you are to make the best of what you are by extending yourself to your fullest capabilities, pursue bliss and the absence of suffering, pursue *moksha* or liberation, and pursue *ikigai* for your existence. You don't want to shed your existence or consciousness like you want to shed unnecessary *koshas*. Instead you want to be living a great life on whatever plane of existence you find yourself that pertains to a certain level of densification, condensing or agglomeration of energies. This is the positive view of your illusory existence as an independent self. So what if life is an illusion in terms of Brahman and you see it incorrectly? You still exist and enjoy the dream with consistency so you must maximize the implications of apparent existence, yet understand what you are and how things really stand precisely so that you use your mind better and make your life better (such as by not holding onto afflictive emotions).

Therefore, another reason you perform these meditations is to try to understand and prepare for the mind of enlightenment. When you attain the stage of the Supra-Causal body or higher Immanence (Buddha) body, the compositional plane of your body is so etheric and refined that it transcends all the denser realms of matter. One can then see how matter is joined with energy seamlessly in one big universal soup of matter-energy that is ultimately energy, or fields, or quantum wind, ... that is essentially a single manifestation substance that in turn is a single motionless substrate.

The realms of the Supra-Causal and Tathagata Immanence bodies are already so etheric that we cannot even sense them with scientific equipment. At those stages your form exists as a bodied-being that is almost pure energy that can then sense all the vibrations in the lower realms of existence across the universe (after training) AND you can also experientially realize that your body is seamlessly united with the many energy fields that interpenetrate the universe that cause it to produce things.

The universe is energy, you are that energy, and the universe is the thing making you – a process within it – out of its single fabric of one taste. Ultimately at the highest stage of transcendence there are no phenomena or different forces and energy types, but somehow that purity gives birth to manifold manifestation. There is just the one universe and transcending the manifest cosmos there is just the single fundamental, permanent ground substrate (Brahman) that never moves or changes, and due to this permanent never-changing nature is always there as our True Self since it dependably never becomes anything different, it never fluctuates and never leaves.

At the highest stages of enlightenment you therefore recognize your unity and oneness with all of Creation, which leads to the *recognition that all men are brothers* despite any differences in appearance. You have an apparent existence that depends entirely upon an infinite number of factors simultaneously interpenetrating, interfusing and defining one another that create the entire universe and then you. You are, therefore, universal. All of the universe participates in making you because you are an essential part of its single body. The same goes for every other thing as well. Your miraculous difference is that you have the attribute of consciousness.

Even so, your consciousness *is also a dependent illusion-making process* instead of something that stands independently transcending the universe as something real-in-itself, and it doesn't belong to any such thing as an independent transcendent being that is out of the universe. You are Nature, your consciousness is a part of Nature. We call ourselves beings but there is no such true thing in the universe for there are just inanimate energies surging here and there and producing all sorts of interacting transformations. That's what you and your consciousness really are. All the conscious minds of sentient beings in the universe are really just inanimate processes and not really accurate or true consciousnesses. However, you can also take the other side and say that the universe is consciousness and living because the highest emanates produce life and consciousness.

Climate affects your consciousness, your anatomy affects it, your diet and circumstances affect it, events affect it, even planets (astrology) affect your thought-making and emotions. Where is there a person in its operations? There is none because the I-sense is a product of its processes, and yet understanding is there in its processes of Knowledge-making.

All spiritual schools teach this because this is the truth as to what you really are. You are liberated and free because you are the Brahman, you are the realm of manifestation and it is that entire realm which is acting as the doer, or you can say that static unchanging Brahman is the Self or doer at the core without doing anything at all. Because of the infinite interdependence of everything in existence participating in the origination of everything else, *when anything within the universe manifests the entire cosmos gets into the act.* When one iota of the universe changes the entire universe changes, and when one part changes it is because the perfect infinite interfusion, interdependence and conditional (relative) origination of all things caused it to change.

The appearance of any one thing within the universe is an *unfoldment* of cause and effect that fully encompasses the entire universe into a *localized enfoldment* or appearance. That is to say, the existence of any single thing depends on the total network of all other things, which are all equally fused with each other, interdependent upon one another, and simultaneously mutually determined by each other so that they interpenetrate one another. This simultaneous interpenetration (interfusion) and co-production is what produces the appearances or existences of everything.

Since everything is perfectly fused with everything else this forms one single manifest substance, which is what you are, and its absolute underlying absolute substratum is the undifferentiated source essence of existence. All things merge in It, the Brahman or Purusha.

The entire universe gets into the act to produce both you and the events and circumstances of your life that are all parts of the universe, seamlessly connected to everything else in a grand smear where there are no real divisions of its body into distinctively separate things since nothing has an absolute border. This is what humans are in the grand scheme of things. You can get a sense of how endless causes or conditions participate in producing what appears to be your body (or anything else) by viewing the "Quantum Cloud" sculpture made by Antony Gormley (check the internet). It reveals how forces unconnected with each other agglomerate into producing a body.

Because you are the universe, your life trajectory, fate or destiny of life events within the universe is called "karma" since absolutely everything cooperates in producing that fate. Most of our karma, since it includes our environment and the world we enjoy, is collective destiny that we either enjoy or suffer from. However, you do have personal karma geared to your birth time and location.

In physics there is a common example used to explain how one can predict the location, speed and direction of gas molecules in a box at any future moment of time if you know the starting conditions for each molecule. Well, because you are really a condensed energy complex whose movements, thoughts and doings are subject to astrological forces, sages have found that your personal karma can be forecast by the positions of the planets in the heavens at any moment in future time when you compare those parameters with those at your birth, which correspond to the starting conditions of gas molecules in our physics problem. Your future karma or trajectory can be predicted by simply seeing where the planets will be in the future, and the rules for determining the meaning of those combinations is the field of Jyotish that reveals your karma.

Masters on the higher planes of existence can see the karma etched out in the lower etheric planes that reveal your fate. Because you are essentially a selfless energy knot of processes subject to surrounding universal forces then even though you think of yourself as a sentient living being there are factors external to your ego-self that determine your life path and future.

You have previously been taught the essential meaning of self-realization, but you must realize what your human physical body, or any of your spiritual bodies, ultimately are as well. Whether a collection of all the atoms in the universe, or a ball of transformations, or an ocean of congealed energy masses that flow along their separate ways, or an effervescent, indeterminate vibration of energies with a unique oscillation or resonance for each moment of time, however you wish to think of the manifest universe it pertains to your existence also.

And what does the human being want during its existence within all this? You've seen that we want *sat, chit, ananda,* and *ikigai.* Furthermore, we pursue *Moksha, Dharma, Kama* and *Artha* in life. One could say that we also try to maximize the benefits and minimize the negatives in our twelve houses of natal astrology and how they express themselves in our life over time. We seek various objectives such as * peak experiences; * the feeling of being truly alive; * healthy relationships; * the wondrous mental state of flow or uninterrupted pristine awareness that is fully and blissfully engaged with the world; * the absence of negative emotions; * the performance of skillful behavior that constitutes virtue and excellence in the art of human life (*arête*); * life satisfaction; * and the state of wellness, well-being or *eudaimonia* that is at the positive extreme of the mood scale with abundant gratification and authentic happiness.

We want to experience a happiness for being a person of whom we ourselves highly approve and we seek all these things even though our self-concept is an illusion, consciousness is an illusion and the universe is an illusion. Nevertheless we do exist even though it is in an empty dream, and yet that dream is stable too even though it changes every moment. Our desire to exist, to feel fully alive with blazing awareness and physical bliss, and joyfully experience life is *sat, chit, ananda*.

EMPTINESS MEDITATION

Some spiritual schools say that to "recognize God" (the fundamental substratum, or Brahman) is the ultimate aim in life. They say that the crown jewel in spiritual studies is to stabilize in the underlying One Without Qualities that is similar to infinite empty space. The ultimate Brahman is That from which everything is born, the ultimate source of manifestation that is Itself unborn, everlasting, and pure in the sense that It is primordially absent of everything that isn't Its singleness beyond matter and energy. Being pure It cannot change into anything else for there is no such thing within It as cause and effect that would produce change. It is also pure in the sense of being free of attributes such as the phenomena or qualities cognized by consciousness that seem to have arisen within It (since those phenomena are exactly It and nothing else).

There are many forms of meditation practice that entail focusing on images of our fundamental substratum in some way which are called "emptiness" or "empty mind" meditations. Yes, this sort of practice will lead to mental quieting but this will never lead to enlightenment. You can rest in empty states of mind for eons and will never achieve the enlightenment of higher, ascended spiritual attainments at all. The major benefits to engaging in such meditations are to calm wandering thoughts, create a detached mental state of clarity and awareness, become able to attain mindfulness of your thoughts and behavior for the purpose of self-correction, and to live in a state of alert presence due to centering yourself in your subtle body as the witness consciousness.

The principle being stressed, however, is that the closer our pristine awareness gets to being like our fundamental nature (Brahman) via formless meditation practices and detachment practices then the less mental perturbations, disturbances or afflictions there will be for us during daily life, and our minds will become more clear and focused during concentration. Formless mind meditation, where there is clear awareness (clarity of mind) in a state of alert presence, centers you in your subtle body thus making you more alive. It also leads to mindfulness or watchfulness of your behavior which enables self-correction.

Everything in this world is in a state of flux so the whole universe is an incessant sea of change except for the fundamental substratum that never changes. Meditation that calms our mind and brings us to a more pacified state of empty clarity, a pristine awareness, is thus championed as a way to become closer to the only thing constant and dependable in our lives – our True Self that is the Brahman.

As already explained, a spiritual cultivation technique similar to meditation is to engage in your life without being attached to your body or activities while holding nothing in your mind. You are not supposed to identify with the relative aspects of your being or expect any results from what you do while still doing what you must for life. Krishna advises us to perform our duties without being attached to the results. You live like someone without a body so that you gradually attain a serene nature.

This is detachment practice to reach liberation from the tendency of mentally clinging. You want your awareness to increase and any limitations caused by mental attachments to decrease. You try to perceive everything as a dance of the supreme original substrate, and try to become detached from the flow of your thoughts by always remembering that you are actually as boundless as space just like your fundamental substance, which is what you are and what the universe is. Not only this, but while going about your affairs you try to make everything you do replete with perfect virtue as if you were standing in the presence of God every moment all day long, which causes you to raise your Yang Prana as inner practice.

These are all techniques with an ulterior motive. No one can possess the attribute of consciousness without a body because the anatomical structure of the brain and nervous system, along with subtle energy, are required to produce thoughts. Thoughts are needed for there to be Knowledge (consciousness), and the ego-sense must be there as well. All we can ever know or experience are the thoughts of our own consciousness and we don't want to give that up to become insentient. Therefore, no true spiritual objective entails having no thoughts at all, which is a state of insentience that would equate with non-existence or extinction since no-thinking (no-thought) entails the annihilation of consciousness.

Even if your mind seems pristinely quiet and empty, as long as you are awake and identifying (recognizing) the objects of your environment through cognition or awareness this means that your thought processes are operating in the background even if the sense of I-ness, me-ness or thinking seems silenced. There is a lot of mental processing going on "in the dark" to produce awareness and that processing is free of any inner feeling that it is happening. But for you to cognize yourself or something there must be an I-thought in those operations of awareness.

THE DEVELOPMENT OF CHILDHOOD CONSCIOUSNESS

When you were a baby your consciousness operated automatically without much reference to an ego-sense. We can describe your consciousness during that early time as a system of disconnected functionings (algorithms) of consciousness, like independent personalities or subroutines, that over time merged into a unity identity ... a personality with an ego-sense ... that has a continuity of memory across time. The self-identity gradually emerges during childhood as you grow because consciousness requires a mental processing mechanism in order for the mind to function and be able to act for the whole person, namely in order for our organism to be able to make sense of reality out of all the internal and external inputs that flood the mind. Consciousness without a self center cannot function, and unconsciousness or thoughtlessness or non-consciousness or insentience is not the objective of spiritual cultivation although you are to understand that your absolute self-nature or True Self is absent of self-thoughts.

This creation of a sense of self in the mind happens to everybody as a consequence of neurophysical development and experiential maturation. There really isn't an ego for our living mechanism but the workings of consciousness invent one over time in order for it to be able to perform higher functionings. It may seem as if you have a monolithic executive or uniform entity underlying all your thoughts and actions – which is the apparent sense of "you" or "I" – but the idea of being an independent, coherent self is an illusion. Selfness does not exist in the way it appears to exist. It is not an eternal self entity but simply a synthesizing, organizing, coordinating, integrating response regulator (regulating mechanism) of all the inputs that we receive to our consciousness so that our consciousness can create a workable worldview for the purposes of survival.

As sentient being we want to experience awareness, or *chit*, where our consciousness is very clear and sharp rather than clouded and fuzzy. We also want to be able to focus and stay with our thought-stream rather than let it jump around from this topic to the next in a wandering manner that we become fused with, thus losing our sense of presence and focus and aliveness that are connected with our higher bodies. Our consciousness forms thoughts automatically in a certain way through its algorithms, but we want to learn the highest method of operating our mind that generates better thoughts where we also allow them to arise and depart without clinging to them. We don't want to be endlessly torturing ourselves with hate, guilt, anger, and so forth but need to let such emotions go. Such emotions naturally arise as a reflex, but we don't want them to dominate our minds and behavior because of clinging.

We also want to be able to change our thoughts and states of consciousness. Our mind operates automatically in many respects and as a life objective you have to learn how to control the operations of your mind, and how to transform the mental states that arise within your awareness.

You want to use consciousness in a way that mimics our absolute self-nature that is all-pervading and allows things to freely arise within It and transform into other things without ever clinging to any of these transformations. However, you want to learn to control consciousness so that you become the master of its transformations! This is your ability, this is your birthright.

You are the consciousness of the fundamental substratum, the True Self, so you always want to know the contents of your mind clearly because that is the purpose of having your attribute of consciousness, awareness of cognizance or illumination. You don't want to destroy that attribute because that's the process you are, created by the cosmos and primordial Self, so that you can thereby experience awareness as part of your functioning. You want to cultivate the clarity and expansiveness and wisdom of your awareness. You also want to learn how to control it, expand its capabilities and be able to change its mental states at will.

You are essentially conscious due to having an appropriate physical body and *atman* composed of transcendental Prana energies that provide the energy of life and consciousness so you never want to try to dull or obliterate your body or mind. You actually want to maximize the potential of your life and consciousness by using your mind in a proper, optimal manner while always giving rise to clear, correct knowing. Then your awareness will become "bright" or blazing and you will seem to shine with energy and light as long as you remain detached from whatever is mentally going on within you.

Your mind within your higher transcendental bodies approximates this optimality because those bodies are closer and closer to pure energy where consciousness functions better due to the life energy of those levels experiencing less friction in its circulation. Your mind seems brighter and more vivid for each new higher spiritual body attainment, but your mind is still just an ordinary mind, like what you have now, for each new level of spiritual beingness although you become capable of more powers because of the nature of your higher body. Because the composition of each spiritual body and its inner vital energy improves for each higher transcendental body the visage of your mental realm seems increasingly more clear, brighter, more vivid or more vibrant. Consciousness is still always just a conditional constructed process, however, and so what you essentially are is still just the True Self or fundamental substratum of the universe that has assumed an apparent form. That is your true I when you say "I" that is what you really are.

If you need fusion with your thoughts for concentration purposes then you do this but normally you should not become deeply entrained with your thoughts and lose your sense of presence and über-observation, metacognition, self-surveillance, mindfulness or self-appraisal because this drops you out of being centered in your higher body potentials. You want to remain in a state of attention where you can observe your thoughts and emotions without being enslaved by them, and by being fully present to oneself you will bring out the full power of consciousness. You don't want to react without awareness like an automaton where you are subject to your old beliefs, habits and conditioning. Rather, you want to see the world right now more clearly and be able to override the automatic functionings of consciousness.

Four examples of using your mind wrongly are clinging to the idea of simply getting revenge, not being able to let go of a broken relationship, clinging to the results of your actions, and clinging to an identity you falsely created to get along in the world rather than being a more satisfied natural self.

The road of spirituality requires that you practice maintaining an extremely clear awareness of your mind, undistracted by afflictions or agitations, while always being an ultra-observer who through attention knows your own thoughts and doings clearly without dropping into them with fusion where you lose that sense of presence and aliveness. Just as we should learn from our mistakes after the fact, in real time we must always observe our thoughts from a higher vantage point so that they are subject to the immediate feedback of appraisal and self-rectification. The purpose is not just to correct ourselves in the moment but to upgrade or rewrite the psychological software that runs our habitual methods for making thoughts and decisions.

We have been given the great miracle of consciousness in a largely insentient universe, and all that the various traditions of spirituality or spiritual practice do is teach us good behavior and how to use our mind properly with countless instructions like this: watch your thoughts so that you get to know yourself and can correct your thoughts and behaviors; be detached from your thinking so that your workings of consciousness flow better; work to develop wisdom and understanding to better your thinking and your decisions and actions and ultimately your life; make sure you do not deviate from the road of virtue since it is at the heart of your happiness; and work on developing the discipline of self-control so that you make less errors in the first place.

That's basically what we are taught: how to be virtuous and ethical and how to operate consciousness properly. We're also given the incentive to start mastering more of its many capabilities – how to take care of our body to keep it healthy and maximize its capabilities – how to achieve through conduct, behavior and activities whatever we want in life (such as *ananda*) – and how to cultivate the higher *koshas* or body vehicles that free us from the lower realms of reincarnation forever while enabling us to experience super living.

THE FOUR VIEWS OF YOUR SELF-NATURE

So as regards spiritual cultivation, awareness and spiritual understanding, you have seen that there are meditations on your self-nature being something of (1) form or (2) formlessness.

As to <u>form</u>, you are essentially the universe of Shakti, Ishvara, Prakirti, Creation, or the realms of manifest existence. Your existence as the entire cosmos can be viewed in many ways well beyond the few meditations provided such as seeing the universe as a combination of space and particles that are the basic components of the manifestation. Whatever fills the universe is to be regarded as your body while their ultimate nature is your nature too.

Yet another perspective of form is that each sentient being is like a tiny cell or neuron within the total universal consciousness where the aggregate of minds makes up the aggregate mind of the universe that exists through all its different levels where *nirmanakaya* give thoughts to different levels to interconnect them and our speaking with others provides interconnections as well. Even so, there is no being standing behind all of these different points of view, vast in number, even though in aggregate these fragments produce actions that cause the universe to become shaped in different ways. In total you might view sentient beings as the embodied mind of the universe.

Another perspective of form is to consider the fact that sages can see your future, which means its pattern is already sketched out in the ether. You are that pattern that extends into the future. At a certain point in time you will be at a certain location doing something, and it has already happened in terms of etheric patterns. That pattern connects with you and therefore is also part of you. You are like a phenomenon centered in the present moment with a big, long trail of history and tracks that trace out your future that sages can see. You can imagine yourself as the form of your present body and the entire wiggly snake trace of your existence from your past to now and into the future.

As to <u>formlessness</u>, the wide variety of spiritual traditions in the world champion meditations, prayers, mantras, and other practices that lead to an empty state of mind with a diminution of the ego-sense and thoughts, so we need not go into them because of the easy availability of such teachings.

You can even meditate with the view that you are <u>both form and formlessness</u> since the manifest universe is one with the absolute nature that is its permeating substrate and container. You are ultimately nothing but at these realms of emanation you are something, yet that something is the whole of manifestation so you aren't what you take yourself to be when you think of yourself as a body. The trinity of Christianity holds for everything – you are the original nature, ALL of manifestation and a particular entity within it.

The one aspect of beingness that has not been discussed in detail is the fourth view that <u>you are a small sentient entity with a physical body that can be unwound into several bodies on different energy planes</u>, each of which remains connected to its previous physical body (as long as it remains alive) while residing on a higher plane of existence. This is what a sage is in terms of manifestation.

Most spiritual schools have you watch your mind in order to purify consciousness, or you are taught to notice the sensations of your body as awareness practice when the real method is to *feel the entire energy matrix of your body*, to feel the flesh in every part of your body since this is then a Prana cultivation technique. From this you move on to actually feeling, moving and thereby transforming or purifying the energy of your body that interpenetrates every atom of your physical nature.

These meditative options solve many of the problems in life regarding *moksha* (liberation), suffering, birth and death and so forth. To achieve *moksha* you must not just cultivate a virtuous character or clarify your mind while abiding in a state of presence. You must also cultivate one of the major capabilities of your mind, which is the ability to direct the movements of your inner vital energy, Prana, that is the essence of the higher bodies. We will next turn to the methods developed to do this in Hinduism, which are at the core of its spiritual practices.

CHAPTER 6
HATHA YOGA TO CULTIVATE YOUR MUSCLES AND PRANA

Hatha yoga is one of the gems of Indian culture. It focuses on different physical postures and breathing methods which specifically preserve and channel the vital energy of your body in order to purify it for ascension. If you don't succeed in attaining the subtle body your yogic practice will still lead to health, physical fitness and spiritual development. Yoga practice is a way to develop your inner subtle body, or life force that assumes the shape of your physical body, to a state where it can finally leave its physical shell, the *annamaya kosha*, as the first step to achieving the *atman*.

Patanjali's Yoga Sutras say that the ultimate aim of Yoga is to reach "*kaivalya*," emancipation or freedom, which is the experience of one's innermost being. Remember that *moksha* means "the state of being released." Therefore the highest value a yogi aspires for lies in shedding the primary constituents of their various unneeded sheaths in their own world-ground (planes of existence), thus "negating" them while achieving a higher transcendental existence having consciousness, i.e. while still retaining a body-mind-energy complex that fulfills the requirements of maintaining *sat* and *chit* so that one might experience life (existence) and *ananda*.

Such an achievement depends upon a sequential separation, decomposition or deconstruction of the bodily life into lower and higher components until one goes as far as one can go in achieving a higher living existence with a pristine state of consciousness.

Hatha Yoga, kundalini yoga, *kriya* yoga, laya yoga, and so many other Yoga types have developed from Patanjali's original Ashtanga Yoga but practitioners have forgotten that this was its main purpose. The purpose is to attaint he higher bodies of transcendence and thus achieve super living.

The majority of Hatha Yoga texts belong to the Nath siddhas and are associated with the yogis of the Natha Sampradaya. In particular, many of the most important texts are credited to or associated with the ancient enlightened teachers Matsyendranatha and Gorakhnath. Those texts teach methods of raising and directing one's Prana, vital energy or life force (that constitute the higher *koshas* embedded in the matter of your physical nature) through different sections of the body with the intent of purifying the tissues along those routes, and the entire body in eventuality, so that the inner subtle body that is being purified can arise as an ascended life. From the stage of success at attaining a deva's body composed purely of subtle energy (which normally happens only upon death) one next starts work at stripping off other energy layers, through a similar means of cultivation, that still surround the *atman* encased within the subtle body until it stands alone resplendent in glory and perfection.

Hatha Yoga became much popularized under the guidance of Tirumalai Krishnamacharya, "Father of Modern Yoga," whose development of postural yoga combined breathing with smooth yoga movements while switching from *asana* to *asana*. An enlightened master, he used the methods of yoga together with Ayurveda to restore health and well-being to many sick individuals. His brother-in-law, B.K.S Iyengar who was founder of Iyengar Yoga, also helped to bring Hatha Yoga to its modern state of popularity.

Incidentally, most people who practice yoga never develop "ripped" muscles like you normally see on athletes. The key to getting ripped muscles by practicing yoga is to hold an *asana* for a long time until you cannot hold the position any longer, and to control your breathing so that you reduce as much oxygen supply to your muscles as possible. You do really long holds in deep positions where you are straining your muscles, which means you are doing really *long isometric holds* for everything.

Russians do powerlift training by holding positions, such as deadlifts, until they cannot hold the position any longer, which is doing the exercise to maximum effort. In isometric training you hold a position until you cannot do so any longer so the holding is like pushing on an immovable object. To get ripped muscles from yoga you have to do this too, which is go into deep positions and hold them for about two minutes or longer while controlling your breathing. This causes you to exercise while contracting your muscles, which closes your blood vessels and stops the blood flow of extra blood going to your muscles that accumulate lactic acid from the exercise strain. That forces your muscles to go into hypoxia, which is a state of lower oxygen that causes a whole cascade of different hormones to be released such as growth factors, testosterone and neurotropic factor. It also wakes up stem cells.

This is like blood flow resistance training. Here you are stretching and moving your body into positions where the deep, prolonged holding of stressed muscles causes you to reduce the blood flow to those muscles naturally, which is like wearing resistance bands. You hold each position to maximum effort, which is about two minutes for yoga compared to what you'd normally hold in a typical yoga routine. This is what builds your strength, stamina and resilience.

Bruce Lee did this type of exercise — functional isometric training where he would press, pull, push and curl against immovable objects — which is why he became really strong and ripped. He used a simple routine of eight different isometric exercises where each exercise was performed with maximum effort (the muscles fatigue with the effort) for 6-12 seconds.

Now in terms of physical comfort or bliss (*ananda*), the better that your Prana circulates throughout your body without bottlenecks, obstructions, or impediments the greater will become your ability to feel the entire Prana of your body as a single unit, or the ability to forget the feeling of your body entirely because its Prana flow becomes so smooth and comfortable due to that higher perfection. The more spiritual and physical exercises you do the more you will strengthen and purify your inner subtle body and prepare it for "birth by transformation" where your Prana-body breaks free of its physical *annamaya kosha* shell.

Hatha Yoga tells us that postures held for spiritual practice are an *asana* and sometimes recommends unusual or uncomfortable *asana* positions in order to circulate your Prana in hard-to-reach regions of your body where it is difficult to stretch the muscles, tendons and ligaments. This produces benefits for your health and your spiritual practice.

While one of the highest objectives of Yoga is to gain complete physical control over your limbs, organs and other parts of your body, some of the best stationary poses are those which gradually lead to the dissolving of Prana circulatory blockages in your physical and subtle bodies. Overall, better Prana circulation will purify its nature and thereby raise its vibrational rate so that the inner pranic body can eventually separate from the physical nature and its coarser energies due to a greater and greater differentiation at all their places of interconnection. This is one of the many reasons why Yoga is associated with the term "dissolution." You dissolve your connection with your physical nature.

If you achieve the frictionless circulation of Prana within your body this will help to purify and strengthen your inner subtle body that is the aggregate of your *pranamaya* and all higher *koshas*. Improving your Prana circulation will also help you to tame your thoughts and emotions because the more perfect your Prana circulation the greater its perfusion in all your tissues. As you achieve a greater fullness of Prana within all your tissues, this will produce a subtle bliss of smooth vitality *that radiates* while you also experience greater calmness and clarity.

Stretching your muscles by holding yourself in an *asana* posture not only increases your physical dexterity and flexibility, which is what ordinary people usually think of as the ultimate purpose of Yoga, but stimulates the Prana throughout your muscles, organs and tissues to improve its circulation. Some postures, such as the sitting lotus posture used for meditation practice, are uncomfortable at first, which means that your body must force its own Prana through the muscle energy channels in order that you can master the position. However, uncomfortable postures once mastered allow you to engage in prolonged Prana cultivation efforts for a long continuous period of time.

If we reference other physical exercise traditions, it can be seen that the standing *san ti shi* "trinity posture" of *xingyiquan* martial arts is also an *asana* that you hold for a prolonged period of time. Holding this special stationary posture allows for enlightened masters and their students to possess your Prana during that time, as is also the case for Yoga, and use their own energy to help improve your Prana circulation. This is why holding stationary muscle stretching postures for a long time is so effective for spiritual practice.

When you automatically engage in Hatha Yoga poses where you don't seem to be controlling yourself – which also manifests as martial arts "shadow boxing" and the spontaneous Trulkhor movements of Tibetan Buddhism – this too is also sometimes due to spiritual masters or devas possessing your body in order to temporarily help your Prana circulation rather than due to psychological causes such as the release of pent-up energy.

Yoga can have a major spiritual benefit of purifying your inner subtle body by washing it with Prana in this way and that if you understand how to approach the objective of gradually freeing your subtle body from its physical shell. Yoga can lead to this result because correct yoga postures will stretch your muscles to reduce circulatory impediments to your internal energy flow and that stretching, of a particular form, will bolster circulation pathways in specific muscle groups and regions. When your Prana circulation improves it is because frictional blockages inside you are removed, which is "purification" of your inner subtle body. This will purify it by freeing it of impurities that are frictionally rubbed away so that it can achieve a greater vibrational rate free of imperfections. This is why Yoga becomes a spiritual practice, for otherwise it is just exercise.

(1) For the most effective Yoga practice you can assume *asanas* while also *mentally focusing* on those muscle groups being stretched (or others) to draw Prana to them in order to wash them with energy. This means holding your focus and intent on your Prana in a certain area of your body being stretched since this will draw Prana to that area.

When your mind concentrates on a region inside your body this will pull your Prana to that area because your consciousness and Prana are linked where your thoughts can always guide it. This is the mind-body connection of science where consciousness and Prana are linked because the mind operates due to being powered by the Prana of the subtle body. Prana powers consciousness because consciousness is essentially happening in the subtle body, so your thoughts can affect your Prana because consciousness is of the same nature as Prana.

By accumulating Prana in a body region due to mentally concentrating upon feeling the energy inside that locale, or by imagining that the area becomes bright with light, this will to some extent "wash" or purify your underlying subtle body in that area. *Bandhas* or locks, for instance, are used for concentrating and holding your Prana in certain body locations for this purpose of washing your subtle body, which Yoga calls "opening the *nadis*."

(2) You can also *use physical force to pump or push your Prana* through specific body locations, as in pumping exercises like *mula bandha*. Pranayama is another cultivation method that uses the power of breathing and its connection with your Prana to forcibly push your Prana through body regions to open their circulatory obstructions.

The *Hatha Yoga Pradipika* and other texts have introductory instructions on pranayama for how to do this. Over time, by pushing your Prana through various regions of your body you will help to strengthen and purify its circulation through those regions and purify your body in total.

(3) You can also *wash* a body region with Prana by using your will (intent) to circulate your Prana in various revolutions within that area. You do this by leading it around inside yourself with your mind, namely your willpower or thoughts. You feel that energy to connect with it, and then lead its circulation in various circular revolutions, or lap the energy upon itself, or try to condense it or inflate it, make it hot or cold, and so on

You can also use special circulatory or vibrational techniques to help wash your Prana in specific anatomical parts, and of course you must repeat those exercises over and over again to improve your Prana circulation within those parts.

Here are three examples: (a) humming "mmm" when trying to feel or push Prana through your upper palate; (b) reciting the sounds "Cha" and "Chr" to push or pull the Prana through your teeth and gums; (c) or pushing the tongue up against the palate to exercise the muscles of the *thyroid and throat* (because this moves them) while simultaneously reciting "Jha" since this sound vibrates the Prana in the throat and thyroid region.

Another way of stimulating the thyroid is by each day placing your two palms, turned backwards, on each side of your neck and pulling backwards for several dozen times as a daily throat massage to bring blood into the area. This quick and painless exercise, discovered by Ninon de L'Enclos, also helps people maintain a youthful appearance well into old age.

Touching the palate with your tongue curled backwards (some incorrectly call this the "tip of the tongue") additionally provides a bridge so that you can push-circulate your Prana through your tongue to your palate, nasal cavity, cerebellum, back of throat and so forth in various circular rotational patterns that are guided by your will.

(4) When your body is held motionless in *asana* or *mudra* positions that stretch muscles you can practice stimulating, exciting, energizing, invigorating, moving, circulating, pushing or pulling your Prana through those muscles being stretched by combining that stretching with other inner energy exercises. This includes * mentally focusing strongly on feeling the muscular energy to sense the shape of the muscles; * using visualization efforts on the muscles being stretched that will bring Prana to those areas; * reciting resonating mantra sounds on the muscles or as if from *within those muscles* in order to stimulate their Prana (the best sounds vibrate the Prana within the part being cultivated because they are *bijas* for selected body parts); * or giving rise to Yin or Yang emotional attitudes to overall stimulate your masculine or feminine (Yang or Yin) energies into moving while stretching.

Wherever you put your focused concentration within your body your Prana will automatically follow to that spot because your Prana and your consciousness are linked since your subtle body, composed of Prana, is connected with your consciousness. By adding emotional content during your practice session you will during that time also stimulate your overall Prana into having a certain quality.

You must wash your Prana by changing the energy through all sorts of moods and then during that time you need to use various inner energy methods of circulating it so that, through friction, the movement of your Prana with that new energy tone will purify it. This is one of the secrets hidden in Hinduism on how to cleanse and purify the Prana of your subtle body.

(5) You can guide your Prana through various *pratyahara* circuits in your body, moving it from point to point and location to location

through the guidance of your mind. To do this you mentally concentrate your Prana at various locations within your body, circulate it within that region and then move it to a subsequent region. This will wash selected body sections in sequence, and then you must link the Prana of these regions as a unified pathway.

The *Yoga Yajnavalkya* has a special sequence for how to sequentially move your Prana to open up all the sections of your body. Chinese Taoism also has a Small Circulation and Great Circulation practice where you revolve your Prana along certain large energy meridian pathways within your body, guiding it along these routes, and this practice is also used in the martial arts.

For instance, you can lead your Prana up into your brain using the pathway of your spine or lead it up by concentrating on spinal nerves or even the skin and muscles surrounding the spine. Yoga encourages people to do this by talking about the *ida, pingala* and *sushumna* channels within the spine whereas the truth is that you just want all of your Prana to be washed by revolutions meant to do this.

After leading Prana to your brain you should then *wash* the brain's anatomical structure using Prana revolutions of countless different patterns. You should use anatomical and DTI (diffusion tensor imaging) brain images as maps to guide your efforts to revolve your Prana along the brain's various nerve pathways. Normally when the brain is filled with Prana it becomes energized and functions more fully so this is a possible benefit. Better blood flow or energy circulation within the brain promote heightened states of quiescence and clarity, which is the basis behind meditation and this work.

Various *pratyahara* pathways are revealed in *Yoga Yajnavalkya, Nyasa Yoga (Bodri)* and *Neijia Yoga* (Bodri). As another example methodology from yet another spiritual tradition, in the *boran kammatthana* Esoteric Theravada School of Buddhism you are taught to concentrate "spheres of light" (which actually means Prana) at the tip of your nose and then move it to the back of the nose between the eyes, between the eyebrows, top of the head, back of the head, epiglottis, heart, navel, and then around the navel. You progressively draw your Prana from the intranasal cavity inside the nostril down to your lower abdomen. In other *boran kammatthana* cultivation methods you place the Prana (light) spherical-concentrations in different arrangements within the body both horizontally and vertically at points such as the navel, at points on the level of the navel surrounding the navel, at the heart and so on. The various tantric schools of Yoga have endless techniques along these lines which are usually practiced under the guidance of an enlightened master.

(6) Eventually after using all these techniques you can build to the point where you can feel all the Prana of your body as a single unit or unified whole – which is the ultimate target – and this becomes possible because the Prana of all individual parts gradually becomes connected through such efforts. This is when you can feel yourself as a pranic deity, or subtle energy-bodied being. You feel yourself as a single entity of energy, which is your subtle body that you want to eventually emerge from your physical shell as an independent life entity capable of the eight *siddhi*.

There are various exercises available that can lead you to being able to feel the entire Prana of your body as a single unit. The point of all these techniques is to try to first move your Prana through your muscles by pulling them with stretching exercises, mentally focusing (concentrating) on them, or by guiding your Prana along special pathways, and in this way "wash" those pathways with Prana that then purifies your underlying subtle body. This is called inner energy Yoga, Tantric Yoga, Tantra, *kriya* yoga, kundalini yoga, laya yoga, Vajrayana, *anapana*, inner alchemy, *nei-gong, neijiaquan, nei-dan, boran kammatthana*, etc.

Many spiritual traditions have such exercises, and in India the main sources are the Yoga and Hindu tantric traditions, but people don't understand their purpose or how to practice correctly because the principles are hidden.

Tibetan Buddhism, which we find in some monasteries of northern India, has calisthenics-like practices called Trulkhor ("magical movements") that combine some basic yoga exercises with inner energy work but Hatha Yoga, being more extensive in stretching all your muscles and teaching you to gain control over the functions of internal organs, is *without question far more beneficial and powerful* especially when combined with inner energy exercises such as those explained herein or in *Neijia Yoga*.

Eventually from inner energy work you will be able to feel the entire Prana of your body as a single unit, and its internal circulation will become orderly and free without obstructions or dysfunctions. The reason that devas are capable of the eight *siddhi* of *anima* (shrinking), *mahima* (enlarging), *garima* (heaviness), *laghima* (lightening) and so on is because their body is Prana energy, and so they can make it bigger or smaller or denser or lighter upon thought after training to do so. The Causal body has even higher capabilities while the "formless" Supra-Causal and Immanence (Buddha) bodies have capabilities still higher because their energy bodies are of an even higher transcendental nature.

When practicing such techniques you should always try *to physically feel the Prana within the location of your body being emphasized rather than just imagining that you are moving that Prana*. Otherwise you will often find yourself thinking you are moving your Prana *but it will just be an imagination in your head that doesn't connect with your energy rather than actually moving your energy due to genuine Prana circulations*. Devas will come rushing in to practice mental manipulations of your thoughts that are disconnected from your Prana, so whenever you work at moving your Prana within you must *feel that energy* and impel the movements to actually happen. Don't get caught up in the illusions of devas who are practicing their abilities at thought manipulation without ever connecting with your Prana.

You could spend years in wasted efforts if your mental thoughts do not actually connect with and grab the Prana throughout your body where you want to be feeling and moving that energy. You still cannot practice visualizing events in your mind without connecting with, touching, grabbing or feeling the actual Prana in your muscles. Thinking about moving your Prana is different than actually doing this, which is the point of such practices, so always make sure that whatever energy flows you visualize, imagine or lead within you are actually doing that and are *being felt within your physical body* because you are supposed to connect your will and intent with your Prana in those regions to actually lead the energy within them.

After all body areas are stretched you should try to feel the Prana energy of your entire body as a single unit because you want the energies of its different parts to become seamlessly threaded together as a single unit without any obstructions between various sections. In particular, you want the top and bottom sections of your body to be joined. The Prana everywhere within your body should become naturally connected for seamless circulation because then you are really cultivating the fullness of your subtle body and preparing it for emergence.

SUMMARY

The entire purpose of Yoga is to greater health and longevity and to *purify your subtle body so that it can emerge from its physical shell*, which normally happens at death when the connection between the two snaps. Unfortunately, most people don't know that this is the first spiritual objective. Once all your Prana is purified and linked so that it feels as if it is just one single unit then the birth of the spiritual body can occur. Since that event comes after completing the task of frictionless inner Prana circulation then at that stage of cultivation your body will feel blissful, and at times almost as non-existent. Furthermore, the smooth internal Prana flow will produce a calmer temperament of peace and quiescence that you might also term blissful.

This is the *sat, chit, ananda* of Hinduism where the mind (consciousness) becomes open, clear and empty (blissful) while your body is so comfortable it feels is as if it is not there. To transform a body into the healthiest state possible you will find that diet, medical/nutritional remedies, exercise, detoxification and physical manipulation are also important. For optimizing your body's structural alignment, if possible you should first undergo chiropractic treatments to align your bones and then AMIT therapy to reactivate all your muscles whose loads have been shifted onto adjacent muscles due to accidents. Then you should engage in either passive stretching exercises (Yoga, Pilates, etc.) or active exercises (dance, rebounding, pogo stick bouncing exercises, martial arts, Ginastica Natural, sports, athletics etc.) in conjunction with inner Prana exercises and mental work.

The best physical development work includes yoga (and Pilates) practice, the soft martial arts, acrobatics or sports, and dance. Classical Indian dancing will help you develop exceptional physical grace and elegance while also stretching all your muscles and circulating your Prana in ways designed to cleanse your subtle body. That is why it uses unusual movements, which is because they have been proven to move your Prana in special helpful ways rather than just serving as beautiful exercise. Dancing is also a form of beneficial cardiovascular exercise, but it especially produces an elegance of physical movement seen in your legs, arms, shoulders and other areas while forcing you to open the *nadi* meridians in all your body parts through movement.

The best yoga teacher is not the one with the highest personal attainment, or the one who is the best teacher/instructor, but the one who is enlightened and uses his own energy to push open the *nadis* of your body when you are doing stretching routines because this is what frees the independent subtle body whilst alive, thus giving you the deva body attainment that makes you a *jivanmukta*.

Yoga master Yogeshwara Ramamohana Brahmachari and Master Tirumalai Krishnamacharya are examples of the many Indian sages who attained the subtle body attainment of enlightenment through the pathway of Yoga practice that must always include internal energy exercises in additional to stretching poses and meditation work. Krishnamacharya was once taught in a dream by the Vaishnava Saint Nathamuni, author of *Yoga Rahasya (The Secrets of Yoga)*.

Many masters in China have become enlightened through the road of martial arts practice with its inner energy exercises – such as Sun Lutang and Guo Yunshen (see *The Secret Inner Teachings of Daoism*) – but what is especially hidden in Hinduism are the spiritual benefits of Yoga in helping you achieve transcendence.

CHAPTER 7
PRANAYAMA TO OPEN YOUR *NADIS*

Before we get into the topic of pranayama, the first principle to understand about breathing is that we should all be nose breathers instead of mouth breathers. The science is very clear: you want to learn to breathe slowly, through your nose, and breathe less. When you breath in through your nose the air undergoes a process of pressurization, heating and purification whereby each nasal inhalation increases blood oxygenation by about 20% more than that achieved by mouth breathing. This amount of oxygen, which is energy to your body, will produce a big transformative effect on your life.

Spiritual schools have said for centuries that the right side of the body is related to masculine (Yang) Prana that produces stimulating or heating body effects while the left side is associated with feminine (Yin) Prana that produces relaxing body effects. Twenty years of scientific studies prove yogic teachings that breathing through the right nostril increases your body heat, heart rate and circulation which are stimulating effects on the body. Right nostril breathing also stimulates the left side of the brain that is associated with logical mental functions. Left nostril breathing, on the other hand, calms us, decreases our heart rate, and is more associated with creative mental functions.

Your body automatically alternates between left and right side breathing throughout the day while stimulating these different results, and the alternate nostril breathing practices of yoga help you to optimize the benefits you receive. If you breathe through the mouth you are getting zero of these benefits while possibly contributing to serious health issues.

There are many mysteries concerning breathing that we simply do not understand yet. For instance, the famous *tummo* breathing of Tibet can raise your body temperature by seventeen degrees. Researchers found that some Tibetan *tummo* practitioners are able to reduce their metabolism more than 60% – the lowest amount ever recorded – while superheating their bodies and yet no one understands how. Their breathing methods create thermogenesis that produces heat in the body. The truth is that they are stimulating their Yang Prana.

As to the various pranayama breathing exercises promoted in the Yoga schools of India, they aim at stabilizing your mind and have therapeutic effects on your body. They can expand your lung capacity, increase your blood flow, oxygenate your blood and temporarily alkalinize your body (which in turn affects your thinking processes). Changing your pH will affect your internal chemistry and therefore your mental states through the route of altering the processes of consciousness.

The first important step in learning pranayama breathing exercises is to master the *asana* of a stable posture. Afterwards you can start to master pranayama, which is basically a set of practices for regulating your breath that will, in turn, help to harmonize the Prana of your body and thereby purify your inner subtle body.

Anapana exercises, which originated in India, involve a subsequent step of using the power of your breathing to push your Prana around inside your body to wash its tissues. You breathe in and out and use that pumping power together with your thoughts to push your internal energy around your body to wash all its parts such as your arms and legs, genitals, head and trunk.

In the ancient Indian *anapana* exercises that were revealed in Buddhism you were taught to "breathe in and experience (feel) your entire body, breathe out and experience (feel) your entire body; breathe in and calm your entire body formation, breathe out and calm your entire body formation; breathe in while internally arousing the emotion of joy, breathe out while internally arousing the emotion of joy; breathe in while arousing the sensation of pleasurable bliss within you, breathe out while arousing the sensation of pleasurable bliss within you; breathe in and calm your mind, breathe out and calm your mind ..."

While doing this you were also taught to notice the "hotness" and "coldness" of your breath, which means the Yang Prana and Yin Prana of your body (its masculine and feminine energies) since they are considered hot and cold or heating and cooling by nature. Nearly everyone misses this meaning. The purpose of pranayama and *anapana* is to cultivate your Prana, so the two modalities of masculine and feminine were designated by the words "hot" and "cold" in ancient India whereas "Yang" and "Yin" are prevalent in China.

As I mentioned previously, the grand objective of spiritual liberation is so important that you must open your mind to accept useful teachings from all sorts of traditions. If people, for instance, want to focus on stretching and gaining control of the Prana in every muscle of their body then they should focus on Yoga from India whereas if they are interested in martial arts and how to channel Prana energy into the legs or arms for punches and kicks then they should focus on the Asian martial arts traditions such as those from China.

The idea is of ancient pranayama and *anapana* teachings is that after you breathe in you should try to feel the Prana of your entire body as a unit, namely the sensation of your entire body as a wholeness that is felt not just because you have nerves but because your body is enlivened by Prana energy which animates it. Furthermore, what is not mentioned are the more complete instructions that you should at times do this while experiencing or holding different attitudes such as the positive Yang emotions of joy, pride, authority, confidence, egotism, anger, exuberance, success, winning, love, closeness to others, pleasure, happiness, etc. ... and the negative Yin emotions of feeling guilt, anxiety, fear, humility, self-surrender, powerlessness, shame, sadness, disgust, despair, hopelessness, depression, and so on.

If you try to strongly feel positive or negative (Yang or Yin) emotions in such a way that it stimulates your appropriate Prana accordingly this is basically the secret basis of the *Viramarga* (Path of Heroes) method of Kaula Tantra that is related to the Nyasa Yoga practices of Hinduism.

This is also the basis of * the *bhakti* reverence practice where you identify with a deity such as Shiva, Murugan or Krishna, * the *yidam* deity yoga techniques of Newar and Vajrayana Buddhism that have you do similar exercises, * the basis of the *boran kammatthana* techniques of Southern Esoteric Buddhism, * Guru yoga where you identify with an enlightened spiritual master and invite his energy into your body while visualizing that you two become one, * the Four Immeasurable Attitudes meditation practice of Buddhism, * and the *nei-gong* inner alchemy methods of Chinese Taoism.

In the Nyasa Yoga practices of Hinduism, for instance, you touch various parts of your body, which means bringing your mental focus there, while chanting specific mantras for that body part and simultaneously envisioning that a divinity's energy comes into your body to energize those parts.

Shri Vidya followers practice Nyasa Yoga and *Sahasranama* recitation, which is a Hindu hymn of praise where a deity is referred to by 1,000 or more different descriptive names. It is said that if you read such hymns every day with devotion and attention you will attain peace of mind, patience, prosperity, mental stability, memory and reputation. By reciting the "Thousand Names of the Divine Mother" (*Sri Lalita Sahasranama*) on a daily basis, for instance, people have sometimes become cured of mental disturbances or physical imbalances and become like a new person. The same can be said for reciting the *Sahasranama* of other deities because this consistent practice invites their attention for an intercession of grace to intervene in your body, consciousness and life to help what can be helped.

For instance, Bhaskararaya Makhin was a great enlightened spiritual master in the Srividya tradition of Shakta Tantrism (Shaktism) who popularized the worship of Sri Lalita Tripura Sundari, which is a practice that helps to purify your Yin Prana. She once materialized on his shoulders to help him defeat a group of scholars in religious debate. Bhaskararaya Makhin also wrote the remarkable *Khadyota* ("That which enlightens the sky") commentary on the *Ganesha Sahasranama* and advised people to recite these or the *Sahasranama* of other deities.

As you recite the descriptions within a *Sahasranama* your Prana changes with each praise because your mind associates it with thoughts that cause a response in your Prana. Proceeding through that flow of washings every day will purify your Prana from this effect, as well as from the effect of enlightened beings in that lineage coming to bless you with Prana washings. If you concentrate on the energy aroused within you when you ponder each praise within a *Sahasranama*, rather than just recite them, the practice become hundreds of times more effective.

As stated, anyone who performs such a tantric *bhakti* practice also attracts the attention of enlightened beings sworn to protect or sponsor it, who will emanate a *nirmanakaya* to wash your Prana. For instance, during a *yajna* ritual the chanting of a mantra pertaining to a particular deity calls forth that deity or some enlightened individual within that lineage of enlightenment that helps take on the role of representing that deity and performing that deity's sworn duties. The same happens when you read the *Sahasranama* of a deity, such as Ganesh, because an enlightened someone will generate a *nirmanakaya* to come and wash your tissues. How much that happens depends upon how deeply you arouse different Prana excitations within yourself when reading the *Sahasranama*. If you are doing a better job then everyone else in arousing your emotions one by one during recitation by "extending and fulfilling," then they will use you as the demonstration piece for how to wash people correctly so that your work will be rewarded.

This secret event of your Prana becoming washed through a *nirmanakaya* emanation happens when someone worthy performs other Hindu pujas or rituals too for you cannot become enlightened unless you first attain the subtle body, and you cannot attain the subtle body unless your Prana is washed by enlightened masters and the guardian spirits of your locale, and this will not happen unless you are a virtuous person of good character who performs the practices that attract their participation in your case.

When you perform yogic practices, however, you are usually relying on your own efforts to wash your *pranamaya kosha* until you reach a stage where your kundalini awakening begins. When and if that happens it involves higher beings working on your inner purification efforts without you knowing about their involvement, and that is the big secret within Hinduism and its various spiritual *sadhana*.

These techniques are essentially versions of the *anapana* method just mentioned where you move your Prana, using the pulsing and pushing power of your breathing, while focusing on either positive or negative thoughts to arouse corresponding energies that flavor your Prana while it is being washed. No one has ever made the connection that these methods of inner energy work are basically the same but they all constitute kundalini yoga.

The basic commonality is (1) changing your attitude or emotions to either a Yin or Yang state that alters the quality of your Prana energy accordingly, and (2) then feeling that Prana energy state throughout your body while sometimes churning, rotating, revolving, lapping, shaking or guiding that energy within you. You can push that energy around using the power of your breathing, which is the technique of *anapana* and some forms of pranayama, or use other methods to help circulate your Prana in order to entirely wash your bodily form. Mantra practice moves your Prana through sound while you can also just lead it around your body using your thoughts and will rather than push it around with your breathing power.

The basic practice is to hold onto a special attitude that is deep enough to shake your body's energy state while you actively wash your body everywhere with that unusual energy. You want to wash all the energy modalities within your subtle body, instead of always remaining in one energy mode alone, which is why students going through the twelve-year kundalini purification process are put through a roller coaster of different emotions and attitudes that alter the energy of their Prana.

Anapana and certain pranayama practices use your breathing to push the Prana around within your body but the secret instructions in Hinduism are that you should do so while holding onto a dominant attitude that changes its tonality. What determines your energy vibrations at any given moment is your attitude because of the mind-body-energy connections, and so you must do this for both Yin and Yang (masculine and feminine) impacts on your Prana energy.

This is the secret principle of the highest pranayama techniques of Yoga. When breathing you should try to feel the entire Prana of your body, and then try to purify your next immediately higher spiritual body made of Prana (your yet-to-emerge subtle body) by washing it with moving energy while holding different Yin or Yang emotions such as the "sensation of pleasurable bliss," or admiration of a deity's greatness evoked during worship or when reading a *Sahasranama*. You can also do this while listening to mood altering music during extensive sets of inhalation-exhalation cycles. There are lots of ways to do this.

Most pranayama techniques that people practice involve alternate nostril breathing where you control your breathing in a rhythmical fashion that alternately focuses on the left and right sides of your body. These are the feminine and masculine sides of your body, respectively. When you practice alternate nostril breathing you actually should feel the entire Prana of each side (half) of your body because that holding of your Prana in an entire body half, and then switching the focus of condensed energy to the other side, will make a little bit of inroads in helping to transform it.

The ultimate aim of alternate nostril breathing is to help you purify your Prana by using your breathing that moves in and out to push your Prana on your left and right sides if you concentrate on feeling that energy on each side of your body. Alternate nostril breathing instructions focus you on controlling your breathing – and thus ultimately your Prana circulation – while leaving out the important detail that this is supposed to be Prana cultivation. Instead they are usually described as calming your energy and mind such as by harmonizing your body's energy. This is a trivial, mundane result compared to what we are truly after. Nevertheless it is a start.

When breathing you should feel the entire Prana of your body, or the Prana on the sides of your body according to the practices being used, and then wash that energy by holding different Yin or Yang emotions during extensive sets of inhalation-exhalation cycles where you really try to make contact with those energies and excite them.

Pranayama expertise begins with developing harmonious respiration where you also feel the energy on each side of your body, or your body as a whole in total. It then gradually proceeds to the stage of washing/purifying your Prana through rhythmical breathing that gently works to open *nadi* pathways on each side of the body when stimulated with intent, and then works at gaining control over the pranic life-currents or inner vital force of your entire body as a whole.

Our thinking is connected with the rate and other dimensions of our breathing, so pranayama is one of the avenues for gaining control of the mind but through breath control.

Despite all the talk about calming your mind the truth is that pranayama ultimately aims to help you start gaining control of the life-currents of Prana within your body through the avenue of mastering your breathing, breath and their ability to link with and move the Prana of your body. Gradually through experience and then mastery you will become able to direct your internal energy to go to any area of your body you desire to "wash" those tissues. Then pranayama becomes a spiritual method used to help purify your subtle body.

When working on the Prana within your body it is especially important to wash the lower regions of your torso from the pelvis down to your feet, including your genitalia, as well as your ears, nose and the hands and fingers. These are areas of the body where Prana flow is bottlenecked and difficult to improve as evidence by thermal heat mapping pictures of blood circulation. Wherever a thermal heat mapping picture shows poor blood circulation in the body it is also the case that there are problems with perfect Prana circulation in that area too, which is why you should especially work on circulating your energy (rotating it in countless revolutions) any areas of the body that show up with low temperatures in such heat images. Another technique is to expand and then shrink your Prana through your skin in various locations, or draw Prana into your skin from the environment at pertinent daily times when those energies are strongest.

By learning to move your breath in the certain specific ways advocated by pranayama exercises such as those in the *Hatha Yoga Pradipika* as well as *Bhastrika* "bellows breathing," *Visama Vritti* "uneven breathing," *Anuloma* "with the grain," and *Kapalabhati* "Skull shining" exercises, you can end up moving your Prana because your breathing can push your Prana, and moving your Prana across your body will end up purifying it because of the friction it undergoes. Eventually with much practice and experience you will become able to simply grab and move your Prana by your will, which then becomes kundalini yoga, *kriya* yoga, *anapana* or what the Chinese spiritual cultivation schools call inner alchemy, *nei-dan* exercises, *neijia* or *nei-gong* work. As part of his cultivation efforts, the enlightened Yogi Nagendranath Bhaduri mastered the pranayama breathing practices of *Patanjali's Yoga Sutras* that enabled him to be able to perform miracles due to his consequential enlightenment.

During advanced pranayama exercises the yoga practitioners will focus their breathing exercises on moving their body's Prana and affecting specific *nadi* channels or body regions in order to improve their Prana's circulation, which of course then affects your subtle body that is made of this energy. Practitioners will wash entire body sections associated with the supposed astral chakras, and wash the tissues of their body so that their subtle body's energy becomes significantly elevated or markedly more refined and different than the coarse vitality of the rest of your body, and thus able to separate from it because of its refinement or purity difference. When you compare the energy of a crude individual from that of a refined yogi or even educated college graduate you can understand the difference that we are talking about.

As an alternative to holding dominant attitudes or emotions during practice, when pranayama can be accompanied by the rhythmical recitation of specific mantras (that vitalize your Prana or ask enlightened beings to come to help you) this then makes it hundreds of times more powerful than when practiced without mantra recitation. As stated, certain mantras request help from spiritual beings for purifying your Prana while other mantras just rhythmically move your Prana on its own because of the resonating vibrational power of the sounds, especially when they are *bijas* for specific areas of your body.

If during pranayama practice you visualize Prana currents moving within you along certain pathways, or you hold your Prana stationary at specific locations within your body (while perhaps rotating at those spots), and if you also simultaneously try to feel these energies while engendering certain emotions or concentrating on feeling the sensations of Prana … then this will do more to purifying your Prana then just moving or holding your Prana stationary. This addition of emotional input will increase the power of the practice, namely its ability to purify your subtle energy so that you are ascending in spiritual purification.

By purifying your inner subtle body you burn away ages of accumulated karma (because it enables you to escape the human material realm forever) through these and other cultivation acts of purification. Because you can ascend to a higher spiritual body this is why Hinduism says that such and such a spiritual practice will "purify your karma."

You can also visualize that the pranayama efforts are purifying you by creating mental images of poisons leaving your physical body through your feet, which is a common Buddhist visualization technique. Sometimes people will get dreams of various sorts showing them what to do, or which simply symbolize that they are purifying their body. You might also visualize your body becoming as transparent as crystal during various relevant practices, such as pranayama, through images of vaporous black energy being expelled upon your exhalations or images of your body shining as a brilliant light because it has excreted all poisons.

Pranayama exercises begin with the regulation of your respiratory breathing. As you gradually master them they proceed to a subsequent stage of washing (or purifying) your Prana until you reach a final stage of gaining control over that Prana. You want to reach a stage where you have complete control over the life-currents or movements of inner vital force within your entire body although perfect control only really happens with the highest transcendental bodies of existence since they are nearer to being pure energy.

In other words, pranayama has the aim not just of improving your breathing but aims to help you start gaining control of the life-currents of Prana within your body since this washes your subtle body and prepares you for the higher existence as a deva whose shape you can somewhat manipulate because your entire body is composed of Prana. That's why the devas can shrink their body in size, or make it larger (with limitations), make it heavier or lighter and so on. In Hinduism there are various stories where two spiritual masters were having a contest with one another and one turned his body into an insect, which actually means they shrank their body down to a small size via the *anima siddhi* hoping that they wouldn't be noticed. Hanuman used the same power to shrink his body when he was swallowed by a female demon named Surasa.

Gradually, after lots of practice, you can direct your internal energy to go to any area of your body you desire. You can then "wash" those tissues through special patterns of rotating your Prana and thereby purify your inner subtle body so that it becomes purified enough to become differentiated from the coarser, cruder, denser energy of your unpurified material nature. Then it can ascend out of your physical shell as a transcendental body attainment, otherwise you must simply wait for this decoupling upon your death and arise in a body that is the impure stage of the Srotapanna Arhat that needs to be purified to avoid rebirth on the physical plane.

This is what you go through during the twelve years of the kundalini awakening experience that all enlightened saints go through, but they will not reveal these or other details because the procedure is at times quite brutal in terms of suffering and they don't want people to be scared away from the exact practices that will lead to ascension. During the first several years of the process you want the various Prana revolutions to speed up, then in later years qualified heavenly students are all tested as to whether they can find something you feel guilty about in your past behavior, they'll make those memories and guilty feelings arise and then they'll explain them away so that the feelings immediately disappear. In the last years of the process it will concentrate on your legs and feet, which will become very cold due to Yin purification work, and the masters will continuously crimp your right flank, give you pain around your right teeth and under their nerves, hurt your asshole, play with your ears, do fairy brushing all over your head and face, and give you pain in all sorts of unusual ways near the end. At times it seems unbearable.

These attacks will differ by tradition, and it bodes well to have an enlightened master nearby who will protect you from extremes. This is a terrible process where you will get pummeled so much that no deva will ask with jealousy, "why him and not me?" It is best if you go through this while living in the remote countryside rather than live in a major city because your ready availability to all the local devas in a city who don't have to travel to see you will certainly mean extra visitors and troubles rather than just completing your process. It is also dangerous to go through the kundalini purification process under a Saturn, Mars, Neptune, Pluto or Uranus astrolocality line. The best situation is when you live with an enlightened master when going through the process.

Thermal pictures of the human body show a big temperature drop at the region of the hips and extending to the legs, which is why this region undergoes a lot of Yin purification during the kundalini years. Martial artists train to have their feet feel like they are blending into the earth to help perform some of these Yin transformations. It is especially important when doing Prana exercises to open up the lower regions of your body from the pelvis to the feet – as well as your genitalia, ears, nose and the hands and fingers – since the thermal heat map pictures show these all suffer from low blood circulation and Prana circulation bottlenecks or inefficiencies.

Chinese Taoism has special exercises for improving Prana flow to the male genitalia that have circulation issues because they stick out from the rest of the body in an awkward fashion to lower their temperature. Unbeknownst to most Yoga practitioners, the *vajroli mudra* exercises are also designed to do this by teaching men to draw energy into themselves through the tip and sides of the penis during breath inhalations in order to cleanse it with Prana rather than to actually suck substances into the bladder. You certainly must never do this to a women (try to suck away her energy) during sexual congress as it will hurt her, and Taoism warns against this.

By learning to operate your breathing in certain specific ways you can end up stimulating or moving your Prana because the two are connected, and when you force your Prana to move within your body this will end up purifying it because you are frictionally churning it against itself. As often explained, churning your energy will gradually wash it of impurities just as the friction of a *dhobiwallah* washing clothes against rocks in a river will cleanse them of dirt and stains. A continuous circulation of Prana along well-defined *nadi* routes will force the more pure pranic energy to differentiate itself from the impure fractions within the body, and in that way you prepare yourself for an ascension from gross matter.

Eventually with skill you can simply grab and move this Prana by your will, which then becomes *anapana* practice, kundalini yoga, *kriya* yoga, or the *nei-dan* exercises, inner alchemy, *neijiaquan* or *nei-gong* work of Chinese Taoism. In Tibetan Buddhism the Tsalung Completion phase practices focus breathing exercises on the body's vital energy and channels, which is also akin to these practices of inner *nei-gong*.

My books *Neijia Yoga* and *Nyasa Yoga* give an entire set of Prana exercises that accomplish the same thing along with many explanatory principles and details. *Arhat Yoga* explains the overall procedure. Also, when pranayama is further conjoined with mantra recitation it becomes one hundred times more powerful than when practiced alone. This is because sound power rhythms will move your Prana through resonance and mantra recitation also requests help from spiritual beings to purify your Prana through *nirmanakaya* emanations. Sometimes they respond and sometimes they don't. It all depends on the mantra you use, area you live in, your natal astrological configuration and transits impacting you, and the individuals charged with responding in your locale.

If during pranayama practice you simultaneously visualize Prana currents moving within your body or hold the Prana stationary at locations within your body and try to feel those energies, *while also trying to arouse strong emotions or dominant attitudes that will provoke Prana excitation* (just as great fear or great joy would give rise to inner energy sensations) then these emotional extras will also increase its power. Certain breathing patterns can also affect the oxygenation of your blood (your biochemistry) and some can stimulate your emotions, both of which can impact your internal energy as well.

Pranayama attainments greatly depend upon the intensity of the practitioner's efforts. It is recommended to practice them two to four times per day when you have an empty stomach and are not tired or worried.

Wim Hof breathing practices, freediving breathing practices, and other forms of breathwork (such as Buteyko breathing, coherent breathing, hypoventilation, holotropic breathwork, embryonic breathing, *tummo* breathing, *sudarshin kriya*, etc.) are just a few of the many types of breathing exercises than can enlarge the scope of your pranayama efforts if you remember what you are ultimately trying to do, which is affect the flow of inner energy within your body so that it washes itself by either changing its tone quality, or by changing the attributes of its movements including its speed, strength and direction of inner movement.

These other types of breathing exercise are different from traditional yoga techniques but are especially good at lengthening the amount of time you can remain in *kumbhaka* pranayama retention states that are one of the most important types of pranayama exercise.

WIM HOF BREATHING

The one scientifically tested pranayama technique that ancient Yoga masters had not discovered but which individuals might daily practice is Wim Hof breathing, which is a type of controlled rhythmical power breathing (hyperventilation) followed by a period of breath retention.

To practice Wim Hof breathing you take in a powerful breath that fully fills your lungs. Then you almost immediately breathe out, but not forcefully, which brings a lot of oxygen into your system because it is similar to hyperventilation. You repeat this at a steady pace thirty to forty times, which may produce some harmless tingling sensations in your fingers and feet as well as some light-headedness.

After completing thirty to forty cycles of this controlled hyperventilation, on the last inhalation of this series you take in one final inhalation as deeply as possible and let it out completely. Then, you stop breathing and hold your lungs empty for as long as possible until you feel the urge to breath again. When a strong urge to breathe in occurs, you must draw in one big recovery breath to fill your lungs, chest and belly. Hold this recovery breath for around 15–20 seconds and then let it go.

In summary, you have controlled hyperventilation done in three to six sets of 30-40 breaths, and on the last breath of each set you exhale and hold your lungs empty for 1-3 minutes before taking a deep recovery breath that you hold for 15-20 seconds. If you so desire you can repeat the recovery breath three to four times.

Wim Hof found that this breathing technique stimulates an individual's stress response. It increases an individual's metabolism because the special hyperventilation breathing increases the body's temperature although the breath retention phase is actually the most important part of his method.

Breathing through your nose stimulates the parasympathetic nervous system in the lower lungs. In cold temperatures it is hard to breath through your nose while breathing through your mouth creates more heat and fire because you are stimulating sympathetic receptors. The Wim Hof method uses hyperventilation (with mouth breathing allowed) where you breathe in twice the length of time as you breathe out, thus doubling your breath intake time by forcing an inhalation to go longer than normal. This produces adrenaline and heat thus creating thermogenesis.

The *tummo* breathing methods of Tibet are also designed to create heat within the body whereas in India, because it is a hot country, the yogis, sadhus and sannyasins usually train on cultivating their cooling Yin Prana because they need it. A famous yogic exercise for doing so involves *Panchangni tapsasya*, which is a special type of Prana purification that involves arousing your internal Yin energy symbolized by female Devas. In *Panchangni tapsasya* you sit in meditation throughout the day surrounded by four burning fires while sitting under the hot midday sun. To survive it you must increase the generation of inner cooling by demonstrating mastery of your Yin Prana.

The Wim Hof method combines *bhastrika* (fast rhythmic

breathing) with *nisshesha rechaka*, which is breath retention beyond the comfort zone where you are holding your breath until you've reached the point of maximum effort and have to breathe in again.

The Wim Hof method tricks you into being able to hold your breath for longer periods of time. This exercises your mitochondria and trains them to become more efficient in their use of oxygen. Also, by holding your breath you create an intermittent hypoxic state (a lower level of oxygen than is normal) and your body, in response, produces more blood cells.

Over time you end up with better vascularization – more capillaries and blood vessels – that make you more efficient at using less oxygen because you're teaching yourself to adapt to low oxygen. More capillaries and better oxygen utilization is beneficial for better Prana circulation. Tibetan, for instance, because of their genetics have many more capillaries than others but much less hemoglobin flowing through their brains.

The Wim Hof breathing has many benefits, and it also produces a calm state conducive to meditation. Because of those benefits it can be performed *just prior* to meditation practice. As with many other cultivation techniques, it actually energizes your body's Prana but does so through controlled hyperventilation.

Yet another quick pre-meditation breathing routine you should know about, called "Ahh-Breathing," can also be performed just prior to sitting meditation practice because it produces an instant stilling of your thought-stream. This method, invented by Lee Shu-Mei, should be taught to everyone who practices meditation and wants to immediately enter a quiet state of mind when they sit down to practice.

To practice Ahh-Breathing you breathe in through your nose and then exhale slowly through your mouth three to five times in succession. Every out-exhalation should be long and slow *as if you are letting go of every possible thought or concern bothering you in life*, and you silently say "Ahhh" when exhaling while shedding yourself of worries or anxieties along with your breath.

The exhalation should be about twice as long as your inhalation, and on the exhalation you let go of all the tension and concerns that are burdening your mind. After you do this several times in a row and feel "now life is perfect," you can *instantly* enter into a quiet meditative state that would normally be impossible without this preliminary breathing exercise.

Ahh-Breathing and Wim Hof breathing (and possibly *Jiujie Fofeng* "Nine Bottled Winds" practice if you want to increase your lung capacity and number of capillaries) should become part of your daily cultivation practice just prior to meditation sessions. As with all pranayama techniques, the Wim Hof breathing method should be practiced two to four times per day on an empty stomach when you are not tired or worried. Ahh-Breathing is practiced just prior to meditation practice because it instantly calms the mind so that you start off in meditation with a quiet mind to begin with.

THE IMPORTANCE OF PRANAYAMA

As a point of mundane physical culture, yogis hold *asanas* for health and well-being, but they practice pranayama to *eliminate sickness and lengthen their life span*. Therefore they usually become interested in maintaining longer and longer breath retention times because this clears out their *nadi* channels, and this is the reason why many yogis can live to a very old age.

The great enlightened yoga master Tirumalai Krishnamacharya said that as you get older you need to do more pranayama because it will help improve your health and longevity. In particular, *kumbhaka* pranayama will expand your lung capacity (VO2 max) and open up Prana circulatory passages, which will have a positive impact on your longevity. If you expand your lung capacity an athlete can get faster at running as well.

The spiritual reasons for practicing pranayama are that it expands your lung capacity, enables your body to hold more Prana, and it also improves the internal flow of that vital life energy because it blasts through any obstructions in the routes of your inner Prana flow. Thus it helps to purify your subtle body that is contained within your physical body.

As a general principle, the more *you become energy yourself* the more transcendent your stage of beingness. This truth arises from the fact that each new spiritual body sheds its impure layers of denser energy in order to arise through "negation," "extinguishment," "purification" or "stripping away," and thus each body within Saguna Brahman, the universe (Prakirti or Shakti), progressively rises towards getting closer to the purity of the primordial essence plane. Of course the first emanation would be a singular energy that could not be turned into a composite body structure, so there is a limit as to how high you can ascend in producing transcendental bodies out of energies because you still need particles for a body structure to have linkages that produce form. At the highest extreme, or highest body possible, you can only keep purifying its nature by raising its frequency or vibration through practices that improve its purity and inner energy flows.

Once you touch the innermost energy matrix of your body and can go no higher you reach the apex of spiritual practice where your *atman* is then enlivened by a higher life force that also illuminates your mind, but no further body can be produced. This is when you become one with Vishnu, Shiva, Krishna, Lalita Devi, Shakti, Ishvara, Ganesh, Brahma and so on since that more transcendent realm of higher energy penetrates and powers all other living beings and their consciousnesses too. We can colloquially say that these energies are thus "the enjoyer of all experiences (of sentient beings)" and the "enjoyer of all consciousnesses" even though, lacking a body and ego-sense, it is not a sentient being but just many inanimate energies that don't form any special pattern. To say it is a deity is only a manner of speaking to help motivate your spiritual progress, and if that formlessness of surging energies could somehow be turned into a deity we would then call it the Supreme Deity such as Ishvara.

Ramana Maharshi explained, "Iswara, the personal God, the supreme creator of the universe really does exist. But this is true only from the relative standpoint of those who have not realized the truth, those people who believe in the reality of individual souls. From the absolute standpoint the sage cannot accept any other existence than the impersonal Self, one and formless."

Sri Nisargadatta also said that our vital force is really *Pranesvar*, the Lord of Energy, the effective God of our lives and world, "the highest principles," the "Great Power of Great Energy without which there cannot be consciousness." He said that "This (ultimate) life force is God and God is this life force." Beyond the *atman* is the supra-personal universal life force that merges with the light or illumination of the mind of the *atman*.

In other words, only the fundamental substratum truly exists while everything else is an impermanent construction that will one day decay, so the foundational substrate is the only true status of

God. If you want a personal God who is a Creator then you have to proceed to an emanated level that is an evolute serving as the manifesting Mother of all Creation. Thus Shakti, Ishvara, Saguna Brahman, Brahma, or the Womb Matrix would be the Creator God if you want to assume there is a Creator being. However, the absolute nature is actually inanimate and so would be any Creator energies.

Conventionally, you can consider the highest energies of emanation a deity because those unattainable energies span the universe as the life force surging within you that also enlivens all beings, and all sentient beings are permeated and composed by those energies. You can then, as a way of speaking also consider their illusory minds a portion of the universal consciousness. However, this is a realm of moving energy rather than the ultimate non-moving source nature of the universe, Nirguna Brahman (Parabrahman, Paramatman, Purusha, Nondual Reality), that can be considered the True Self or absolute unchanging source of all life, manifestation and consciousness.

This explains why Hinduism sometimes refers to the highest manifest planes of vibrational, energetic existence as "consciousness" or "life force" since they power those manifestations whereas the highest planes, if they are not composite energies, are not in any sense living or animate. They are simply fields or energies that move. Nevertheless they pervade your life force and consciousness as the animating force and we are all composite, conditional illusory beings of energy that exist for a period of time and then disappear forever … unless there is such a thing as reincarnation to manage our re-emergence as life, or a state of transcendental attainment so refined in terms of pure energy that it can last nearly forever without decay, or a body of transcendental energy which can duplicate energetic copies of itself to continue living in place of the original energy body should it decay, or …

We call ourselves sentient beings with life and consciousness, but from the aspect of the Brahman there is no such thing as the manifest universe, life or the processes of consciousness, while from the manifest aspect of Shakti or Creation we are just interfused composite agglomerations of various energies in greater or lesser degrees of condensing, compression or vibration rather than actual intrinsic selves with lives and a sentience that stands apart from the universe as an independent process. Sentience or consciousness is actually just another insentient process within the universe rather than actually something that transcends it as real consciousness. There is no such true thing as a true self, *jiva*, soul or sentient being, but those are the names we call ourselves within the delusion of an existence that comes about due to a *Maya* consciousness. To understand this is part of the understanding required of Advaita Vedanta, and is called self-realization.

Now you understand how things stand. But still you must live life, and should maximize your life experience to include the full expression of your consciousness, free of limiting mental patterns, where you also experience the glory of *joie de vivre* during life as much as you can.

What you must realize is the following: you will always exist at some stage of condensed agglomeration rather than as an insentient formlessness that does not have a body, and so while you realize that your level of densification is not the way the universe really exists, and while you can realize that the way you see the world at your level of densification is also an illusion, it does exist for you so you should pursue the *ananda* of existence that comes from relationships, accomplishments, respect from others, health, *Artha*, *Kama*, and so on.

These books have already been recommended for further explanations and are again recommended if you want to understand Purusha-Prakirti or Nirguna-Saguna Brahman: *Avadhuta Gita of Dattatreya* (Swami Chetanananda), *Astavakkra Samhita* (Swami Nityaswarupananda), *Traditional Theory of Evolution and Its Application in Yoga* (Gharote, Devnath, Jha), *Maya in Physics* (N.C. Panda), *The Ribhu Gita* (translated by Dr. H. Ramamoorthy), and *Dasbodh* (Sri Samartha Ramdas).

Spiritual schools say that the ultimate source of life as its absolute substance or substratum called the Brahman or Parabrahman (Nirguna Brahman), or you can alternatively say that the source of life is the body of manifest existence known as Saguna Brahman, Shakti or Creation. It depends upon your perspective as to what you are trying to communicate. It is actually all an irrelevant argument because you find out, upon the subtle body attainment, that *you are simply trying to achieve higher transcendental bodies to escape life and death in the lower realms of existence forever and you want to go as far as you can go, and if you can go no farther in attaining a yet higher transcendental body because of the structure of the universe makes it impossible to further dispose from your body unneeded energetic constituents and still retain a sentient existence then so be it.* It doesn't matter what you then call the ultimate, or whether errors are being communicated to you in order to help you make progress because the only important thing is that you want to go as far as you can go.

You want to retain consciousness in that process of ascending transcendence and continue your existence with pleasantness, namely bliss. The goal of the *atman*'s unity with the Brahman is not a *nirvana* liberation of insentience, annihilation or extinction otherwise destruction is the spiritual path, and no one says that thoughtlessness is the pathway or end target otherwise constant sleep is preferable to aware living. You can instruct people to meditate on the state of pure being that is essentially thoughtlessness but that is nonsense as an ideal since it is also insentience. It's just a method of practice (that you cannot actually achieve) meant to trick you into letting go of thoughts where you also center yourself in a freer and more clear state of mind. The ideal of achieving a state of selflessness but existence, where the self-center drops out, is also nonsense because then you are no longer self-directing your efforts at all, and the drive to improve drops out. Even though it is true that you are characterized by selflessness you only need to understand this to know the truth, but you need the self-concept in order to function as a living sentient being so you don't want to lose it. You simply want to live as a "self" at your level of emanation but know your ultimate self-nature.

The important point is that you must try to achieve the first transcendental subtle body attainment during this life, and then the rest of the teachings, free of religious coverings and mistakes, will be given to you in the earthly heavenly realm when you enter it. The heavenly plane of the earth surrounds us, invisible to our eyes but populated by countless devas that can know our thoughts and see everything we do so there is nothing you can hide when you are called upon for an accounting of deeds after your death.

We are surrounded by devas every moment of our lives, all the devas know the true pathway of transcendent spiritual practice, the fully enlightened guardians and rulers of the heavenly realms are not members of any of the religions humans developed on earth (which all contain errors but aim to train people in good conduct while pointing them towards cultivating the higher spiritual bodies), spiritual masters readily demonstrate the higher spiritual bodies and their capabilities to devas (who can also observe the processes of reincarnation, etc. so there is no use keeping secrets from them), and so everyone knows the true spiritual path and has faith or belief in those teachings just as Mencius said.

To achieve this spiritual ascension requires the task of purifying your Prana, and the best way to do so is to follow a number of spiritual cultivation practices simultaneously – *bhakti*, yoga, pranayama, mantra recitation, *pratyahara*, etc. – under the guise of an already enlightened master.

Along these lines, pranayama practice can help you with the mundane objectives of health and longevity as well as spiritual practice. Various forms of breathwork can also open up your *nadis* or excite the Prana everywhere throughout your body, which is why they are practiced since this is the basic transformational method of purifying your subtle body for its independent emergence from your physical shell. Therefore, spiritual aspirants should undertake daily pranayama practice with the methods chosen being left to your own decision or the recommendations of an enlightened teacher with experience.

Because pranayama practice can open up the *nadis* within your brain and cause better Prana flow into your head, pranayama exercises can also sharpen your intellect, sharpen your senses, and help quiet a wandering mind due to that superior Prana flow within the brain. Practiced with consistency, pranayama certainly helps produce greater mental clarity, calmness and concentration. From the mundane aspect, Pranayama develops the brain, the head, your lung capacity, the strength of your breathing, and your longevity. Through the power of pranayama you can also develop strength in your bones, bone marrow, and heart.

There are many breathing methods, pranayama techniques, and breathwork exercises for "harmonizing the breath" (such as harmonious 5.5 second coherence breathing), but the highest goal is to wash your body with stimulated Prana, produce better pranic circulation everywhere, and either lead you to a state of energetic stimulation (where you feel blissfully alive and full of energy) or to a state of quiescent mental calmness. Particularly useful are the *kumbhaka* pranayama exercises that expand your lung capacity (VO2 max) because you hold your breath and they have a large positive effect on your longevity.

As to the specifics of *kumbhaka* pranayama, the *Yoga-sutras of Patanjali* states, "Regulation of breath or the control of Prana is the stoppage of inhalation and exhalation, which follows after securing that steadiness of posture or seat." This is *kumbhaka* pranayama, which forces your Prana to circulate throughout your body to keep it alive due to the fact that you stop breathing, just as the lack of food during fasting forces your physical body to rely on its pranic life energy for survival. Additionally, holding your breath through *kumbhaka* practices also dilates your capillaries throughout your body, and that dilation or stretching of the capillary structures is a way of exercising those tissue tubes, which constitutes a form of inner yoga practice. It helps to transform the suitability of your tissues for better blood and Prana circulation.

Some breathing exercises are a form of breathwork that moves the Prana within your body to wash your tissues, as in *qi-gong* and martial arts "guiding your Prana" practices, but *kumbhaka* breath retention exercises force your body to dilate tissues and open up all its internal energy pathways.

The standard pranayama exercises of yoga include *Bhastrika* "bellows breathing," *Visama Vritti* "uneven breathing," *Anuloma* "with the grain (natural)" pranayama, and *Kapalabhati* "skull shining" pranayama that use your breathing to move your Prana within you. Yoga texts also contain many other *kumbhaka* breath retention exercises, which can be learnt therefrom, and the most impressive advanced yoga exercises involve *moving your body into different positions while holding your breath.*

To explain, most methods in yoga teach you to hold your body stationary in certain positions while you mentally guide, pull or lead your Prana along acupuncture meridians to open those channels. Some advanced pranayama techniques, on the other hand, have you move your body through certain postures while holding your breath and guiding your Prana.

There are many different *kumbhaka* techniques, such as holding your breath in a "vase" in the lower belly abdomen. Another popular method is to perform subtle contractions of the pelvic muscles without inwards respiration, and there are many techniques where you pump your breathing in order to heighten wakefulness, mental clarity and awareness.

If a breath retention technique is not practiced according to rhythmical ratios of exhalation, inhalation and retention, and instead for the purpose of just holding the breath for as long as possible, the general principles are to: (1) hold your breath as deep within your body as possible, (2) for as long as possible, (2) using as little force with as few muscles as possible, and then (4) forcibly expel it as quickly as possible (although some methods specify a slow release). Basically, follow an enlightened teacher's guidance or *use whatever classical instructions are provided within the instructional text you are using.*

Another breathing practice is to inhale to fill your entire body with breath, and then hold that state for as long as possible while feeling the Prana everywhere within you in order to open up its circulation within blocked meridians. At the same time you can (1) visualize that all your flesh is red in color or your body is flaming on fire in order to arouse a Yang state, or (2) hold onto the *bhava* of intense ecstatic stimulating joy, and (3) you also visualize that your bones are shining with a bright white light as you exhale (and you feel or move the Prana energy inside them). After exhalation, you hold your lungs empty while maintaining the visualization of your bones giving off a shining light. At the final stage of this visualization you abandon all such images and rest your mind in an empty state where you don't deliberately think thoughts, and stay in that state as if you were just infinite empty space with a bodiless awareness that allows all things to arise within it without clinging to anything (since empty space cannot grab anything). In Hinduism this meditation practice of infinite space (after arousing the Yang Prana of your body) is called becoming established in the Self. Appendix 2 has several related formlessness meditations based on the teachings of Kashmir Shaivism.

It is not so much your breath that you want to feel within your body while inhaling, holding, moving and exhaling your breath in pranayama exercises. You want to be feeling and circulating the vital energy within you because that is how you wash your inner subtle body composed of Prana. You can combine various pranayama techniques with freediving or Wim Hof breathing exercises if you want to hold your breath longer, and should periodically measure and record on a graph the length of your retention period so that you can track your progress as a visual method to help motivate you to improve upon best efforts.

Any of the pranayama methods explained here should be considered simply indicative because you can receive fuller instructions from genuine masters who may differ on principles or procedures so rely on their instructions rather than those herein. In particular, you can hurt yourself with *kumbhaka* breath retention techniques if you are too strenuous so you should train in the advanced techniques under the guidance of a living master to avoid self-inflicted harm.

CHAPTER 8
BHAKTI DEVOTIONAL WORSHIP

Vedanta interprets the *Vedas, Upanishads* and *Bhagavad Gita* in a way that defines Hinduism and gives foundation to Indian culture. It is concerned with a few key concepts, the first of which is that the Brahman is the ultimate reality and source of all things including all the gods and deities of Hinduism which are considered just aspects of universal power. Secondly, the *atman, jiva*, or soul of the individual – what we call our innermost self – is the same as the Brahman. Naturally our highest self or *atman* is already in unity with the Brahman, *as are all things*, but it must experientially recognize this unity on a very elevated plane of energy existence for the blissful *moksha* of spiritual liberation that puts an end to reincarnation in the lower realms forever.

Generations of historians tell us that the world has been populated by a moving parade of civilizations that appear for a certain period of time, prosper, and then eventually pass away. Sometimes they don't even leave behind a trace of their former existence. This is the nature of reality: the appearance or birth of a phenomena, its maintenance or continued existence or a period of time, and then its disappearance. This is a progression symbolized by Brahma (the Creator), Vishnu (who offers support and maintenance) and Shiva (the Destroyer).

All past civilizations had populations that worshipped various gods and goddesses. This includes the inhabitants of various River Valley civilizations such as the Indus valley civilization of ancient

India, Ganges River valley civilization, Nile River civilization of the ancient Egyptians, Yellow River basin civilization of China, and Mesopotamian civilization that formed around the Fertile Crescent on the Tigris and Euphrates Rivers.

When a society worships various gods or deities its citizenry supplicates them for the favors of protection and the boon of benefits. Society is pacified and runs better when people act in virtuous ways to gain their approval so that their personal requests might be answered by the gods. Since enlightened beings with higher transcendental bodies masquerade as deities this charade helps to keep them motivated and interested in helping such individuals if they are indeed virtuous people who call upon their name for help. Individuals can win over the intercession of higher beings through their devotion and thus there is a benefit to believing in gods and goddesses, or even just one supreme deity, even if it is all a masquerade of outright falsity.

A civilization's belief in Big Gods usually leads to a belief in supernatural surveillance and punishment – karma – and as a result of believing that there are inescapable consequences for one's bad behaviors this belief increases the ability of large groups to sustain complex social organizations and successfully expand. The belief in *Big Gods makes possible big societies* because a population believing in and worshipping Big Gods leads leans towards more virtuous behavior and this leads to more unity and cooperation within the social order. In order for a large number of people to live together peacefully and cooperatively they must subscribe to shared assumptions, and when a society believes in the existence of Big Gods with special powers these beliefs fit the bill.

One power of all-seeing and all-powerful supernatural beings is that they will see when people do wrong and punish them, which will sometimes happen in this life (by bringing misfortune on their heads) and sometimes in the after life. The end result is that "watched people are nice people," and the social order of society consequently becomes more peaceful because of these fears.

Whether the watchers of your behavior are supernatural gods, your friends and neighbors, a police state, or even karma the end result is that people who think they are being watched (or will have consequences for their bad behavior) act nicer to one another. This is a result we want and something that enlightened spiritual beings want as well. The problem is not just antagonism and violence against one another but the tendency for the powerful and elites to enslave, exploit or oppress the public.

The common beliefs of humanity are that Big Gods, such as the major deities of Hinduism, can look inside your mind and know what you think such as whether you plan to cheat or keep your side of a bargain. They know if you are being fair or selfish. They care about morality and whether you are trying to be virtuous or unethical. If you are bad they can and will punish you, and they will reward the good because they care about morality. They can be harnessed through propitiation to advance your interests or protect you.

Basically, one of the end results of worshipping deities is that people end up policing their own behavior to keep it clean, and this leads to a better society. When you cultivate virtuous ways this too is a very slow but definite way to purify your Prana, which can easily be proved by the fact that you can instantly tell the energetic difference between a crude individual and someone who has cultivated themselves through self-study, ethics and self-correction to raise themselves above the stage of animal vitality. Nevertheless, the big point is that to manage society it is a great idea to promote the idea of Big Gods or all-powerful, all-seeing deities.

Now returning to the philosophical school of Vedanta that has helped to shape Hinduism greatly in various ways, the Advaita school of non-dualism is the most famous of all its traditions. It stresses the correct understanding of the sacred texts of Hinduism, and of course the objective is *moksha* or liberation. However, there is also the Vishishtadvaita school of qualified non-dualism, the Tattvavada (Dvaita) school of dualism, and other schools of Vedanta as well. These schools sometimes disagree among themselves and can even take opposite positions of one other on certain matters. For instance, Advaita Vedanta does not emphasize worship but many of its other schools promote the worship of Vishnu.

For Adi Shankara, founder of Advaita Vedanta, reality is monistic: there is only the Brahman that is the sole reality, entirely without attributes, and the Brahman is the only thing that is. There is nothing else that exists other than the Brahman, and the Brahman has nothing to contain for is just itself without any second thing. All things are essentially the Brahman and our experience of an appearance of objects is the result of the operations of our sense organs, consciousness, its ignorance and *Maya* (illusion).

Forms that we perceive with our mind are basically a combination of Shakti (Prakirti or Ishvara or the manifested universe), sensory inputs, consciousness and *Maya*. While Adi Shankara recognizes worship as a step on the way to the final liberation, which is an importance allowance, there is no reason to worship the Brahman since that is what you are and the Brahman has no need of it. However, remembrance of your true beingness is importance because it leads to detachment from the physical body while centering your awareness in the metacognition of your observing subtle body, which strengthens it.

Everything is the Brahman so mental liberation entails realizing one's existing identity with the Brahman rather than worshipping what one ultimately is. You also don't need to worship the elements that make up the manifest universe as the building blocks of your beingness such as atoms, energies or the five elements. The teachings of Vedanta simply point you towards realizing what you are in order that you correct your ignorance.

Therefore, properly speaking we can say that worship and *bhakti* are not Advaita Vedanta's yogic path to self-realization. Adi Shankara prefers Jnana Yoga, the yoga pathway of knowledge to realize one's true identity as one with the Brahman as the way to reach liberation. By speaking of the *koshas* he let you know of your highest possible existence that puts an end to suffering in the lowest planes of manifestation forever if you tread the path of spiritual practice. Through cultivation you can achieve a state of transcendence where you can experientially perceive your *atman* and its unity with the universe and with the Brahman. This involves stripping away unnecessary coverings over the *atman* so that it can rise to new realms of etheric existence.

Shakyamuni Buddha, founder of Buddhism in India, sought for a solution to sorrow in life and taught that desire was the root cause of all suffering. The cause of desire was, in turn, *Maya* or illusion where release from *Maya* (illusion) would result in enlightenment, or *nirvana*. *Nirvana*, or deliverance, is a state of liberation that dispels *Maya* (ignorance) and Buddha offered various cultivation methods, gleaned from the Indian culture of his day, for cultivating to attain *moksha*, liberation, enlightenment, or release from suffering and the attainment of *nirvana*. These spiritual cultivation methods are similar to many of those in various Hindu yogic and tantric traditions of today. They involved yogic experiential paths and intellectual study for attaining liberation by breaking free from the *skandhas*, or *kosha* coverings that obscure the possibility of complete and perfect enlightenment, which is basically the same achievement of the naked *atman* as posed by Shankara. This makes sense since everyone is achieving the same ultimate enlightenment.

In Buddha's explanation of *nirvana* there is no *Maya*, no desire and no suffering but this sounds so much like a state missing *sat, chit* and *ananda* that it did not appeal to Hindus. In actuality, *nirvana* does not mean thoughtlessness or selflessness since they entail an abandonment of consciousness akin to extinction or annihilation. It equates with a purity of mind, and the highest purity you can reach is when you attain the *atman* or inner Buddha body that you can achieve via a route of ascetic-like cultivation.

Instead of leading mankind in the way that Buddha did, Hinduism instead focuses on Avatars such as Rama and Krishna who had human qualities as well as divine auspicious attributes. Like us they are also married, had children and experienced the joys and sorrows of the world. This is a positive view of life as opposed to the "no intrinsic self" emptiness view of Buddhism that is, in many respects, similar to Advaita Vedanta. Both of these schools are too high for ordinary people who want teachings that touch their lives. The Avatars of Hinduism fit the bill because they ruled over kingdoms and did not tolerate outrages against society but waged war successfully against the forces of evil, wickedness, oppression and exploitation. Ordinary people want to hear these stories as guides for their lives rather than talk about Adi Shankara's teachings on not having an intrinsic self.

Ramanujacharya differed with some of Adi Shankara's views on how to lead people and therefore developed Vishishtadvaita Vedanta (qualified non-dualism) that practiced devotional worship *(bhakti)* to Vishnu or his Avatars (Krishna, Rama, etc.) as a means to liberation. Ramanuja taught that all things are parts of the Brahman where the Brahman is like the soul that moves the body – a universal ego – and where we are separated parts of the Brahman. This is a non-dualism that upholds a degree of difference between God and human so that there is room for devotion to God as a path of Prana purification yogic practice to attain the higher spiritual bodies that enable you to attain *moksha*. Vishishtadvaita Vedanta espouses devotional practices to Vishnu, such as worship, by proposing that Vishnu and the Brahman are equal.

Madhvacharya, the founder of the third major school of Vedanta, Dvaita (dualistic) Vedanta, like Ramanuja also embraced Vaishnavism where Vishnu was not just another deity but the Supreme Being. He wanted to create a pure devotional path of worship (of Vishnu) as a way for people to achieve spiritual liberation too. Madhvacharya taught that the Brahman and *atman* are different and the only way to reach liberation is through worship, which is actually only because worship is a way to purify your Prana inner subtle body so that you can attain the next stage of spiritual ascension. Madhvacharya's lineage of Davaita Vedanta became the Uttaradi Math, Raghavendra Math and Vyasaraja Math of Hinduism.

It is actually irrelevant whether you worship Vishnu, Surya, Shiva, Ganesha, Kartikeya, Devi or anyone else including Jesus, Buddha, Mahavira, or Guru Nanak as long as you are purifying your inner Prana body so that it can emerge from your physical shell. Upon that achievement you will be introduced to extremely clear spiritual teachings without garbage. You will discover the truth beyond all the spiritual practices we espouse in the world, which is that they aim to get you to purify your higher *koshas* for separate unfused existences from one another until you ultimately achieve a naked *atman* without any sheaths whose attainment equates with liberation from the material realm forever. It does not matter whether or not you believe that there is one Universal Being behind the minds of seemingly different individuals and sentient animals and so forth and through them all has the experience of duality. All that matters is that you cultivate as high a transcendental body as possible. At each level of attainment you will be given new teachings so it doesn't even matter if you subscribe to errors here and there, or even if this book transmits some errors, *as long as you target the first objective of attaining the deva body to get started* on the path.

The miracles that Madhvacharya performed throughout his life proved he attained enlightenment, meaning he had attained the five transcendental spiritual bodies, and he believed that worship was the best way for a largely uneducated population to achieve some degree of spiritual purification via devotional practices. Therefore he strongly promoted the devotional worship of a personal God that had an enormous impact on Hindu culture.

Was his philosophical stance correct or not? It doesn't matter because he caused many people to correctly cultivate towards enlightenment whereas they would not have done so without the influence of his teachings. All the religions of the world promote incorrect teachings in order to elevate the populace and bring them closer to final liberation through self-cultivation. The important point is to pacify society by elevating human behavior. You want to structure society in such a way that people cultivate a high inner life, virtue and ethics, good deeds and their higher bodies. Worship is a way to train their behavior and transform their Prana.

Lord Krishna, an Avatar of Vishnu, is known for several magnificent characteristics. *Bhakti* devotees sometimes mentally imagine they become unified with Krishna as a form of worship. Sometimes they focus on imitating a dominant trait of Krishna that they greatly admire and strive to become like him. The work to do this washes their Prana for as long as an aspirant holds that absorption on being Krishna and experiencing or exhibiting his qualities.

You can cultivate your Prana's purification in this way, and achieve a measure of personality transformation as well depending on how hard you work, such as by doing deeds that Krishna would do even if you don't feel like it but elevating your spirit, at those times, to be in tune with his heart and mind. By cultivating in this way you tend to act in alignment with Krishna's values and behavior, and the ideal is to slowly get closer to becoming a more admirable individual.

As practiced in Vaishnavism, Shaivism and Shaktism, the general purpose of worshipping Krishna, Rama, Lakshmi, Vishnu, Durga, Kali, Lakshmi and so on is to generate an ardent emotional feeling of loving devotion to such a deep extent that you arouse intense positive emotions inside you that you hold in a steady manner in order that the energies aroused are strong enough to significantly penetrate and wash your Prana. If you are an individual who worships a deity you also tend to act more ethically than others because you always want the eye of approval for your deeds. What you want to avoid, said Swami Vivekananda, is degenerating into a hideous fanaticism in your *bhakti*, and once you have chosen a deity to worship you need to avoid denunciation and hatred against other deities or paths.

Bhakti is just a method to help you reach the great divine, namely to attain the first of the transcendental bodies of enlightenment that free the *atman* from its shells so that you can proceed onwards from there, and has nothing to do with denouncing the ideals of any other religion while championing the peculiars of one's own decisions. You don't want to become like a barking dog who protects only his own master's house from intrusion.

Rapture is a positive emotion that produces a Yang response in your Prana while longing is a negative emotion that produces a Yin response. Deep emotions such as these, stimulated by loving devotion towards a deity, will end up creating sensations inside your body that will provoke its Prana into moving and therefore stimulate your internal subtle body. If you do this correctly, worshipping deities becomes a method for internally purifying your pranic life force, or impure subtle energy, in preparation for its emergence as a life independent of the physical body shell.

This is why Sri Ramakrishna Paramahansa would cry daily before Mother (Kali) with a sense of longing and separation (which stimulate Yin Prana) saying, "I only want you, don't give me anything else." His acts of devotion were not the important thing. The fact that he was washing his Yin (feminine) Prana through strong emotions of longing and separation was the importance of the practice, yet no one realizes this because they do not understand the principles of Hindu deity worship. They only see the surface events and do not comprehend what is truly going on in such practices.

Of course, Ramakrishna would also experience many positive, ecstatic visions projected into him by enlightened friends that served to raise and wash his Yang (masculine) Prana. It is well-known that Ramakrishna experienced many types of visions during his years of cultivation prior to enlightenment, and they were usually positive because he was a spiritual master reborn (who are usually treated through the kundalini process much easier than first-timers because his old buddies are doing all the transformation work on his new body) and his astrological configurations for positive for that sort of thing. In *The Visions of Ramakrishna*, it is explained:

> Most of his visions, especially of the Mother, were of great beauty. Swami Saradananda tells us that Sri Ramakrishna saw at this time limitless forms of the Devi, from the two-armed to the ten-armed. The Master himself

speaks of meditating under the tree when 'Sin' appeared before him and tempted him in various ways. It came in the form of an English soldier (pointed symbolism!) wanting to give wealth, honour, sex pleasure, occult powers, etc. 'I began to pray to the Divine Mother!" I still remember that form of the Mother, Her world-bewitching beauty. She came to me taking the form of Krishnamayi, but it was as if Her glance moved the world.' The most beautiful of all these visions, he said, was that of Raja-rajesvari, 'Queen of queens,' one of the traditional ten forms of the Divine Mother, who is also known as Sodasi. 'It looked,' he said, trying to put this into language, 'as if the beauty of the person of Sodasi had got melted, spread all around, and was illumining the universe in all directions.' ...

In this period, the close of Tantric sadhana, the Master had visions also of various male figures such Bhairava, companion of Siva; under the vilva-tree where most of these practices were undertaken, he had many 'flaming visions' and other mystical experiences the contents of which he was not able to reveal.

'There were then so many extraordinary visions and experiences in the Master's life day after day,' says Swami Saradananda, 'that it is beyond the power of man to mention all of them.'[4]

The hidden principle is that if you purify your subtle body sufficiently it can eventually break its bonds with the *annamaya kosha* because you etherize its energies far beyond the normal thickness of union where it interfaces with the physical matrix. You can "thin" them enough by raising their frequency, purity or vibration to become vastly different from the undifferentiated cesspool they used to be part of so that they break free due to that elevating differentiation. Enough vitality will remain with the physical body so it does not die, but it must also get used to the loss of some vitality.

When *Bhakti* devotional practices involve extreme love for a deity this is similar to the Four Immeasurable Emotions practice of Buddhism where you cultivate a tremendously large Prana of positive

---

[4] *The Visions of Sri Ramakrishna*, Swami Yogeshananda, (Sri Ramakrishna Math, Chennai: India), pp. 43-45.

heart emotions that nourish love, compassion and kindness in order to wash your internal energy with that Prana. *Bhakti* devotional practices should not be matters of bargaining with a deity or asking the deity for anything. The purpose is to but cleanse your mind by cultivating an internal feeling of reverence so that this energy permeates your Prana to wash your personality and subtle body.

You accomplish this through a calm but continuous remembrance of a deity just as a wife holds to a constant remembrance of her husband's companionship. When you practice this correctly, which is possible because it is an easy and natural practice, you become satisfied because you become filled with a full feeling of Prana that washes your body and mind. For instance, when we feel love we feel pleasant. Similarly, when our thoughts are peaceful, full of divine love and goodness because of *bhakti* worship then we can feel the joy of life and encounter a divine peace that purifies our Prana. *Bhakti* is a method by which we may feel love in fullness and thereby elevate our life as well as transform our vital energy. The fullness of love cancels evil in the mind and also purifies our Prana far above its animal nature.

Most people in life never raise themselves higher than the daily concerns of eating, drinking, sleeping and procreating while chasing after sense enjoyments as their only means of gratification. After brief thrills the pleasure of experiencing them quickly wears off leaving them unfulfilled. However, by engaging in the easy route of *bhakti* where you cultivate love and leave hate behind, you can enjoy positive emotions for a prolonged period of time as long as you keep your deity in mind, and you can start raising yourself to something higher than the mundane life.

Bhakti worship involves constant remembrance of a deity and usually also entails the singing of emotional *bhajans* that give rise to higher spiritual thoughts and emotions, and by washing your Prana through such sounds and emotions it is a way to purify your inner subtle body.

A similar *bhakti* method is to repeat mantras while holding onto certain states of mind, or simply to recite a mantra whose intent is to elevate your mind and take it to God. You try to foment the conception of a certain state. As a Hindu, perhaps this method will suit you according to your nature and if not there are many other spiritual practices for transforming, refining or purifying your inner subtle body to achieve spiritual progress. Mantra recitation, or *japa*, is just one of the many diverse spiritual practices available in Hinduism.

Many *bhakti* devotees also dance as they sing *kirtans*. Dance is a form of moving yoga where you wash your body's tissues by circulating your Prana through special movements that ancient enlightened masters have found move your Prana beneficially, which is why they developed special dancing forms. This is also a proper form of Prana purification yet few know it.

Why or when are practices considered spiritual? When they can help you change your character, personality or behavior for the better (thus enhancing your life) by building up memories that create new neural patterns that change your brain mapping. Repeating good spiritual practices can rebuild the nerve pathways in your brain that produce default behaviors, and thus they can elevate you if you adhere to virtuous practices that build you into a better person and improve your life.

Every time you repeat the same actions or activate a specific neural pattern in your brain it becomes more defined as the preferred neural pathway for consciousness to use. This makes it get closer to becoming your default behavior in your way of doing things. Spiritual practices are designed to produce admirable neural behavioral pathways so that you become an elevated, non-violent, cultured human being. Secondly, spiritual practices purify your inner subtle body or Prana that becomes released as a deva body for the path of spiritual ascension. Without this ascension you will never attain true *moksha* or liberation since it is at its heart an existence attainment, meaning a body-entity attainment.

Pranayama practices, kundalini yoga and even sexual intercourse tackle the task of stimulating, energizing, moving and simultaneously purifying your Prana via friction in entirely different ways but most spiritual masters would encourage *bhakti* worship as the primary means of Prana purification (spiritual practice).

Thus Krishna instructs, "Immerse your mind only in me, be devoted to me, worship me, bow in obeisance before me. I am pledging that you will attain me because you are my beloved." The story of Krishna reveals a personality that most women dream of being with and most men want to be like, hence for many individuals he is a perfect focus for *bhakti* as a superior companion or admirable example for their lives. By becoming devoted to a deity or some entity as our guru a human being can become more like that deity or entity.

This is why the Bengali saint Chaitanya Mahaprabhu, founder of Gaudiya Vaishnavism, stressed Krishna worship through *bhajans, kirtans*, mantra recitation (such as the Hare Krishna Maha-mantra) as well as dance and prayer. These are all means of moving and purifying the Prana of your body to achieve the spiritual purification necessary to separate your subtle body from the coarse, denser, unpurified and undifferentiated vital energy that envelops it. Chaitanya Mahaprabhu, who also demonstrated many miracles during his life that verified his enlightenment, worshipped Krishna not only through *bhajan-kirtan* but through dance. He was even eventually seen as an Avatar of Krishna himself. Mirabai, a celebrated *bhakti* saint, was also a devotee of Krishna but other saints have recommended the *bhakti* route of other deities too.

Chaitanya promulgated pure devotion to Krishna as a way to attain liberation because he felt this avenue of spiritual practice was the most appropriate means for common men to purify their character and inner Prana, and because Krishna was the easiest to worship, identify with, and because he had essentially vowed to help people attain liberation, which means enlightenment, who did so. Krishna also stated that non-liberated *jivas* or souls are under the influence of matter but in the liberated state the *jivas* are free from the influence of matter which is precisely because they attain the spiritual bodies of higher purified energy that transcend it.

Even those bodies, however, Chaitanya considered separated parts of the Lord Krishna whom he took as representing the Supreme Absolute Truth endowed with all energies. Other sects in Hinduism use Shiva or Vishnu or other deities to represent Nirguna Brahman (formless Ultimate Reality without attributes or quality) or Saguna Brahman (manifest Reality with form, attributes and qualities). It does not matter which deity you choose, or whether you are equating Him or Her to the ultimate substrate (Purusha), its first emanate, the entire realm of manifestation (Prakirti or Shakti), or just the highest energies beyond our reach as physical body components as long as long as you achieve the final result in a virtuous way.

Many "Krishna consciousness" devotees, when they practice properly, are put through many deep emotional experiences of Yin and Yang to purify their Prana, but this also happens if you worship

Kali (Ramakrishna), Shiva (the Shaiva Nayanars), Vishnu (the Alvars) or other deities where a large host of enlightened beings stand behind each particular tradition to help followers who have also chosen that pathway because it accords with their liking.

For instance, the Tamil saint Arunagirinathar succeeded in enlightened because he worshipped Lord Murugan due to his preferences. He created the *Tiruppukai* (a book of Tamil devotional poems in praise of Murugan) just as Chaitanya and others created dances, hymns, *kirtans,* and *bhajans* in praise of Krishna. Arunagirinathar's *Kandar Anubhuti* is another of his works that contains hymns requesting Lord Murugan, a deity both with and without form, to help him in overcoming *Maya*, the illusory nature of the world. Naturally this requires the attainment of the highest transcendental spiritual bodies of enlightenment.

You will only attain the first of the higher spiritual bodies that sets you on the path of ultimately attaining full *moksha* if you practice *bhakti* fully while also using *other spiritual cultivation methods as well* as shown in the example of Ramakrishna. When you pick an Avatar to worship that has a set of enlightened spiritual masters behind that lineage, little by little their *nirmanakaya* emanations to purify your Prana will have an effect, so we say that little by little the grace of the deity will fill you during your exercises.

The experience of the deity will feel like it becomes a living one when these masters use *nirmanakaya* emanations to possess you in order to transform your Prana using their own, and then you will feel as if your relationship with the deity is as a living one as someone who exists near you or even walks with you. Of course, this is all the result of feeling a projected *nirmanakaya* emanation from someone who fills you with energy and gives you such thoughts. Nevertheless you will feel as if the experience of Krishna, Vishnu, Shiva, Murugan, Ganesh, Sri Lalita Deva or any other deity you choose for *bhakti* becomes a living one.

Sometimes you might pray to a deity for guidance, and then receive an answer that is "a deep idea that is a palpable force of determination, a kind of conviction, and an intense feeling" of what to do. This too is from an enlightened master who has reviewed your situation and given you an answer via a *nirmanakaya* emanation that takes possession of your mind to give you instructions that you think come from yourself. This is how enlightened masters normally help people, which is by giving them thoughts or by giving other people thoughts to help you. It is not God that does this but enlightened beings although people usually attribute everything over to God. How did you think it really happens?

The "Fools for Christ" are the *bhakti* aspirants within Christianity who similarly use deep worship of Christ as their road of spiritual practice only in this case Christ becomes the deity of focus. Once again, the secret target is not the activity of worship but the accomplishment of purifying the Prana of your inner subtle body. A true deity does not want or need worship. In fact, it also *does not even matter whether a deity you worship is real or fictional* as long as enlightened spiritual masters handling your case are using the emotionally stimulated arousal of your Prana to wash your internal energy body!

Your own Prana becomes cleansed when more refined Prana penetrates your pranic matrix to pass through it, and then the higher quality energy must frictionally stir your Yin and Yang Prana against itself to differentiate them from one another. This process is essentially higher heavenly Prana rubbing against your own, which produces frictional warmth, the separation of the higher from lower energies, and the pushing aside of dregs through the process just as seen in the story of the *Samudra Manthana* that also produced poisons.

Our feelings or emotions and strong attitudes produce vibrational responses in our internal energy that are initiated according to our existing concepts, so we can use them to generate sensations within our physical nature (*annamaya kosha*) that move our Prana so that this internal Prana stimulation, when prolonged, can wash the various qualities of our energy. This principle is commonly used in many forms of spiritual cultivation without practitioners knowing about this basis. It is hidden in Hinduism as well but is an essential part of the secret pathway of the saints.

As previously explained, the classical Indian Bharatanatyam dance form from Tamil Nadu, which uses mudras to tell stories within the dance, is designed to move your Prana, and because of this the dancing becomes *divine movement* because it is then a form of spiritual practice. There are other classical forms of Indian dance involving *bhakti* as well as well including Odissi, Kuchipudi, Manipuri, Kathak, and Kathakali. The point is that we want to master a form of dance that moves our internal energy to wash our tissues and internal energy because then it becomes spiritual practice and divine movement. Otherwise it is just dance exercise.

Japa, or mantra repetition, can calm your mind depending upon the sounds of the mantra being used and your practice technique, but what is interesting is that the sound power of some mantras is designed to rhythmically move your Prana without a need for the intercession of heavenly beings to help you.

Most mantras were given to us from enlightened masters as a way to invite the attention of enlightened beings to come into you and wash your Prana through a *nirmanakaya* emanation that they would then project to help you, but if you use the wrong mantra it is like making a telephone call where no one picks up the other end of line. In other words, reciting the wrong mantra that has no lineage behind it means that no one will respond with *nirmanakaya* help as an intercession. Because of this possibility it is usually best to use the mantra connected with the deity of a local temple, or a mantra given to you privately by an enlightened Paramahansa or *jivanmukta*. Unless, of course, the mantra is composed of *bijas* that vibrate your Prana on their own.

You don't want to waste your spiritual practice time on useless methods and pursuits. No matter how religious or virtuous you are you can do better by practicing yoga methods where you circulate your own Prana within your body using your mind, by reciting mantras that naturally vibrate and energize your Prana through resonance, or by singing *bhajans* where your emotional involvement together with the sound power and your breathing rhythm will also move your Prana even if no one comes to aid you with *nirmanakaya* washing.

Naturally you don't have to neglect participation in religious rituals and ceremonies or reading spiritual texts and reciting hymns since this will help you with the overall goal. The purpose of all these methods, one and all, is to move you to the realm of realization, namely the body attainments that equate with enlightened liberation from matter. They usually entice enlightened beings to help you because of your participation.

The foundation behind all these techniques is your personal effort to improve your character and behavior because if you are an unethical or violent-prone human being the enlightened spiritual masters of this world will not invest much time in helping you attain the higher transcendental bodies that give you power over others.

This is common sense. Spiritual progress is for the virtuous who have left evil ways behind, and who work on rewiring their mental circuits so that they are naturally good people and help others rather than use them.

The emotions of tremendous admiration and awe that you might normally feel during devotional worship can move your Yang Prana and thus wash you inner subtle body. Your Yin Prana becomes energized during religiously motivated crying such as when you feel yourself separated from your deity because of an intense longing. When you truly humble yourself through devotional worship through a deep feeling of humility this will also wash your Yin Prana. *Bhakti* can cause you to wash your inner spiritual body by arousing all sorts of emotions in an easy manner without much instruction or oversight necessary.

Sometimes enlightened spiritual masters and enlightened guardian spirits will give *bhakti* practitioners spiritual visions with the intent of having them abide within a state of highly energized Yang Prana for awhile, and sometimes they will scare them terribly, as is done in the Aghori schools of India, in order to strongly stimulate their Yin Prana for the purposes of washing it. When it isn't done simply because someone wants to show off his skills it is done to help people purify their pranic subtle body but the danger is that the supervisors of the process go too far and put you into danger or lead you astray in some way.

For instance, in the Shugendo spiritual tradition of Japan practitioners are tied up and hung upside down off the side of a mountain in order to cause extreme nervousness and anxiety because that fright will temporarily raise their Yin Prana even though people supervise the process to make sure nothing goes wrong. When spiritual masters put you through such experiences they often go to extremes because of the fun in manipulating you, which is why masters warn you not to lose your head during these events. In any case, the purpose of many practices is to wash the Yin or Yang Prana of your inner spiritual body.

Many enlightened spiritual masters will cause their most ardent practitioners to undergo unpleasant experiences such as intense fear or terror, anxiety, depression, dejectedness, hopelessness, sickness or even shaking and trembling (during feelings of cold within the body) in order to arouse and purify their Yin Prana. "Krishna consciousness" disciples, when taught properly, are put through many deep emotional Yin experiences to purify their Prana too. The purification process is not accomplished simply through worship that is of a Yang nature.

Now, when going through the kundalini process many *bhakti* devotees will be taken over by devas and be made to perform in unusual ways automatically beyond their control such as to start weeping, shouting, making unique movements, or doing something strange, all of which may make onlookers afraid but have the incomprehensible design to provoke and wash their Prana. At times individuals going through the process may even seem a little bit crazy to others because you might catch them talking to themselves (mumbling) or doing other strange things during the overall process.

The 3rd Alwar, Pey Alwar, would incessantly cry for the Lord Vishnu. When other people saw him cry like a madman they took him to have gone insane or to have become possessed by an evil spirit but he was just like the Greek Orthodox monks on Mount Athos who cry for Jesus Christ and who are washing their inner life force through that process. An example of spiritual possession is when Adi Shankaracharya's student Padmapada was possessed by the "spirit of Lord Narasimha" and then pounced upon a Kapilika and tore him to pieces when he was about to kill Adi Shankaracharya with a sword. During the period of kundalini transformation, Deva *Mara* will definitely exploit situations by entering the body of the spiritual aspirant and cause him or her to do unusual things.

This is why it helps to have an enlightened master nearby who will protect you from excesses during the process, including sexual leanings that are provoked to raise your Yang Prana. Deva *Mara* during a twelve-year kundalini awakening will oppose a spiritual practitioner with desires, doubts, worries, imaginations and all sorts of delusions. If devas gain complete control of you during the process – for they are undergoing the same transformations themselves and will use you to demonstrate to the attending teachers their own progress in being able to control the consciousness of a human being – they will cause you to damage your health, body, wealth, relationships and nearly everything, and then laugh and leave since they have no accountability for what they do. This is why spiritual masters have created the fictitious story that kundalini energy is too powerful for most people, would burn out their body, create insanity and so on. Masters do not want you to become involved in such practices without an enlightened guru as a supervising teacher because when you perform inner energy exercises there is always the danger that some local devas will practice in you and cause all sorts of mischief without supervision. Actually, your relocated astrological natal chart will indicate whether an area is good for you or not in this regard.

You are caused to experience many extreme emotions during the long process of kundalini purification because those energies will help differentiate the Yin from the Yang Prana of your body that is all jumbled together for individuals who do not spiritually cultivate.

You will be put through very painful emotional experiences by spiritual masters who might even use their own *nirmanakaya* energies to cause physical pain within their student's bodies to arouse their Yin Prana, especially during the last years of the multi-year purification sequence. All of this pain is distressing to human practitioners and prompts many to consider suicide due to undisciplined excessiveness during the process. Therefore you must really police your thoughts and actions during the process.

Ignorant practitioners who don't know these teachings are unable to evaluate their level of accomplishments or understand what is happening. Thus they cannot recognize these situations when they manifest, and then may wrongly claim that they have become spiritual and reached some level of attainment. For instance, *bhakti* adherents absolutely must experience sorrowful states of mind, such as feeling cut off from God where they cry in despair since this anguish will raise your Yin Prana and differentiate its internal circulation from your solar energies. Your Yin Prana or lunar energies must be purified within your subtle body through various techniques that are typically uncomfortable. Heavenly beings will help you to generate these states, but few practitioners will understand what is going on and might feel they have reached some degree of *bhakti* mastery when pranic energy starts moving inside them whereas someone else is doing this work for them.

Because *bhakti* yoga often involves states of emotional fervor, *bhakti* devotees are especially prone to experiencing excesses or becoming unduly influenced by Deva *Mara*. Remember that the enlightened Greek sage Socrates reported he always heard a *daimonion* (divine spirit) that frequently warned him – in the form of a "voice" inside his head – against mistakes. The Indian sage Hariwansh Lal Poonja ("Papaji") reported that he was always playing with a (visionary figure of) Krishna in his mind when young, and some saints report that they were able to continuously talk with a guardian spirit or some deity since they were young too. These are just two examples of masters playing with your mind.

Deva *Mara* and enlightened masters will practice giving you thoughts that you take as your own during your lifetime of spiritual practice. Plenty of Christian monks report being tormented by devils and demons that were actually just devas playing tricks on them to stimulate their Yin Prana. All sorts of things like this are bound to happen during the kundalini transformation period that prepares for the liberation of your subtle body, especially illusory events that stimulate your mental fear module for periods of time.

This is why the sage Tulsidas said, "Take the sweetness of all, sit with all, take the name of all, say yea, yea, but keep your seat firm." You have to stay centered during all of this and not lose control of yourself or your sense of reality.

Shakyamuni Buddha of Buddhism gave a non-denominational warning to spiritual practitioners about devas possessing them and leading them astray during the twelve-year kundalini purification period so in the *Surangama Sutra* he warned the spiritual practitioners of all religions, schools and traditions: "Do not allow Deva *Mara* to take advantage of you, but be on guard and strive to realize supreme enlightenment." He also explained to his student Ananda, "Many states associated with spiritual practice of dhyana arise in a meditator's mind. Ignorant and wayward practitioners do not evaluate themselves. When such reactions manifest, deluded people do not distinguish these states or reflect on them, nor are they able to understand the causes. They may wrongly claim that they have attained sainthood and falsely proclaim enlightenment. After my *nirvana*, in the Dharma ending age, you must transmit this teaching so that all living beings may awaken to this message, that Deva *Mara* (heavenly demons) cannot take advantage of such states (to have their own way), and that practitioners can be on their guard as they strive to realize supreme enlightenment." You now have these warnings and even greater explanations than Shakyamuni Buddha gave us.

During advanced stages of Prana transformation practitioners will also experience many Deva *Mara* emotional testings. Enlightened masters and their students will provoke strong emotional responses in practitioners, produce imaginary visions in their minds, or move their internal energy in various ways to demonstrate their skill level and show other heavenly residents how to do this. The big goal is teaching others how to create thoughts and emotions using their *nirmanakaya* projections, which is a skill that the newly enlightened must learn since it doesn't come naturally without instruction and practice. Where do they practice? They practice in you who are going through the process they went though! They also want your Yin or Yang Prana to arise so that they can see which *nadis* are open or still thwarted with circulatory obstructions so they can help clear those pathways but they won't tell you that.

The older enlightened individuals like to show off their skills to all the seniors assembled at these times, which can number in the hundreds or even thousands of Arhats and Great Golden Arhats who have gathered to get worked on by each other and learn new skills. What is impressive is when someone demonstrates generating countless *nirmanakaya* (one for each audience member) that can act as independent personalities from one another and handle problems separately on their own. This takes years of training to master. What is even more impressive is using three different types of *nirmanakaya* – one from a Supra-Causal body, one from an Immanence body and one from the *nirmanakaya* of their Immanence body's *nirmanakaya* – to act as separate personalities in one individual to affect their thinking and emotions. They will demonstrate this skill on you!

These types of mental experience you will suffer are called "trials" or "tribulations" (although you could also call what is happening "trickery" or "torture") and the process can last for years as the entire matrix of your subtle body *kosha* is washed and elevated and you are being used for training purposes. The process is usually overseen by the masters of your tradition along with many other saints and sages who help out since the process requires tons of work and everyone helps one another. They'll be working on countless local devas in your area as well so it's worth the effort. Even though the process is being supervised it is still difficult at best because the devas, who are being worked on and taught at the same time as you are, cannot control themselves due to their joy at being able to play with your mind and display their skills to their enlightened teachers or test themselves against each other. They have been raised to do this to people all the time so they tend to look down upon humans since they have a lower status, and you fall into this category.

No one wants to tell you that this is going on so you can hardly find these teachings except from the *Surangama Sutra* of Shakyamuni Buddha, the enlightenment story of Lu Dongbin, the story of Naropa and from the thermal pictures I've mentioned. Everyone else just sanitizes the process by calling it a stage of cleansing and harmonization of the elements of the body, which in Yoga calls opening the body's *nadis* or chakras. They say it's difficult but don't mention any details. Masters will tell you they spent "twelve years" with their teacher but won't provide any details, so now you have some.

Religious practice also follows this pattern of purifying your Yin and Yang Prana in more orthodox ways such as when monks and nuns are led to meditate on topics such as glorious heavenly rewards (which raises their Yang Prana), the fear of Hell (which stimulates Yin Prana) or the necessity for humility, obedience or repentance for sins (that also stirs Yin energies).

Cultivating deep emotional states on purpose is done within the Kaula Tantra "Path of Heroes" that instructs you to hold onto an emotional mood or attitude during an activity or for a prolonged period of time in order to help transform your Prana and thinking patterns.

Some tantric yoga teachings of India instruct you to invite deities into your body in order to tune your Prana to different qualities and help with the purification transformations necessary to wash your subtle energy (Prana) that eventually produces a transcendental body. That is the actual purpose of *bhakti*, but devotees do not know this fact and enlightened masters do not want to tell you either because it involves too much knowledge that the uneducated masses cannot easily comprehend. The public just isn't ready for it, or for the fact that devas are passing in and out of you all throughout your life and use everyone to learn how to give the human stage of existence various thoughts and emotions. It has always been best just to provide instructions on mantra practice, singing *bhajans* or reverential worship and so on without lifting the cover off of matters, but now people are more mature and educated.

Nyasa Yoga similarly instructs you to associate with the energies, disposition and personality of a deity as another way to cultivate your Prana. The practice of envisioning that you become one with a deity, spiritual savior or spiritual master will not only move your emotions but can also be used in personal development efforts to move you in the direction of developing any admirable character traits they possess which you desire. After all, one of the goals in human life is to build a strong, virtuous character so that you act properly in all situations.

Because Tibetan Buddhism has entered India, over time many of its techniques (which actually originated in India) will return to mix again with those already established within Hinduism. Because of its practices you should probably consider it a *sampradaya* (tradition, sect, spiritual lineage or religious system) of Lamaism, rather than a division of Buddhism, because its real focus is on guru worship since the guru is supposed to be enlightened and take you to the other shore. One of its related practices is deity yoga where you imagine that you become a deity, and is said to be accompanied by a degree of spiritual risk for the reasons we just went over.

In returning to *bhakti* practice let us emphasize that it is not about worship because no one needs to be worshipped. It is actually about strongly stimulating devotional attitudes that will arouse internal body sensations in order to stimulate your Prana so that this energizing will act to differentiate (clarify or purify) your Prana. States of deep devotional crying and longing will stimulate your Yin Prana so that it separates itself from the great mass of undifferentiated energies within your body, while joyous states of rapture and ecstasy will similarly separate out and purify your Yang Prana.

Kaula Tantra, on the other hand, instructs practitioners to mentally visualize fantastic imagery, often with erotic arousal, to help excite the Prana of the body which is a different method other than worship. The way purification works is that Prana that rubs over other Prana will wash it of impurities through frictional rubbing, and differentiating Yin or Yang Prana from your great mass of internal energy will clarify their circulatory routes, so most spiritual methods try to get you to move your internal energy to do this for prolonged periods of time.

Songs or hymns of worship that move your Prana internally (because they arouse emotions and because the sound power moves your internal energy in different areas of your body) are also *bhakti* or reverence cultivation practices since they strongly color and move your Prana through emotional songs, hymns and the attendant breathing. When singing religious hymns such as *bhajans* you should always make the sounds resonate within your body while feeling deep emotions since this stimulates your energy into moving, and then this becomes true spiritual worship and transformation instead of just simple singing. It turns your singing into a divine movement towards spiritual ascension that will liberate you from the material realm forever.

Mantra recitations of deities, or *japa* practice, should always be performed in the same manner with the intention of vibrating (activating or energizing) the Prana of your entire body, or just certain body sections, and should be combined with feeling strong emotions and your internal sensations at the same time since this will help in that effort. The practice of chanting hymns, mantras and other religious sounds should *never be monotonous* because you should try to vibrate the Prana in different areas of your body on purpose, or your whole body at once, and then the practice becomes effective at spiritual development. Then these efforts become true spiritual practice whereas otherwise they are just voicing sounds.

To feel strong emotions when singing bolsters the effect of inner Prana stimulation and purification. You might notice, for instance, that some professional singers seem to become more etheric over time. Religious reverence, as practiced in spiritual ceremonies and rituals, is also a cultivation exercise for quieting and purifying your mind in addition to transforming your Prana.

The reason that devotional rituals or religious ceremonies can often help you cleanse your consciousness (and thus Prana) by temporarily freeing your mind from impurities is because they require either humility and selflessness, or concentration, and both of these avenues banish wandering thoughts. During occasions of spiritual worship and religious reverence, such as when visiting a temple or attending a spiritual service, you should engender a feeling of deep awe or reverence because that attitude felt throughout your mind and body will shunt aside wandering thoughts and emotions, and the temporary purity of devotional feelings will then be fully transforming your Prana for ascension. This is what is important during *puja*, for instance, rather than performing the mechanics of the activity. You might also cultivate a state of humility or self-surrender by "surrounding your thoughts to God" during that time, which is a type of mental emptiness that also cleanses your mind and Prana to a state of natural purity.

The deity Hanuman, hero of the Ramayana who was the devoted companion of Rama, always kept Rama in his heart by continuously reciting "Ram" as a devotional mantra. That is because this sound successfully vibrates the Prana of your entire body (just like "Om") as a cleansing cultivation method. Hanuman represents the power of devotion that enables animal man, who is an ape like Hanuman, to reach the higher spiritual bodies of ascension that constitute spiritual evolution. Hanuman never deviates from his singular *bhakti* Yoga practice on Rama, his ideal, having said in the Ramayana, "Though I know that the Lord of Shri, Vishnu, and the Lord of Janaki, Ram, are both manifestations of the same Supreme Being, yet my all in all is the lotus-eyed Rama." This is the correct way to proceed.

Hindus worship many incarnations of God and all are legitimate paths as long as the pathway and practices are virtuous and lead to good results. Krishna said in the *Bhagavad Gita*, "Those who are devotees of other gods and who worship them with faith actually worship only me." He also said, "All these forms are mine." As the Sage of Kanchi reminds us in his book, *The Guru Tradition* (page 192), "The sastras proclaim that the obeisance paid by a devotee to the different forms of Divinity attain the one and the same Isvara. '*Sarvadevanamaskarah Kesavam pratigacchati.*' It is the One and Only Paramatman that is manifested as different forms of the godhead. ... So the *namaskara* or obeisance made to any form of Divinity – one must add, the obeisance made to any *asami* – attains the One and Only Paramatman."

The secret hidden in Hinduism is the objective through *bhakti* of pranic cleansing aimed at purifying your *pranamaya, manomaya, vijnanamaya* and *anandamaya koshas* that are all condensed in your inner subtle body that is released upon death or released when you become a beginner sage after undergoing the many years of kundalini transformations. This is the pathway to becoming free from the lower realm of existence forever. Most individuals cannot complete this pathway during life, but they can do so in the afterlife as a deva if they are a virtuous individual, which is a development fostered by *bhakti* activities since they push you into becoming a better human being.

Yet another aspect to the practice of religious rituals is that they purify your mind of wandering thoughts when the ceremonial performance requires a high level of concentration by the celebrant. When you must perform many actions at the same time this will quiet your thoughts of distractions due to the necessary concentration you must expend, and afterwards you can abandon any focused concentration to rest as a relief in a mental peace empty of burdens. This shedding of mental activity afterwards because you expended so much concentration sometimes then becomes a transcendent experience due to the grace of heaven.

Prayer is also a form of *bhakti* worship and there are many types of prayer for spiritual cultivation purposes. Repetitious prayer should eventually lead to a quieting of your thoughts and mental peace. That internal peacefulness from prayer is a type of internal illumination where your inner narrative quiets but you become filled with energy due to the inner peace and contentment that comes from quieting thoughts.

When praying you should pay close attention to the words of the prayer. This is where your attention must be at all times and you must ignore any images that arise in the mind. You must ignore distractions that are sometimes the result of deva students playing with your consciousness. When reciting some prayers it is appropriate that you should focus your mind on feeling the meaning of the prayer inside you so that it affects your Prana, but normally each time you repeat a prayer your awareness should be sharp and clear as ever. You should be concentrating on the present moment and the words of the prayer while forgetting all previous repetitions and ignoring any other mental distractions.

Another type of praying instructs us to let go of our ego and "give all your mental concerns over to God." Many religions commonly explain that prayer helps us reach a state of supreme solitude centered entirely on the presence of God that is a "union with God," hence, prayer is also a *bhakti* means for reaching the experience of God. Profound inner silence is considered a deeper connection to God because it is unusual and feels blissful. This experience of being free of coarse thoughts or inner quietude can be achieved either through meditation practice, prayer recitation or mantra practice since they all quiet your thoughts and silence the inner narrative of mentally dialoguing with yourself.

Thousands of men and women over the centuries have achieved the independent subtle body attainment through the religious pathway of prayer, worship and reverence. This includes Chaitanya Mahaprabhu and Ramakrishna Paramahansa, who each attained the initial enlightenment stage of the deva body via the cultivation route of religious practices that included prayer, worship and reverence. After their initial attainment of *Homo Deus,* which is the stage of attaining the subtle body, they went on to complete the entire spiritual path of attainments that nearly everyone normally completes who attains the subtle body achievement.

Incorruptibility (a non-decaying, non-rotting corpse after death), which was exhibited in the body of Yogananda Paramahansa after his death (and by the saints of countless other traditions), is a typical result of undergoing the extensive Prana purification process of the kundalini transformations rolling around your body necessary to generate the higher spiritual bodies. As a result of success in achieving the higher body attainments – which makes one the equivalent of an enlightened saint, sage, guru, *jivanmukti,* Satguru, Paramahansa, Arhat, spiritual master, etc. – individuals become worthy of prayers (mantras) for intercession by supplicants requesting their heavenly aid just as you would normally do for deities. When they attain the highest Immanence, Superconsciousness or Tathagata body of Perfect and Complete Enlightenment they become qualified for such supplication.

An incorrupt body attests to genuine spiritual attainments and proves an individual *truly succeeded through the pathway of prayer, worship, spiritual devotion and reverence* which led to the multi-year kundalini transformations that made their physical body pure and incorruptible. Those who succeed can usually display miraculous abilities such as being able to read people's minds, heal the sick, foretell the future, know what is happening at a distance, project physical body doubles (*nirmanakaya* emanations) in multiple locations that you can see and touch (which Chinese then call *yang-shen*), etc. as commonly demonstrated by Neem Karoli Baba, Bhagawan Nityananda and many other Hindu saints. With practice you can even generate a *yang-shen* emanation that does not even look like you.

Here's the point about this that most people miss, especially television and movie writers. A physical *nirmanakaya* emanation that you can touch, or body double, is not projected from the physical body. It is from an entirely different person than the one you see in the physical world. It is projected from either an Supra-Causal or Immanence body, which are the enlightenment stages of the full Arhat and Great Golden Arhat. The person who generates a *yang-shen* body double isn't even a citizen of earth!

Let's say that you attain the Supra-Causal body and generate a *nirmanakaya* body double that is then accused of a crime in the material world. People would then arrest your physical body because it looks like the *nirmanakaya* body-double that committed the crime. However, the physical human being did not commit the crime. The human body is just the home base for all the higher transcendental bodies upstairs; it is a shell they can withdraw into or appendage they can use rather than the real man who committed the crime. It is just a physical shell that the real man is indifferent to discarding.

The human in front of you did <u>not</u> project a *nirmanakaya*. The Supra-Causal individual did it. He has an entirely different birth time and different personality and resides on a different plane of reality than the human body, subtle body and Causal body from which he initially arose. You cannot arrest him because he's living on an entirely different plane of existence. You cannot bribe him or blackmail him, impel him or coerce him in any way. You can even torture the human body but the Supra-Causal guy doesn't care and cannot be forced into doing anything for you. The human form in front of you did nothing and has no power over a *yang-shen* emanation that looks like him. That individual or body *did not generate that body double*. The transcendental guy living on a higher plane did and you cannot touch him or hurt him in any way nor force him to do anything by threatening his human original template that is now just a disposable shell. The guilty party is living in another realm where your laws don't apply to him and don't touch him. It could even be someone entirely unrelated to the individual you see because masters practice generating solid *nirmanakaya* that look like other people all the time; countless western masters, for instance, have their own versions of Jesus images or solid *yang-shen* they generate to satisfy the great demand in the world for idealized images of him.

Millions of Arhats with transcendental bodies, as well as billions of devas, are invisibly intervening in human affairs all the time across the world and everyone is oblivious to this fact while also being powerless to do anything about it.

Sci-fi movies always make this mistake of thinking that a human being can emanate a tangible body double, which is a capability way beyond the powers of even devas and Causal-bodied individuals. They assume that an ordinary person can generate a body double to go do tangible things in the world but no human can do that. Only an Arhat or Great Golden Arhat (possessing a Supra-Causal or Immanence body) can generate an energy body duplicate capable of bilocation and other feats, and such individuals don't exist on this earthly plane. *They are individuals who reside on higher planes of existence. Those are the only guys who can do it.*

Because they reside on a higher plane of existence they generate and project *nirmanakaya* in order to physically interact with us on this plane of existence, and when they are really good at it they can appear in multiple places at once. As Meher Baba explains in *God Speaks*, they typically just give people thoughts, dreams, visions, feelings, inspiration or energy (as in performing healings) with their *nirmanakaya* emanations but if they want a tangible presence then they need to emanate a normal *nirmanakaya* made entirely of energy but then condense the energy into form that can have various levels of density (which is why you can sometimes see through one when it isn't an illusory vision). More examples and explanations are found in *The Secret Inner Teachings of Daoism*.

Everyone might think that a spiritual master's material body is the individual at fault if a *nirmanakaya* committed some type of infraction whereas it is an entirely different individual from the upper realms that would be responsible for a crime. The Supra-Causal body is an independent person and the physical body we see is like an empty sleeve or shell.

A last point of note related to devotional prayer, *bhakti*, *pujas* and so on is the fact that many Hindus say that "God is the one who illumes our senses, causes us to move around to perform activities, and even illumines your mind to think. He is showering us with His grace, love and blessings every moment of our lives." However, we should instead say that it is the whole universe as a single entity that causes this, or we can say that the real Self, the unchanging Brahman, is the ultimate mover and doer. All the while we must remember that there is no such thing as living beings and conscious entities in all this, nor is there a conscious God. The whole universe is doing it.

The Brahman is not a person but a non-composite substrate so the Brahman never does anything at all. As for life, while it is an illusion our own existence is self-evident and does exist even though it is an apparent illusion in terms of its absolute essence. It exists on a plane of densification, crystallization or agglomeration of energies so it is not that it doesn't exist. It just doesn't exist in the way it appears to us. Therefore, and this is KEY, the best course of action is to seek out the joy and bliss possible to life and direct our life in positive ways including the pathway that takes us to transcendental states of beingness. Our life is a process that is always becoming so rather than settling for nihilism or annihilation you should take it to more permanent states of elevation and enjoy what consciousness has given us. After all, with the attainment of the higher bodies we have the means to extend life nearly forever.

To realize what we are, which is the meaning of *self*-realization, simply means to dispel ignorance as to the real state of affairs behind our existence. It does not mean nihilism because we know that we *do exist* at our level of densification, we will always exist at some level of densified agglomeration we do have consciousness even though it is faulty in making errors, and there is a real world surrounding us at our level of agglomeration even if we experience everything imperfectly. The fact is that we perceive things *in a consistent manner* for every possible realm of our existence, and this is what matters. This doesn't produce nihilism but leads to the fact that we should strive to enjoy our lives and make of them the best that we can while also helping others to do so.

ASTROLOGICAL INDICATIONS

Vedic astrologer James Braha states that when Jupiter occupies the 1st house in an individual's natal astrology chart, or aspects the 1st house ruler, then the person tends to spiritually cultivate using the *bhakti* pathway of devotion and prayer (like Krishna devotees), and the same if Jupiter aspects the individual's Sun (which represents the soul) or Moon (which represents the person). This is good information to have if you are pondering *bhakti* as a pathway.

People who follow austere spiritual cultivation paths that strongly involve meditation, introspection, fasting, detachment of the senses, non-attachment to the world and monkhood will usually have Saturn occupying or aspecting the 1st house or Saturn aspecting the 1st house ruler or Sun or Moon.

People who are attracted to the pathway of Advaita Vedanta (non-duality), astrology, the *Vedas* and *Upanishads*, intellectual inquiry, spiritual seminars and associated mental paths tend to have Mercury occupying or aspecting the 1st house, or Mercury aspecting the 1st house ruler or Sun or Moon. This is a pathway that focuses on dispelling the mistakes of the intellect and ascertaining truth with the assumption that "the truth will set one free."

These three spiritual cultivation paths are symbolized by Krishna (a Jupitarian *bhakti* type path), Shiva (a Saturnian austerity pathway of yoga) and Vishnu (a Mercurian mental type pathway that emphasizes thoughtful analysis). Indian culture has many other spiritual paths to add to this so this information is just to get you started thinking about which path might be best for you and letting you know that the right Vedic astrologer can sometimes tell you which path or practices are suitable for your spiritual progress.

CHAPTER 9
MANTRAYANA

Reciting prayers or mantras while listening intently to the words/sounds quiets your mind and calms your Prana circulation to help you attain an internal state of quiescence. A mantra also invites into your body the energies of a particular family of spiritual saints promoting a deity who have vowed to help practitioners who recite the particular mantras they sponsor, which thus helps to purify the Prana of your inner subtle body that then hastens your spiritual development.

The recitation of an artfully constructed mantra will also transform your Prana directly, without need of any transcendental intercession, if the resonance of the sounds vibrates the Prana within your body, thus washing it a bit if the sounds are harmoniously constructed to have the impact of vibrational power.

When you continuously recite prayers in tune with your breathing this will also help to give your pranic circulation a push and purify it as well. Any rhythmical breathing used during recitation will also help to *push* your stimulated Prana in a regular circulatory pattern where the resulting friction will slowly purify it over time. This gradually produces Prana purification of your inner subtle body just as the churning of milk produces its transformation into butter.

Sometimes after continually reciting a mantra it may seem as if the mantra starts being internally recited *automatically* within your body at a specific location without you doing the recitation. It is as if the mantra is being recited on its own, which is a good sign of progress because it means someone else is doing the work and purifying your Prana as well. For instance, after many repetitions you might feel and hear the words of a prayer or mantra being recited from your heart where the recitations are happening automatically without you originating them.

This is actually the sign that an enlightened master has entered your body and is showing students how to move your Prana in tune with the recitation. The expectation is that after he (or she) leaves they will also perform this work for you, which is part of an underlying kundalini purification process disguised as *japa* being self-operational. Many sadhus attained the higher bodies through the method of continuous *japa* practice such as reciting "Ram" because spiritual masters have made vows that they will start washing your Prana when you recite their mantra a sufficient number of times.

Some mantras therefore result in Prana purification due to higher spiritual beings. Some work on transforming both the Yang and Yin Prana of your body, and some primarily purify just your Yang or just your Yin Prana through direct sound resonance.

The same outcome of moving and cleansing your Prana through the power of sound rhythms happens due to singing *bhajans* when they are artfully, harmoniously constructed to embody strong emotional and sound correspondences that move the energies inside you. As you sing *bhajans* the waves of emotion and energy you feel will wash your internal energy, and thus this is a form of spiritual practice not because *bhajans* pay reverence to a deity but because you can use sound energy connected with emotional stimulation to purify the internal energy of your inner subtle body or soul.

Different mantras, prayers, devotional hymns (e.g. the Hanuman *chalisa*) and *bhajans* (as well as books and spiritual texts) when recited, sung or read are "answered by," "protected by," "attended to" or "receive a response" from enlightened masters who through their vows have assumed responsibility for them in order to help human beings spiritually ascend. You cannot help everybody so various enlightened Vedic masters have vowed various types of intercessory aid, dependent upon their interest, to those who perform specific types of spiritual activity that they want to sponsor that they feel connected with. This is due solely to their compassion and grace.

A mantra, *chalisa*, *kirtan*, *bhajan*, prayer, song, hymn etc. will create a certain emotion in the mind that then becomes reflected in an individual's Prana by changing its quality, movements or vibration. Some create peace, some create happiness, some create calm or the feeling of protection because they affect certain neurons and *nadis* in the brain and because they provoke emotional reactions. Prana and the mind (thoughts) are linked because consciousness runs on the same pranic energy. Therefore your thoughts can affect the Prana of your body which is why you can lead your life force around inside you.

Vedic mantras properly pronounced repetitiously will produce the mental effect of well-being without baser emotions dominating your mind. This spiritual result is also sometimes due to the intercession of spiritual masters projecting very fine *nirmanakaya* into those individuals to fulfill their vows of helping those mantras succeed in such tasks. Naturally these are spiritual masters who have attained the long-lived transcendental bodies and fill their time with this as one of their compassionate activities which is achieved through *nirmanakaya* projections. In response to their Supra-Causal or Immanence (Buddha) body hearing the recitation of a mantra, prayer, *chalisa, kirtan, bhajan* or text they have chosen to protect they project *nirmanakaya* emanations to work on purifying the Prana of the practitioners reciting them, or help to solve their mental problems of understanding by giving them ideas, and so forth.

Therefore a good mantra or prayer is one that you feel moves the Prana within your body because this shows you are receiving a response for your work. Just as some enlightened masters become the spiritual protectors of temples, towns or cities, the hidden truth of Hinduism is that higher spiritual beings will also respond to mantras, prayers, spiritual texts or rituals being performed due to their personal vows to help those who recite the chosen mantra or prayer, perform the ritual, or read the scripture they have vowed to "protect" or "patronize" through "sponsorship." This is the secret compassion of the "deities" of Hinduism, although the "deities" are just enlightened spiritual masters masquerading as deities.

Even without this help there are certain mantra *bija* sounds that can *naturally resonate, vibrate or stimulate* the Prana within particular parts of your body. Therefore some mantras with the right *bijas* in the right order will also help to strongly purify your Prana through the power of those sound vibrations alone even without heavenly aid. When mantras are constructed of specific seed syllables that vibrate specific areas of your body then reciting these sounds can help vibrate and elevate the Prana in those locations. This is often better than hoping that reciting a mantra with discordant sounds will invite an enlightened master to do this for you. The *Yoga Yajnavalkya* has a list of useful *bija* and body part correspondences.

To make *japa* (mantra recitation) practice, *chalisa* practice, or prayer practice even more effective, you can:

(1) Generate strong emotions at the same time you practice your recitations in order to better arouse your Prana so that it is fully stimulated and moving.
(2) Think of possessing in yourself the most ideal model of a particular personality trait during that recitation and amplify the feeling of that core *bhava*; you should create a full body feeling of having that desired trait or attitude that you wish to incorporate into your life, and in daily life you should work towards becoming a person of whom you highly approve because you work on developing those traits.
(3) Combine this type of mantra or prayer recitation with visualization efforts (when appropriate) that also stimulate your Prana into moving, or use them to concentrate it at a selected location in your body (such as when you visualize that a certain portion of your body shines with light).
(4) When reciting, use your willpower to try and stimulate (energize) the Prana in different areas of your body according to the sounds or their meaning.

When you do these things then *japa* mantra practice, *chalisa* chanting, *dhoon* singing and prayer recitation becomes Mantrayana, *which is a more effective type of spiritual practice than simply rote recitation alone.* You either want to be calming your mind and Prana due to recitation or you want to be stimulating your internal energy so that a new quality of Prana washes over all your tissues. The principle is that you are using sound to move your Prana throughout your body, and you color it by arousing different attitudes or emotions simultaneously so that different flavors of Prana are being washed throughout your tissues during your efforts.

Basically, whenever you recite a prayer, *chalisa*, or mantra *you should try to move the Prana within your body*, and it's even better if you impregnate the Prana of your entire body with a specific Yin or Yang feeling, attitude or emotion to help energize your Prana for purification purposes.

By moving your Prana through rhythmical breathing and resonant sounds that vibrate its energies, and by actively impregnating it with various emotional tones simultaneously, you will actively cleanse your subtle body's Prana in a much diluted fashion than what goes on during the twelve to fourteen year kundalini transformation period. This is therefore a portion of the intensified yoga practices, or path of preparation, that prepares for your birth in an independent deva body.

During Vedic mantra recitation, if you recite the Sanskrit words with the exact proper tone and proper regulated breathing it will vibrate your *nadis* and Prana naturally in a particularly intended region of your body whose cavity or structure harmoniously resonates with those sounds. This is why it is a spiritual practice, otherwise it is just rote repetition.

ENVIRONMENTAL AND EVENT PRANA

You can actually change your Prana by changing your *environmental Prana too*, such as by changing the city where you live so that you absorb different energies from the place. You can adjust the placement of objects within your house, or its décor, for the similar reason of making the energy feel better because you will be absorbing the energy of that natural environment as long as you live there. As an example, if you cultivate in a cool cave made of limestone or having (calcium carbonate-based) stalagmites then that environment of cool Yin Prana will enter your body and affect your own Prana when you do recitations.

If you cultivate in a cremation ground at midnight in pitch blackness, which is done in Aghori traditions to raise your fear, those strong fear and anxiety-based Yin emotions will stimulate your Yin Prana into arousing in that Yin environment, and at that time you should try to use various methods to push that Yin Prana around your body to wash its tissues. If you were to cultivate in a dry desert or simply an arid environment, this would be beneficial to certain types of Prana cultivation too.

The western field of astrolocality lines is absent from Vedic culture but can be used to pinpoint certain exact locations where you will experience certain modes in life and associated types of feelings that will equate with different Prana responses inside your body. In this case the response of living under such lines will be correlated with the meaning of planets in different houses and signs in your natal astrology chart, and this will produce a particular Yin or Yang or five element correspondence in your Prana, life and fortune. One need only visit those locations to feel the corresponding energy, and together with relocation astrology (which is far, far more important than astrolocality lines) you can wisely change the environmental Prana of your residence.

The energy of a location can also be classified as hot-cold or dry-wet, which will have an effect on your Prana just as the weather does, and even if you live far inland the calculation of solunar forces (used for hunting and fishing) may have some influence.

If you were to cultivate in a room with a working Van de Graaff generator that was filling your environment with strong electromagnetic fields this would also be another way to expose your body's Prana energy to an entirely different type of energy. If you are sitting in a hot mineral bath (as done in Japan) where the heat penetrates your body, raises your temperature and thus spurs the speed of chemical reactions then this too would be a way of using environment Prana to affect your own inner energies so that you could use that time for special internal Prana washing exercises. Nyasa Yoga or *pratyahara*, whose equivalent is the Chinese *nei-gong* practices, either invite enlightened masters to change your energies using their own or have you change your own energies yourself without regards to the environment.

Naturally, it goes without saying that living an ethical life by cultivating virtuous ways (the *Yoga Yajnavalkya*, for instance, stresses non-violence, non-harmfulness, truthfulness, not stealing, celibacy or fidelity to one's partner, kindness and compassion, sincerity, forgiveness, fortitude, moderation, cleanliness and purity, persistence, contentment, generosity, and modesty) is taught to us as a way to purify our minds, but the über-intent is that holding ourselves in this manner (of non-harmfulness to others in thought, word or deed and the highmindedness of always trying to do the right thing) is also a way to continuously color your Prana and thus transform it over time. Rituals and rites that help center your mind back on this pathway of being a good person, which is elevating ourselves above baser instincts from our animal nature, thus serve as an assist to transforming your Prana to a state of ascension.

Of course, *events* will also temporarily change your Prana to an extreme extent such as mourning a loved one's death (that activates your Yin Prana), confessing one's faults or crimes (which raises Yin Prana), begging for food (raises your Yin Prana), attending peppy music concerts, sports events, happy ceremonies or popular cinema (that raise your Yang Prana), watching a scary movie (that evokes your Yin Prana), winning a contest (that stimulates your Yang Prana) and so forth.

YIN PRANA CULTIVATION TECHNIQUES

As events, the Aghoris are famous for putting initiates through frightening *sadhanas* involving dead bodies in order to raise and wash their Yin Prana.

The spiritual masters in the Chöd tradition (from the Yundrung Bön tradition of Tibet) create frightening visions of ghosts and demons in practitioners to stimulate their Yin energy and help cleanse those channels.

In the Shugendo tradition of Japan, practitioners climb a mountain and then are hung upside down over a cliff to arouse their Yin Prana due to the anxiety, fright and fear of the event.

In Hinduism there are many happy celebratory holidays that praise deities where the population raises its Yang energies in total. Various *yajna* ceremonies or Vedic rituals are designed to stimulate your Prana as well.

There are also special cultivation practices, *tapas* or spiritual *sadhana* meant to arouse your Yin or Yang Prana for extended periods of time. The Jains are famous for going naked, which at first makes them embarrassed and ashamed until they get used to it, and during that initial embarrassing discomfort their Yin Prana is stimulated. Christian Greek Orthodox monks are instructed to continuously recite a prayer that arouses guilt, humility and surrender in order to evoke Yin Prana: "Lord Jesus Christ have mercy on me a sinner." I know of a situation on Mount Athos where a monk was kept in a state of fearful anxiety for months (on purpose) because his monastery would not register him as a monk, which at that time would prevent the government from inducting him into the army. He remained in hiding for several months on the island while government officials looked for him, always in fear and worry, until the monastery finally registered him after the enlightened masters deemed he had done enough Yin purification.

In another situation I also know of a Tibetan tulku who was supposed to take over a monastery because of his title but was refused for a period of time by an enlightened master occupying it in order to arouse within him specific emotions, but of course the monk had no clue.

The sage Ramakrishna wore women's clothes for a period of time so that the temporary mental feminization would stimulate his Yin Prana. A similar cultivation method is hinted at in the Buddhist *Vimalakirti Sutra* that was thrust upon the aspiring sage Sharipputra. Several great warriors with strong Yang Prana were also said to have passed through this feminization method, namely Hercules, Thor, Arjuna, and Krishna. This particular method needs some more detailed discussion because it is often thrust upon practices and they should not go astray.

In the *Vimalakirti Sutra* the story reported is that countless Buddhas (enlightened masters) and deva students enter the enlightened layman Vimalakirti's small room, which symbolizes heavenly beings using the *anima siddhi* to shrink down and enter his brain. This actually describes what happens to you during the twelve-year period of kundalini transformation where enlightened masters bring their students inside you to teach how consciousness works, and to transform your Prana and their Prana at the same time. Sharipputra, who was an ascetic with a reputation for great knowledge about the nature of reality that would equate with Advaita Vedanta, is present in Vimalakirti's small room. Flowers fall down and stick to him and the other students who haven't yet achieved full enlightenment, which means those less than the stage of the full Arhat. The many flowers represent the fact that the accomplished ones use many methods to change their Prana but don't get attached to the methods.

At this time Sharipputra is said to have been changed into a women by a goddess (it was actually just a mental feeling rather than an actual sex change) and he could not through his own mental efforts change back to restoring the feeling of his masculine Yang Prana again, so after a while the goddess then "changed him back into a man." The actual meaning is that a female Arhat projected a *nirmanakaya* to enter into him to help purify his Yin Prana, he felt the difference of this energy, but now could not shake the feelings of being a woman due to her thoughts and the prevalence of Yin Prana. He had to bear it until she stopped doing this.

The fact that he could not shake off the feeling of Yin Prana thrust upon him is why the flowers stuck to him, although another reason is actually a warning to Varjrayana students who use sexual fantasies (imagining they are young girls or imagining having sex with female devas) as a cultivation method. They often drop into the imaginations through the loss of self-control, which is a clinging also symbolized by the flowers sticking to Shariputra and the other students. This type of scenario is also mentioned as a warning in the second set of fifty Demon *Mara* states within the *Surangama Sutra*.

In fact, the story of the thunder god Indra having to bear 1,000 marks of a vagina all over his body is actually equivalent to Shariputra's story of his temporary transformation into a woman featured in the Buddhist *Vimalakirti Sutra*. The thunder god Indra, who is a symbol of excessive Yang Prana, had made love to the Sage Gautama's wife, Ahalya, and for his adultery was then cursed by the enlightened sage to have these marks appear on his body. Gautama also cursed the moon and his wife, both additional signs of Yin Prana in the tale.

The secret meaning of the story is that Indra was either engaged in sexual intercourse with someone, or just mentally imagining sexual congress as a practice, to transform his Yin Prana for the enlightenment path. It is not mentioned in this tantric story, but part of this sexual methodology usually involves a male practitioner imagining that he is a woman in order to stimulate his Yin Prana into being excited and washed. The image of adultery (a Yin situation) was used to indicate that this is an unorthodox path forbidden to most people, and you will also find instances of Adi Shankara or Matsyendranatha also engaging in forbidden sexual activities.

The fact that the 1,000 vaginas on Indra's body later turned into eyes symbolize the omnipresence of enlightenment achieved after Indra passes through some strong stage of Yin Prana purification assisted by the sage Gautama. When the vagina marks appeared Indra initially hid himself because of embarrassment (another Yin emotion) and these facts, together with hiding in darkness and the plethora of vaginas upon him, clearly indicates his cultivation of Yin Prana that only initiates understand correctly. To remove the vaginas Indra had to worship the goddess Adi Parashakti, another sign of great Yin Prana, who turned the marks into eyes. Overall the story means that Indra obtained omniscience (enlightenment) after passing through a prolonged period of cultivating his Yin Prana that involved a short period of mental feminization ... although many other cultivation methods and time were no doubt also required.

The *Devi-Bhagavata Purana* narrates a tale where once Shiva was making love with Parvati in Sharavana ("The Forest of Reeds") but they were intruded upon, so Shiva cursed the forest so that all-male beings entering it became female. This later happened to a man named Sudyumna who became a woman Ila due to the magic. As a woman Ila married Budha, the god of the planet Mercury. Sudyumna was related to King Ishvaku, founder of the Solar dynasty, and as the woman Ila bore a son Pururavas who became founder of the Lunar dynasty. Thus the story indicates a similar secret tantric meditation in order to transform the Yin and Yang Prana of your body.

Yet another story concerns an incident when Lord Rama was leaving for a fourteen year exile from his Kingdom of Ayodhya, which could be taken as an analogous period to the twelve to fourteen year kundalini purification period. Many people followed Lord Rama to the edge of the forest and then returned to his kingdom. Everyone returned except the Kinnars (transgenders) who stayed out and waited near the edge of the forest for his return, which possibly insinuates a Yin Prana process similar to Indra's during Rama's forest exile, which certainly involved the Yang processes of fighting.

The sage Ramakrishna similarly dressed and acted like a women for a period of time in order to stimulate and purify his Yin Prana but few people are qualified to understand such tantric practices. Ramakrishna practiced sixty-four ancient tantric purification techniques, with this being just one of them, and few people have the teachings or wisdom to know that this he used this technique to further differentiate his Yin Prana from Yang Prana.

Ramakrishna's behavior had nothing to do with transgenderism, homosexuality, homoeroticism or any other type of sexual offshoot.

The same applies to Shariputra's case where the Yin Prana feelings were thrust upon him by an enlightened woman (goddess) as a means to help purify his Prana through Yin divinization, and the story was created to pass this secret tantric information onto practitioners who must go through the process so that they won't get worried. In yet another Buddhist story a monk was going through the kundalini process felt like he had been transformed into a woman, and then ran away from his monastery to hide because of his embarrassment.

The Indian mythologist Devdutt Pattanaik collected many such stories in *Myth = Mithya: Decoding Hindu Mythology*, but he did not know this principle behind many of the stories. Since so few people understand this technique that we should discuss it in some detail to provide insight, and will focus on the Greek myths since so few people recognize that they too contain spiritual knowledge just as the Hindu myths and legends do.

The Greek story of Hercules has a tale where the hero was forced to wear women's clothes and take up a woman's work of knitting (working on his *nadis*) for one year. The German-Norse thunder god Thor dressed in women's clothes to retrieve his hammer (cultivate his Prana) from a giant, and in the *Mahabharata* Arjuna dressed in women's attire for one year which also illustrates this method.

Another related tale is the Greek story of Tiresias, the prophet of Apollo whom the Goddess Hera (symbolizing an enlightened woman once again) transformed into a woman for seven years after he started beating two copulating snakes that he encountered on a road. The two mating snakes represent the Yin and Yang Prana of his physical body that he had finally purified and differentiated due to his spiritual cultivation practice, so the story was simply saying that this method was imposed upon him after he had reached a certain stage in his cultivation efforts.

This famous gender-change story also refers to cultivating Yin Prana through imaginary feminization in order to develop an enlightened subtle body with all its powers. It is said that Tiresias was later changed back into a man but was blinded by Hera. Zeus, however, then gave him the gift of clairvoyance (the ability to divine the future) and a lifetime of seven lives. This long lifespan of seven generations and his superpowers were basically indicating that he attained the deva body, which lives for hundreds of years if it is purified through the pathway of spiritual cultivation, which is what

Tiresias was doing as the priest of Apollo. His blindness was a symbol that his physical body was "negated" because he now relied on his subtle deva body for sight rather than his human eyes after his Srotapanna attainment. The deva body has the power to see things far away, hear things far away, and typically gives one small clairvoyance, which also explains his gifts of foresight.

It was only after Tiresias had initiated the kundalini awakening that separated out his Yin and Yang or masculine and feminine Prana (the two snakes) through purification that he was exposed to the more advanced Prana purification technique symbolized by being transformed into a woman (female Buddhas possessed his body with their *nirmanakaya* so that their Yin energy would further differentiate and purify his own Yin Prana). Doubtless he used other Yang purification techniques as well, but the point is that this experience was thrust upon him since that is what happens to most practitioners.

Narada, Krishna's student in the *Bhagavata Purana*, also becomes a woman after bathing in water which symbolized that he also used the imagination of having a woman's Prana to cultivate the Yin Prana of his body.

Another story related to Krishna and Radha is that Sudyumna and his horse (who represents Sudyumna's Prana just as Hanuman's mace represents Hanuman's Prana) were also turned into females in the forest of Shiva-Parvati lovemaking. All men who entered this forest were turned into the opposite sex, which carries a meaning related to the tantric purification processes we are discussing.

To cultivate their Prana, after specific instructions from an enlightened master tantriks sometimes employ this type of imagination during sex or as a standalone sexual fantasy during appropriate conditions. If you are not under the tutelage of an enlightened master and receive such instructions, such as with imaginary *karmamudra* practice, you will make mistakes and go astray. Once again, this is why the flowers that fell from heaven in Vimalakirti's brain stuck to the bodies of all the low-level practitioners.

The Vajrayana *karmamudra* practices of Buddhism use imaginary sex with a visualized consort in order to change one's Prana, which is also found in some Indian practices of Tantric Yoga since most of the Vajrayana methods came from India. Their purpose is to excite your energy through imaginary sexual congress that stimulate it through visualizations and strong attitudes, and then one blazes or spreads that awakened Prana to wash one's body tissues.

The Indian Sufi Meher Baba disguised the real meaning of these tantric methods for public consumption, but did us a great favor by commenting a bit on this imaginary feminization technique in his *Discourses*. He wrote:

> If one is transcending sexual duality and trying to understand the experience associated with the opposite sex, sometimes one actually exhibits the traits usually associated with the opposite sex. Thus, for example, some aspirants in the male body at one phase or another actually put on the clothes of women, talk like them, feel like them, and take on their habits. But this is only a passing phase. When inner understanding of the relevant experiences is complete, they neither experience themselves as male nor as female alone but as being *beyond* the distinction of sex. The experiences connected with the male and female forms are both accessible and intelligible to the aspirants who have transcended sexual distinctions. They remain unaffected by the limitations of either, because through understanding they have freed themselves from the limiting obsessions characteristic of sex-ridden imagination.[5]

In many spiritual traditions a practitioner is told to cultivate Yang Prana through masculinity practices where they identify with a heroic deity with tremendous courage, strength or power in order to arouse their Yang Prana for an extended period of time. This is what is done to women although some men are instructed to generate divine anger or divine pride to raise their Yang Prana for a short while. When they are young, girls are also often given dreams where they are a virile young man in order to stimulate their Yang Prana, such as being an adventurer riding a horse or a warrior going off to battle. The thermal heat mapping images which show where emotions are felt within your body can explain many such methods, especially dreams where you appear in various situations in order to affect your energy in specific ways.

Countless individuals throughout history have used singing,

---

[5] *Discourses*, Meher Baba (Sherira Press, South Carolina, 2000), pp. 325-326.

prayer or mantra recitation as a means to calm their mind and transform their Prana as part of the intensified preparatory internal work necessary for attaining the deva body of spiritual enlightenment. The main practice in religious avenues have usually focused around visualizations or "imaginary cognition" of some type. When you continuously recite mantras or prayers this is just another technique designed to affect your Prana through resonance or by calling for heavenly aid in Prana purification because those words have no magic to them. They are especially effective if you do this while holding onto strong attitudes that color your Prana with a dominant energy that is out of the ordinary and far beyond normal.

BIJA SOUNDS TO VIBRATE YOUR BODY IN SPECIFIC LOCATIONS

As stated, certain mantra sounds or root syllables (*bijas*) are incredibly effective at vibrating (stimulating) the Prana in certain sections of your body through natural resonance. Three short examples are the consecutive sounds of "Om Ah Hung," "Om So Hum" or "Ah Rah Ham" whose syllables (*bijas*) affect the Prana in your (1) head and arms; (2) chest region; and (3) abdomen together with legs, respectively.

Many people know about these three mantras, and there are many more. They are equally effective in vibrating the energy within different sections of your body when you focus each sound on a particular body region. Actually, when reciting the syllables of these mantras they should be felt in all parts of your body equally, as is the preferred case for all three-syllable mantras, unless you are specifically reciting each syllable within a smaller section, or rotating the sounds through sections, for the purposes of *emphasizing Prana purification in that region*. Sometimes you do this by attaching a large emotion to each region as well.

"Aim Hreem Shreem" (where "Aim" is pronounced "I'm") is another popular mantra that can also be used to excite or vibrate the Prana of your entire body or to stimulate it in your three body sections consecutively.

"Om So Hum," "Om So Ha" or just "So Ha(m)" are mantras usually associated with breathing methods. The sounds of many mantras, such as "Ah Rah Ham," can also be used to *pulse* the entire

Prana of your body in rhythmical fashion when recited to do so with that intent.

Once again, usually you try to feel each syllable in your *entire body matrix* when each is pronounced. Or you might move the energy in your body starting from your head and push it towards your feet as you hold the syllable, such as when enunciating the "Ah" sound. You can also start from your feet and move the sound power upwards inside you. You can start within your stomach area and move the sound outwards everywhere. You can recite the sound as if from the perimeter of your body and have the sound pour inwards, and so forth for each syllable respectively.

There are many ways to move energy within yourself with the basic principle being to do just that: move the energy inside your body with your mind as you pronounce the sounds, and to be simultaneously stimulating different emotions at the same time to further energize your Prana with energies different than normal.

Another alternative is to try to feel the effect of the sounds along certain acupuncture meridians (energy channels) or within certain body parts and pathways. You can also recite mantras on certain *bindus*, *marma* points, acupuncture or acupressure points in order to stimulate the Prana around those locations.

An example is the following mantra that uses *bijas* to vibrate special body parts in sequence so that the sound power washes your Prana rather than just calls upon spiritual beings for aid. When you recite each line you can concentrate on a certain elevating attitude or emotion that elevates the Prana of that region, such as joy and generosity extending from the heart to the arms and hands, and so on.

Here is a mantra designed to vibrate separate sections of your body due to the *bijas*:

Om Ah Chr Jha Rah
Rha Bha Hreem Shreem Tah
Hoo Ssss Foo Shoo Vam
Lam Tah Bam Dam Tam.

You can think of it vibrating the body in this way, and can in fact focus your concentration on vibrating those sections as the appropriate *bija* is recited:

Om (head) *Ah* (nasal cavity and forehead) *Chr* (teeth and gums) *Jha* (throat and thyroid) *Rah* (heart and chest torso)
Rha (chest torso) *Bha* (shoulder bones and shoulders) *Hreem* (upper arms) *Shreem* (lower arms) *Tah* (hands)
Hoo (stomach) *Ssss* (lungs) *Foo* (kidneys) *Shoo* (liver) *Vam* (lower abdomen with *dantian*)
Lam (*dantian*) *Tah* (private parts) *Bam* (thighs) *Dam* (lower legs) *Tam* (feet).

You can recite one, two, three, four or five syllable mantras in order to cultivate the Prana of that many different sections of your body respectively, and if you simultaneously hold onto an emotion at the same time, or simultaneously hold onto the idea of being one with some spiritual great like Krishna, the practice will impress your Prana with the influence of those extras.

In special versions of Tantric Yoga you even envision and intone certain *bija* seed syllables within your body to vibrate its Prana while you identify with being a beautiful, opulent, heroic, fierce or ecstatic deity). The mantra and your visualization efforts notifies enlightened masters that you are doing this practice so that they might learn of your efforts and then help you.

If you recite mantras while trying to feel, move, excite or stimulate the Prana in different areas of the body, naturally this effort can be helped by also simultaneously using emotional excitement or other vitalizing and invigorating techniques such as visualizations and rhythmical breathing. And, if you also put your mind/will on those areas to move your Prana in conjunction with reciting and feeling those sound syllables then you will quickly stimulate your Prana into oscillating throughout your subtle body. This will thus purify and strengthen its structural integrity.

VISUALIZATION ADD-ONS

Adding visualization efforts to the relevant body sections at the same time – by using your imagination to mentally flood an area with bright light or change its color (which instantly changes your energy because of mental energy-light connotations you've built up in your memories during life) – will also help to energize and purify its Prana because those actions will bring energy into the region while the color will change the temperament, flavor, quality or frequency of your energy.

Aside from using visualization with mantra practice, you can also independently practice visualizing certain colors and shapes as a way to cultivate mental stability, which is a result of concentration practice. You practice holding images steady in your mind for as long as possible to build your powers of concentration, which is a necessity for many tantric *sadhana*, or you can practice mentally rehearsing moving scenarios.

You can even practice visualizing light and/or colors at certain points within your body, and can visualize special shapes or pathways inside your body in order to stimulate your Prana. Sports figures use mental rehearsals (visualizations) to train their body to perform athletic activities with excellence. This is explained in *Sport Visualization for the Elite Athlete* (Bodri) and *Visualization Power* (Bodri).

Visualization practice is just a superior way to develop the mental skill of concentration. You can use it to hold your Prana at one place in your body in order to open up all the *nadis* in that region, which is done in certain branches of Yoga.

The ability to hold a stable concentration in your mind leads to a stronger mind, i.e. stronger powers of focus and concentration and the ability to ignore mental distractions. When you develop stronger mental powers of focus you can more easily ignore afflictions, annoyances and distractions that spontaneously arise in your mind without your invitation – "mental defilements" that are recruited into your mind depending on circumstances – and thus make headway into mastering the functioning of your mind. After all, you are not the commander-in-chief in control of most of your mental functions (thoughts, emotions, or willpower) since they happen automatically. You are not in control of the algorithms for your conduct and actions since they are determined by a multitude of bottom-up processes without an "I" or monolithic executive in control of them. Nonetheless this is one way to seemingly gain control over some of the mind's functioning.

Your consciousness is not in control of your brain, meaning the things that arise in your mind because mental events are a product of these processes rather than their master. For instance, you fall asleep despite not wanting to and then lose the presence of a witness, so the self-ego must then *not be the ultimate master* of your configuration of mental processes. Remember, you are an organism with consciousness that creates the illusion a self completely in control of consciousness. However, you can learn how to gain control over some of these processes including how to change unwanted mental states at will, but it requires practice.

For the cultivation purpose of gradually purifying your subtle body you should especially practice holding bright images of Prana such as flames, fires, lights, the sun, etcetera in your abdomen, heart, brain, and other areas of your body as is also done in various religions, *and do so while reciting mantras* because this will cultivate both your Prana and exercise your mental powers of focus and concentration.

Visualization or "imaginary cognition" is commonly used in various Hindu spiritual practices for visualizing deities and feeling the deity's energy inside yourself by imagining that you become one with them or because they enter into you. When you perform such *sadhana*, spiritual masters who previously succeeded with that technique will often come to lend you their energy to help purify and transform your subtle body.

As explained countless times, this is what happens when you recite particular mantras as well. As previously stated, the hidden aspect within Hinduism is that certain mantras will naturally vibrate (and thus purify) your Prana all on their own because those sounds resonate strongly with certain body sections while other mantras are actually requesting an enlightened being to send you their aid.

The best mantras are composed of *bija* sounds that actually vibrate your Yin or Yang Prana naturally without the need of heavenly intercession because they change your body's energy temperament through oscillating your energy naturally. As examples, "Om" seems to vibrate the energies of the head and chest while "Ah" resonates more so in the chest. "Ram" (Rang, Rahlam, Rah) and "Vam" (Vah, Vang, Lam, Lang, Lah, Nam, Hum, Hung) are very useful sounds for vibrating the Prana within the top-bottom or left-right sides of the body.

Several famous Hindu mantras for stimulating the Prana or kundalini of your body with impact include "Aim Hreem Kleem Shreem Yam Ram Lam Sham Dam Van Tam" and "Om Lam Hah Hreem Rah Aim Hum Souah Rah." It is the most beneficial when you recite each *bija* syllable in the body section where it vibrates your energy the most.

The point is that some mantras can particularly vibrate the Prana in specific sections of your body to "raise your kundalini." Afterwards you can try to "blaze the energy and spread it" throughout your body. This is how you quickly transform and purify the Prana of your inner subtle body, which is by vitalizing different modalities of your Prana by the simultaneous emotional tones you generate, and then spreading the feeling of that energy everywhere within you to wash all your tissues.

For the best results you should always combine *japa* (mantra repetition practice) with pranayama, meditation and other spiritual exercises. Don't just rely on one cultivation technique but *simultaneously practice several that work according to different principles*. Through the repetition of sounds and the practice of special breathing rhythms you can gradually activate the potential of your inner energy that is already there within your body's structure. You can thereby provoke it into responding, which is the same goal as in kundalini yoga and other spiritual practices.

Remember that the power of sound can impact your body's energy so it can alter your body's Prana, which means that it can help to purify your internal subtle energy. Just listening to music will help change your energy too, but a more significant method is to sing *bhajans* or recite mantras. Because certain enlightened masters have vowed to respond to certain mantras and *bhajans* they will emanate a *nirmanakaya* projection body to envelop your body and help transform your Prana as you recite a mantra or sing *bhajans*, or they will send their students to help you.

That is the hidden spiritual secret of Hindu cultivation methods. This discussion touches upon many issues explaining why reverential *bhajans* work and why mantras work too. Different enlightened masters will respond to different mantras, *bhajans*, hymns, etc. according to their vows of intercession or not. If you work at becoming an expert in the sound yoga of *bija* physical correspondences and use the recitation or singing of *bijas* to move your Prana on its own then this cultivation method can ultimately help you to attain the supreme reality.

CHAPTER 10
TANTRIC YOGA FOR INNER KUNDALINI PRACTICE

The commonly held view of kundalini cultivation, which is the precursor to the twelve or more years of internal Prana rotations that purify your inner subtle body for the enlightenment of its emergence from your body, is that your kundalini is pranic energy lying dormant in your *muladhara* root chakra within your pelvis, and that this life force is the energy of your astral (subtle) body. The view promoted by many Hindu texts is that this energy is sleeping like a coiled snake but you can make it arise by concentrating on different chakras in the body one after the other. This is all designed to mislead you.

The popular theory of kundalini cultivation is that by mentally focusing on the chakras this will supposedly cause the real Prana, life force energy of the body or your kundalini energy, to start traveling upward through all your chakras until it reaches the top of your head and you achieve samadhi, or some type of ecstatic state or mystical experience such as "becoming one with the universe."

This is all simply rubbish.

Your real Prana is not lying dormant in your *muladhara* root chakra but is subtle energy permeates every cell of your body just as you would expect if you understand the theory of the *koshas* and your subtle body. Also, your Prana is, like blood, always circulating within your body and passing through your head so it is not true that when your Prana reaches your head (because of spiritual exercises) that you will feel that you are out of the body, not your body or encounter some mystical state. Many spiritual exercises have you leading your pranic life force energy up and through your head in countless revolutions to wash those tissues and you normally only feel the energy washing. Where is the mysticism or mystery in that? There is none.

The profound mental experiences described in ancient texts are due to enlightened spiritual masters possessing people and giving them strong inner energy experiences by moving the energies of their *nirmanakaya* inside them. This also enables an enlightened sage to take control of your conscious experience because a spiritual master can use his or her *nirmanakaya* to overlay mental states they have mastered upon your own thinking to give you particular positive, motivating mental experiences. They come up wilt all sorts of misleading visions and explanations because they basically don't want people to know that enlightenment is a body attainment.

The truth of spiritual development is that your Prana must revolve through all the tissues of your body to wash them, which means washing your inherent subtle energy body, in order for you to arise in a purified transcendental body to achieve liberation from the material realm, and this is a process requiring more than twelve years of work by innumerable enlightened spiritual masters who must use their own energies to wash yours. *Their energies* are the strong kundalini energies you read about. Any special mental states you experience also come from them demonstrating to their peers and students different types of ecstatic projections they have mastered. When you become enlightened and your body is basically energy and you basically have thousands of years to live, then a good portion of your time is spent figuring out a life purpose and mastering all the various capabilities of your body and your *nirmanakaya* projections, and this is when you get a chance to show off and demonstrate your skills to peers.

So kundalini purification is a critical principle hidden in Hinduism and many other religions who might call the subtle body attainment a stage of Arhatship, heavenly transcendence, *Homo Deus* or a stage of super-living with longevity. Many masters mention this process of kundalini purification without going into the details. It is a process besought with difficulties and takes *at least* twelve years (usually more) in a quiet place with a good teacher.

To reach this stage is the actual purpose of Hinduism. Hindu culture is designed to enable people to find inner peace and live together with one another in a peaceful, harmonious, cooperative way. It is also designed so that through adherence to its codes of conduct and standards for relationships we naturally become moral, ethical, virtuous beings with a high inner life above the animals, and that through our practices of spiritual devotion and worship we expose ourselves to countless opportunities for washing our Prana so that our subtle body also becomes gradually purified in this way as well. The ultimate worldly target of such practices is to reach this outcome where you begin to experience the kundalini awakening of radical Prana transformations within your body so that a purified subtle energy body can emerge as a spiritual life independent of matter.

Remember that your Prana energy *is in all the cells of your body* and not just resting in the *muladhara* chakra that symbolizes the region of your pelvis. That fullness of Prana, the basis of your subtle body, is why an entire subtle body emerges from your corpse upon death.

Another common misconception is that your *sahasrara* crown chakra is some astral flower above your head whereas the hidden truth is that the "crown chakra" means your brain with all its nerves and neurons. In addition, the *ajna* chakra refers to your two-part brain stem that is described as a masculine-feminine composite through the symbolism of the Shiva-Parvati *Ardhanarishvara* combination in the *Brihadaranyaka Upanishad*. The half male and half female Vishnu-Lakshmi composite of *Vaikuntha Kamalaja*, which is worshipped in some parts of Nepal and Kashmir, also represents the brain stem.

These figures are said to represent the union of *Purusha-Prakriti* or *Shiva-Shakti*, as well as a harmonious natural balance of energy within your body, but in terms of chakras they represent the brain stem that produces our thinking rather than a third eye on the forehead. Sometimes they represent the two halves of the brain, or two halves of the body.

A Shiva lingam, which among other things is said to represent Shiva and the power of creation (generative power of existence), *is also a symbol of consciousness* because it is another representation of the brain stem. The brain stem is the *Kaustubha* divine jewel of Hinduism, the most valuable jewel in the universe that is spun out of the Ocean of Milk. The brain stem is that part of our brain responsible for thinking so it is the "wish-fulfilling gem" of Buddhism too.

Traditional kundalini teachings state that when your Prana reaches the brain and the *sahasrara* chakra it means that the awakened power of kundalini (Shakti) unites with Shiva. This is called the union of Shiva and Shakti, but it actually refers to the Prana going through the two-part brain stem (*ajna* chakra or *Ardhanarishvara*) since this is responsible for consciousness and thinking. Every part of the brain will go through hundreds of thousands of washings of kundalini, or divine energy, when your subtle body is being purified but yoga texts and the *Upanishads* call attention to this event and talk about special mental states in order to make aspirants work hard at their *sadhana*. They want spiritual aspirants to do lots of preparatory inner circulation and energy work to make the twelve years of kundalini washing revolutions possible.

The true meaning of the chakras, which is part of the hidden Hinduism that is taught to worthy adepts and initiates, is explained in Appendix 1. Basically, to become enlightened through the liberation of achieving the subtle body, and then to attain the yet higher transcendental bodies, you must engage in activities of worship where higher beings use their energies to purify your own or you must perform energy exercises yourself to rotate the Prana in your body sections to purify your inherent subtle body. This includes pushing or pulling Prana up your spine and then down the front of your body and down your alimentary canal in the center of your body ... and circulating your Prana in your appendages, including sexual organs, to wash the tissues by the friction of revolution. Various Yoga texts teach us to do this.

One popular way you can work at this is by approaching the body in cross-sections delineated by the sections of the spine, which are basically the chakra horizontal sectional designations. You can segment the body in other ways too, but most *Upanishads* refer to chakra sections and you are supposed to understand the principle that there are many other ways to segment the body as well. The *Yoga Yajnavalkya* gives us some examples as well as the Appendix.

Although your Prana circulates everywhere within you, many yoga texts emphasize that your Prana ascends into your head because at the earliest stages of spiritual cultivation you spend a lot of time moving your Prana up your spine through mind-led visualizations and other efforts.

It is easiest to clear these Prana circulatory routes just by guiding your Prana to move in an upwards and downwards circulatory orbit hundreds of times per days for about three months. A common introductory practice is to especially work on moving your Prana up and then down your spine into your brain hundreds of times per day, or to circulate it in circular orbits (loops) up your spine into the brain and then down the front of the body *and* through your alimentary canal, or to hold it at various places along this route. The first times you do this you might feel wrecked the following day where your muscles are all tensed up, but after this initial muscle locking that initiates matters the progress will go smoothly.

Practicing Prana revolutions or holding patterns in various parts of your body will bring different results ("delights") to a practitioner in accordance with their ability to move their Prana to these spots and rest it there. Just as in martial arts you should practice moving your Prana hundreds to thousands of times per day for the quickest results.

When you start doing this you will no doubt start to receive heavenly intercessions, or you can say the "interference" of the local devas who will use you for their own training purposes. So that this does not get out of hand, this is why spiritual masters rarely teach such things to the uninitiated but expect them to receive empowerments before attempting tantric teachings. You must understand what is going on instead of this intercession remaining hidden. This information should help innumerable Hindus who are practicing various *tapas* and *sadhana*.

If you have enough merit to receive the help required for the twelve-year kundalini transformation process, at the completion of the process your subtle body (astral body) will finally be able to disentangle from your physical body and detach from that shell according to your will. You will have achieved the subtle body attainment mentioned by the Hindu sages and freed yourself from the physical body *kosha*, which is the first genuine step of spiritual liberation.

Buddhism calls this subtle body achievement, which is the stage of Srotapanna Arhatship, "entering the stream" whereas when you finally achieve the "formless" Supra-Causal and Immanence body attainments (equivalent to the full Arhat and Great Golden Arhat or Buddhahood attainments) that can create *nirmanakaya* energy copies of themselves, this is called "crossing the stream" or the Great Transformation (Transition) since you transcended the Causal body and the lower planes of form. You have then thereby freed yourself from the lower material realms of reincarnation forever.

Buddhism calls the subtle body's emergence the first stage of enlightenment, or "entering the stream," that leads to the higher body attainments. You might arise as either a Srotapanna Arhat or Sakradagamin Arhat depending upon how much purification work you performed for your subtle body's emergence. Buddhism segments the subtle body attainment, where your new body's energy can be of higher or lower grade of purity, as the first or second dhyana attainment while Hinduism calls these the *vitarka* and *vicara* samadhi and matches the achievement with heavenly *lokas*. Because your consciousness is a bit more purified between these stages of achievement it means that your body is more purified as well, or you can say that because one body is more purified its consciousness is more purified.

What is hidden from the public is that the religions of Hinduism, Buddhism, Taoism, Jainism, Sikhism, Shugendo, Christianity, Sufism and so forth are actually about spiritual body achievements, which explains why masters can perform miraculous superpowers, but they hide the true path of spirituality as mental attainments in order to motivate people to practice meditation. They obfuscate, obscure, misdirect, and evade the truth ... they lie. This is done as a function of skillful means because they think people aren't ready for the truth and wish to protect them due to their immaturity, but now the public is educated and mature. The problem is ready for such open truths.

Because the Brahman, the true reality, is a non-conceptual state there are natural analogies of this fact to desirelessness, detachment, naturalness, tranquility and empty mind meditation practices. This analogy justifies people working to purify themselves and their behavior through mindfulness where you stand above your mind to watch your thoughts and actions. This self-observation leads to moral and ethical progress as a natural character trait, and thereby uplifts society because everyone is policing their mind and behavior.

As stated, if you start doing many kundalini exercises then lots of local spiritual residents will start using you as their own practice vehicle especially if you live near an ashram, *matha* or temple since that is where devas often congregate. Their involvement in your life can be either good or bad depending on your fortune, and the danger is that it can lead to all sorts of mischief and abuses on their part. This is why spiritual masters don't normally teach kundalini yoga, or require that those training this way do so under their close supervision so that you are somewhat protected. This is also why initiates go to practice in the countryside far away from cities so they won't have so many heavenly visitors except those devoted to helping them. Temples are sometimes located in the wilderness for similar reasons.

Nevertheless the yogic path, which is one of your own control rather than the path of *bhakti* and worship where you just wait and hope for spiritual progress to be graced upon you, is one where you *take matters into your own hands* and work to bring the fruits or results of the path into the process of the spiritual path in order to kick start it into commencing, thus saving many reincarnations in the process. Yogis thus separate themselves from society to intensely commit to spiritual practices to prepare for the many years of automatic Prana rotations that result in true enlightenment rather than just some intellectual realizations that people think is enlightenment but which are just a bunch of thoughtful insights.

Very few people can achieve the genuine rotation of the automatic Prana circulation within their body where it circulates among all your limbs and meridians in addition to rising up the spine and descending down the front of your body. Even fewer will be able to achieve the stage of separation of their subtle body from their physical body, which is the generation of the deva body that is the first stage of enlightened attainment that makes you an Arhat or the Arahant of Jainism. After this stage, a person goes beyond earthly things and enters into the metaphysical realm of the various heavens. Even if a teacher wished to describe this in detail, a student with the wisdom and experience to receive these instructions beyond the realm of the human world would be exceptional. But now you know the way hidden in Hinduism.

According to traditional Yoga teachings that try to bring about spiritual ascension, we know that after great cultivation efforts (*tapas*) and spiritual practice (*sadhana*) the kundalini inside you is awakened. According to the yogis there are three special *nadis* in the spinal column – *ida, pingala, and sushumna* – and along the *sushumna* channel are six lotuses or chakra centers with the lowest known as the *muladhara*. Then comes successively the *svadhisthana, manipura, anahata, visuddhi, ajna* and *sahasrara* chakras which are actually code words for various segments of your body.

Your kundalini, when awakened through spiritual practice, supposedly passes through the lower centers and after passing through the six centers reaches the thousand-petalled lotus in your head known as the *sahasrara*, and the aspirant supposedly then goes into samadhi or encounters some type of wondrous experience. No such thing happens unless an enlightened individual gives you that special experience which they themselves create. Actually, during the twelve years of Prana purification the energy flows throughout your body in waves over and over again washing everything, including your brain, and you don't experience ecstasy at all. Ancient yoga texts provide fantastical descriptions of wondrous mental states, however, in order to encourage spiritual cultivation work and to also give aspiring devas some target objectives of experiences they might try to reproduce in human beings using their own abilities to shape consciousness.

The hidden truth of Hinduism is that its corpus of teachings contain all sorts of nonsense or misdirections like the chakras in order to encourage you to do special types of inner Prana practice. Every religion has this sort of misdirection or misinformation. Many teachings in Hinduism are conveyed through stories pregnant with symbolism but told in such a way that an enlightened master still have enough material to be able to reveal the real truth to striving adepts. What you have just read is a standard explanation of kundalini along with the real truth that most masters of the past did not want people to know about, but now society has progressed and it is time for the full pathway to be revealed.

Devas and spiritual masters are passing in and out of your brain your entire life giving you thoughts, emotions, inspirations and energy but regular people never realize this. This is how enlightened masters train devas to be able to help people, and how they also test whether they are pure enough to deserve enlightenment themselves because they remain virtuous in dealing with you rather than abuse their powers.

If you start practicing inner energy work then the local devas will all start to practice within your body because a spiritual master will probably send a *nirmanakaya* emanation to start helping you, and them if they are inside you. This is happening to everyone throughout their life, so it is no worry. You just didn't know about it even though countless tantric pictures show various spiritual beings within a person's body to prepare you for this fact that you personally observe and do after you pass away. The problem is when they start using you to test their powers such as giving you thoughts, flashing images in your mind, blocking your memories so that they will not come to mind, making you talk in rhymes, playing music in your head, or assuming control over your body in various ways. This will produce all sorts of troubles for you that you cannot stop or control.

Unfortunately, Hinduism lacks the literature for what to expect when this happens and you have to either find a good master or turn to the *Surangama Sutra* of Buddhism to guide you when you do tantric yoga so that you don't hurt yourself and go astray. However, with this book Hinduism finally has this material, which is concentrated in Chapter 2 and throughout. Most spiritual schools simply warn people to pay no attention to such things when they happen because they are *Mara*, but they are indeed a nuisance that can harm you if you let yourself get taken in, which will definitely happen at times due to the superior power of enlightened elders who will also want to use you to demonstrate various skills to their peers.

Always remember the truth of Hinduism that enlightenment or spiritual liberation is a spiritual body attainment of freeing your *atman* of your unnecessary *koshas* that allows you to escape from every plane of existence until you can do this no further. First you escape the material realm with the subtle body achievement, and each higher transcendental body you achieve carries within it the potential for an even higher transcendental body attainment that allows you to transcend (escape from or "negate") that realm of existence.

The highest bodies are so energetically refined that they live for very long times, and are therefore said to be immortal even though all composite things suffer from entropy over time so even "immortality" is a false teaching. Chinese Taoism even calls them stages of immortality and we learned from the story of Tiresias that a purified subtle body lives for hundreds of years. However, because of the nature of those bodies there are various types of continuity to new existences.

With each new body attainment (ascension) comes an attendant higher clarity of one's mind and greater vividness of consciousness because each new body's composition is nearer to being that of pure energy, and a higher form of life force energy for each body circulates in your brain to power consciousness without as many obstructions or impediments to its circulatory flow. Consciousness is always more pristine and clear with each new body attainment.

To put it another way, the universe has many layers or planes of existence where the gradations can be counted as actually infinite. The transcendental bodies represent planes at higher levels on this vast spectrum, which Hinduism has partitioned into *lokas*, due to their composition of a more refined type of energy. Those bodies are achieved through yogic *sadhana* that involves churning the vital energies or life force within whatever present body you have. This is the same process of salvation, liberation or ascension for the living beings of every world system across the universe although in some worlds they use technology to help with the energy transformations required to produce a new body out of a lower one.

Naturally, many spiritual practices can be used to help transform your Prana because it is beneficial to change the frequency, tone or quality of your Prana and move it *via many different techniques* since they all get different results. Just practicing good behavior, for instance, will refine your Prana to highly differentiate it from animal Prana, which is why virtuous behavior is a cultivation method in itself. Nonetheless, for our world system achieving a higher body will require the help of spiritual beings higher up on the scale (who are the inhabitants of these higher planes of existence) temporarily loaning you their energy to purify yours, which is why we engage in spiritual reverence and worship to establish connections with them for blessings.

Only if you are a virtuous person who has risen above egoity, greed, selfishness, violence and carnality, and only if you have the tendency to do good deeds, will many agree to help you in performing this great time-consuming deed of washing your life force energy. The energy of your subtle body must become refined enough to become substantially differentiated from the coarse vital energy of your physical nature in order for your subtle body to break its bonds with the realm of materiality and ascend out of your physical shell. It requires many heavenly helpers and a large number of enlightened masters working on you continuously for years in order for your subtle body to become sufficiently purified for this, which is why so few spiritual masters become enlightened in this world. If it was so easy and quick then there would be many more enlightened masters, and of course there are more than you know about because most hide their attainments from the public for very good reasons.

After you achieve the independent subtle body it requires about three years to achieve for each new higher body attainment. Thus after the attainment of the astral deva body (subtle body), which takes about twelve to fourteen years of active around-the-clock kundalini transformations where your Prana is constantly rolling around your body to purify its energies through frictional contact, it requires another three years to attain the Causal body and then three years to attain the Supra-Causal attainment and so on.

When Sadguru Sadafal Deoji Maharaj said that he practiced Vihangam Yoga for seventeen years it means that he attained the subtle body, Causal body and then Supra-Causal body attainment. It took him about twelve years for the subtle body achievement and then five years for the subsequent two bodies.

When the Advaita Vedanta master Nisargadatta Maharaj, who is equivalent to the Subhuti of Buddhism because of his mastery of emptiness, said that it only took him three years to awaken after meeting Siddharameshwar Maharaj, he was editing out the fact that he had already achieved the subtle and Causal bodies. It took him three years under Siddharameshwar's guidance to achieve the full Arhat's Supra-Causal body of enlightenment, and we know he achieved enlightenment because he was invited into the Inchagiri Sampradaya as one of its leaders.

In his book, *I am That,* Nisargadatta explained, "I find that by shifting the focus of attention, I become the very thing I look at, and experience the kind of consciousness it has; I become the inner witness of the thing. I call this capacity of entering other focal point of consciousness, love; you may give it any name you like." This, of course, is a veiled reference to using *nirmanakaya* emanations (or the powers of his higher Arhat bodies) to enter into people's minds to understand their thoughts or to give them thoughts or energy. Once can only do this at the attainment stage of achieving a Supra-Causal body or Immanence (Buddha) body, both of which can emanate *nirmanakaya* projections.

Whenever anyone finally reaches the Supra-Causal body attainment – which is also known as the Prime Causal body, light body, *vijnanamaya kosha* body or wisdom-knowledge sheath, and the stage of the full Arhat of Buddhism or Arahant of Jainism — they are often asked to take on the leadership helm of a great temple, monastery or spiritual lineage even though there is yet one more body to go. They have crossed the stream in attaining the stage of a full Arhat, and it only takes a little more work to attain the final body. Shakyamuni Buddha said that only he had attained it but everyone attains it. Countless Hindu masters prior to his emergence attained it and it is just that no one public revealed teachings in India on these matters as fully as Shakyamuni, so he had to create some claims to grab attention for his fuller teachings. This is called skillful means.

Some masters go into secluded retreat during the first of the two-and-one-half to three-year periods required for attaining higher bodies beyond the subtle. They do this so that their spirit can leave their body and they can then travel around without being disturbed, or so that they can avoid other heavenly individuals possessing it while away since they might inadvertently cause troubles when using it. After their enlightenment they usually have someone else take over their body when they are away, and at that time the resident possessing their body in their place will simply use their memories to deal with people and events.

This explains, by the way, why many spiritual masters develop cancer. It sometimes occurs because of spiritual trips they take that remove most of their higher life force energies from their physical bodies. They don't keep up with supplying enough vitality to the physical body, which develops cancer. However, natural protocols that use ivermectin, fenbendazole and tocotrienols are effective at curing cancer and might help many masters solve this problem caused by low vitality due to their spirit bodies traveling all the time rather than remaining inside their physical nature.

When Adi Shankara occupied the body of King Amaruka to learn the sexual arts for his contest against Mandana Misra's wife Bharati, his students hid his body in a cave. You must use your wisdom to decide whether the part of the story about the king being dead was really true or not. There is also a story where Gorakhnath calls Matseyendrath away from sexual pleasures with the Queen of a kingdom ruled by women only, which just goes to reveal the secret that yogis in their higher bodies are engaged in sexual cultivation to help transform the Prana of their transcendental bodies.

As stated, in their later years many enlightened masters die from cancer because their higher spiritual bodies spend too much time away from their physical body that then suffers from prolonged periods of Prana deficiency. Because of prolonged periods of insufficient Prana circulation (due to the absence of the higher body energies resting inside one another within the mortal frame) and then not repairing themselves upon return through special pranayama and inner energy techniques to balance inner harmony, cancer becomes a common possibility such as happened with Sri Ramakrishna. However, daily deep breathing methods to clear their body's Prana can prevent cancer while ivermectin together with fenbendazole and tocotrienols (along with adjunctives like Carnivora, Chaga tea, Essiac tea, the Brazilian recipe of *aloe arborescens* and honey found in *Hydrogen Peroxide and Aloe Vera* by Conrad LeBeau, etc.) are a possible remedy to help such masters if they use it along with other alternative medicine modalities. Decades from now I'm sure that new natural remedies will be developed.

The mind you have for each body on each plane of existence is considered a different level of consciousness even though it is just the same ordinary normal mind you have now but for a new body on a new plane. Its only specialness is greater clarity and the ability to connect with the energy of lower realms that then produces superpowers in those worlds. Remember that our consciousness can control our Prana energy so if your body achievement ascends high enough then its own higher consciousness energies can produce overriding control over the energies of consciousness in lower realms, and you can even learn how to manipulate energies in lower realms to produce superpowers. Devas of the subtle heavenly plane around us have very limited superpowers that primarily revolve around manipulating the energies of their own bodies.

At each level of existence there is no magical mind. There is just an ordinary mind like you have now but it's your mind for that body with the addition that its sensory capabilities expand because the energy plane of that body penetrates through the lower, denser planes of material existence ... just as the ultimate substratum of all existence penetrates and permeates through everything as its ultimate substrate or substance. Being composed of a transcendent energy that penetrates the lower realms of existence you can sense vibrations in those fields.

When you hear all these descriptions of chakras mentioned in kundalini yoga texts you must also remember that there are no such thing as "astral chakras" within the body or on heavenly planes. The chakras refer to sections of your body – horizontal sections – delineated by the standard partitionings of the spine according to nerves of the spinal vertebrae. In *Neijia Yoga* and *Nyasa Yoga* I provided other alternative ways of partitioning the body as well.

Since many spiritual traditions instruct you to do Prana-work on your body according to sections the idea of chakras was invented to guide people who weren't being personally taught kundalini yoga methods. It was just an expedient method meant to help you. In other spiritual schools you don't need to know anything about chakras at all because they don't exist. You just have to circulate energy up your spine and down the front of your body, and in every other way as well, to wash it continually day by day.

The kundalini energy is basically *your Prana that resides in all your body cells since your subtle body interpenetrates your physical body*, so "unawakened kundalini energy" does not primarily reside in any chakra such as the notion it is coiled up inside the *muladhara*. It is everywhere within you and comprises an energetic duplicate of your physical body that is released as your "soul" (subtle body, deva body or astral body) upon death. When you feel strong energies welling up inside you we term it the kundalini energy, but truth be told this is usually the energy of a higher being using his or her energy to temporarily move and wash yours.

Through the ordinary religious practices of Hinduism you run through a variety of cultivation techniques to work on purifying (vibrating, moving, awakening, rotating, churning, lapping, washing, etc.) this Prana throughout your life. However, it is through *intensified yoga practices* that you actually start deeply purifying the Prana of your subtle body after much spiritual effort ... and *only if* you are qualified for the grace due to your long accumulation of good deeds, a higher inner life and virtuous character. A massive amount of organized labor must be provided to you through the grace of countless spiritual masters will commence where for years they will use the energy of their bodies, namely *nirmanakaya* emanations, to move your own energy within you to wash your tissues ... *while also doing this for local deva residents as well who also qualify for enlightenment*. There will always be a big hubbub of activity around you when this happens.

The enlightened masters never work on one person alone because they are expending a lot of work and energy, so they wait until not just you are ready but a large number of local devas are ready for ascension too. Many local masters will also come, during the long process, to learn new tips and tricks from their peers as well as to obtain personal purification work on themselves and their own *nirmanakaya* emanations to help upgrade them. Many Supra-Causal and Immanence masters have to prove their proficiency to their peers in a number of skills, including whether they can simultaneously handle a certain number of *nirmanakaya*, so that they can be certified as qualified to run this multi-year process in their own locale for it is the only way that devas also rise to enlightenment.

Therefore, if you start undergoing the process it is not you alone but countless devas surrounding you who will also undergo spiritual ascension, and many masters will come to use their *nirmanakaya* emanations on the many devas that congregate around you, using you as the central focus ground, and in that way their own *nirmanakaya* from their Supra-Causal (Arhat stage) and Superconsciousness-Immanence-Buddha bodies will become purified from powerful masters working on them so that those *nirmanakaya* can themselves achieve their own Immanence (Buddha) bodies, thus upgrading them.

It takes more than twelve years of ceaseless work to purify your subtle body's Prana during a kundalini awakening, which is tiring work for the core set of masters involved in the process, so enlightened masters across the world have created little games that automatically draft others into the process of purifying your Prana such as by requiring an enlightened master to work on someone if the student discovers an error in their writings, or requiring that someone discovered by the practitioner to be enlightened (because of reading some book for instance) to also work on the hapless practitioner regardless of their tradition.

This is yet another reason that the enlightened do not want anyone to know that they are enlightened and what it entails, including the possession of higher spiritual bodies with special powers and capabilities. Secrecy maximizes their freedom and minimizes problems such as requests by people for help. These are some of the secrets to the process of helping someone become enlightened.

The Sufi Meher Baba commented that the great saints are like strong trees you can rely upon because they have many, many offshoots of *nirmanakaya* emanations that independently do things in the world. They produce them throughout the centuries because of countless efforts to purify sentient beings on the lower planes of existence. When Krishna showed his *Vishwaroop* (universal form) to Arjuna during the Kurukshetra War in the *Bhagavad Gita* this was just a mental projection into Arjuna's mind representing the greatness of the many bodies Krishna had emanated over time that belonged to his *sambhogakaya*, which is the collection of all of someone's main spiritual bodies and *nirmanakaya* emanations.

You will most likely mistake the heavenly energy of enlightened beings for your own kundalini when the rolling chariot of kundalini energy commences inside you, but it is actually *their energy that seems to be automatically rolling around inside you*, and they just take shifts at the effort. This is one of secret, hidden aspects of Hinduism and Hindu spiritual cultivation, with another fact being that India is one of the best places on earth to go through the process because of thousands of years of masters and their expertise at doing this. Some nations, because of a low culture, have barbaric traditions they force upon you as you go through the process. You will undergo many "spiritual" experiences during this process which lasts for years and it is best undergone under the watchful eyes of a mortal enlightened master nearby.

It takes many years of organized labor to purify your Prana and produce the subtle energy or deva body attainment, which is the subtle body attainment of Hinduism or the Srotapanna-Sakradagamin Arhat stage of enlightenment in Buddhism. When an aspirant's thoughts stop *it is also because an enlightened being intervenes to make them stop rather than that you attain some mysterious exalted state of consciousness on your own due to ardent meditation practice*. Otherwise you could perform this feat at will.

Enlightened masters practice controlling thoughts so they become expert at giving people various types of spiritual experiences through their own *nirmanakaya* projections. When you cannot cognize your body because it seems "empty" it is because they have projected this experiential state into you. From ignorance, students call this "samadhi" and falsely attribute it to their own progress such as self-generated kundalini Prana rising into their brain when the experience is being projected into you by higher beings. Another example of this is the experience of *shaktipat* where an enlightened master sends a *nirmanakaya* into you with the ability to stop your thoughts.

To achieve the initial rotation of the Prana and the kundalini transformations they entail you must perform many different types of Prana exercises. One might during a single day practice thought-free meditation, *japa* practice or mantra recitation, singing *bhajans*, pranayama work or *anapana*, yoga stretching while visualizing your muscles to energize them, and inner *prayahara* work to move your Prana, etcetera.

By practicing *multiple techniques simultaneously* rather than just a single cultivation method alone you have the best chances of purifying your inner subtle body made of Prana. Using multiple methods means that each one will have an effect on transforming (purifying) your Prana via a different set of principles which is better than concentrating on just one and hoping it is the most effective one for you.

For instance, *anapana* means that you use your breathing (and mind) to push your Prana around within your body, and *anapana* thereby washes your inner subtle body with your own vital energy by using the connection between breathing and Prana to push energy everywhere inside yourself while there is also mental guidance as well. As your breathing goes in and out you can push your Prana to various areas of your body (guiding it with your mind) such as above and below, to the left side or right side of your body, to the arms and legs and so on to wash them with energy.

It is especially easy to push the Prana of your body upwards or downwards into your upper or lower torso or limbs with the assistance of your breathing and mental guidance. As is usual, the frictional rubbing of Prana over itself causes an abrasive (frictional) cleansing of its nature where the pure or more refined energy eventually separates from that which is less pure (refined) and of lower vibration (denser) due to the presence of impurities. The more refined or purified Prana is what escapes as your spiritual body at the initial stage of enlightenment or liberation that is the twelve-year subtle body attainment. It is more purified than the angelic deva body that ordinary mortals arise within when they die and leave their physical shell.

One famous cultivation technique used by yogis in *charnal* grounds is to watch bodies burn to bones and dust in order to arouse feelings of sadness or disgust that stimulate Yin Prana in this uncomfortable environment of ugly sights. Then the yogis concentrate on feeling their bones inside their own bodies while visualizing them as shining with bright whiteness in order to inspire their Yang Prana into moving through them. This method washes your inner subtle body with Yang Prana around the shape of your skeleton. Rather than use chakra sections of the body you use the body's segmentation into bones to guide your practice.

This practice entails mentally concentrating on feeling internal sections of your body to send your Prana there through the principle that wherever you put your mind within your body your pranic energy will follow because consciousness (thought) and your vitality (life force) are linked to one another. Once again, rather than chakras it uses bones as the progressive segments for your concentration and Prana work.

While *anapana* uses breathing to push your Prana around inside your body to wash its tissues, Mantrayana uses sound energy to stimulate your Prana and move it around within your body to thereby wash its tissues to purify your inner subtle body. You can also use the singing of *bhajans* to do this, or you can arouse strong emotions within yourself to change the tonality of your Prana by singing along with regular music. These are yet other different ways to wash the Prana of your body.

By listening to music of various types – energizing, defiant, triumphant or heroic, amusing, calming or relaxing, dreamy, annoying, nostalgic, happy, inspiring, joyful or cheerful, fearful or tense, sad or depressing, etc. – you will create internal energy sensations that wash your Prana *if you let the music move you*. This constant washing of your Prana with emotional sound responses in their inner energy is why some "pure" musicians often seem "lighter" than regular people. This is because the Prana of their subtle body has been continuously washed with emotional Prana pressure over the years, thus rarifying (purifying) it.

In Buddhism, which originated from the cultivation practices of Indian culture, there is a *Bramavihara* (Four Immeasurable Emotions) practice that uses the arousal of great emotions or dominant attitudes to energize and thus wash the Prana of a practitioner who wants to attain enlightenment. By enveloping yourself in infinitely large emotions beyond your comfort zone you will evoke strong internal sensations that fully arouse your body's Prana with positive energy while coloring that energy with a different quality to wash it as singing *bhajans* does.

What contributes most to your energy vibrations at any given moment is your attitude, so you can practice this technique using many types of deep emotions to help wash the energy of your inner subtle body that is the basis of your consciousness and all your higher transcendental bodies too.

Nyasa Yoga, and the *pratyahara* method of leading your Prana around within your body with your thoughts or will, both have you guiding your Prana movements around inside your body to wash its parts through the guidance of your thoughts and will because of the mind-body connection of Prana and consciousness (thoughts).

By using your mind to connect with your Prana in *pratyahara* you can rotate your energy around your bones, organs, cavities and appendages. Your willpower enables you to lead your Prana around inside yourself so that you can wash your inner subtle body with rubbings of your own vital energy. Through frictional churning that constitutes your own internal *Samudra Manthana* you will eventually refine and purify the Prana within the matrix of your subtle body thus enabling its emergence as an independent spiritual body on its own. As with concentration practice, this technique relies on the principle that your Prana energy will follow your thoughts so you can guide it around your body to go wherever you want. Thus you can guide it and rotate it according to your will.

During Hatha Yoga practice you hold your body motionless in stationary *asanas* but you should also practice moving your internal energy to the particular muscles being stretched in order to help purify and inner cleanse them. Yoga and the martial arts use stretching, muscle control and Prana control (mastery of your internal energy guided by your will) to cultivate the Prana of your body. However, with Nyasa Yoga or *pratyahara* you do not employ any physical exercise while rotating your internal energies around inside you.

Kumbhaka pranayama is yet another different technique that uses breath retention in order to force open the impediments or obstructed pathways to the proper Prana circulation within your body. It helps to increase the number of capillaries within your body and also pushes your Prana through certain tissues. When practiced correctly, pranayama will help to clear out the pranic circulatory pathways within your body that then speeds your attainment of the independent deva body.

The idea of pranayama is to learn how to control your breathing and your Prana because the two are linked, and the mind-body mastery of the "thought guiding your Prana" interconnection is what you use to cultivate your inner subtle body. Every part of your body can be filled with Prana, and when you are able to actually do this you can eventually become able to control your entire body. Then you – through expertise in yogic practices – must practice to gain control of the Prana in every muscle of your body to quickly develop your independent spirit body. This objective, which takes a long time to accomplish on its own, can be hastened immensely by other physical practices involving movement such as dance, acrobatics, sports, the martial arts and any other physical exercises that teach you to master your inner Prana circulation.

Running and other cardiovascular sports that involve strong mental concentration to achieve states of extremely coordinated physical movements with special breathing rhythms, optimal blood flow and Prana flow will also transform your Prana very well when these systems become all become synchronized together into a harmonious state of unity and flow. The harmony of these functions all working together creates a state of dynamic balance where one's physical nature is no longer just a physical vehicle but part of the awareness process that brings greater aliveness to the inner subtle body.

Cardiovascular sports use the coordination of movement, breathing, blood flow and Prana flow at their optimum peaks to drive your Prana flow to an optimum state of harmony, and then movements cause it to wash your body. Many young sports stars just exude positive vitality because they were able to cultivate their health and inner vitality, namely Prana, to a state of optimal flow where it even seems to emanate from their body.

When during sports your concentration, breathing, Prana and blood flow reach optimal peaks that are synchronized into a harmonious unity then you will be truly cultivating the Prana of your underlying subtle body so as to speed the attainment of the subtle body's emergence from the human shell. This is how you also cultivate the state of sports "flow."

SUMMARY OF INNER ENERGY METHODS

Let's put this in review:

Basically, *anapana* uses your breathing to wash or purify your Prana where you change your emotions while breathing in order to wash your energy with different Prana frequencies or tones.

Pranayama uses control of your breathing to move your Prana and wash your inner energy.

Kumbhaka pranayama uses breath retention to force open up your Prana channels and improve inner Prana flow.

By visualizing that your skeleton shines with a bright light while feeling its bones and overall structure you are using mental concentration to mass your Prana around the bones and surrounding tissue areas, and thus washing them entirely.

Taoism has you draw energy from the environment into your bones at their ends in order to wash them with purifying energy.

Pratyahara uses your thoughts and willpower to guide your Prana internally through special circuits routes within your body to wash your tissues. This is similar to the *nei-gong* practices of Chinese Taoism that use this method of mental guidance as well. You might focus on a body region to bring Prana into that area, or use your will to circulate it in various patterns elsewhere (and especially in particular areas you select for a work session) according to a schedule you set up. The entire purpose of incessant Prana stimulation is to gradually eliminate impediments to the flow of Prana within the *nadis* or circulatory routes that penetrate all your tissues, and to circulate your Prana over the molecules and their atomic bonds again and again to purify them.

Mantrayana uses sound power to vibrate your Prana (to a different frequency, tone or quality) and breathing to push energized Prana around your body to wash its tissues. In Orthodox Christianity many Hesychasts ignite the kundalini transformation process by continually reciting the Jesus Prayer until they eventually start hearing the prayer automatically being recited on its own within their heart, the energy within their body starts rotating and they see signs such as flames within their body. This also happens to Hindus who recite mantras continuously. What occurs is that a spiritual being temporarily assumes control over washing the Prana of your body and they perform the automatic recitation of mantras inside you that you think is your own self automatically doing so.

Singing *bhajans* with emotions also uses the power of sound to transform your Prana.

You can use the practice of holding onto very large dominant attitudes – like the four boundless emotional states of infinite loving kindness, infinite compassion, infinite joy and infinite equanimity – to energize and color your Prana. Naturally, other positive emotions can also be used. While doing so you can feel yourself radiating those energies into the environment everywhere to wash your internal energy.

There are Yoga methods of *absorbing the essences of the sun and moon (that constitute masculine and feminine energies)* to flood your body with Yang and Yin Prana respectively, especially while also reciting relevant sun or moon mantras or the mantras of very masculine or feminine deities. Sadguru Bhausaheb Maharaj, founder of the Inchegeri Sampradaya who achieved "Advaita Siddhi" (the highest stage of realization of the Self that is the Immanence or Buddha body achievement), had specially built a space measuring two feet in the wall of his house where a person could stand and would stand there at night, from 12:00 am to 2:00 am to absorb Yin Prana.

The traditional ways to absorb Prana are through your skin, the top of your head, special points in the palms of the hand or at the bottom of your foot (such as the Yongquan KI-1 acupuncture point or *kurcha marma, talahridaya marma and kurchashira marma*), at your joints, and at special places used by tantric traditions that offer special instructions. Taoism has you draw energy from the environment into your bones at their ends in order to wash them with purifying energy, an example being to draw energy into your hands at the end of each finger joint. Absorption into the body is a method of pulling environmental Prana into it during the inhalation phase of breathing. While some texts talk about absorbing the light of the sun or moon using the eyes this should only be done under the supervision of an enlightened master.

Bhausaheb Maharaj's standing absorption practices have an exact correspondence with the *xinyiquan* martial arts "trinity pile standing" posture of *santi shi* that can be performed to increase either your Yin or Yang energy. To increase Yang energy you extend your left hand while facing South (wherever environmental Yang Prana is strongest) when the sun apexes in the southern sky, and in the evening you stand in *santi shi* with right hand extended and facing North during 11:00 am – 1:00 pm, which is the Chinese time to inhale Yin Qi (Prana) and nourish one's blood. You try to draw energy in through the hands.

The enlightened martial artist Sun Lutang would use this technique and for 36 breaths would try to feel the accumulated Yin energy around his body and then for 36 more breaths try to direct it to his *dantian* (lower abdomen), and afterwards stand for 30 more minutes to allow the Yin and Yang energies to mix and settle. Many special times, directions, places and practices can be used to absorb Yin or Yang Prana from the environment to replenish one's body, wash the inner subtle body and cultivate one's spirit.

The *Viramarga* Path of Heroes method from India has you rest in a *bhava* absorption that is the pure mood or feeling of a hero. You do this by fixing yourself in a given positive attitude for a prolonged period of time where you feel the Prana energy of that attitude penetrating all throughout your body in order to wash your Prana with the total penetration of that flavor.

The School of Kaula Tantra has you practice ecstatic visualizations, often with an arousing erotic content, to excite your inner energy so that you can then more easily move it using your will to wash your channels and tissues via mental guidance.

The Newar and Vajrayana deity yoga methods of Northern India used by Buddhism, which are originally derived from various Hindu sects, use imagined unification with a *yidam* deity or Buddha (such as Avalokitesvara) to invite enlightened beings into your body so that the presence of their energetic *nirmanakaya* emanations within you will wash your Prana and thus purify it.

In Hindu Nyasa yoga you similarly "invite deities" to transform your body and mind since such strong sentiments of unification will stir, affect, vibrate or stimulate your vital energies (Prana). In this manner you try to recreate yourself as a perfected being in line with the chosen deity by strongly emulating specific emotions. The practice diffuses energy into the body by associating mantras with every part of the body and the whole of it. For the best results you need to stay on each spot for as long as it takes to energize the Prana of that region, and visualizing the targeted area as shining with light will open the *nadis* quicker. Because it helps you generate the deva body Nyasa Yoga is said to *divinize* a practitioner's body.

The Wim Hof style of breathing uses hyperventilation to wash all the Prana of your body although the most important part of this pranayama exercise is the breath retention part. The *Jiujie Fofeng* "Nine Bottled Winds" practice uses breath retention to help open your *nadis*.

Fasting forces your body to rely on its inner subtle energy body rather than material food (just as breath retention forces your body to rely upon its Prana for survival when breath is unavailable), thus strengthening the integrity and efficiency of your inner subtle body. Fasting and kumbhaka pranayama both force you to temporarily rely on your vital energy to survive.

If we put a variety of spiritual practice techniques from across the world's traditions into a table, we find this result that can help decipher many hidden aspects of Hinduism. This is probably the most important table you will ever see for understanding the various methods of spiritual cultivation across India and the world:

Circulating Your Prana Internally Without Engaging Your Emotions (Emotionally Neutral)

- Pranayama
- *Pratyahara*
- Nyasa Yoga
- *Anapana*
- *Qi-gong*
- *Nei-gong*
- Stable concentration that focuses on a body location (e.g. abdomen, energy center, chakra, limb) that consequently brings Prana to the area of focus
- Developing the attitude of an unattached witness of your thoughts and deeds, which is *centering yourself in your subtle body* that strengthens it
- Vipassana practice of observing body sensations and then *feeling the physical sensation* of your entire body as a single unit, or focusing upon physically feeling various segments of your body in turn (which brings Prana to those regions)

- Visualization of light or fire with warmth at different body locations and also visualization of water or cold feelings at different body locations
- Combining inhalation and exhalation and (the subsequent movement of energy within the body moved by your breathing) with visualizations of energy, light, color, heat/cold, etc., which is a form of *anapana*
- Accumulating energy in certain centers (e.g. abdomen) and channeling it through certain pathways (e.g. spine, microcosmic circulation), which is basically *pratyahara*
- Listening to singing bowls or a gong and feeling the corresponding vibrations and energy moving within your body. Humming or droning continuously, reciting *bija* sounds in synchrony with optimal hand movements, or singing while moving your internal energy are also techniques
- Mantrayana where you vocally repeat certain words/sounds while in tune with your breathing or while leading pranic flow within your body; Also, repeating mantras while focusing on specific points within the body or different sections of the body
- Yoga stretches where you also concentrate on feeling the Prana of your limbs
- Absorbing Yin and Yang energies by standing motionless at certain times of the day while facing the direction where Yin or Yang energy is strongest and drawing energy into your body through your lungs, your pores, the top of your head, etc. and allowing it to accumulate in your solar plexus

Moving Your Prana Internally While Engaging Your Emotions in Order to Color the Qi of your Body with a Different Flavor

- Kaula Tantra ecstatic visualization meditations
- Nyasa Yoga methods of internally moving your Prana while imagining that you receive the help of a deity or become a deity
- *Boran Kammatthana*

- Chanting while feeling strong emotions, or singing religious songs or sutras or glories of a deity with strong emotion while using the sound energy to move the Prana inside your body
- White Skeleton Visualization practice where you arouse repugnance visualizing how a dead body slowly decays and decomposes, and joy at giving away your flesh while becoming a shining white skeleton
- *Anapana* where you push your Prana by moving your breathing while engaged in emotions of joy, bliss, confidence, triumph, pride, … Also, combining inhalation and exhalation with visualizations of energy, light, color, temperature changes, etc. along with dominant attitudes or emotions to arouse whole body Prana
- Repeating an affirmation and feeling the corresponding Prana that is evoked throughout your body and along any particularly relevant Prana channels
- Attending sporting events or music concerts that move your emotions and internal energy

Coloring Your Prana (With Prana Rotation Being Stationary) by Holding onto Large Yin or Yang Emotions

- Simply holding onto a dominant attitude (that overwhelmingly perfuses your Prana) or intent for a prolonged period of time
- The Four Immeasurables concentration practice (infinite joy, infinite compassionate, boundless equanimity, infinite loving kindness)
- Absorbing oneself in the color and five element *kasina* meditations of the *Visuddhimagga* to feel the texture of that Prana
- The four Buddhist formless absorptions of infinite space, boundless consciousness, infinite nothingness and neither thinking nor not-thinking that are basically "formless" meditations on being bodilessness, with detachment to the things within one's awareness, while engaging in a peaceful but expansive mental experience of emptiness and equanimity in some way
- *Viramarga* Path of Heroes

- Bhakti devotional yoga
- Self-cultivation in continuously emulating your highest ideals in their most perfect forms; creating ideals of perfection that continually inspire you to levels of ever more perfect realization

Cultivating Large Emotions While Imagining that One is an Active Deity

- Nyasa Yoga
- Bhakti devotional yoga (Ex. a Fool for Christ, Krishna bhakti devotee ...)
- Guru Yoga
- Deity Yoga
- Buddha Yoga
- Taoist deity possession
- Shamanism
- *Boran Kammatthana*
- *Viramarga* Path of Heroes

Movement Exercises Where Strenuous Stretching or Cardiovascular Activity, Sometimes Combined with Aroused Emotions, Can Circulate Your Body's Prana

- Martial Arts
- Tirumalai Krishnamacharya Viniyoga
- Dancing
- High cardio sports such as soccer, basketball, dancing, swimming, acrobatics, track and field, ...
- Sexual Intercourse (you excite and move your Prana while washing it with joy)
- Special moving Yoga postures that involve simultaneously engaging in special *kumbhaka* pranayama methods as you move through the *asanas*

Location and Event Examples

- **Yin Locations**: cool cave, limestone formations, cold waterfall, crematorium, funeral home, morgue, hospital, hospice, opium den, scary forest, nighttime desert (cold and dry), battlefield littered with corpses, refrigeration unit, polar region, in close proximity to a Van de Graf generator, in close proximity to high frequency electron spinning ...

- **Yin Events**: mourning at funerals, sadness after a loss, shock after a robbery, fear during a scary movie, depression after a divorce, performing thievery, attending a séance ...
- **Yang Locations**: temple, ashram, some fertile and vibrant mountains, flower gardens in bloom, hot springs, hot sauna, fertile jungle or forest, martial arts dojo, active construction site, sports stadium during an event, an active shopping market, sea shore, daytime desert (hot and dry), in the proximity of an ozone generator, in close proximity to a magnetic vortex (formed by high speed spinning magnets arranged in a geometric design) ...
- **Yang Events**: music concert, sporting event, wedding, military battle, happy meal with friends, comedy movie, a race, awards ceremony, dancing, making a flower arrangement, singing happy songs, prayer, giving a gift, doing charity ...

Countless kundalini cultivation style exercises are used across the world to purify the Prana of your inner self, which is basically differentiating the purified high-grade energy of your body from its undifferentiated, impure, denser, coarser or more unpurified energy. To do so successfully you must daily practice a set of different types of spiritual exercises, which all work at purifying your Prana via different principles, in order to start transforming your Prana for the first spiritual body that leads to the most perfect union of *atman* with the Brahman where all unnecessary koshas have been stripped away.

The general rule of cultivation progress is: *the more practices of different types that you simultaneously practice with consistency the better and quicker will be your results*. The harder you work – the more types of methods you practice and the longer and more consistently you practice – the higher will be your chances for success at liberation, and the quicker your success if success is to come. Success is the result of consistent effort applied to various *sadhana* and cultivation methods across time. The longer and deeper you practice the more profound will be your results.

There are many ways to choose from to start transforming the internal energy of your physical body because many other spiritual practices are available. If you purify your physical energy then you will live healthier and longer. If you transform it profoundly then you can attain a stage of spiritual ascension, which entails cultivating an independent spirit body while alive as explained. This achievement is technically the first but lowest rank of enlightened liberation, and yet to the human body this is the highest achievement possible for its existence.

To become enlightened (attain the higher transcendental bodies) is not a matter of study, worship, meditation, mantra, introspection, yoga, improved behavior or other similar efforts. These practices are helpful but *it is primarily accomplished through inner energy work together with meditation practices*. Either you do the work yourself by *taking the result of the path into the practices of the path*, or you wait and wait and wait many lives hoping that spiritual masters will do this energy purification work for you because you are a good and kind human being.

Hindu culture offers both routes – the fast and slow path.

Nonetheless, you absolutely must cultivate inner *nei-gong, neijia*, Prana or kundalini energy work for the attainment of enlightenment. Paramahansa Yogananda and Swami Muktananda are just two of the many individuals who attained their deva body through the pathway of kundalini cultivation or *kriya* yoga.

Thus, while you need to practice meditation to cultivate mental stillness and clarity of mind, the practice of formless mind meditation where you let go of your thoughts and your vital energy allows higher beings the opportunity to more easily move your Prana with their own because they don't have to fight your thoughts and their grip on your Prana circulation when they subsequently attempt to purify your body. The general key to success is *inner energy work* that involves moving the Prana within your body and gaining control over its properties and movements.

After the preparatory work of more intensified yoga practices than we normally find through reverential worship, you have to proceed to the stage where the twelve-year kundalini transformation cycle of inner alchemy commences. Hundreds of masters and their students will take shifts working on your body continuously during this long kundalini transformation process if you have the merit, which can only happen after years of devotion to intensified inner energy yoga, and this is absolutely necessary for the subtle body attainment.

Masters never discuss the details of the process but simply say "I spent twelve years with my master." However, now you know many details that are missing from or hidden within Hinduism. This will make it an even more powerful vehicle for *moksha* or liberation.

CHAPTER 11
SUPERPOWERS

Now let's explain some stories of superpowers based on our new understanding.

The Bhagavan Ramana Maharshi (d. 1950) used to regularly talk with animals who would enter his meditation hall such as monkeys, squirrels, dogs, a mongoose who once came and sat on his lap, and a frequently visiting cow named Lakshmi. Many saints across the world are involved in stories where they communicate with animals and the methodology is simple. They simply project a *nirmanakaya* emanation that goes into the animal's brain to give it thoughts and to understand its thoughts, and then there can be some communication.

On a situation where an animal seems to talk, which happened in the case of Sant Dnyaneshwar (d. 1296) who placed his hand on the head of a mistreated buffalo that then recited a Vedic verse, someone used a *nirmanakaya* emanation to speak the words and also to open the animal's mouth and move its tongue as if it were talking. Of course the sounds came from an invisible *nirmanakaya* speaking rather than from the buffalo, but since the animal was moving its mouth and tongue under the control of the *nirmanakaya* then everyone believed the buffalo was doing the talking. In the Old Testament a talking donkey speaks to Balaam and it is exactly the same thing going on.

It takes training to understand the mentality of different types of animals in order to do this, but nevertheless this is what is happening when an enlightened master communicates with elephants, cobras, tigers, horses, dogs and cats, parrots and so forth. You can even control animals using higher bodies or *nirmanakaya* emanations, which is why the yogi Changdev could ride on the back of a tiger. We commonly say that tigers, lions and other such wild animals forget their enmity and are found living peacefully around sages, such as Matsyendranatha, owing to their "occult powers" but no one ever explains that it is due to *nirmanakaya* emanations. Through them, or by using one of your own higher bodies itself rather than a *nirmanakaya*, you can take over an animal.

The Bhagavan Nityananda (d. 1961) once froze in the air the arms of a thief who was assaulting him, which was also accompanied by emanating a *nirmanakaya* projection body that took control of the man's body and mind to stop his actions. A *nirmanakaya* emanation has a higher *vasitva siddhi* capability (the ability to force influence upon anyone) than physical, subtle and Causal bodies, which is why an enlightened master can override a lower Arhat's ability to produce superpowers since they require the application of his discriminatory mind (called the sixth consciousness sin Buddhism).

Another interesting story about Bhagavan Nityananda involves a widowed mother who visited him with her blind child. The child said to Nityananda, "I would like to see my mother once," and it happened later that day that the child could see after the two left him, but the joy of the child lasted only minutes before her blindness returned. Nityananda had generated a *nirmanakaya* projection of his body, or used one of his own higher bodies, and used it to enter into the child and project what it was seeing into the child's mind so that she could see her mother. He also gave the child the thought of recognizing her mother. When individuals have visions of spiritual greats they never wonder how they know it is that special person since they have never seen them, but that is because *those thoughts are being projected to you at the same time as well.*

Once Ramalinga Swamigal (d. 1874) was riding in a cart with another individual who was taking him back to his village. The cart was attacked by two bandits who raised a cudgel against the saint in order to beat him. Suddenly their hands became immobile and their eyes lost sight, which was due to his projection of *nirmanakaya* emanations into them in order to take over their bodies by freezing their movements and blocking their vision. After they expressed sorrow for their behavior and prayed for the Swami's pardon they were instantly restored back to normal.

Krishna at one time caused Durvasa Muni and all his men who were visiting the Pandavas to feel satisfied of their hunger by projecting *nirmanakaya* emanations into them and through those projections gave them the feelings of satiation.

In the many cases where a sage can see the future with clairvoyance it is because they have attained the Supra-Causal body past the Realm of Form, and learn to see the patterns in the etheric energies that foretell the fortune of people or look at those patterns to see their past. The Immanence body also has this capability with greater depth, length and precision. The reason this is possible is because the lower realms of vibration originate from the higher just as the pattern for the subtle body originates from the Causal body, and the Causal body originates from the Supra-Causal body and so on. Before anything significant happens in the world there is always a pattern in the higher etheric realms that can be seen by someone whose body and sensory perceptions transcend those realms. This is why clairvoyance of the future and past become possible whether for the fate of an individual or nation.

Furthermore, someone with a Supra-Causal, Superconsciousness or Immanence body can sense vibrations in the lower planes of existence, hence they can know when someone is thinking of them from far away. When an individual reads some strange or unusual story about them, or they recite their personal mantra, then a Supra-Causal or Superconsciousness master will know about it. They do not need *nirmanakaya* emanations to understand someone's thoughts on the earthly plane but in order to give people thoughts, energy, or healing they are usually necessary. A spiritual body can also check someone's memories in their brain neurons and thereby know all the secrets of a person, as well as their personal doings for the day, week, month, or even years ago. It is common when going through the kundalini purification process for an enlightened master to arrive with his retinue of students in the practitioner's brain, and then recite everything that happened to that individual that day by reading their neurons.

Let's look at an astrological remedy, other than a simple astrological mantra which asks a deity for help with a situation, to see how such things work and to dispense with the idea of magic being performed by reciting special syllables. Here is an example of a typical Vedic astrology remedial measure to enhance your finances or increase your earnings. It entails having you go to a temple for six consecutive Saturdays and offering six red roses to Hanuman at that time, so it is best to go to a Hanuman temple. This should be done in the afternoon (past 12:00 noon) until night with the best time being 5:00-7:00. This, supposedly, will then increase your finances.

The reasoning behind the remedy is that the second house of money (income) in an astrological natal chart is ruled by Venus, whose number is six, and Venus is represented by flowers. The eleventh house of extra income in a chart is taken to be Aquarius whose lord is Saturn, so you would do this on Saturdays since that is Saturn's day. How many Saturdays and how many flowers? Six, because of Venus ruling the second house of Taurus.

You would offer the flowers to Hanuman because he represents the lagna (ascendant) lord of Aries, and they would be red because this is the color of flowers typically offered to Hanuman (although as you will soon see any color you like or flowers you choose would probably work). This, then, would be a typical astrological remedy for increasing your income or finances.

If you did not know the astrological reasoning behind this remedial measure it would just be a set of instructions to "go to a temple and offer six red roses on six consecutive Saturdays for Hanuman" while asking for income assistance. If this works at all then it would be due to some type of magical activation of a response using some unknown cause and effect laws of the universe, as is done with *feng shui* remedies. However, this assumption of some type of mysterious "chemical reaction" that manifests a physical result due to your consistent actions in the temple is nonsense.

What you are actually doing is attracting, through your ardent activity and persistence, the attention of enlightened individuals (masters) who have chosen to act as wealth deities, who will then try to help you over that time period to bring about a positive result. Or, things might just get better over time naturally in tune with a placebo effect.

This is why *any type of flower or color would work* because if this works at all it is because all you are doing is attracting the attention of enlightened beings to alert them that you need help, and your persistence in doing this consecutively over time through a deed that attracts their attention prompts a response and effort on their part if it can be achieved at all through their compassionate assistance.

When you go to a truly enlightened master in our world they will know your problems and offer advice if they can, and sometimes they can solve simple problems. Sometimes they can only lighten your heart and mind of burdens and nothing more. Here you are alerting enlightened masters in the upper realms and they have vowed to help people in certain areas of their expertise if they can. You are just notifying them through this "ceremony" performed consistently over time, which attracts their notice, that is called a remedial measure.

In the spiritual cultivation school of Swami Muktananda (d. 1982) people will often see a little blue sparkle floating in front of their eyes, and in other schools the masters project a different trademark vision to practitioners. These are all illusions where Causal-bodied and higher beings are practicing their powers of visualization projection within your brain. In other words, they are not natural phenomena. It is not that you will definitely see them or regularly see them when you perform the same spiritual practices; it is not under your control. They are simply due to spiritual masters playing with the powers of projection within people's minds that are available due to the fact that they have higher energy bodies that can affect consciousness since the mind runs on those energies. They simply overlay their consciousness, or a *nirmanakaya's* mental workings, on top of your own and then your mind is controlled.

The Hindu sage Neem Karoli Baba (d. 1973) was commonly known for being seen in several places simultaneously, which is the case for many Hindu saints, and could take things from one location to another. This means he achieved the Immanence body attainment to be able to do so. The superpowers of the subtle body are the eight *siddhi*, but the superpowers of the Supra-Causal and Immanence bodies include the ability to make energy copies of themselves (*nirmanakaya* emanations) that can instantly appear in different places to give people thoughts, energy and feelings such as motivation, fearlessness, inspiration, and so forth. When a spiritual body can carry things from one place to another this is higher than the stage of a *nirmanakaya* being seen as a tangible entity.

Once Bhagavan Ramana Maharshi was caught by his childhood friend Ranjan (Velacheri Ranga Iyer) emanating a *yang-shan nirmanakaya* whilst asleep. Ranjan returned from a trip away from the ashram and saw him outside sitting on a bed and then went inside his room to find his sleeping body lying down. When he told Ramana the master replied in his typical way to dismiss any matter involving miraculous powers, "Why didn't you tell me at that time? I could have caught the thief!"

Bhagwan Swaminarayan also generated multiple visible *yang-shan nirmanakaya*, each standing beside a different horse in a stable, to thwart the thief Joban Pagi of Vartal.

Robert Svoboda, author of *Aghora: At the Left Hand of God*, once talked about a time when his enlightened Aghori teacher Sri Vimalananda was talking to an Indian who had been working abroad and sending money back to his family. The man had just come back to India and was telling Sri Vimalananda that he was tired of working, was ready to retire in India and would expect his family to take care of him. The man's family did not want this and Sri Vimalananda did not think this was a good idea either so he just stared at the man for a few seconds. The man stopped talking, and then suddenly he announced he had decided it was actually a better idea to return overseas and continue sending money back to his family rather than retiring in India at that time.

Later Sri Vimalananda told Svoboda that this man was the *tamas* type of individual which are easy to change because they're going to assume that whatever they think comes from themselves and if they thought it then it must be right. The man was originally thinking one thought was right, then suddenly changed his mind and then thought the new thinking was right. Sri Vimalananda said that's all he had to do, which was make sure the man thought that his new thinking was right. Naturally he gave this man these thoughts through either one of his higher spiritual bodies or a *nirmanakaya* emanation.

This is how it is done.

CHAPTER 12
TAKEAWAY SUMMARIES

CHAPTER 1:
You have the potential of five spiritual bodies which are recognized not just by Hinduism but by many other world religions that simply refer to the same transcendental bodies by different names. To attain a higher spiritual body you must purify the inner vital energy of whatever body constitutes your present mind-body-energy complex. This is the pathway to full and complete spiritual enlightenment. The energies of your consciousness and life force both come from the presence of higher bodies compressed or entangled within your physical nature, which is the meaning of the Hindu *koshas*. To attain the naked *atman* free of all lower pollutions you must step by step arise in new spiritual bodies that progressively separate from each lower level of being and you achieve this feat by internal energy (kundalini) purification efforts.

CHAPTER 2:
You are given an explanation of the multi-year kundalini purification process that purifies your inner vital energy so that it can arise in the first of the higher transcendental body attainments. This is the subtle energy or deva body that people normally attain after death, but the one attained through spiritual cultivation is much more purified and is immediately ready to attain the next higher body attainment called the Causal body. This process of purification involves spiking your

emotions and rotating your inner energy during that enlivened, dynamized state, which is explained through the story of the churning of the Ocean of Milk (*Samudra Mantham*), thermal heat mapping pictures and tantric pictures of deities inside the human body. It is also explained in the *Surangama Sutra* of Buddhism and in the stories of the Indian Mahasiddha Naropa and Lu Dongbin from China. Now you have a guide (which is missing from Hinduism) for going through the kundalini transformation process as well as warnings from Ramana Maharshi and Shakyamuni Buddha.

CHAPTER 3:
The Brahman somehow gave birth to the universe, the universe evolved within itself complex life with consciousness, and its higher civilized life (such as ourselves) pursues several goals among which is *moksha* or spiritual liberation. Avatars have previously set examples for guiding mankind at various stages of evolution and we are at the present stage where ordinary men can now guide themselves due to their stage of maturity, education, wisdom, ethics, skillfulness and knowledge. Many spiritual traditions have evolved in the world and with differences in dogma, but this is usually irrelevant in the big religions as long as they point us towards cultivating a higher inner life, more elevated behavior, and offer us pathways to the higher body achievements that they encourage us to tread through worship, meditation, prayer or mantra, and so on. In addition to helping society stay peaceful and function cooperatively, now you know several key purposes of religion for managing the masses.

CHAPTER 4:
In this chapter you are provided with the highest teachings of Advaita Vedanta regarding your True Self, or self-nature. You can now dispense with the need to spend years studying Hindu scriptures to glean the relevant teachings regarding enlightenment, liberation and self-realization. This one chapter supplies explanations to fill in many of the gaps of both Hinduism as well as Buddhism as regards enlightenment teachings.

CHAPTER 5:
You are taught how the *Mahavakya* correspond to elemental meditations that show you how to envision the universe in different

ways as either Ishvara (a form of manifestation) or the Brahman. You are also taught various detachment meditations used by sadhus and sannyasins to help them stop identifying with their physical body as their self. Now you have several meditations for envisioning that you are the entire universe, which *is* your manifest body, or for dispensing with the idea of materiality altogether. Appendix 2 is an adjunct to this information.

CHAPTER 6:
Hatha Yoga is taught as a way to cultivate your muscles and the Prana of the individual body. The method of getting ripped muscles through Yoga practice is by engaging in long isometric holds. You also have various *asanas* for cultivating the Prana of individual body parts and then linking them together as whole. Various methods are taught to supercharge Yoga practice in order to cultivate the Prana of different body appendages or sections that then prepares you for the subtle body achievement. The *Yoga Yajnavalkya* is highlighted as a dependable study guide. Appendix 1 is an adjunct to this information.

CHAPTER 7:
Pranayama is taught as a way to open up your *nadi*s in your subtle body. Anapana is taught as a way to use the power of your breathing to move the Prana around within your body to your tissues. Nyasa Yoga is taught as a way to use mantras on body parts to divinize them through *nirmanakaya* or sound energies. Reciting various *Sahasranama* is taught as a method of transforming your Prana too. Wim Hof breathing is introduced as an adjunct to well-known Yoga pranayama techniques and Ahhh-breathing is introduced as a method to be used just prior to meditation since it instantly silences thoughts. *Jiujie Fofeng* "Nine Winds" breathing is recommended to increase your lung capacity and the number of capillaries in your body.

CHAPTER 8:
Many spiritual masters masquerade as Hindu deities in order to respond to the needs of the people, and the existence of all-seeing Big Gods (deities) with supernatural monitoring helps to regulate society because "watched people are nice people." The fear of Hell or karma is usually stronger than a desire for Heaven so it helps to regulate group behavior. The various methods of *bhakti* (devotional

worship) are explained as safe but very slow methods to help purify your Prana, so there are special ways to elevate the *bhakti* of deities and other spiritual cultivation techniques to make them more effective. Now you will know those secrets to advancing your practice and can understand the reason for various quirks in many cultivation practices of Hinduism. A Vedic astrology method is revealed that can tell whether *bhakti*, ascetic Yoga or Vedanta is the right pathway for you.

CHAPTER 9:
Other than using mantras to calm your thoughts, two basic types of mantras for purifying your Prana are explained – those which call for assistance from enlightened beings to help transform your Prana due to their *nirmanakaya* emanations, and those constructed of *bijas* that vibrate, energize and purify the Prana of body parts through special resonance on their own without need of external assistance. The importance of environmental Prana, and usefulness of astrolocality lines is introduced. The importance of emotional *bhajan* singing is stressed where you also move the aroused energy or mood around inside your body. Visualizations are a powerful add-on to devotional practices. A basic primer on emotional Yin or Yang (lunar or solar energy) cultivation techniques is given again as well as insight into the mystery of tantric Yin feminization stories in Hinduism, which are just one type of Yin purification method among many.

CHAPTER 10:
Nearly two dozen types of cultivation techniques are explained in terms of how they purify your Prana using different principles. The general rule is to simultaneously use as many different cultivation exercises as possible that are each based on different principles for stirring, moving or purifying your Prana because you don't know which methodology will work best for you since everyone is different. There are methods for stirring your Prana without engaging your emotions, methods for moving your Prana while fully spiking your emotions to change the tone of your Prana, methods for absorbing yourself in incredibly large emotions to permeate your Prana with different qualities, methods for changing your Prana by imagining unity with a deity or spiritual master, movement exercises that can be combined with advanced Prana cultivation techniques,

and special events or locations that can be used to stimulate your Yin or Yang Prana. This is the secret basis of Hindu spiritual cultivation.

CHAPTER 11:
Some secrets behind various miracles performed by Hindu saints are explained, which are usually due to using their higher bodies or the *nirmanakaya* emanations of their higher bodies to perform certain tasks.

APPENDIX 1:
CHAKRAS

This is an excerpt on the real meaning of chakras taken from my book *Correcting Zen* that has been appended with additional examples. Similar information can be found in *Neijia Yoga*:

Most chakra visualization techniques use a seven-part scheme to segment the body into seven segments for energy work, yet since people don't know the real meaning of the chakras they don't know what these segments are. Hence, here is the lost information that can be used for the purpose of cultivation practice.

The four-petalled *Muladhara* root chakra, often symbolized by a four-sided square, four-legged elephant or four-armed deity, represents the bottommost section of our torso containing the perineum. This is supposedly where the power in our body torso comes from. When visualizing this chakra you are actually supposed to be focusing on the flesh, bones and energy within the pelvis in order to wash these tissues. The reason that an *elephant* is sometimes used to symbolize this chakra is because male genitalia are similar in appearance to the head of an elephant.

Power is symbolized by an elephant, and hence we have another reason for the symbol of an elephant since this region of the body is said to be where our torso's power originates. The reason that this chakra is also often represented as a *square* is because a square represents the foundation of a building and the major muscles around the perineum form a square of four sides. In mandalas, a foundational four-sided square with doors represents this chakra and its four muscles. Seen from below there are two ischiocavernosus muscles that form a corner of a square, the diagonal is the superficial transverse perineal muscle, and the ileococcygeous muscle forms the rest of the square. On the internet you can find pictures to confirm this and see the square.

This chakra simply represents the lowest section of our torso, and our energy is supposed to originate from this area although it doesn't produce any special energy generation. The idea is just an analogy although in the martial arts the power of our legs below has to pass through this region to get to the upper body. Buddhist mandalas have four sides to represent the energy within this part of our torso, and Buddhist deities commonly have four arms to represent the power of this region as well with the insinuation that the energy is used for virtuous celestial purposes.

The *Svadhisththana* six-petalled sacral chakra corresponds to the sacrum. This chakra is often represented by a crocodile because rough crocodile scales remind people of the bony protrusions of the sacrum, and its six petals refer to the six nerves protruding from each side of vertebrae S1, S2, S3, S4, S5, and C0 within the sacrum. If you look at a picture of the sacrum from the internet and find these nerves you'll quickly see why it is said to be composed of six petals.

In Indian culture the goddess of the Ganges River, Ganga, is represented as having four arms (representing the four-petalled root chakra) and riding a crocodile-like creature called the makara (the six-petalled sacral chakra) on the river. The overall symbol represents the Qi/Prana running from the pelvis (containing the two chakras) and traveling up the spine.

In the *Surangama Sutra* Samantabhadra Bodhisattva stated, "World Honored One, I always use my mind to listen in order to distinguish the variety of views held by living beings. If in a place, separated from here by a number of worlds as countless as the sands in the Ganges, a living being practices Samantabhadra deeds, I mount at once a six-tusked elephant and reproduce myself in a hundred and a thousand apparitions to come to his aid. Even if he is unable to see me because of his great karmic obstruction, I secretly lay my hand on his head to protect and comfort him so that he can succeed."

This is actually referring to *nirmanakaya* emanations where

Samantabhadra's "six-tusked elephant" represents his pelvis (waist), thus meaning his entire person, because the six tusks represent the sacral chakra and the elephant's head represents the root chakra and both are in his pelvis. When he says he rides an elephant *it just means he is standing there resting on his pelvis*. Buddhism has encoded the chakra lessons into this one image but this information has become lost over the ages.

The ten-petalled *Manipura* navel (solar plexus) chakra corresponds to the section of the body served by the left and right nerves protruding from the L1, L2, ... L5 lumbar spinal vertebrae, and represents the lower *dantian* belly of the body. It is basically our body's abdomen within which are the intestines used to draw energy from food and excrete wastes. The twelve-petalled *Anahata* heart chakra corresponds to the regions of the body controlled by (the body section in front of) the T1 through T12 thoracic vertebrae nerves, which includes the heart and lungs in the chest region. The sixteen-petalled *Vishuddha* throat chakra is the set of C1, C2, ... C8 cervical vertebrae and their surrounding tissues of the neck, face and upper chest ruled by the nerves extending out of those vertebrae.

The two-part "third eye" *Ajna* chakra represents our brain stem and the two halves of the brain that have left and right, Yin and Yang sections, and thus in Hinduism this synthesis of masculine and feminine energies (Surya and Chandra) is represented by *Ardhanarishvara* (a form of Shiva conjoined with his consort Parvati). The male-female deities of Harihara, Jumadi and Vaikuntha Kamalaja also represent the two-part brain stem that we say is partitioned into a Yin and Yang side. It is ashamed that no one knows this. Even the Shiva linga represents the brain stem, which gives us consciousness, and that is why it is worshipped. It is the wish-fulfilling jewel of the human body.

The famous Indian legend of Garuda the magical bird being ridden by Vishnu also symbolizes the brain stem controlling the two wings or halves of the brain. Incidentally, garudas are said to "eat dragons" because your Qi rises up the spine into your brain stem (garuda) and this Qi is a snake or dragon. In Hinduism, the deity Skanda is known as "the rider on the peacock" to symbolize the brain stem surrounded by the web of neurons in the brain that are symbolized by peacock feathers.

The top chakra is the thousand-petalled *Sahasrara* crown chakra that symbolizes our brain with all its neurons and nerves, which are also often represented as colorful peacock feathers or the hairs of Yang-type animals. The *Sahasrara* crown chakra is not located above our head but instead represents *the brain and all its neurons* inside the skull! Its nerves can be seen in modern DTI diffusion tensor images that you can and should use to guide internal Qi rotation patterns that you perform to "wash your brain" to help open up its Qi channels.

What most people don't know is that our brain also represents Kamadhenu, the wish-fulfilling cow of Buddhism. As can be seen from pictures of Kamadhenu, she becomes the Sphinx of Egyptian mythology and the Chimera of Greek mythology (where the tail is the spine with its triangular sacrum and its fiery breath is the kundalini hot Qi necessary for some of the purification processes involved in the processes of spiritual transformation). The Tibetan Wind horse (Lung-Ta) that carries the wish-fulfilling jewel of enlightenment, which is the brain stem, is also a symbol of Kamadhenu and the brain as well. In the Hindu epic *Mahabharata* the warrior Arjuna meets the mythical creature Navagunjara (a manifestation of Vishnu) who also represents the human brain and spinal cord.

This information should cause you to have greater faith in your cultivation practice that absolutely should include inner energy techniques such as the white skeleton visualization *sadhana*, or even Qi rotational schemes using chakras and appendages as body sections. It is no crime to use tantric yoga, or Vajrayana/Newar Buddhist methods as well since the goal is enlightenment and such methods are virtuous and clean. This is why many people use the Indian partitioning scheme of seven chakras based on spinal vertebra, and in *Neijia Yoga* you will find an eight-part sectioning scheme based on fascial planes within the body that is even better since it is more relevant to Qi flow inside us.

This is an excerpt from Chapter 7 of *Neijia Yoga* ("Cultivating the Body's Qi in Sections") and teaches you how to cultivate your body in sections instead of the segments defined by chakras:

Fixing your Qi for a long time at various points within your body, and holding visualizations at those points or simply washing them with Qi, is one way to cultivate the Qi of your entire body in sequence.

If you partition your body into logically defined sections such as torso segments, body cavities, limbs, muscles, glands, internal organs, bones, etcetera then you can subsequently work at cultivating your entire body by using your mind-guided Qi to wash all such areas one by one. Eventually you can link the purified Qi of all those body segments into one undivided whole and thereby create permanent power. Power becomes permanent after sufficient internal Qi cultivation work to cleanse and unite your internal energy, whereas force (the usage of power) is temporary.

There are several ways to work on purifying and transforming the Qi of body sections. Using your mind you can try to feel the Qi of an entire region by concentrating on internal sensations within it, and simply hold onto the feeling of the "energy" or "substance" of that section. You might also mentally wash it with a visualization of bright sunlight or moonlight while pushing your Qi around within that area.

You can use your mind to push your Qi energy throughout all your various body parts and sections. You can ultimately guide it in this way to wash all the sections of your body and their interior components. However, it takes time to learn how to perfect mind-guided movements of your Qi. Bodhidharma's "marrow cleansing" technique within the *Xi Sui Jing* follows this principle as applied to bones. Daoism has various systems of inner washing as well and Hinduism has the method of Nyasa Yoga to wash body parts step by step.

You can also recite mantras or *bija* sounds on body sections, or as if from within body sections to stimulate/activate their Qi and thereby wash them through excitation. Furthermore, you can recite *bija* sounds on top of strategic *bindus* (points) such as acupuncture points, pressure points, *Dim mak* points, or marma points because by emphasizing those points you will affect the Qi connected to its network of associations. Reciting a sound as if at a point or upon a point will stimulate all the Qi around it, thus serving as a force for Qi activation and frictional purification.

While performing such practices you can try to arouse positive (Yang) or negative (Yin) emotions within yourself in order to stimulate the Yin Qi or Yang Qi of your body, and in particular you must then try to feel the Qi in this way within that section. Emotions can used to stimulate, arouse, excite, energize, invigorate, and transform the Qi within your body as they change its quality or tonality and all the possible tonalities of your Qi must be washed in this way. Martial artists and yogis tend to think that you should only cultivate your Yang Qi but your Yin Qi must be cultivated and purified as well.

Here are some classical ways to partition the body into various sections so that you can work on transforming the Qi within each segment.

TWO SECTIONS:

Left side, right side; Top and bottom; Front and back; Up the spine and down the front of the body through the *du mai* and *ren mai*; Up the spine and down the Alimentary canal (the tube from mouth to anus) and everything surrounding it ... these are some ways of partitioning the body into two parts.

The Buddhist and Hindu sutras recommend that you use the sounds of Om, Ah or Ram, or recite the Rah-Vah (also Ram-Vam) mantra, within the different body sections in order to transform the Qi of your underlying energetic nature. This work will help to improve Qi flow throughout your body, which is essential for the highest level of martial arts proficiency.

Leading your Qi upwards or downwards in your body, or to the left or right, or in a clockwise or counterclockwise direction, or in spirals or in caressing bones or limbs or organs, etcetera are all ways of moving your Qi internally to wash your tissues.

Traditionally the right side of your body is considered Yang and the left side is considered Yin. The traditional cultivation method of Buddhist Arhats is to concentrate on feeling heat and fire on one side of the body (that is envisioned with the color red), and feeling cooling water on the other side (which is envisioned with the color blue or white). After sufficient practice, the hotness and coolness (Yang Qi and Yin Qi) are switched to the other side of the body. This is practiced within the top and the bottom sections of the body, and for the left and right sides of the body.

This is essentially the Daoist practice of *Li* and *Kan*, which is working to purify the Yin Qi and Yang Qi of your body. Yogis and the supreme martial artists use a variety of methods to cultivate the Yin and Yang energies of their bodies. Rather than using the visualization spur of fire and water to change the texture or quality feel of your Qi, you can practice feeling the energy of the sun on one side of the body and the energy of the moon on the other, and then switch them.

Another martial arts practice is to feel that one half of the body is empty while the other is heavy, and then to switch sides again with those feelings. Or, you might try feeling that one side of your body is light while another side is darkness, and so on.

This sort of technique is like practicing under a cold rushing waterfall and then in a hot spring or dry sauna.

THREE SECTIONS:

Head with neck and arms, chest and middle torso, thighs and legs to feet; Head and neck, arms and chest and trunk to pelvic waist, legs and feet; Head, chest and arms to waist, thighs and legs to feet; Backside of the body running upwards, front side of the body running downwards, inner core of digestive organs and alimentary canal ... these are some of the ways to partition the body into three sections that you tackle one-by-one through inner Qi washing exercises. The most famous three-part sectioning scheme is the three *dantian* of Daoism.

Om-Ah-Hung, Om-Ah-Hum, Om-So-Hum, Om-Aum-Hum and Hreem-Shreem-Kleem are some of the three-syllable mantras used to stimulate and purify the Qi in each of the three body sectional schemes. Each syllable of these mantras is to be recited within a different segment of the body so as to vibrate the Qi within it.

For instance, Samantabhadra's mantra of "Om-Ah-Hung" is used extensively in the Esoteric school of Buddhism. To use this mantra to transform your body's Qi quickly you would recite "Ah" while trying the feel the Qi of your head, neck and arms. This is the upper part of your body according to one partitioning scheme. You would then recite "Ah" while trying to feel the Qi within your arms and torso. This is the middle section of your body. You would then recite "Hung" or "Hum" while trying to feel the energy in the lower section of your body from your waist down to your feet.

Other three-syllable mantras are available to be used in a similar manner.

Daoists concentrate on feeling their internal energy within the three *dantian*, but few realize that one reason to favor this tripartite scheme is because each section contains organs with the most nerves, and nerves are responsible for consciousness.

The upper *dantian* contains the brain, which is the major organ of consciousness. The middle *dantian* contains the heart, which has lots of nerves and neurons that can also store memories, which is why heart transplant recipients often start exhibiting the likes and dislikes of their heart donor that were impressed within the heart tissues as memories. DTI (diffusion tensor) images of the heart easily show these nerves. The lower *dantian* contains the intestines (alimentary canal), gut or "second brain" that can also store memories although to a lesser degree. Through these and other mechanisms people often carry over their own personality tendencies and even fears from a past life.

If you arouse attitudes or emotions within these sections then those neural tissues will become imprinted by them and they can be more easily carried forward to subsequent lives. Hence you can use "dominant attitude" meditation to not just transform the Qi of this body but help design the personality of your next incarnation. Even now, you can alter this life by altering your attitudes of mind.

FOUR SECTIONS:

Head, neck and arms, arms and chest (middle torso), lower abdomen and pelvis, legs and feet; Upper left quadrant of the body, upper right quadrant of the body, lower left quadrant of the body, lower right quadrant of the body … these are just some of the ways to partition the body into fours.

Om-Ah-Vah-Lah, Om-Hreem-Shreem-Kleem, and Sah-Rah-Vah-Nah are some four-part mantras that apply for the head, chest, abdomen, and waist to legs. One can also use the five-syllable mantra Ah-Vi-Ra-Hum-Kham where the first four syllables are apportioned to four sections of the body while the final "Kham" should shake the Qi of the entire body in total, or just be used on the spine.

FIVE SECTIONS:

While the body can easily be partitioned into five sections, your Qi can be partitioned into five different qualities or categories as well.

According to the five *Vayus* (winds or Qi-types) principles of Hinduism our head and arms correspond to the ascending Qi called *Udana;* the region of the chest with lungs and heart corresponds to *Prana;* the mid-trunk of body containing digestive organs corresponds to *Samana* Qi; the lower abdomen and pelvis corresponds to the Qi called *Apana;* the entire body is pervaded by *Vyana* that is especially located in the legs to the feet. Some yoga schools differ on this attribution scheme, so this is just one of the many ways to partition the body into five parts.

Om-Ah-Vah-Lah-Hum is one of the many five-syllable mantras you can use to cultivate your Qi in these five body sections. Another is Om-Ah-Vah-Rah-Hum.

Besides the five Prana, martial artists are often taught to evoke different internal feelings in their training that correspond to different flavors of Qi. They must not only learn how to make their Qi surge, ebb, be stored and be guided to wherever their mind directs, but must be able to change the quality of that Qi. The quality, flavor, feeling or nature of your Qi is often represented by the characteristic temperament of an animal such as a snake, monkey, tiger, dragon, crane and so forth. Thus, students are sometimes taught to practice the spirit and movement of a Yin or Yang animal in order to master particular movements as well as temporarily transform the quality of their Qi.

Similarly, you can also recognize for each of the five elements – earth, water, fire, wind and space – a different type of Qi energy within your body. Each type of element Qi can be purified through a different type of Qi training. In fact, you can practice Qi purification exercises for your Yin and Yang Qi, a different Qi feeling for each of the five elements of your body, a different Qi feeling for the planets of our solar system since they affect us, a different Qi feeling for each season or for the 28 lunar mansions, and other partitioning schemes that segment Qi into different types. To do this, you must focus on feeling that type of energy within your entire body, perhaps by first stimulating it, and hold onto that Qi sensation so that it suffuses the segment with some type of mild or overt excitation.

Earth represents the solidity of your body, is especially felt within your flesh and bones, and is usually cultivated by imagining that your body becomes solid, heavy, yellow earth. Often masters teach students to merge with a boulder, mountain or wall that they train next to (or feel its energy) in order to help them cultivate their earth element Qi.

Water represents fluidity and the Yin Qi of the body, which is 70% water, and is cultivated by imagining that your body's entirety becomes cool blue water, or simply white in color. Often Daoist and Buddhist masters teach students to train next to a lake whose energy they might feel or try to merge with in order that they cultivate their water element Qi or Yin Qi.

Fire represents the heat and Yang Qi of your body, and is cultivated by imagining that your body becomes a raging fire.

Wind represents just the Qi or vital energy of your body, which is often referred to as the wind element, and is cultivated by imagining that your body loses its structure and is just a matrix of coursing energy everywhere.

Space represents the ultimate nature of your body that is empty like space, and is cultivated by imagining (and feeling) that your body becomes like an empty sack, or is abandoned entirely and becomes universal empty space.

A practitioner should progress through these contemplations one-by-one to purify the Qi of their body and end them by abandoning all notions to rest their mind in emptiness by imagining that they become empty space.

The *Visuddhimagga*, or great treatise of Theravada Buddhist cultivation written by Buddhaghosa, has teachings on cultivating the five elements within the body through concentrations, called *kasina* meditations, but these lessons are incomprehensible without this information. You should not just concentrate on merging with a certain type of element but on feeling the energy or Qi of that element within you. This is how you wash the Qi of your body with different flavors or textures.

In the martial arts, special attention must be paid to each of the elements within five elements cultivation. For instance, the earth element represents an integral combination of all the elements together (they all exist within the earth element). It is the embodiment of both Yin and Yang essences combined together.

For martial arts it is important to practice the earth element cultivation method of feeling rooted in your feet so that you develop firmness in your stepping. You practice feeling the earth element below your feet united with the Yin Qi in your foot. Or, you can practice sinking your Qi into your legs and feet as if the entire Earth empties its weight into your shape, and then mix this feeling in your feet with the Qi of the Earth. When martial artists practice heaviness in the legs or feet in order to develop this firmness, they must make sure that the feeling doesn't transform into sluggishness. Nevertheless it is common and proper to imagine that your foot becomes very cold, like Yin Qi, and to spin that cold Qi within it to wash its tissues. This is superior martial arts as well as superior Buddhist and Daoist cultivation.

SIX SECTIONS:

Heart, lungs, stomach, liver, kidneys, and triple warmer ... this is one of the ways to partition the body into six internal organs.

The organs correspond to the Daoist six healing sounds Haa (heart), Szz (lungs), Hoo (stomach), Shoo (liver), Foo (kidneys), and Shee (the three sections of the upper, middle and lower warmer). Different traditions will use different sounds for the organs, and the proper sounds are the ones that help you feel or move the Qi of the organs. While practicing, you can try to feel the positive or negative emotions associated with each organ.

SEVEN SECTIONS:

The body can be partitioned into seven sections using a symbolism of "seven chakras," which corresponds to body sections delineated by spinal vertebrae and their nerves. The top chakra is the thousand-petalled *Sahasrara* crown chakra that represents our brain with all its neurons and nerves. Its nerves can be seen in DTI diffusion tensor images, and those pictures should be used to guide any internal Qi rotation practices that you perform to "wash your brain" and help open up its Qi channels. This will result in higher mental quietness, clarity, and speedier reflex responses over time.

Incidentally, the brain is Kamadhenu, the wish-fulfilling cow of Hinduism and Buddhism (that becomes the Sphinx of Egyptian mythology and Chimera of Greek mythology)[6], and the Qi channels within it must be opened through countless Qi washings. The Tibetan Windhorse (Lung-Ta) that carries the wish-fulfilling jewel of enlightenment, which is the brain stem, is also a symbol of Kamadhenu and the brain as well.

As stated, Kamadhenu has its equivalent in the Sphinx of ancient Egypt who could ask questions of humans since the Sphinx symbolizes the brain. The hairs of the Sphinx represent the nerves or Qi channels in the brain, its wings represent the two brain lobes, the four paws represent its four sections and the tail of the Sphinx represents our spinal cord.

The Lamassu or Sadu of Mesopotamia (Sumerian and Akkadian mythology), which looks like the Sphinx (and Kamadhenu), also represents our brain. Furthermore, the strange creature Navagunjara that the warrior Arjuna meets in the Hindu epic *Mahabharata* represents our brain as well, which is a fact unknown to scholars.

The Greek Chimera also represents the brain through its many lion hairs that are the brain nerves, its two wings that are the two brain lobes with neurons (feathers), the two goat horns that are the two protruding nerve bundles that ascend upwards from the spinal cord, the snake tail that represents the spine and cobra head-shaped coccyx, and its fire represents the *kundalini* energy necessary to transform it.

The two-part "third eye" *Ajna* chakra symbolizes our brain stem that has conjoined left and right, Yin and Yang sections like the Shiva-Parvati *Ardhanarishvara*. This is the "muddy pellet" of Daoism, and the hump on the back of Kamadhenu the wish-fulfilling cow. Its two horns represent two ascending spinal nerve bundles that reach from the spine to the top of the head. The great sage yogi Gorasknath named Kamadhenu's four teats Ambika (mother), Lambika (eyes at the summit), Ghantika (sound) and Talika (clapping) in order to represent the two nodes of the superior colliculus and two nodes of the inferior colliculus in the brainstem that process visual and auditory information.

The sixteen-petalled *Vishuddha* throat chakra is the set of C1, C2, ... C8 cervical vertebrae and their surrounding tissues of the neck, face and upper chest ruled by the nerves extending out of those vertebrae.

---

[6] See *Nyasa Yoga* and *Buddha Yoga* for details.

The twelve-petalled *Anahata* heart chakra corresponds to the regions of the body controlled by the T1 through T12 thoracic vertebrae nerves.

The ten-petalled *Manipura* navel (solar plexus) chakra corresponds to the section of the body served by the left and right nerves protruding from the L1, L2, ... L5 lumbar spinal vertebrae, and represents the "*hara*" of Japanese martial arts or lower *dantian* of Chinese medicine.

The *Svadhisththana* sacral chakra corresponds to the sacrum. This chakra is often represented by a crocodile because rough crocodile scales remind people of the bony protrusions of the sacrum, and its six petals refer to the six nerves protruding from each side of vertebrae S1, S2, S3, S4, S5, and C0.

The four-petalled *Muladhara* root chakra, often symbolized by a four-sided square, a four-legged elephant or a four-armed deity, symbolizes your pelvic girdle muscles along with your asshole, perineum and genitals (male genitalia are symbolized by the head of an elephant).

The major muscles around the perineum form a square of four sides because seen from below two ischiocavernosus muscles form a corner of the square, the diagonal is the superficial transverse perineal muscle, and the ileococcygeous muscle forms the rest of the square. Hence, mandalas have four sides to represent this area of our torso, and Hindu deities commonly have four arms to represent the power of this region as well. In other words, the four-petalled chakra just represents the bottommost section of our torso.

Power-possessing Hindu deities are shown with four arms to represent the muscles of this square that is the primal source or foundational basis of power for all the muscles above. The center of the square contains the perineum or *huiyin* DU-1 acupuncture point, which is the *haidi* or "bottom of the ocean" from which Sun Wukong retrieved his staff. Thus the pelvic region in general is usually symbolized by the root chakra together with the sacral chakra, which are sometimes together represented by an elephant (who symbolizes great power). The Goddess Ganga, who is symbolized as having four arms and riding a crocodile in the Ganges River, also symbolizes the pelvis, sacrum and spine together. The Ganges River she rides upon represents Qi ascending through the *du mai* into the brain.

All of these sections can be washed with Qi that can be vibrated by traditional *bija* sounds recited within them. You have to vocalize various sounds to see if better ones than those used in your own tradition can be found to vibrate/affect the Qi in various body sections.

The *Mahavairocana Sutra* of Buddhism and *Yoga Yajnavalkya* recommend the same set of sounds to help wash each body part with Qi, which is called the "disposition of letters" or "disposition of syllables." However, these are not to be taken as definitive. The best mantra sounds to use are those that vibrate the Qi within the section being concentrated on, and sometimes you can find sounds to do this that have not been recorded in ancient scriptures. If a tone vibrates the Qi channels within certain sections of the body, it is considered a *bija* or root sound for that body part and you can use it.

Daoism needs to do some research work on this to find the best sounds for vibrating the Qi within each section of your body. After those sounds are discovered, they can be turned into mantras that you recite to vibrate/wash the Qi of specific body parts in sequence. This type of mantra recitation will help you make progress in purifying your Qi even if an enlightened spiritual being is not there to help you was your Qi at the same time through one of his *nirmanakaya* projections. Whenever you recite a sound you would focus on feeling the Qi of the body part with which it has a vibrational association, *and possibly add a strong emotion to each sound as well*, to wash the Qi of that section as you proceed from one region of your body to the next.

Each spiritual cultivation school in the world recommends different *bija* sounds to help resonate the Qi within separate body parts, and that information is usually incorporated into mantras or prayers. Sometimes a mantra is designed to vibrate the Qi of your body, and sometimes it is designed to call for the assistance of a Buddha, deity or Immortal to use their own Qi to work on purifying the Qi of your body segments and cleanse the underlying subtle body within them. You might inquire of a master as to which mantra may work best for you.

EIGHT SECTIONS:

Another torso partitioning scheme[7] of eight sections can be made using seven fascial meridians or meridians of latitude called "bands" that segment the body into eight parts. While the seven sectional scheme based on chakras is delineated based on nerves and spinal vertebrae, this sectioning scheme is based on fascial planes within the body, and hence is more relevant to the Qi flow inside us.

The first meridian is the eye band that is a horizontal plane starting from the bridge of the nose and running to the back of the skull. The section of the body delineated by going upwards thus contains the eyes and the brain.

The chin band is the angular line formed by the bottom of the chin slicing upwards to back of the skull. This band to the eye band contains the bottom region of the head including the nasal cavity, teeth, tongue, palate and cerebellum. As with all other body structures, these parts must all be washed over and over again by revolving your Qi inside them in many diverse ways.

The collar band is a strap running around the bottom of the neck centered on the clavicle (collar bone) and continuing towards the back on the upper border of the shoulder blade (scapula) ending at the junction of the cervical and thoracic vertebrae. The body region delineated contains the neck with thyroid gland.

The chest band is the area just below the nipples running horizontally as a band around the body. This band running upwards to the collar meridian contains the heart, lungs, thymus gland, shoulders and arms.

The abdomen (belly or umbilical) band starts at the belly button and then wraps horizontally around the body. This band upwards to the chest band contains the internal organs of stomach, pancreas, spleen, liver, gall bladder and kidneys.

The inguinal band runs across the lower abdomen starting at the back of the buttocks and running atop the pelvic bones until falling at their front, slightly dipping downwards, thus taking the shape of an inverted arch. From the inguinal band to the umbilical meridian are the bulk of the intestines.

The pubic band extends from the pubic bone (pubic symphysis) in the front of the body across the groin to the bottom of the

---

[7] Dr. Louis Schultz and Dr. Rosemary Feitis discovered these horizontal bands within the body's myofascia, which are thickening in the deep layers of fascia and connective tissue. See *Anatomy Trains* by Thomas Myers for illustrations.

buttocks in the back. From the pubic band to the inguinal band above it is the region containing the sacrum and coccyx as well as the genitals.

The lowest section of the body below the pubic band contains the legs and feet. This section starts from the public band that stretches like a gentle arch from the pelvic bone to the bottom of the buttocks, thus defining the beginning of the legs.

APPENDIX 2:
SAMPLE "EMPTINESS" OR "FORMLESSNESS" MEDITATIONS FROM KASHMIR SHAIVISM

This is an excerpt on formless meditations taken from my book *Correcting Zen* but perfectly applicable to Hinduism. The meditations are based on the *Vijnana Bhairava Tantra* of Kashmir Shaivism, possibly authored by Guru Keyuravati.

Here is a large list of a variety of "emptiness meditations" you might practice that involve mental stations of infinite space, infinite consciousness, infinite nothingness, infinite emptiness, infinite Allness, infinite oneness, infinite bodilessness, infinite ungraspability and infinite detachment. The purpose of such meditations is to help you arrive at an experience of mental quieting, *shamatha*.

- Set your mind on the highest realm of consciousness that is above all thought-constructs. Let go of thoughts and remain there.

- You should concentrate intensely on the idea that this universe is totally an ephemeral, effervescent illusion populated by transparent images. Phenomena are ungraspable like mirages since they are transient affairs that lack inherent existence. Let your mind therefore let go of clinging attachments to this emptiness and become like the empty space itself within which they appear.

- Go to an empty field or top of a mountain and stare into space. Take no notice of any clouds but let go of your body become the space itself that infinitely extends in every direction. Let go of everything and become bodiless space that possesses awareness but no body. Rest in that state of infinite bodilessness but stay detached from anything that now arises within your awareness. Through your awareness you should maintain a knowingness of whatever that arises in your endless body but don't attach to anything since space cannot attach to anything.

- Imagine that, like a fish, you are swimming in an infinite ocean of pure consciousness without any obstructions whatsoever. Then imagine that you are a bodiless observer in that same boundless pure consciousness.

- Imagine you are a pot of water immersed in water. Next, imagine the pot breaks and there is you are now also the water outside of you so you are just one endless water everywhere. Now imagine you are a pot of air resting in space, and similarly the pot disintegrates. What are you like? Be that. Rest there.

- Imagine that you are a point of light within an ocean of infinite light. Let go of your ego and become one with that body of light. Let your body dissolve so that you are that endless ocean of light, which has no borders or bodily form. Make that point of light merge in the infinite ocean of light.

In some of these approaches (1) you try to feel that you or your consciousness becomes infinite, and in others (2) you try to feel that you are part of the infinite by taking an infinitude as the subject of your consciousness while thinking of yourself as a part of that infinite.

You must try each method to see what works best for your meditation progress.

When you find that your internal energy stirs because of practicing some technique, that is a good sign of progress just as Buddhaghosha noted in the *Visuddhimagga* (*Path of Purification*). You can practice becoming the energies related to the four elements or ten planets, for instance, but for practice to be successful you must stir your internal energy in a related manner (such as becoming surging cold water or flaming wild fire) at the same time otherwise you are just performing a stale visualization that doesn't wash your internal energy with the friction of a different energy modality.

For instance, you can imagine embodying the energy of the ten planets in yourself just as you can imagine absorbing (and becoming) the essence of the sun or moon (which is a method mentioned in the *Surangama Sutra*), but unless you strongly stimulate, shake, or arouse your Qi with each new energy state you will not effect any positive benefit from your imaginative efforts at all. For instance there is a school of water cultivation techniques where you imaginatively stimulate various turbulent water states (running water, bubbling water, cold surging water, breaking sea waves, etc.) within your body in order to arouse and thus to cultivate (purify through stimulation that leads to friction) your Yin Qi. One can experience the heat warmth of fire penetrating your body during Shingon fire ceremonies where you are to arouse energetic joyful feelings to match with the inner sensations of Yang Qi at that time. The instructions to change your energy state and stimulate your internal energy for all these methods is used to wash your Qi, but the meditation methods in this Appendix are designed to help you achieve *shamatha*.

The *Vijnana Bhairava*, which is a how-to meditation book from Kashmir Shaivism, contains instructions for practicing over one hundred different types of emptiness meditations for *shamatha*, many of which have made their way into different schools of Buddhism such as Vajrayana. You can also find relevant methods within the stories of the *Yoga Vasistha* from India.

Several of these meditation practices embody far different methods for cultivating mental emptiness. In order to avoid getting into a mental rut where you cling to the realm of emptiness that you are generating as an image within your mind, I suggest you devote yourself to a new one each week and cycle through them during the course of a year. This is one of the quickest ways to develop your meditation progress.

Some other emptiness meditation methods are as follows:

- Visualize the Qi of your body arising from your root chakra (from the bottom of your pelvis) as getting subtler and subtler until at last it dissolves into emptiness and remains there. Let your mind become empty like the final dissolution of that Qi.

- Visualize the Qi of your body that arises from your root chakra as getting subtler and subtle, dissolving your body as it proceeds upwards, until your body dissolves into empty space that merges with the universe, that also then becomes empty like endless space. Stay in that final state of dissolution.

- Fill the center of your brain with Qi (visualize it coming into the brain from your spine, or visualize it entering into the top of your skull from the cosmos) and keep letting go of any thought-constructs while so doing. Let your mind become un-minded. Continue with knowingness but let your thoughts go to the state of being unmanifest. Your consciousness will eventually become empty if you continue letting go of whatever arises within your mind after first bringing Qi into your head. Another way of bringing Qi into your head is by taking in a deep breath and letting it out slowly through your mouth while feeling the energy go up your spine into your head as you exhale. You can do this several times in a row and then rest in mental emptiness.

- Meditate by locating your consciousness in your heart, and hold your thoughts and energy at that location until discursive thinking dies down. Upon the disappearance of your thought-stream stay absorbed in that emptiness. Alternatively, restrain your mental activities in the heart chakra (in the lotus of the heart or within a flame you imagine at that location) and try to cultivate an empty mental state that eventually envelops your body.

- Slowly recite the sound "Ohm" or "Aum" and observe the void of emptiness at the end of the protracted syllable. Doing this many times, you will eventually attain a state of mental emptiness after the syllable ends, so remain in that state when it happens and don't begin another enunciation until thoughts arise again. For some people "Ohm" works better than "Aum," so you must try both sounds to see which works best for you.

- Imagine that you are the empty space in all directions simultaneously without any thought-constructs, so you are a nothingness yourself surrounded by emptiness all around you. Imagine being the spatial emptiness in all directions around you and rest your mind in that state. If anything arises, let it arise within you because you are just infinite emptiness – bodiless, boundless and limitless like space. Being empty space you cannot grasp anything so just refuse to cling to whatever arises within your mind and let go of it.

- Imagine there is endless space above your head, below your feet and within your heart. Rest your mind in that visage of empty space without holding onto any thoughts that now arise but just let them appear and pass away naturally. Simultaneously imagine that the upper part of your body is void and the lower half of your body is void. In your consciousness there is nothing, in both halves of your body there is nothing, and in empty space everywhere there is nothing. Rest in that mental state.

- Contemplate that the constituents of your body (the bones, limbs, organs, etc.) are pervaded with mere vacuity (emptiness). In other words, imagine that all your body components are empty inside and you are like a walking empty sack. In time, the contemplation of having empty body parts will become steady and you can then extend the idea of emptiness to resting your mind in empty space as well.

- Contemplate that the skin of your body is like a thin outer wall and that there is nothing inside your skin but empty space. After you imagine that your body becomes like an empty sack, imagine that your mind becomes limitless and infinite in all spatial directions. All things you experience appear within this infinite spaciousness, but you know them without attaching to them because nothing is you – you are just empty space that cannot attach to anything. Rest your mind like that.

- Bring your mind and your senses into the interior space of your heart – the Qi energy or voidness of the heart – and exclude everything else from consciousness.

- Penetrate all parts of your body by consciousness, feeling all the parts of your body as a unified wholeness of soft energy, and then bring your mind into the brain and let go of your thought-stream so that it turns into emptiness.

- This very moment stop and recognize that everything that you are seeing, hearing and perceiving are just images within your mind. You are just perceiving your own mind-consciousness and only your consciousness rather than the real external world. Even though you are experiencing only your consciousness instead of the world it seems as if you are experiencing a world outside of yourself because somehow your mind inverts these images in a type of projection so that they manifest as external objects, but everything is happening only inside your head. Stay within this recognition that everything is consciousness-only, and learn to detach from the picture as if you are not the doer involved in anything because even your I-sense is consciousness-only; it is only a figment of imagination created by that algorithmic operations of the consciousness running you. Recognize that "All things I perceive are my consciousness, and I am a figment of the consciousness running my mind. Therefore there is no reason to become attached to anything. Cultivate that detachment."

- Imagine that the whole universe is successively dissolved from a gross state into a subtle state, from a subtle state into emptiness, and then from emptiness into an even more transcendental, formless, supreme state that lacks any attributes at all. This is called the technique of *sadadhva* where you trace the entire universe back to its source. Allow your mind to dissolve in the same way into the purity of primal empty consciousness and then let it become an emptiness of unmanifestation.

- You should concentrate intensely on the idea that this universe is totally void, without substance or parts, and completely empty in its fundamental nature. Imagine that it is practically a nothingness because even atoms are mostly empty space and intangible energy. Their smaller components of protons, electrons and muons are condensed energy, energy is an excitation in quantum fields, and those fields of energy are ultimately empty themselves. In that ultimate emptiness that is void of all matter and energy and attributes let your mind abide.

- You should cast your eyes in the empty space inside a jar or any other empty object while leaving aside the enclosing partitions. Remember not to push the Qi forward in your head while so doing but let it circulate evenly even in the cerebellum. Let your mind get absorbed in that empty space, and then imagine that your mind gradually becomes absorbed in infinite empty space. Let yourself become identified with that infinity of endless, boundless nothingness.

- Cast your gaze on a region in which there are no trees, such as when you are on a mountain plateau or high wall, and then look into the empty sky. Let your mental state become empty, like the empty sky you observe, by merging with it. Let thoughtfullness become thought-lessness as you try to merge with that empty space. Let your thoughts die away as you become the empty space. Cast aside your body and ignore the fluctuations of your mind as you become the empty space you see that is bodiless but has awareness, and so does not attach to anything.

- Contemplate with an unwavering mind that your whole body and the entire universe simultaneously are the nature of consciousness. Since your consciousness is what sees everything as pictures, then anything you are seeing is only consciousness (only images within your consciousness). Therefore the body you normally take yourself to be, and the universe you see, are just mental images that are ultimately consciousness-only. You are only experiencing consciousness – not a world – and only consciousness, which is a creation of your mind. Your mind created this knowledge so it isn't ultimately real but just a false fabrication of thoughts. Now realize that the "you" ("I") that you take yourself to be is therefore also only pure consciousness rather than anything real. Your sense of being a self or observer is a fiction you can abandon because that false imagination robotically arises naturally without any need of effort on your part. It is a mirage that arises within you that is pure and empty just like empty space. Just let go of everything and see what you turn out to be that is already there.

- Contemplate that your whole body and the universe are simultaneously filled with total bliss. After fully saturating yourself with this bliss, let go of all streams of consciousness and let your mind rest in this blissful feeling without using your thoughts. Don't even cling to the bliss but just let yourself be infinite bliss that permeates and bubbles you and the universe with its excitation.

- Concentrate on yourself in the form of a vast firmament, infinite and unlimited in any direction whatsoever.

- One should contemplate thus: "Within me the inner apparatus consisting of the mind does not ultimately exist for it is just brought about by a combination of atoms and energy in a particular structure that makes Knowledge happen. In the absence of thought-constructs I will be rid of all mentation and will abide as pure emptiness." Try to become that ultimate state free of thoughts, but let go of thoughts rather than suppress thoughts in order to become thought-free. Let yourself evaporate into an emptiness of nothingness.

- Sit in meditation to witness your mind and observe any desires or afflictions that spring up. When you observe a desire or affliction that springs up, put an end to it immediately. Don't let it function at all but halt it immediately. Do not let it disturb you. Let your mind become absorbed in the very place from which it arose. In time your mind will become pure and clear.

- Towards whatever object the mind goes, one should remove it from there immediately by that very mind, and thus make your mind supportless by not allowing it to settle down anywhere.

Just push your mind away from any point upon which it settles. Wherever the mind moves to, withdraw it to non-clinging emptiness. Do not attach to any thoughts that arise within your mind. Let your consciousness become perfectly free.

- Consider, "When knowledge has not arisen in me, then what am I when in that condition?" Become absorbed in the reality of your primal existence without thoughts.

- Go about your daily activities without a sense of involvement.

- After rejecting any attachment to your body, you should with a firm mind that has no consideration for anything else, contemplate thus: "I am everything, I am everywhere," and let go.

- Cast your gaze on an object, withdraw it and slowly eliminate the knowledge of that object along with any thought or impression of it so as to abide in a non-knowing state of consciousness.

- When a person perceives a particular object, absence is established regarding all other objects (including what you perceived just prior to this object). Contemplate on this vacuous absence until you settle into a tranquil state.

- Fix your mind on the vast, limitless outer space that is empty and without support. By prolonged concentration practice on becoming boundless outer space you will gradually acquire the capacity of mentally becoming like supportless, objectless, vacant space. Let your mind become absorbed in this experience.

- First, think deeply: your fundamental substratum is without attributes so it cannot be perceived or fathomed. You can never know it because there is nothing there as an attribute or distinction. The dependent reality about you, however, it is always ceaselessly changing so can never be grasped because it never stays one thing, and what you think you see of it is just a poor similitude of a mere-representation in your mind. You see an imperfect illusion that lacks countless dimensions but which is created within your mind simply so that your object-type in the universe – a "living being" object – has even fitness functionality to be able to survive. You can never truly know the attributes of the external reality surrounding you because the mode of reality for you is only your limited, faulty, and imperfect consciousness of perceptions and ideas that simply amount to subjective false imaginations. Remember that even your I-sense behind your knowing is also a falsity automatically produced by your consciousness; your I-ego is a false creation that automatically arises within sentient living processes otherwise they could not survive as the adaptable moving energy objects they are. Realize that you have no ground to stand on to know any sort of true reality whatsoever. You do not even truly exist as a self either and your consciousness is a fiction. There is nothing you can actually see or cling to as a real external world because it is continuously fluctuating in a state of flux. Therefore let go of clinging to all thoughts and remain in that state of liberation and freedom.

- Realize that you are just a part of the All of manifestation, everything, so you are everything since you are intrinsically entwined with it as part of its one fabric. You are a drop of the cosmos so you are the cosmos. The cosmos is a oneness or single manifestation and you are that. However, the dancing universe that you are is not absolutely real and with your errant, limited senses and consciousness you cannot truly perceive it either. Do not identify with your (imperfect) mind and sense perceptions. Do not cling to your artificial fake ego. Do not hold onto anything in your mind. Strive to be one with the ultimate without any attachments – since that is what you are – and rest in your desire-free consciousness to find a peace and serenity as if nothing exists.

- You are not the body and should live like someone without a body so that you become detached and attain a serene nature. You are simply beingness that has consciousness, a fraction of the consciousness of the universe that seems embodied in a human form. Rest in that true beingness without a body that is what you really are.

- Use breathing to calm your thoughts and enter into an empty state of mind. First inhale air through your nose deeply into your lungs, and then using your mouth exhale slowly to empty your lungs while saying "Ahhh" while simultaneously letting go of all thoughts and concerns. Your exhalation should last about twice as long as the length of your inhalation, and you should let go of all your mental pressures and tensions upon those exhalations. Try inhaling for a count of four and then exhaling for a count of eight, and continue doing this several times in a row. When exhaling, always let go as if you are finally releasing a big burden off your shoulders where you can abandon all thought concerns, and it is as if "now life is perfect" so that you can rest in a state of empty bliss, even if but for a moment. Every time you exhale make a silent sound of "Ahhh" as if you are so happy to be able to let go of everything in the world and release all your problems and pressures. Eventually you will reach a point where you feel like you have let go of everything, your body feels comfortable inside, and your mind should now be quiet and peaceful.

Buddhism espouses four "formless absorptions" – the samadhi of infinite space (all phenomena are empty like space, and I am bodiless like space but have awareness), samadhi of infinite consciousness (consciousness is infinite and directionless, and I am essentially just consciousness), samadhi of infinite nothingness (the perceptual sphere of nothing whatsoever where this mind does not consist of any entity whatsoever; it is non-existent and empty), and the samadhi of neither perception nor non-perception or "neither presence nor absence" (where the clear cognizance of perception is missing yet a type of perception is there that cannot be made an object of the intellect) – and many of these meditations are a means to gain entry into these four states of mental concentration.

Actually, the last two of these meditations are fake because a human being cannot shut off his consciousness to access thoughtless unless they fall asleep, but an enlightened being can stop all your thoughts using a *nirmanakaya*. It is said that after you leave the samadhi you immediately think, "nothing was there, no mental experience was there." There was no consciousness, mind, experience, etc. That's how the samadhi gets its name. While in it you know nothing but after leaving it you can grasp that there was no experience there. This stopping of your mental functions is something you cannot cultivate but the state is thrust upon you by an enlightened being who then makes you think you achieved it.

As to the samadhi of neither thought nor no-thought (perception or no-perception), this too is an invention that humans cannot create with their minds, which is why other religions do not mention this. The explanation is that "samadhi without thought and without no-thought" means this realm is absent of ordinary discrimination (it's a stage "without thought"). Since discrimination isn't totally absent because consciousness is still operative, it's also a state "without no-thought." Hence this samadhi is a stage of spiritual knowing where thought doesn't seem to be there, and yet it isn't absent. There is still subtle cognition but it doesn't seem to function. Consciousness (cognition or discrimination) is practically non-existent, and so it is said that there is no thought – a state "without thought." However, a very fine trace of thought still exists and so it is called neither cognition nor non-cognition (neither thought nor no-thought). I don't want people wasting their time trying to cultivate states of ignorance and not-knowingness. Your purpose throughout your existence is to always remain in a state of attention with focus and mental clarity.

The realms of samadhi are quiet states of optimal mental and physical well-being *without psychological or psychiatric problems*. They are non-pathological stages of internal peace, just like the samadhi of infinite space, which is what everyone is actually seeking.

In the Theravada, all the practitioners work to cultivate dhyana and samadhi. In the Mahayana schools the approach is different—the practitioners cultivate the *prajna* wisdom of awareness. Mahayana practitioners try to cultivate *presence*, which is the awareness, knowingness or beingness of knowing one's thought-stream while abiding in only the present moment.

Mahayana practitioners train to remain clear every moment so as to always know what they're doing, which we commonly call knowing, witnessing, mindfulness or observing. They cultivate to recognize the mind-moment. This is the real route of Mahayana cultivation, and it is the secret basis of the *Surangama Sutra*. It's the method of direct attainment without stages by cultivating the awareness present in a moment of mind.

As is stated in the *Diamond Sutra*, the past mind cannot be grasped, the present mind cannot be grasped and the future mind cannot be grasped. Therefore you shouldn't chase after your mind or thought-stream. Just abide in a state of presence and know that the whole experience is all unreal, yet function using your mind without the entrainment of attaching to your thought-stream. Use it, but recognize that it is just an illusory construction that arises in your illusory body and mind.

The *Complete Enlightenment Sutra* also tells us: don't add any interpretation on top of things, don't add any verbalization on top of what you experience. Just experience the reality that appears without dropping into attachment. Everything else is just putting one hat on top of another.

These various meditation exercises should always be matched up with refining your Qi into your subtle body spirit, which is related to the *Surangama Sutra's* "body generated by will" attainment. As explained, this is the first dhyana attainment achieved due to freeing yourself from the body (form *skandha*) but to do so you must first purify that inner subtle energy before it can escape its cage. No matter what path you choose in meditation they all involve initially setting up an object to focus upon, as found in these examples, since almost no one can directly attain the skill of non-abiding, which means detachment from thoughts while still allowing for the fullness of knowing. In many of these meditations you are attempting to cultivate a combination of emptiness, lucid clarity and joy where you are pristinely mentally clear and feel a subtle bliss, and yet you are also empty of attachments because you recognize that nothing is real.

OTHER BOOKS OF INTEREST

The author, William Bodri, has written several related titles that may interest you:

Nyasa Yoga – This book was written to reveal the true purpose of Nyasa Yoga, an energetic inner yogic technique for clearing your *nadis* of circulatory obstructions. Many Nyasa and related yoga exercises are described that rarely appear in print, including sectional body cultivation techniques and tantric meditations from a number of spiritual traditions that do not require special empowerments. There is a special focus on the value of the *Yajnavalkya* yogic exercises. Nyasa Yoga *divinizes* your physical body through mantra and deity work on specific body parts, concentrated upon in turn, in order to attain the subtle energy deva body that is the first step of spiritual ascension, enlightenment or liberation. Usually enlightenment is posed as a samadhi attainment (for very good reasons of managing populations even thought this is not true) but it is actually a transcendental body attainment.

Neijia Yoga – This is the first book of its kind that combines the spiritual practices and philosophies of Hinduism with Chinese Taoism in detail. It reveals the *nei-gong* inner energy practices for Yoga and the martial arts, and actually combines the perspectives of Hinduism with Taoism while explaining the symbolism of Hanuman and Sun Wukong in the field of spiritual liberation. There are many techniques designed to help you cultivate the Prana (Qi) of your muscles, organs and bones; meridians or Prana circulatory orbits; muscle force transmission pathways; bindus, marma or acupuncture points; appendages such as arms and legs; body cavities such as the three *dantian*, chakra sections and other sectioning schemes; and simple body parts (such as the ears, eyes, teeth, penis, and so forth). To reach the highest levels of yoga and the martial arts you need to practice these internal energy exercises, revealed in detail. If you want to do a lot of tantric yoga that involves inner energy work then this book will be especially productive for you.

The Secret Inner Teachings of Daoism – This book puts a new framework on Taoism for today by revealing the spiritual pathway to ascension hidden within ancient Taoist texts along with Taoism's specialized internal energy cultivation methods for becoming a "spiritual immortal." Taoism is one of the few spiritual traditions that directly tells you that enlightenment is a transcendental body attainment, and the stages of its spiritual immortals constitute the stages of Arhatship. The book takes the unusual approach of combining the Taoist road to enlightenment with equivalent results seen by enlightened masters in Orthodox Christianity and Hinduism. Many mysteries involving superpowers are explained. There are also many valuable lessons on very practical aspects of astrology, self-healing, geopolitics, military affairs, and political governance that fall within the Taoist framework. This is commentary you will not find elsewhere in print. If you liked this book on Hinduism then this one on Taoism is highly recommended, especially as it gives many more case studies explaining superpowers. In fact, if you truly want to understand Hinduism you really need to get this book! If you want to get involved with cultivation practice then *Neijia Yoga*, *Nyasa Yoga* and *Correcting Zen* are the most important texts you can get. If you want to understand the whole field of spiritual cultivation in one book then *Arhat Yoga* is the one to get. Most of this information is revolutionary followed by *Buddha Yoga* and *Correcting Zen*.

Correcting Zen – While the title focuses on Zen practice, this book was actually written with the intent that individuals in other monastic traditions – such as the Ramakrishna, Swaminarayan and various other Hindu, Jain, Sikh and Buddhist Sampradaya – would use it to elevate their own traditions in various ways. It focuses on (1) reinstituting physical exercise (yoga or martial arts) in monastic training, (2) stresses the attainment of various mundane skills (in preparation for the after-enlightenment state) and (3) values social service rather than just worship and study. Its (4) discussion of scriptures constitutes an advanced understanding of selflessness and comprehensive interdependence found within Buddhist and Advaita Vedanta teachings. It (5) focuses on self-rectification methods for changing one's personality and behavior along with the helpful use of affirmations as done in Stoicism, and is unique in (6) stressing the development of personal vows for the spiritual path. This is an orientation that totally reorients monastic practice, or personal cultivation practice, away from primarily just meditation and worship that typically produces useless individuals without skills. This trio of books goes together: *Buddha Yoga*, *Arhat Yoga*, and *Correcting Zen*. A related but as yet unpublished forthcoming title is *Self-Creation: The Superhuman Protocol*.

Arhat Yoga – A non-denominational *magnum opus* on the single topic of spiritual cultivation for enlightenment and what it entails. Much of the contents will seem revolutionary including: a comprehensive description of "interdependent origination" including the creation of the universe and sentient life that incorporates the *Flower Ornament* view of interdependent arising and phenomenal interfusion; the *Diamond Sutra* enlightenment view of what we are and our origins; an explanation of the spiritual goal of *sat, chit, ananda* and how this necessitates a dualistic mind-body cultivation system that entails physical exercise and inner energy work to achieve physical health and bliss, and meditation practice to achieve the flow state of pristine awareness; how we must cultivate our minds and behavior towards virtuous ways and improving society in order to merit the twelve years of kundalini transformations required for enlightenment; revelation of the five spiritual body attainments within the *sambhogakaya* along with their properties; the five stages scheme of spiritual progress; and the principles of Yin and Yang Qi cultivation inherent in yoga, martial arts and all spiritual cultivation practices. This one book illuminates the basis of cultivating to become an Arhat, or enlightened sage, that is in every spiritual tradition. Its contents dispense with the need for countless years of Abhidharma, Consciousness-Only or Vedanta study etc. usually required by a spiritual sect. You just need this one book and then can dispense with a thousand others. It reveals the hidden meaning within many Buddhist sutras that have escaped scholars for centuries since they don't understand that Vimalakirti's brain is his room, the *Diamond Sutra* is talking about metrological simples and the meditations we discussed in Chapter 5 on the *Mahavakyas*, the waving flags and pennants and blazing lights in the *Avatamaska Sutra* represent the brain activity of neurons firing, and so on. It is the foundational work for anyone who is devoting their life to spiritual training, especially those who have bought hundreds of books on spiritual theory and practices because they are still searching for secret tips or explanations. If you had just this one book, and read it carefully, you could understand the spiritual path pretty much in total and be able to immediately understand when spiritual teachings or methods are incorrect. This book is the crux of Hindu, Taoist, Jain, Shugendo, Sufi, Christian and Buddhist practice.

Buddha Yoga – A non-denominational book that summarizes the path to enlightenment in terms of its two pillars of mental meditation practice and inner energy work for attaining samadhi, namely the transcendental body achievements of the spiritual path that make one a Buddha or enlightened sage. Even if enlightenment is out of reach within this lifetime it teaches how to train to become a Bodhisattva or guardian spirit for all sorts of earthly activities. This includes spiritual careers as protectors of nations, cities, communities or people's personal health, wealth, families and specialized mundane fields such as agriculture, weather making, politics, and so on. It teaches that we should make Buddha vows *now* instead of waiting to become enlightened and reveals recommended texts and bodies of knowledge one must study to become a particular Buddha or Bodhisattva of a specialized type. This book, along with *Arhat Yoga*, provides explanations of the Buddhist Sutras that you won't be understand unless you are a deva so these two together really reveal the true teachings of Buddhism. *Cultivating Zen* deals with practice and is non-denominational. Once you read *Buddha Yoga* you will understand that many Buddhist sutras were written containing instructions on how to understand the formation of thoughts in the brain. *Buddha Yoga* is extremely practical as it also goes into the details of practice schedules for running monasteries or spiritual centers and how to raise money to keep the institution flourishing. Very rare and unusual information.

The Little Book of Hercules – The spiritual tradition of the ancient Greeks in the only one that really revealed the exact steps to purifying your inner energy prior to the stage of kundalini awakening. Using the Greek story of the Twelve Labors of Hercules, which outlines the progressive stages of spiritual development that spiritual practitioners in all spiritual traditions go through, this book presents full details on the step-by-step progression of the physical transformations that occur to practitioners. The companion volume to this is *Meditation*

*Case Studie*s that provides an advanced review of the various kundalini phenomena you are likely to experience on the spiritual path, and the fifty Deva *Mara* states of the *Surangama Sutra*. If something strange happens to you then the mystical experience is probably described in *Meditation Case Studie*s.

Visualization Power – This was written because of many stories that touched me in my youth about prisoners of wars and prison inmates who used the powers of visualization to change their lives and practice skills in just their mental training. It was also inspired by the *Visuddhimagga (Path of Perfection)*, which is a spiritual cultivation book that uses many visualization techniques for cultivating samadhi. Another first, it builds up an entire framework of visualization training for musicians, businessmen, athletes, personal healing, and spiritual practice. The expenses can be used for many fields of endeavor.

Sport Visualization for the Elite Athlete – Written for athletes wishing to improve their skills, this book specializes in visualization and mental rehearsal techniques for improving sports performance. The contents includes stories of dozens of athletes who used visualization in various ways, including many Olympians and world record holders in various sports.

Detox Cleanse Your Body Quickly and Completely – The methods of inner cleansing espoused in ancient yoga texts are no longer powerful enough to significantly help people in today's polluted world because our organs have not been able to keep up with the detoxification demands for so many contaminants. This book supplements the ancient yogic methods by collecting together the best detoxification protocols for every organ system of your body. Found nowhere else, you will learn how to read your blood lab test results to finally discover what organs inside you are not working at peak efficiency and can use some detoxification support. You'll find out which supplements work best for these concerns to either help cleanse an organ or strengthen its functions.

Super Cancer Fighters – This is a book on at home natural therapies that people use for cancer. The discovery of the ivermectin

+ fenbendazole + tocotrienol protocol for fighting cancer is now first and foremost the mainstay for most people, but much of this other information might still be useful. A related book is *Prevent and Reverse Atherosclerosis: Proven Natural Alternatives that Eliminate Cholesterol Plaque Without Surgery (Stanton Reed)* that might contain useful heart help information for those harmed by vaccines.

Look Younger, Live Longer – By combining research on the Blue Zones regions of super human longevity, the latest theories on aging with the nutritional supplements that counteract each of these proposed mechanisms, and the longevity methods of eastern spiritual traditions you then have a formula for anti-aging and longevity better than anything else out there. By doing the right things we can slow or reverse the signs of aging to live longer and better. This book combines the best approaches of nutrition, supplements, and eastern wisdom for slowing aging and becoming more youthful.

Culture, Country, City, Company, Person, Purpose, Passion, World – This book integrates ancient (including Eastern) wisdom and extensive research to help explain the rise and fall of companies, countries, cultures, and more. It provides a grand overview scheme of history revealing several cyclical explanations for the birth, growth and decay of large social organizations from empires down to companies. It is deeply useful in understanding cycles of wealth and prosperity that affect you as an individual and provides rare investment techniques that take advantage of grand economic cycles. It even goes into how to create products that will keep a company profitable for years because they are based on unique selling propositions. Finally, it explains how a person should find their own personal purpose in life, pursue their passions rather than profits, and help the world through mastermind groups and cooperative grand scale activities. This is the favorite of all the books I have written primarily due to its usefulness and the feedback I get from businessmen. It takes large groups of people, reveals the historical principles behind why those groups rise and fall, decreases the group size (while maintaining apropos explanations) until you come down to the size of a single individual, and from there it shows how you join with larger and larger groups of people to save the world. I used to give lectures in China to businessmen and they would always rave about this material, so I turned it into a book because it teaches how to give your business a higher purpose, and how to make sure your products have a higher purpose as well. Therefore it teaches you how to create a unique selling proposition for your products or services, among its many other contents, although you can find specific information on that in my *How to Create a Million Dollar Unique Selling Proposition*.

Super Investing – This book provides a formula for attaining generational wealth, namely wealth large enough that it can be passed onto your children. It provides five investment models, historically tested, that have consistently beaten fund managers and market returns. You won't hear about these tested methods on Wall Street even though they are extremely simple and fundamentally sound. They include Benjamin Graham's final value stock investment method, a market timing model based on interest rates that beats the market all the way back to 1929, a momentum investing method that *consistently* makes over 20% per year, a monthly cash generation method of very rare techniques that beats dividend investing, and a special proven seasonal timing investment technique. This book was written to help people accumulate generational wealth through long-term investing with the intent to pass it onto their family or do significantly large philanthropic work. I worked in Wall Street for years and you will not find these techniques unless you look really hard. *Buddha Yoga* also contains some superlative investment techniques and so does *Breakthrough Strategies of Wall Street Traders*.

Color Me Confucius – If you liked the information on the Confucian ranks for the spiritual body attainments then you might enjoy this book on Confucian cultivation, which focuses on mindfulness or introspection to police and correct errant thoughts and behavior. It focuses on the cultivation of ethics and morality through mental watching. It has a particularly large section on how to avoid becoming an "errant man of business" in today's capitalist society that worships profits, and teaches you how to find a purpose in life (life purpose) that will provide you with life satisfaction and fulfillment. This book goes along with *Culture, Country, City, Company, Person, Purpose, Passion, World* because of its deep discussions on determining a life purpose and guiding your business to avoid becoming a destructive force on mankind due to the pursuit of just profits alone.

The Art of Political Power – While India has the *Arthasastra* – an ancient Sanskrit treatise on statecraft, political science, economic policy and military strategy – this is a translation of the Chinese equivalent attributed to the sage Guan Tzu (Guanzi), who is considered superior to Sun Tzu and Confucius in terms of geopolitical and political strategy. This is a primer for geopolitics on how countries should act to preserve themselves or climb the prosperity ladder to become premier in the world. It also teaches individuals how to rise to national or international prominence. The commentaries, which span the gamut of history and economics, contain eclectic information little cited and are particularly powerful helpmates for leaders. A good companion to this book is *The I Ching Revealed: Tap into the Five Secret Patterns Underlying the 64 Hexagrams.*

Husbands and Wives Were Connected in the Past – A famous saying runs, "Husbands and wives were connected in the past. Whether for good or bad those connections never fail to meet again. Children are basically past debts. Some come to give and some come to collect." This book collects marriage and relationship advice from divorce lawyers, marriage counselors, psychologists, astrologers and ancient sages. While it could be titled, "The secret of great marriages and families," its special focus is on karmic relationships. Soul mates meet again in this life because of their karmic past, and the marriage relationship can be good or bad depending upon how you handle the relationship. Children also come into your life on account of a past karmic relationship as well. This book tells you how to find your karmic spouse that you were connected with in the past, how to improve upon that relationship, how to beget children when fertility problems might be an issue, what lessons to teach them to raise good kids, and how to band everyone together in a strong family unit that grows closer and happier over time.

www.ingramcontent.com/pod-product-compliance
Lightning Source LLC
Chambersburg PA
CBHW072147070526
44585CB00015B/1025